Explorers of the
In Search of a Better World

Gilbert Siegel

UNIWORLD PUBLISHING
Garden Grove, California

EXPLORERS OF THE MIND
IN SEARCH OF A BETTER WORLD

By Gilbert Siegel

Published by: UNIWORLD Publishing
9392 Canterbury Lane
Garden Grove, CA 92641 U.S.A.

Copyrights ©1992, 1995 by Gilbert Siegel

All rights reserved. No part of this book may be reproduced in any form or by any means without permission in writing from the author, except for inclusion of brief quotations in a review.

Printed in the United States of America
Cover and Graphics designed by Susan Siegel
Edited by Janet McDonald

Library of Congress Catalog Card Number: 95-90571
Siegel, Gilbert
Explorers of the Mind: In Search of a Better World
Includes 85 Figures, 7 Tables, 50 Presentations, Appendix with Glossary & References

1. Social Sciences   2. Regional Planning   3. Government Organization

307.7   1995

ISBN # 0-9646514-0-8

Explorers of the Mind: In Search of a Better World

FOREWORD

It is 5 minutes to 12! Mankind is on the verge of destroying its living conditions and making the earth no longer capable of supporting life.

Gilbert Siegel takes on this challenge and discusses the question of survival comprehensively and assertively. The book provides multi-perspectives for this universally important topic. Giving a detailed description of the conditions of human living all over the world, he discusses questions such as the the quality of life, overpopulation, problems of metropolises with populations in the millions, various energy resources, etc. He also offers constructive suggestions on how to solve their problems. He shows that the individual quality of life depends on collective quality. He offers a new concept of social organization, regionalization, as the key to the solution of man's problems. The development of new regions with networked infrastructures, centers and communities seems to be a rational approach taken by the book.

" Explorers of the Mind: In Search of a Better World" serves as a model for imparting and integrating ideas and knowledge. The book can be useful and stimulating for multi-disciplinary seminars or assigned group projects. It can serve as a text in conjunction with course material. It can be read by people of all ages, all levels of education and all ethnic groups everywhere.

The author consciously excludes those scientific details which would ordinarily be understood only by experts. His intention is to examine all of the problems of people and their environmental conditions and to explain how these interrelate. Furthermore, he has avoided the typical scholarly style of writing found in the academic world and did not footnote or include a detailed bibliography.

In order to make the reading lively and to promote an active interaction between the author and the reader, he has three fictitious characters, Neos, Veritor and Pragma, carry on a conversation with each other. They represent the three ways of perceiving, reflecting and responding. Hence, three different opinions, counter-opinions and solutions are presented in discourse. The question and answer method and the style of language make the manuscript easy to read and lively. It gives a good motivation for identifying and coping with the existential problems and for taking responsibility.

FOREWORD

I can highly recommend this book for publication.

Prof. Dr. Magdalena Baus
FR 6.3 Soziologie
FB Sozial-und Umweltwissenschaften
UNIVERSITÅT DES SAARLANDES

ACKNOWLEDGEMENTS

I am very grateful for the considerable efforts and support by all those who have made this book possible. I am thankful to Professor Doctor Magdelena Baus for her foreword of the book and her encouragement, Janet McDonald for her careful editing, my daughters, Susan Siegel for the organization, desk top publishing and graphic design, Charlene Ralston, and Linda Siegel-Aviani for their critical review and finally to my wife, Lore, who has lovingly supported my effort in writing this book. All have positively influenced the form and substance of my writing.

Explorers of the Mind: In Search of a Better World

PREFACE

This book is as ambitious as it is urgent. Its topics are multi-faceted and multi-themic. It is on a global scale, yet is relevant to each of us. As I started to write, I was asked, "Why are you addressing the whole world?" I could only answer with a question, "If worldwide problems are systemic and complex, why not address them comprehensively? "Building a better world cannot be realistically addressed in a provincial, fragmentary or narrow way, particularly when adverse conditions mushroom and population pressures increasingly impact societies everywhere. How can we individually and collectively hope to cope with these pressures? How must our government infrastructures be re-designed and developed to help us anticipate and manage them?

I felt that I could make a difference by presenting the subject in a different way and by encouraging others to also address them in a new way. After years of relevant experience and insight, I began to ask myself, "Was I ready to contribute to a larger vision of a better world, with perspectives that provide new formulas for creating a better quality of life universally?", and I wondered,"What could mankind's future be like - if?"

I have attempted in this body of work to express different viewpoints and ideas that could bring some order out of the chaos in this turbulent world. My intention was to stimulate and challenge others to act, particularly those who might some day assume leadership responsibilities. So new concepts of social organization that have been maturing in my mind have finally been presented. New regional concepts have been proposed to sow the seeds of possibility. It would be a world in which man-made systems would become more concerned with the well-being of humans and would also be more harmonious with nature. As I began to write, I felt that the best approach would be to define problems, solutions and limits in the context of larger environments. I began to realize my own limitations as to how far I could penetrate or expand on the subject matter of this book without losing reader interest. I could only hope to show the big picture, not the whole picture. I realized that a step by step process of awareness was involved and further expansion and detailing would have to be done later. This was most apparent when describing the functions of each regional infrastructure and when defining regional implementation.

I have been aware that many well known and respected humanists and futurists, large scale planners and system scientists in diverse fields have been addressing needs and solutions for a long time. They have demonstrated high levels of dedication in seeking the betterment of all. I am indebted to them for much of the inspiration for this book.

I have avoided the antagonist/protagonist approach to the resolution of issues.

PREFACE

In order to optimize solutions in this ever-changing world, it became apparent to me that long term approaches must be viewed and creatively expressed using more than two extreme perspectives. I felt that if the antagonist/protagonist method is used, it might induce biased thinking, ego gratification, domination and fear. These would tend to obscure key issues, underlying causes and hidden conditions. Further, it seemed to me that many people become increasingly skeptical with simplistic solutions and opportunistic decisions that only end up creating more problems than are solved. I have also noticed that when narrow focusing occurs, positions became hardened, polarized and irreversible stands are taken. Thought processes become imprisoned, and creativity is stifled.

I have been puzzled by persistent human inertia, blind acceptance and gullibility. I wondered about the tolerance of people to accept losses of freedom or to undergo harmful abuse. I wondered why people feel helpless, become indifferent or insensitive, submit to sadism and masochism or foster ignorance and fear? Does it take catastrophic events to finally motivate them for change? Do people respond mostly for immediate gratification? In light of all this negativeness, how then can mankind be expected to adequately meet life crises, facing them squarely and courageously with intelligence.

I found this world has been made more complex and more troubled by a long list of excesses. These included population over-concentrations, uneven technological growth, urgent, socio-economic problems and basic human needs made critical by neglect. There has been a proliferation of narrow interests and a breakdown and disintegration of man-made systems and government institutions. These have led to social chaos and friction and the abuse of natural systems and resources. Major negative factors abound. It became apparent that there was a need to understand critical socio-economic imbalances from wider and higher perspectives. Faltering systems, for example, had to be understood in terms of differences and similarities in cultures, religions, economies and political climates. Intuition and insight from such analysis has proven to be invaluable in discovering where systems were failing or were likely to. Such insights allowed me to sense what more effective structural changes could then be applied.

A broad-brushed appraisal of man-made systems and their inter-relationships with natural systems was essential. I reasoned that it would be necessary to describe new arrangements in which humans and other life forms could live and prosper. I realized that new kinds of social organization involving various essential infrastructure development in a regional setting would be necessary. Such universal models would have to be designed for a world that has a pluralism of life-styles, variations in sophistication, differentiation, resources and geography. Of course, while I wrote, I was ever aware that there exists an enormous accumulation of meaningful knowledge and experience about social evolution. This was more than I could ever hope to fully read, assimilate and utilize. I felt that this great storehouse of information would be well utilized when my proposed concepts began to be expanded and applied. Fortunately, I have been motivated and enriched by many years of experience involving systems management, design, planning and analysis in numerous fields, and I have developed many "cutting edge" concepts relevant in writing this book.

However, when preparing this document, the staggering volume of available statistics and reference material loomed as an obstacle as well as a bonanza. There were sets of statistics to support all sorts of viewpoints. So caution and some test of appropriateness or reasonableness needed to be applied. A common tendency by many has been to penetrate and focus on only one area and to ignore other related ones. Such focusing may have been based on expediency to provide temporary solutions to current problems, to study some specific area in depth, to respond to a contractural requirement or to meet budget limitations. Furthermore, emergency measures have frequently been necessary because mankind seems to live from crisis to crisis. But it is also necessary to understand that such temporary measures may ultimately require further corrective efforts. Whenever the specter of immediate or impending hunger, disease, hazardous exposure or safety posed a threat, of course, I found that it would be wiser and more humane to consider both short and long term solutions. Needs assessments and common sense, but not endless detailed research, seemed ample enough to justify and advocate specific firm action. I have also felt that on-going, long term research and system analysis in re-inventing government will always be essential. In this, all generations must continue the quest for longer-lasting, more satisfying solutions.

In summary, the main thrust of this presentation has been to introduce new comprehensive and provocative ideas. It has been necessary to set far-reaching, high-minded goals and reasonable objectives and to propose preliminary regional designs and schemes necessary to meet them. I have taken these designs and proposed their long-term, phased-in implementation so as to make our world a better place for ourselves and our posterity.

Explorers of the Mind: In Search of a Better World

TABLE OF CONTENTS

FOREWORD iii
ACKNOWLEDGEMENTS v
PREFACE vii
LIST OF PRESENTATIONS xiii
LIST OF FIGURES xv
LIST OF TABLES xviii
INTRODUCTION xix

PART I - URGENT TIMES & CROWDED PLACES 1
   Chapter 1 - Common Cause in a Changing World 2
   Chapter 2 - Gaining Multiple Perspectives 4
   Chapter 3 - Rivalry for Time and Space 6
   Chapter 4 - Quality of Life and Population Congestion 17
   Chapter 5 - How Dense Can We Afford to Become? 27

PART II - JUSTIFYING THE REGIONAL CONCEPT 33
   Chapter 1 - Initial Journey 34
   Chapter 2 - Attributes of Cities 64
   Chapter 3 - Rural Areas and Open Spaces 69
   Chapter 4 - Open Borders & the Territorial Imperative 76
   Chapter 5 - Economic Imperative & Quality of Life 80
   Chapter 6 - Environmental Imperative & Survival 83
   Chapter 7 - Shaping the Future 88

PART III - REGIONAL DESIGNS AND SCENARIOS 93
   Chapter 1 - Introduction of the Regional Concept 94
   Chapter 2 - Functional Design of the Region 106
   Chapter 3 - Regional Infrastructures and Their Networks 110
   Chapter 4 - Third World Infrastructures 171

PART IV - PREPARATION FOR TOMORROW 173
   Chapter 1 - Regional Preparations 174
   Chapter 2 - Feeding the World 178
   Chapter 3 - Water Resources and Crises Management 193
   Chapter 4 - Energy Resources: Dependencies and Alternatives 206
   Chapter 5 - Trees and Restoration 223
   Chapter 6 - Fiber Resources: Dependencies and Variations 232
   Chapter 7 - The Management of Non-Renewables 235
   Chapter 8 - Summary of Continental Resources 238

TABLE OF CONTENTS

    Chapter 9 - Human Resources and Human Potential 248
    Chapter10- Welcome to Innovation 253

PART V - THE CHALLENGE OF IMPLEMENTATION 257
    Chapter 1 - Strategy 268
    Chapter 2 - Concept Networking 261
    Chapter 3 - Motivation 275
    Chapter 4 - Mobilization 278
    Chapter 5 - Initiation of Programs 291
    Chapter 6 - Development of the Region 314
    Chapter 7 - Investing in Life and Living 334

PART VI - EXPANSION OF REGIONALIZATION AND BEYOND 345
    Chapter 1 - Expansion 346
    Chapter 2 - Population Shifts & Regional Influences...348
    Chapter 3 - Reflections..352

APPENDIX
    Glossary
    Specific References & Readings

LIST OF PRESENTATIONS

PART I - URGENT TIMES & CROWDED PLACES
Chapter 3
- Time 8
- Concept of Space 10
- Spatial Constraints 12
- Personal Space & Collective Space 14

Chapter 4
- Optimum Quality of Life for the Individual 19
- Factors Which Modify Quality of Living 21
- Conditions Which Affect Quality of Living 24

Chapter 5
- Collective Quality of Life 30

PART II - JUSTIFYING THE REGIONAL CONCEPT
Chapter 3
- Population Dynamics of the Rural Area 72

Chapter 4
- Territorial Imperative & Borders 77

Chapter 5
- Levels of Economic Imperative 81

Chapter 6
- Excessive and Improper Use of Resources and Environment 84
- Redefinition of the Environmental Imperative 86

Chapter 7
- Shaping the Future 90
- Population Pressures - Rationale for Dispersion 92

PART III - REGIONAL DESIGN & SCENARIOS
Chapter 1
- Definitions 95
- Initial Community Development Premises 99
- Network Linking of Communities and Centers 101
- Community Network & Centers - Possible Disadvantages and Concerns 103

Chapter 2
- Expectation of Functional Competency for Regionalization ...... 108&109

Chapter 3
- Regional Network - Group A 114
- Towards Universal Health Care 123
- Regional Educational Development 136

PART IV - PREPARATION FOR TOMORROW
Chapter 1
- Estimates of Regional Needs Worldwide 177

Chapter 2
    A Different View of the Amazon 188
Chapter 3
    Growing Crops With Salt Water...190
    Irrigation 195
Chapter 4
    Inevitable Move to Alternative Energy Resources...207
Chapter 5
    The Gift of Trees 230
Chapter 8
    General Resource Development Appraisal for..242
        Continents of the World- (Food)
    General Resource Development Appraisal for..243
        Continents of the World- (Water)
    General Resource Development Appraisal for..244
        Continents of the World- (Energy)
    General Resource Development Appraisal for..245
        Continents of the World- (Trees, Shrubs and Others)
    General Resource Development Appraisal for..246
        Continents of the World- (Fibers)
    General Resource Development Appraisal for..247
        Continents of the World- (Non-renewable)
Chapter 9
    Promotion of Human Potential as Humans on a Regional Scale 249
    Enhancing the Potential of Humans on a Community Level.........................252
Chapter 10
    Innovating for Growth 254
    Innovational Dependencies..255

PART V - THE CHALLENGE OF IMPLEMENTATION
Chapter 3
    What Will Motivate? 276
Chapter 5
    Initial Participation : Policy Making for Regions 307
    Policy Making As a Function of Regional Program Phases 308
Chapter 6
    The Development Phase 316
Chapter 7
    Investing in the Infrastructures..342
    The Search for Human Resources and Funding Alternatives 343

PART VI - EXPANSION OF REGIONALIZATION & BEYOND
Chapter 2
    Conversion of the Supercities...351
    Expansion Adjustments 353

LIST OF FIGURES

I-5-A	Population Over-Concentration	29
II-1-A	Mexico City Supercity Expansion	37
II-1-B	Patterns of City Growth	40
II-1-C	Patterns of Metropolitan Growth	41
II-1-D	Saõ Paulo (Brazil) Supercity Expansion	44
II-1-E	Cairo Supercity Expansion	47
II-1-F	Shanghai Supercity Expansion	50
II-1-G	Tokyo-Yokahama, (Japan), Supercity Expansion	53
II-1-H	Moscow Supercity Expansion	56
II-1-I	New York Supercity Expansion	59
II-2-A	Positive Attributes of the City	66
II-2-B	Negative Attributes of the City	68
II-3-A	Occupations of Rural Areas	70
II-3-B	The Nature of Open Spaces	74
III-1-A	Networking for Living	105
III-3-A	Overview - Building the Infrastructures	112 & 113
III-3-B	Regional Network - Group A & Center, Community and Neighborhood Levels	115
III-3-C	Regional Network - Group L & Center, Community and Neighborhood Levels	118
III-3-D	Regional Network - Group D & Center, Community and Neighborhood Levels	121
III-3-E	Regional Network - Group M & Center, Community and Neighborhood Levels	125
III-3-F	Regional Network - Group S & Center, Community and Neighborhood Levels	130
III-3-G	Regional Network - Group H & Center, Community and Neighborhood Levels	133
III-3-H	Regional Network - Group E & Center, Community and Neighborhood Levels	138
III-3-I	Regional Network - Group C & Center, Community and Neighborhood Levels	141
III-3-J	Regional Network - Group T & Center, Community and Neighborhood Levels	146
III-3-K	Two Automated Carrier Systems	148
III-3-L	Terminal Embarking and Disembarking Concept	150
III-3-M	Regional Network - Group P & Center, Community and Neighborhood Levels	153

III-3-N	Community & Neighborhood Patterns & Perspectives	155
III-3-O	Neighborhood Housing	156
III-3-P	Regional Network - Group N & Center, Community and Neighborhood Levels	159
III-3-Q	Regional Network - Group F & Center, Community and Neighborhood Levels	161
III-3-R	Regional Network - Group B & Center, Community and Neighborhood Levels	163
III-3-S	Advanced Research and Development	167
III-3-T	Regional Multi-belief Impact	169
IV-2-A	World Land Cultivation	179
IV-2-B	Diversion, Retardation, Preservation, Restoration	183
IV-2-C	Top Soil Replacement for Cleared Tropical Lands	185
IV-3-A	Removing Salt	200
IV-3-B	Multiple Uses of Sea Water Under the Aegis of Regional and Inter-Regional Development	203
IV-3-C	Scheme Showing Reverse Osmosi /Force Method	205
IV-4-A	Fossil Energy Resources Status	208
IV-4-B	Energy Through the Ages	211
IV-4-C	Alternative Energy Resources	214
IV-4-D	Proposed Concept - Combined System For Energy	217
IV-4-E	Geothermal Tapping of Earth's Furnace	219
IV-4-F	Propelling Vehicles For a Compelling Future	222
IV-5-A	Reforestation & Replanting - Slopes, Mountains	225
IV-5-B	Reforestation & Replanting - Plains, Farmland	226
IV-5-C	Reforestation & Replanting - Rain Forests, Marshes, etc.	227
IV-5-D	Reforestation & Replanting - Arid, Barren Areas	228
IV-6-A	Fiber Resources	233
IV-8-A	Borderless Regions	239
V-1-A	Regional Implementation - From Concept to Prototype	260
V-2-A	The Regional Concept and the Academic World	263
V-2-B	Direct Academic Involvement	264
V-2-C	Direct Government Involvement	266
V-2-D	Direct Business and Industry Involvement	265
V-2-E	Public Networking for the Regional Concept	270
V-2-F	Development of International Networking	272
V-2-G	Networking With Regionalization - The Emergence of Research & Development and Enterprise	274

LIST OF FIGURES

V-4-A	Basic System Relationships for	279
	Regional Mobilization and Beyond	279
V-4-B	Organizing for Regionalization	281
V-4-C	Regional Resource Application for Multi-Levels and Multi-Phases	283
V-4-D	Initial Contributions for Organizing Mobilization	285 & 286
V-4-E	Dealing With the Realities of Regionalization	288
V-4-F	Mobilization Arrangements	290
V-5-A	Program Initiation of Regional Natural Resources	293
V-5-B	Initiation of Human Resource Development Programs	295
V-5-C	Initiation of Food Resource Development From Global to Regional	297
V-5-D	Initiation of Lawmaking From Global to Regional	299
V-5-E	Investigation and General Enhancement of Potential	302
	Regional Sites- (Investigation)	
V-5-F	Investigation and General Enhancement of Potentia	303
	Regional Sites-(Enhancement)	
V-5-G	Criteria for Regional Site Selection	305
V-5-H	Preliminary Design Sequences for	311 & 312
	Subsequent Regional Development	
V-6-A	Development of Regional Infrastructure N	318
V-6-B	Regional Communication Development	321
V-6-C	Regional Transportation Development	323
V-6-D	Public Works Development	325
V-6-E	Business, Commerce, Industry and Agricultural Development	327
V-6-F	Infrastructures M, D and E Development -Medical,	329
	Safety/Security and Education	
V-6-G	Developing Regions, Communities, Neighborhoods & Centers	331
V-6-H	Developing What is Public and What is Private	333
V-7-A	Human Resources - Primary Regional Investment	337
V-7-B	Regional Investments According to Phases	340

Explorers of the Mind: In Search of a Better World

LIST OF TABLES

I-5-A	Preliminary Survey- Selected Over-Populated Cities	31
II-1-A	Conditions Within Some Supercities	63
III-3-A	Social Responsibilities	128
IV-1-A	Proposed Apportionment of Regions	176
IV-1-B	Regional Development Evolvement	176
IV-3-A	World's Water Supply	199
IV-7-A	Global Resources (Mostly Non-renewable)	236

INTRODUCTION

The human race is running out of time! Mankind has fouled the Earth's environment and taxed its resources almost to their limit. Clear thinking individuals must seize the initiative and devise ways to save our planet before the situation becomes irreversible. Not to do so may spell the end of civilization and, perhaps, our species.

Of primary concern are the twin problems of worldwide overpopulation and high local or regional density which bring about environmental deterioration and attrition of resources. If our social systems are to be saved, the concept of the modern megalopolis or supercity must be reevaluated. These gigantic entities have typically evolved in a random, chaotic manner, resulting in monumental problems for their inhabitants. In spite of this, they offer many advantages worth retaining.

Can new infrastructures be developed that would be in consonance with human nature and natural resources and preserve the desirable elements of the supercity while eliminating the negative ones?

Comprehensive, long term planning must replace the piecemeal, short-sighted efforts that prevail today if we have any hope of accomplishing this.

Population growth in much of the world continues to accelerate unabated, placing all forms of life in jeopardy and many in danger of extinction. Acute environmental and resource crises are already evident in many places. The Earth is finite; we cannot exceed its limits with impunity. When the environment deteriorates and key resources are depleted, people of all economic strata suffer. They become vulnerable to disease, hunger, criminal violence, social upheaval, economic chaos, pollution and water and power shortages.

There is a global cry for changes to save our world. It calls for greater individual and collective awareness of existing natural and man-made forces and impending events, cataclysmic or insidious, that are likely to bring disaster.

The world is in desperate need of leaders who are sufficiently concerned about the impact of overpopulation on the environment, resources and quality of life. These leaders must have special knowledge and skills which enable them to direct complex efforts that are systemic in nature. They will be required to have vision, strength of purpose, a sense of responsibility and the character to undertake the great works needed to build and restore our world. Drawn from a wide range of disciplines, they must aspire to provide for the common good of present and future generations. They will respect the old, well-formulated workable methods of the past while being open to innovative ideas. Their challenge is to aggressively build new regional infrastructures and to modify old ones throughout the world. We must find these leaders now.

Supercities cannot continue on their present course without reaching a critical mass of self-destruction. There is hope of avoiding this if population influxes are decreased and people diverted to new, specially planned and prepared regions while supercities undergo restructuring.

These processes take time; the need is urgent; the effort must start immediately.

The creation of new regions worldwide will require the optimum use of time and space so that there can be maximum freedom for all. This means that regional designs must provide safe and effective access to resources and locations within its space while protecting and enhancing the environment.

When the region is designed, all levels of socio-economic activity must be included. It is not a matter of central versus local planning, implementation and control, but the competence of each to perform requisite functions. The region provides a flexible form of organization, employing networking for empowering its various infrastructures. This new look is achieved through imaginative design and planning and pragmatic implementation while sustaining a vision of a better, more civilized world.

Only by avoiding the extremes of both chaos and regimentation can we achieve optimum freedom and fulfillment. The regional concept, as it is applied worldwide, represents a balanced approach. Universal models of the region must be adaptable to accommodate different cultures, social differentiation, political systems, geographical locations, lifestyles, environments and resources.

Implementation of design concepts on a global and regional scale requires multi-faceted approaches and strategies. Such implementation requires a number of years of careful phasing-in with emphasis on system integration. Adjustments must be made gradually to minimize hardship in existing densely populated centers. It takes time, perseverance and insight by the public and private sectors to create new regional infrastructures which will allow orderly population shifts to take place.

New regions must be prepared, finances arranged, resources allocated, laws passed, policies, operating rules and limits determined, and people retrained and resettled. Regional planning requires careful introduction of new community networks and dedicated centers. As they are designed, planned and implemented, the regions will also provide invaluable experiences in the restructuring and restoration of what were once over-populated cities.

The advancement of civilization requires multi-generational continuity. New concepts of networks and centers for living and working must continue to evolve. Each generation must have its chance to make this a better world. Our major imperative is to ensure that coming generations have an opportunity to

INTRODUCTION

survive and thrive. The Gaia hypothesis states, "...the conditions necessary for life are created and maintained by life itself in a self-sustaining process of dynamical feedback". (from "The Ages of Gaia"-J.E.Lovelock)

Is it possible for people of many backgrounds to explore and realize a better world for all? We speak different languages and have different attitudes, but we have common needs. We seek different objectives, but share common perils and pain. Difficult as it may be, we need special ways to communicate with words, pictures and ideas in order to face our several worlds together. How can such complex communication be accomplished? Our diverse ways of thinking need not be a deterrent. If we agree with the need to create new regions, then we have already taken a positive step in the same direction. All of our perspectives are likely to grow. We may have strong imaginations and create new things. We may face life's events in pragmatic ways. We may weigh the behavior of ourselves and others, guided by moral and ethical considerations. I propose that we have the potential for all of these, and that there are inherently three ways of perceiving, reflecting and responding to be found within each of our brains. They enable us to communicate effectively. I have named these three ways Neos, Veritor and Pragma, who, as little characters, explore the topics of this book. These characters become involved in trialogues as they express various perspectives, opinions and relationships on different issues. During these conversations, they attempt to present new ideas in a positive, constructive way. Let me introduce Neos, Veritor and Pragma.

I am Neos. I strive for the ideal, the optimum and new. I am that part of you that creates, innovates and reassociates. I am that potential within you that strives for freedom of expression. I am the part of you that wants to try new things. When you address challenging issues, I help you utilize intuition and keep an open mind. You may be reluctant to seek my participation at times because it is risky to express and implement new ideas and strive for what is different. The ideas that I give to you may be subjected to ridicule, skepticism and denouncement. How do you know that I inhabit your very thoughts and actions? I have always inhabited the minds of humans. Every man-made object, setting or system that exists today and that has been accepted as a reality has at one time been an idea or concept waiting to be discovered. I enable you to express your creativity. You may do this by helping children to discover new things; you may express it by artistry; you may pioneer innovative enterprises.

I am the potential that heightens your awareness of the esthetic significance and uniqueness of what you observe, think, feel and do. I prompt and encourage you to design, compose, fashion, build, integrate, synthesize, project, teach and share your creativeness, however expressed. I enable you to channel your creative endeavors towards any field of interest.

I am always with you when you sense the wonders of nature with its designs, beauty, harmony, chaos and variety. I am always present in your quest for a new tomorrow, a world reborn. Because I am a part of every human's creative nature, I encourage each person to communicate and to combine ideas with others.

INTRODUCTION

I am Veritor. I am that part of your thinking and feeling that ennobles and enrichens. I am your resolve to invest in life in order to promote well-being and self-worth. I am that part of you that is sensitive to the joy and pain within yourself and others. I help you to achieve vision and gain insight. I am your understanding of natural and spiritual interrelationships. I am your conscience, your sense of self-esteem and your awareness of self, others, and your environment. I am that special potential gift that has been given to you to feel profoundly, to weigh values and to establish levels of significance. I am the capacity within your mind that is either enhanced or inhibited according to your cultural, religious and political environment. Within such limits, I determine your compassion, sense of social justice, cooperation and willingness to communicate with persons of different backgrounds.

How do you know I am that potential? You are secure in helping those who are in need because your wellspring of empathy for your fellow humans never dries up. You have continued to rely on me. How much so? You will know by how and what you value in life, by what you are doing to develop yourself into an exemplary person, and by how you treat your fellow human beings. You will know by your respect for human dignity, limitations, strengths, weaknesses and potential. You will know by your reverence for the gift of life and your continued quest for wisdom, knowledge and understanding. You continue to seek to know more about yourself and how you fit into the universal scheme of things.

I am that part of your insight needed to make this a better world for yourself and others. I am within each human mind and spirit, the promoter of the best that is in you and others. It is this commonality that makes humans civilized.

Explorers of the Mind: In Search of a Better World

I am Pragma. I help you analyze in a practical way so that you can be efficient and effective in all that you do. You then learn to be expedient and decisive and to become results-oriented. This helps you prepare for most eventualities. I assist you in organizing your time and space so that you are able to bring order to your life. I enable you to think, communicate and act precisely and without ambiguity. This permits you to compete, cope and get along in all circumstances. I persuade you to accept and accommodate new situations which you cannot change. I help you to analyze 'risk and gain' for all issues.

How do you know that I am a part of your basic nature? You are able to manage your everyday affairs, plan for the future and assume responsibility. You have relied on me during all stages of your development and experiences in life from infancy through adulthood. You have always depended on me to help you confront conditions that you felt threatened by. I have also been part of your primal instinct for flight or fight in the face of impending danger.

I continue to sharpen your perception of the changing world about you. I make you conscious of history and the lessons of survival. I am that part of your reasoning that deals with the pragmatic aspects of life. I am also a part of every other human being as well, and this common ability allows all who call on me in themselves to communicate and reach mutual accord for a better world.

INTRODUCTION

We, Neos, Veritor and Pragma collectively form the patterns of your thinking and profoundly affect your very being. When we are called upon to act singly or together in your brain, it is to provide you with potential for a life of hope, meaning and fulfillment as well as the intellectual and emotional means of effectively facing adversity.

Because we three are collectively within all minds, we are formidable. When we act in unison, people with receptive minds, will be able to devise ways to enhance, protect and conserve life on our planet.

We are ready to induce the best thoughts and feelings within each of you. We will prevail and guide you in your quest for a future filled with promise, peace and prosperity. Together, we offer you balanced thought processes and an effective means of communication to achieve these goals.

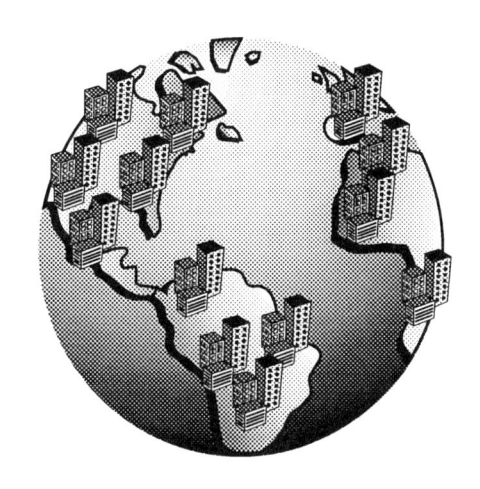

PART I
URGENT TIMES &
CROWDED PLACES

Part I - Urgent Times & Crowded Places

CHAPTER 1 - COMMON CAUSE IN A CHANGING WORLD

It matters not where one lives. There is no escape. People everywhere are vulnerable not only to the inexorable forces of nature, but to human nature itself. Our responses to both are often unreliable and inadequate.

This may hardly be a revelation. Humans have always attempted to cope with and control environmental influences and limiting characteristics. In doing so, mankind has created conditions that have ravaged earth's bounty. Conditions created by rapid population growth and increasing density in specific locales exacerbate demands on environments and resources. The higher the density, the greater the demands and the more critical the problems that result.

Efforts to master the environment and exploit resources have been a factor in producing a variety of socio-economic systems. Most existing designs, however, are obsolete and ineffective in the face of rapid population growth and higher densities of living. When so many people vie for the same living spaces and limited resources, what is likely to happen to their prospects of a better world? One human denies another's survival. Groups do the same. Countries follow suit. Conflicts ensue.

In contemporary times, experiments in social organization have been spawned by a multitude of political ideologies with narrow visions of a better world. None, however, has been concerned with the preservation of the environment or conservation of resources. Furthermore, their obsessions with specific ideologies exclude all others from any benefits to be accrued in their "better" worlds.

Evolutionary progression of new social structures has produced highly differentiated, complex socio-economic systems and governmental designs. Marked contrasts exist between undeveloped and developed countries today. However, despite the comparative sophistication of the "advanced" countries, their socio-economic dysfunctions are widespread and persistent. Obviously, mankind has not reached the apex of functional design in socio-economic organization.

It takes vision, new concepts, planning and the will to grow, remedy or change existing conditions. There is an urgent need for significant improvement of functional interactions for all elements and levels of social organization and governance. Widely divergent groups must be encouraged to participate. Contrary to narrow ideologies, the search for a better world must be inclusive and not exclusive so all may benefit.

Although there exist many ideas for the improvement of world conditions, still more are needed. Concepts must address the development of new regions and the re-development of distressed supercities. New approaches must include extensive networking of human endeavor. Obsolescence must give way to revitalization and restoration. New areas of progress must emerge.

CHAPTER 1 - COMMON CAUSE IN A CHANGING WORLD

The human race has a common cause in making this world more livable for present and future generations. But how is this to be accomplished? What can be gleaned from experience? How can innovation and system concepts be introduced? How can thinking be reshaped and efforts re-directed to provide cooperation, harmony and beneficial growth?

The profusion of cultures and customs worldwide suggests that there are many variations in perspective as to what the good life means. People are likely to formulate divergent goals. In spite of this, a common vision of what may be accomplished for the greater good of all societies would have far more meaning. Such societal goals would need to be based on fundamental human needs.

The absence of key resources and the existence of environmental adversity undermines and modifies human perspectives, expectations and potential. Consequently, conditions for betterment exist unevenly throughout the world. Any universal model for the future must include the capacity to grow.

Our efforts to define and design a highly functional, universal, socio-economic model must be for the purpose of attaining a greater quality of life within the limits of prevailing environment and resources and within the boundaries of time and space.

Part I - Urgent Times & Crowded Places

CHAPTER 2 - GAINING MULTIPLE PERSPECTIVES

Self-interest must be balanced with the interests of others in the search for a better world. How else can people with divergent views arrive at a consensus for planning and acting? What does it take to develop common goals so that resulting changes can make life better, not worse? Rational, creative and ethical thinking are essential.

Of what value is pragmatism alone if it is unethical, simplistic and devoid of innovation? Of what value are high ideals alone if they cannot be applied with imagination, understanding and relevancy? Of what value is creativity alone if it is destructive, vague or trivial? When the virtues of all three perspectives are combined and commonly understood, goals can be made significant and wise, design and planning can be made comprehensive and programs can be implemented effectively. Diversity can make for enrichment.

Designs for better living are appropriate and valuable only when they are derived from balanced thinking. Otherwise, the predominance of one perspective may distort design and subsequent implementation. But how does one integrate complex, comprehensive concepts and designs that have multi-perspectives based on human need? Design functions, in turn, must be inter-related by using a comprehensive systems approach and by communicating with those who will be involved during planning, implementation and operations. This approach must guide us as we strive to fully develop new concepts of social organization.

What communication methods would help us in our quest for a better world? They must help as many as possible to be on the same wave length (like tuning a radio) and stimulate increased comprehension. Perhaps new ideas and perspectives might best be expressed in a special way. The use of presentations and a trialogue could promote greater common understanding.

In order to further this approach, three imagined characters (perspectives within each human mind), Veritor, Neos and Pragma become involved in expounding a central theme (see Introduction). They represent different ways of looking at things. These perspectives may conflict at times, but the characters are of one mind. They share a common purpose of evaluating human conditions and creating a model of a better world. All humans have this potential of multiple perspectives. They may not always share a common purpose, and each individual may have conflicting thoughts. There can be no communication and no hope of attaining unanimity of purpose without identifying and sharing issues, conditions, expectations and solutions.

Each of the imagined characters presents special information. These presentations concern the philosophical basis, prevailing conditions, design and preparation, implementation and operation of a universally applicable social organization model.

GAINING MULTIPLE PERSPECTIVES

Our characters view this world we live in, mindful of the grandeur, intricacies and complexities of nature. They also witness the beehive-like activity of people worldwide as they attempt to prosper. They are impressed by the extent of man-made enterprises, monuments and special pursuits, but they are aware all is not well in the social systems of the world. They realize much must be done.

Symptoms of decay and disarray everywhere need to be investigated, understood and acted upon. Earth-shaking problems are rapidly emerging. They must be addressed intelligently and comprehensively now.

Part I - Urgent Times & Crowded Places

CHAPTER 3 - RIVALRY FOR TIME AND SPACE

Designers of social structures must seriously consider the use of time and space. This is critical because high densities of population often lead to rivalry and friction. More rules and regulations are required. Furthermore, there are more delays and interruptions in transportation and communication, less room to live, work and play and more pressure for all. The costs involved are not only monetary. The greatest cost is degradation in quality of life.

Time and space may be shared, given or taken. When shared, it is by mutual consent; when given, it is through the donor's initiative; and when taken, it is against the recipient's free will. Because humans are conscious of time and space in various ways, their patterns of specific behavior are also likely to differ. In particular, people in industrial societies spend much effort trying to control the influence of acute time and space constraints. The notions of time and space, however, may be linear, cyclical or random and are subject to the variables of nature, man-made designs and strategies for living. Lifestyles of people in various parts of the world differ accordingly. Some people make fewer demands and are more passive.

Veritor, Neos and Pragma are discussing the dimensions of time and space. The characteristics of the latter are of particular interest to them as they sit in their mountain retreat and gaze across the lake before them to a distant city below. They are concerned with underlying interrelationships that effect human behavior within different environments.

Pragma is troubled. "I think when people live too closely together, conflicts are difficult to avoid. What forces people to live that way?"

Neos asks, "Don't people who live in crowded areas have too many distractions? Some of them must be involved in things not of their choosing. I think these unwanted activities infringe on personal time."

Veritor glances up and answers, "As for over-crowding, we can see that many live together in relatively simple ways, and their use of time coincides with nature's changing events and seasons. They perform their daily tasks and celebrate according to the cycles and episodes of their lives. Even in densely populated cities, people sometimes try to isolate or insulate themselves, but this is difficult."

Pragma objects to this, "Is this what is really happening? It seems to me people are attracted by all the excitement, sounds and sights. Distractions and new encounters are pure adventure, especially for young people. All their waking moments must be charged with activity. Chaos and conflicts for time and space-sharing look to them more like opportunities."

Veritor counters, "It is hard to imagine chaos resulting in greater individual freedom, unless it is to exploit the unwary or the ill-advised. I believe more harm and

CHAPTER 3 - RIVALRY FOR TIME AND SPACE

hostility would probably occur for most, and more time and effort would be needed to cope and compensate. It occurs to me that people in densely populated areas have to face three environments involving time and space: one that is self-induced, the second from man-made conditions, and the third that which exists in nature."

Neos has a puzzled look, and notes, "We have only briefly mentioned people who live in very different cultures. Won't it be difficult to communicate with them about new concepts of social living, even if it would improve their lives?"

Veritor responds, "That's an important observation, Neos. Later on, when we design for better living, the concepts of time and space for different cultures will have to be seriously considered, particularly for Third World countries. Of course, it will not be easy to communicate because they will have different views of how to live with time and space. Some will be conscious of time constraints and time sharing while others won't. Some will recognize individual ownership of space; others won't. When we talk about the fundamentals of quality of life with them, perhaps we will have things in common to discuss as we describe new concepts for living and how they might utilize them.

"In industrial and highly technological societies, friction occurs because impersonal systems often demand time commitments from people, leaving less time for individual freedom. Those who control the scheduling and use of time derive tremendous power and privilege. For communication and transportation in a modern setting, timeliness, time-sharing and schedules become all important for synchronization, safety, economy, legal and social contracts and for access to different kinds of space.

"I would like to briefly present some of the time concepts we will need to consider. Some of this is quite esoteric, but it suggests that there is more than the linear time concept of western, industrial cultures."

Time

The concepts of time are many, and one or more of them play a part in all cultures. Such concepts may affect receptivity to new designs for living (i.e. in communication, transportation, commerce, industry, medicine, living arrangements, etc.)

Some see time as:

- *an attempt to precisely measure when and how fast something takes place.*

- *an internal biological clock that resides in all living things governing life cycles.*

- *a perception of successive events happening to oneself, others and the environment.*

- *a dependency of earth's events on cosmic time and space.*

- *a psychological concept of elapsed time dependent on whether desirable or undesirable events are taking place (i.e. time goes by "faster" when pleasant things are happening).*

- *a cultural concept that is "monochronic"(linear sequence) or "polychronic" (simultaneous events with no schedule)-Ref.E.T.Hall,"The Dance of Life, the Other Dimension of Time"*

- *a merging of past and present as with Hopi Indians or of the present and "dream time" of the Australian aborigines.*

- *a measuring tool, not an absolute flow or a substance or a dimension that is a secondary quality in nature.-Ref.Prof. J. Wheeler, Physicist*

CHAPTER 3 - RIVALRY FOR TIME AND SPACE

Veritor begins again, "Concepts of space are inseparably linked with those of time. They help us understand human migration and settlement throughout history and appreciate how mankind may need to live in the future. For instance, consider the premise that living things do not really own space; they only occupy or borrow it for a finite period of time. Furthermore, mankind's existence in this world is in constant flux, completely dependent on time and space and their utilization.

"We have been talking about spaces that hold something of value for humans. We live in a world where people constantly move about. The spaces of yesterday may have different occupants today. Life, past, present and future is forever part of a universe of change."

Pragma thinks about this a moment and says,"It's apparent to me that people attempt to define 'ownership', to organize spheres of influence and master the spaces of their environment."

Veritor answers, "Yes, and they continue to invent new rules to control the exchange and utilization of space such as land and its resources or buildings and their contents. The more spaces and the greater utilization of their contents, the more new rules and regulations are required. Governments are formed to create and enforce them, sometimes for the collective benefit of many and sometimes for special interests.

"The concepts of space are many. Humans have need for certain kinds of personal and collective space. I believe they can be described in terms of physiological, biological, psychological and developmental spaces and their combinations. In other words, people need room to live and grow. Spatial needs of humans interact with the available spaces of their environment. But how should one describe these environmental spaces? Do they include outer space, the atmosphere, land, oceans and even the earth's interior? Should we also count spaces within the mind in the visualization of virtual space?"

From this bewildering array of insights Neos, Veritor and Pragma consolidate their thoughts and expand them in terms of what future societies could be like. But before attempting to offer concepts of such viable societies, they feel it is necessary to further discuss human space needs and interrelationships.

Concepts of Space

- *Everything in the universe is forever changing, subject to the conditions of environment and space. Humans, therefore, must face many transitions.*
- *Space and time are not mutually exclusive and are forever linked. Human occupancy of a specific space will always be modified by time. Designs for living must consider this.*
- *Outer space, atmospheric space, land space, ocean space and the earth's interior space are dynamically linked. Restoration of environments and designs for living are affected.*
- *Earth and cosmic space perpetually interface and interact. Awareness of this is essential for timely preparations, for coping with recovery from cataclysmic events.*
- *There is personal space and collective space. Each individual requires its unique space. Groups require common spaces which may also be unique. Variations in design are needed.*
- *Personal and collective spaces may be given, shared or taken. Human relationships and transactions are involved and affect quality of life.*
- *There is a physiological space required for freedom. This must be considered in the design of habitation, recreation, the workplace, etc.*
- *There is a biological space required for survival. This must be considered in restoring and preserving the environment so that it remains suitable for humans and other living things.*
- *There is a psychological space required for thriving. This must be considered for human health and the enrichment of life.*
- *There is a developmental space required for growth. This must be considered for the redesign and improved utilization of existing spaces to enhance productivity and promote effectiveness.*
- *Thoughts are dimensionless but can discern space limitations and provide imagery of spatial content. It is essential in design to appreciate limits and to utilize imagery.*
- *Space can never be owned, only borrowed and utilized. This recognizes the futility of acquiring space without need and the importance of utilizing the contents of such space wisely.*
- *Territorial imperatives represent individual or collective drives to control and occupy space. Designs must counteract this tendency so that territorial sharing will result in an inclusive world.*

CHAPTER 3 - RIVALRY FOR TIME AND SPACE

Pragma observes, "It's apparent that individual space is needed for carrying out everyday basic functions. It would be torture to deny individuals their basic space for standing, sitting or lying down. There may be a sharing of space for working or intimacy during short periods if time, but cultures vary in their treatment of this."

Veritor reflects and comments, "This is very interesting. A bounded space can be either a prison or a sanctuary. The difference is whether an individual is free to come and go. It also occurs to me that the mind or internal space is free to project images of other real or imaginary space and its contents. This is important because imagery is essential when attempting to create new living and working spaces."

Neos finds this line of thought exciting, "Don't you think the dynamics of time and space also need to be considered in design? People need to be able to move about to perform work and enjoy leisure time. This is a major problem in the industrial, high density cities of today where it's common for people to intrude in the functional spaces occupied by others. Various means of transportation, which afford people freedom of movement, require extended space, for example. But what happens when someone doesn't want to share space and intentionally contests the space of another? There are bound to be many costly conflicts."

Veritor answers,"Yes, you're right. This takes place even when there is relative freedom of movement. Conflicts are bound to happen if there are no rules for regulating behavior and traffic flow. Local governments have to create legal rights of way and specify how they are to be used. In the future, control centers will be necessary to regulate extensive traffic. In some cases physical barriers will need to be erected to avoid collisions. We will expand this further when transportation systems are discussed."

Pragma adds, "I am quite interested in why people select specific spaces to occupy, use or traverse. Does it reflect status, strategic locations, central areas, convenient access to resources and services? Are they for protection or defense? There are obviously many combinations of reasons to explore."

Spatial Constraints

When designing for humans, consideration must be given to constraints lest they prove excessive. Various cultures have different space tolerances. Such preferences may be due to conditioning. How does this affect human behavior? How much space do individuals basically need to survive, thrive and develop?

Seated in bus, train, plane or boat

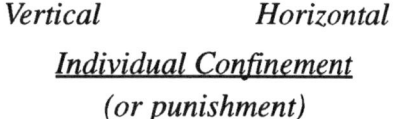

Vertical   Horizontal

Individual Confinement
(or punishment)

IMMOBILITY

Standing in a crowded elevator

Collective Constraints
(Conditionally Given)

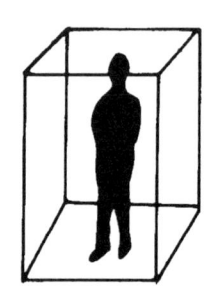

Small room with four walls, floor and ceiling, no windows

Restricted Individual Movement
(Physio-psychological conflicts exist)

Room for more than one with four walls, ceiling and floor and no windows

MOBILITY

Collective Restricted Movements
(Friction induces need for rules in sharing time and space)

Overcrowding produces friction which may result in aggressive/passive behavior and psychological disorders.

CHAPTER 3 - RIVALRY FOR TIME AND SPACE

Veritor speculates. "I wonder what kind of space is needed for mankind to survive. Isn't need for physiological space dependent on immediate surroundings for resources? We know there has to be water, oxygen, nitrogen and carbon for the many biological cycles to occur. There also have to be means of growing food. There have to be enough green plants with unobstructed sunlight to promote photosynthesis for plant growth, absorb carbon dioxide and add oxygen to the air as well."

Pragma looks towards Veritor and says, "What concerns me most is the attrition of resources and the increasing demand by people in heavily populated areas. It is likely to be very difficult and costly to supply such people with key resources. Yet people still keep crowding into the most congested spaces in the world."

Neos brightens, "I have an idea. Perhaps we can examine how much living or working space individuals and groups actually need and indicate when such space will be needed. We know about 'time sharing'. Isn't this related to space sharing? Can't we think of such sharing in terms of 'usership' instead of 'ownership'? There may be reason for optimism when more people become aware and cooperate in planning for space use. This takes into account, of course, physiological, biological and psychological factors. Everyone would then be able to thrive in a new golden age."

Pragma ponders this and asks,"When we are talking about psychological space needs, do we mean spiritual, cultural and sociological needs? Free expression? Art, music and theatre? Recreation and sports? Is it all of these?"

Veritor responds, "I would include all of them because they enrich life. They are nessessary emotional outlets. Most people require space, not only for their own activities, but for other activities that promote, supply and support them."

Neos add, "People must escape at least occasionally from crowded conditions. Recreational areas such as parks, lakes, mountains, seashore, etc.provide freedom where the spirit can soar, the mind can wander or be in peace and the body can be active or passive."

Personal Space and Collective Space
Preliminary Considerations for Regional Design

Survival Dependency - Cyclical and Seasonal Biological Space Needs

- *For growing and processing of food*
- *For providing health and hygiene*
- *To produce clothing*
- *To provide shelter and housing*
- *To ensure key elements exist in order to live*
- *For providing and supplying pure water*
- *For controlling and eliminating pollution*
- *For converting or disposing waste safely*
- *For developing, conserving, processing and recycling natural resources*
- *To provide safety and security provisions*

Thriving Dependency -Psychological Space Needs

- *To satisfy the spiritual*
- *To provide cultural and social interaction*
- *To allow recreational activities*
- *For stimulation, identification, relaxation*
- *To promote and perform the arts and music and a sense of well-being*
- *To promote and produce theater*
- *To perform sports activities*
- *To develop, encourage literature and information exchange*

CHAPTER 3 - RIVALRY FOR TIME AND SPACE

Spiritual needs are of concern to Veritor. "Religions of the world can bring solace and act as a bulwark against the harsh realities of life. People often worship with others in shared spaces. People everywhere share spaces for stimulation, identification, relaxation and a sense of well-being. Psychological space provides the emotional and mental freedom of individuals to interact and improve group relationships. Its availability enhances human behavior and inter-dependencies."

Neos's face lights up, "Many feel that music, drama, the arts and communing with nature offer spiritual experiences. This allows them to transcend time and space, to escape into a personal realm of imagination. Sometimes they may try to share this with others. Sometimes these spaces of the mind are filled with ideas that can materialize into creative expression like art, writing, acting, dancing and so forth."

Pragma looks sharply at Neos. "That may be all well and good, but in the real world, people do not become involved. There are quite a few who prefer to be spectators living vicariously in the lives and imaginary spaces of others. Even so, I can see that sharing of space does take place even when it is displayed on a TV screen."

Veritor sums up"Psychological space starts with people's minds and emotional make-up. All humans need to manage stress in a non-destructive way. Collectively, they need to provide for common psychological spaces where there can be respectful exchanges. These promote cooperation and assistance to those who have acute problems. Family settings and places of worship may offer this. Many cultures encourage space-sharing and group support. However, in some cultures feelings are suppressed and the sharing of space and time is minimal."

"If time and space could be allocated for healthy sharing experiences worldwide, what an antidote for war this could become!" Neos exclaims. "Also, it's by far preferable for people to become involved in sports and common creative endeavors than engage in destructive activities."

There is a lull in the conversation as Veritor, Neos and Pragma consider developmental space needs that must be provided to allow individuals and groups to grow. They recognize that it is critical to the well-being of future societies. Basic public and private functions need to be performed. But special spaces must be set aside to do so. Great emphasis must be made, therefore, when designing and planning, to designate appropriate spaces for such functions.

Pragma breaks the silence,"There are so many people throughout the world who control space that is beyond their capacity to utilize. There is also a good deal of disparity in how people use their spaces. Some lifestyles are simpler and less demanding; others are complicated, requiring more space-sharing. There are also great differences in technological and economic development, commerce, use of natural and human resources, governmental infrastructures, financial sophistication and complex transportation and communication systems. But do these diverse man-made conditions have anything in common?"

Veritor responds, "Basic considerations exist for different activities, lifestyles and circumstances. Technologies need room to experiment, manufacture, process, assemble, store and transport. Commerce and communication need space for centers, storage and distribution networks. Resource gathering and extraction need access, processing, storage, rights of way and shipping spaces. Government functions of all types and at all levels require space to plan, manage, administer, safeguard, operate and maintain public works. Areas for health and education functions are constantly needed. All of these general functions are necessary for populations throughout the world."

Veritor adds, "For these prime functions we also have to consider the service functions that support them. Water and fuels must be supplied, energy generated, transformed and delivered, maintenance and repairs made for roads, bridges, harbors and airports, legal and medical services provided, food processing and distribution made, waste processing and disposal furnished, and many primary, secondary and tertiary services, as well. All require special spaces. Industrialized countries, in particular, have become heavy consumers and overly dependent on service functions."

Pragma reflects and states,"I think the test for dependency is to see what would happen if such services were missing or scarce. Could a densely populated center or country continue to survive, prosper or grow if they were not available?"

Veritor thoughtfully concludes, "It is my observation that inter-dependencies are not adequately recognized by opposing interests vying for the same space. Multinationals have often waged wars because of unyielding positions and short term gains. Instead of collective or universal sharing or the peaceful exchange of human skills and natural resources, including common land utilization, there is dominance and over-competition. Promotion of competition may serve to stimulate humans to achieve the best utilization of a space that is uncontested. However, excessive competition can prevent optimum use and be enormously wasteful and detrimental, creating inequities."

Neos adds, "Fortunately, we can see positive examples already happening. Countries have agreed to share and protect Antarctica. Also, the laws of the sea are gradually evolving to promote sharing and protection of the world's oceans, waterways and resources."

Veritor challenges the others. "How effective can governments be in the promotion of space and time-sharing? Governments are the most powerful man-made regulators of space and time utilization. Of course, the forces of nature and environmental conditions are even greater. How can mankind achieve a better understanding of nature's space, and how can governments become more mature in their comprehensive planning of space utilization? The results should be of historical significance. This is what we must explore!"

Part I - Urgent Times & Crowded Places

CHAPTER 4 - QUALITY OF LIFE AND POPULATION DENSITY

Quality of life pertains to the enrichment of human existence which emphasizes not only surviving but thriving. It implies that many fundamental values and needs transcend differences in standards of living. For example, we may consider the need for creature comfort to be a universal goal, desirable by both the bushman in a primitive surrounding and the cosmopolitan sophisticate. Despite quantitative differences, they both desire this quality in their lives.

What contributes to or detracts from quality of life? There are internal and external forces that modify living conditions. Over-population and congestion, for instance, create adverse changes which, when extreme and unaddressed, seriously reduce quality of life. Demands and rivalries become acute, resources are dissipated, conflicts multiply and people dehumanize.

Neos, Veritor and Pragma are keenly aware of the prevalence of social problems. They know that there can be an glut of things of questionable importance as well as a dearth of those things that have greater significance. In a philosophical mood, they reflect on what quality of life means, particularly as it relates to population density and conditions. They seek a better understanding of what people yearn and live for. They speculate on scenarios that would promote better living conditions for people in all cultures. They hope to gain insight by comparing how people could live throughout the world if there were improvements in the design of critical socio-economic infrastructures.

Veritor begins,"We can expect to find a great variety of life styles and people in widely disparate economic circumstances during our journey. We need to test our ideas as to what an optimum quality of living means for people of different cultures. Can they share a universal concept of this? People adapt to or tolerate adverse circumstances in many ways in order to survive. They often try to salvage whatever they can and consider this to be the best quality of life they can achieve. Still others live in complete misery and destitution, buried in a mire of hopelessness."

Neos considers this and asks, "Isn't it amazing how well some people are able to create their own special environment in the midst of a larger, more hostile one?"

Pragma grimly responds, "I think that these people ultimately have to face up to this problem, especially when their immediate environment is threatened. How many 'protected' and isolated societies are there that are immune from the influences of the world at large? Some affluent people live in enclaves for security or prestige. But what happens when the natural course of events in their lives are disrupted, security breaks down or they lose control? Was General Cedrous of Haiti secure?"

Veritor reflects and says, "We have mentioned the giving, sharing and taking of time and space.

What happens when indigenous people, their possessions and way of life are threatened? Other than survival, what must they safeguard? They may lose everything, but they must never lose their self-esteem, sense of humanity and capacity to over-ride adversity."

Pragma answers emphatically, "You're right. History is filled with accounts of conquerors and invaders. Yet, many who were oppressed not only survived but retained their feelings of self-worth and hope for a better life. We have an example of this in concentration camp survivors."

Veritor thinks out loud, "I wonder if overly aggressive people lack awareness? Their concept of what quality of life means must be extremely limited or distorted. Perhaps they don't even recognize their deficiencies. After they have disrupted, ruined or taken the lives of many other people, what quality of life do they have left? For instance, in the former Soviet Union, over fifty years of aggressive, despotic efforts were expended to establish central economic planning, domination and absolute control, ostensibly to provide collective quality of life. Still, there was little awareness by those who ruled as to what constituted an acceptable individual quality of life. Human freedom and dignity suffered. The people who were discouraged from participating became passive and indifferent. Lives were disrupted; oppression prevailed. Although this aggressiveness has since been confronted, residual aggressiveness remains. Materialism has been increasing as people seek to compensate for deficiencies in their lives. The quality of life remains unsatisfactory."

Neos is curious, "Isn't materialism related more to quantity rather than quality? Could it be that we often mistake one for the other? Some people build taller buildings, others seek acclaim, others accumulate land and property, many collect objects for the sake of accumulation while still others acquire money, heads of cattle, even wives and children as property. People everywhere have the notion of quantity as an indicator of worth. But isn't this at the expense of a life with quality which could prove more rewarding?"

CHAPTER 4 - QUALITY OF LIFE AND POPULATION DENSITY

Optimum Quality of Life For The Individual

Life has optimum quality when it is given meaning and is appreciated, when there is hope for the future and, within limits, the freedom of choice.

Quality of life occurs when there is/are:

- *sufficient food, clean air and water to sustain life*
- *adequate protection from the harshness of the elements.*
- *relief from illness and the availability of medical care.*
- *respite from continuous labor.*
- *the capability of supporting self and family.*

- *sufficient resources.*
- *confidence in one's skills.*
- *a feeling of security.*
- *freedom to be mobile or at rest.*
- *freedom from oppression and abuse.*

- *freedom to learn and grow as an individual.*
- *creature comforts.*
- *recreation that brings joy.*
- *an enjoyment of all kinds of beauty.*
- *the opportunity to create.*

- *a sense of fulfillment from one's accomplishments.*
- *the expression and experience of love.*
- *a process in which one relates to the Divine.*
- *a sense of harmony with oneself and the environment.*
- *friends to share various aspects of living.*
- *a feeling of belonging or associating.*
- *others*

Veritor notes, "A life that is based on materialism can never prove to be enough. This seems to be consistent throughout the world. I see this acquisitiveness in affluent countries where people consume more than they need, accumulate multiples of everything and throw things away indiscriminately."

Neos reflects and asks,"What do people require at the very least for quality living? Isn't it essential that they have sufficient food and water, shelter, relief and care when ill, and respite from too much labor? Don't they need to be capable of supporting self and family, both now and in the future, and to feel secure from oppression and abuse? Who doesn't want to enjoy leisure, creativity and fulfillment? And what of love and friendship in a world often made alien by perverse human behavior? Spiritually, isn't true that people need solace and understanding of themselves through concepts of divinity?"

Veritor responds,"Your perceptions have merit and give us much to ponder. They should also prove to be helpful when we observe different elements of society, particularly when they are brought together as a result of migrations. New relationships caused by the mixing of cultures can modify quality of life, sometimes in a negative manner, with disruptions and friction."

Pragma nods,"I agree. New relationships don't necessarily mean better relationships. Some individuals will assume leadership roles and may dominate others, some become followers and still others remain independent or indifferent."

Neos adds,"It seems that many leaders crave power, prestige and admiration. Becoming archetypes may be part of their concept of quality of life. Leaders often play parent or boss roles. Followers appear to take the role of children or workers who may be subservient and seek protection, guidance, comfort, direction, limits and some degree of acceptance. Some may attempt to imitate their archetypes. Whatever the roles played, they modify concepts of status and expectations in life."

Veritor continues,"As you began to say, Pragma, there are individuals who don't see themselves as leaders or as followers. They assumed the role of adults, independent in thought and action in their association with others. They interact, exchanging ideas and possibilities, participating in many activities on a voluntary basis and initiating joint ventures with full cooperation and partnership. Their's is certainly a different concept of quality of life."

Factors Which Modify Quality of Living

For the individual

As a Leader
- Power
- Prestige
- Admiration
- Acclamation
- Achievement
- Heroism

Parent or Boss Role and relationships

As a Follower
- Protection
- Guidance
- Imitation
- Praise
- Acceptance
- Limits

Child or Worker Role and relationships

As an Associate
- Interaction
- Exchange
- Identification
- Feedback
- Participation
- Partnership

Adult or Colleague Role and relationships

For Nations and Cultural Groups

In Collective Leadership
- Economic growth and dominance
- Control of resources
- Acquisition of wealth
- Achievement

In Collective Fellowship
- Supplying natural resources
- Supplying human resources
- Economic survival
- Growth dependency

In Cooperative Association
- Exchange of knowledge
- Exchange of resources
- Mutual Assistance
- Communication and interaction

Neos suggests, "Let's look at similar relationships that exist between different countries and cultural groups. Some nations see their roles as leaders of economic growth. They exert control to maintain or influence utilization of available resources both within and outside their domain. The United States and other industrial countries are economically structured to be high consumers and must exploit their own resources and those of others to satiate their appetite. They find it necessary to do so because of market driven demand. But this demand is based on a narrow concept of what quality of life means. It sees the acquisition of wealth and material goods as being all important. Educational, cultural and spiritual accomplishments are also considered, but as secondary achievements. In a way, industrial nations assume the boss or manager role in international economics and in a larger sense a 'parenting' role. I question whether they have a parental sense of responsibility for the members of their own societies and for underdeveloped nations."

Pragma responds, "But other countries submit to dominance. Third world countries in Central America, Africa, Asia are heavily populated and primarily agrarian. Many have valuable natural resources and all have abundant cheap labor that may be attractive to industrial nations to exploit. The less developed countries become dependent for their very survival on the dominant nations. The rate of economic growth of underdeveloped countries is largely controlled by others. In the meantime, their very rapid population growth increases their own deterioration. They assume the role of dependent workers or 'children' of the world."

Veritor reflects on this and continues, "I think you have expressed some provocative ideas, but I also think many more countries and cultural groups have been 'maturing'. They neither dominate nor are they being dominated. For instance, the Scandinavian countries have evolved through the years to become stable societies which appear well organized and progressive. They show a spirit of cooperation and association. Inter-communication, social interactions, economic trade and cultural exchanges are encouraged. Competition and ventures are healthy and productive. The relationship between countries is that of colleagues and 'mature adults'."

Neos, Veritor and Pragma now turn their attention to overpopulated and underpopulated areas and their quality of life. These areas have very different kinds of environments and availability of critical natural resources, conditions which directly affect human quality of life. Environmental degradation is common in most populated areas of the world. Too many people in affluent countries demand, consume and waste limited key resources. This leads to multi-national exploitation and domination in order to seize or maintain control of human and natural resources. As a result, the powerless are manipulated and left with a marginal subsistence, tenaciously struggling to survive. Eventually, everyone living in or near densely populated areas with depleted resources suffers a reduction in quality of life. When population exceeds the capacity of the land, there is pollution.

CHAPTER 4 - QUALITY OF LIFE AND POPULATION DENSITY

Over-population and compression of population are of grave concern to Veritor, Neos and Pragma. They feel it is necessary to investigate its impact on different parts of the world. How else will they be able to intelligently produce meaningful concepts of new societies?

Veritor is the first to speak. "It is difficult for people living in crowded parts of the world to be objective. Some with money and influence who live there in comfort do so under increasing threat from those who have had little or nothing. Having so much to lose, the affluent take special security measures, pressing for protective or restrictive laws. Ironically, these precautions make for further isolation and are often accompanied by further indifference to the plight of others. What do you think, Neos?"

Neos replies, "I think that wherever abject poverty, hunger and disease prevail, the wealthy and the powerful remain indifferent at their own peril. History shows us that eventually, as corruption and decadence grow, the oppressed react with violence. The radical changes that follow are not necessarily favorable to those who have been deprived, especially without a planned restructuring of society."

Veritor adds, "The sad part of it all is that the privileged often do not recognize their opportunity to use their wealth and power to promote the health of their society. They would have more to gain in terms of quality of life, themselves, by doing so before the resources of their land have been depleted and their populations impoverished. To what avail is the special status of the powerful in that situation? Will they transfer their wealth and interests elsewhere and desert their countries? When world resources are depleted or inaccessible, what then? Will the earth be a 'sinking ship' in which all drown?"

Neos, Veritor and Pragma must now begin their travels to the far reaches of the earth to evaluate quality of life in densely populated areas. They expect to witness curious anomalies in which an acceptable quality of life exists despite the crowding. These, they suspect, will be the exception. They will be particularly concerned with resources and man-made as well as natural environmental conditions as they affect quality of life.

Conditions Which Affect Quality of Life

Natural Conditions

- *Altitude and Latitude*
- *Geographic Location*
- *Climate Characteristics*
- *Accessible Water Resources*
- *Energy Resources*
- *Arable Land*
- *Mineral, Chemical, Resources, etc.*
- *Forests and Foraging Land Conditions*
- *Suitable Land for Construction*
- *Earth Stability and Volcanic Activity*
- *Ocean, Lake and River Effects*
- *Mountain Barriers*

Man-made Conditions

- *Water Acquisition Systems*
- *Agricultural Activities*
- *Industrial & Processing Systems*
- *Mining/Extraction Activities*
- *Energy Systems*
- *Transportation Systems*
- *Communication Systems*
- *Education Systems*
- *Economic / Financial Activities*
- *Public Works*
- *Health Care Systems*
- *Recreation & Cultural Activities*
- *Government / Political Systems*
- *Business and Commerce*

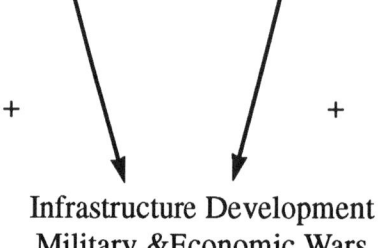

+ +

↓ ↓

Infrastructure Development
Military & Economic Wars
Distribution of Populations
Cultural Preferences & Habits

↓

Extent of Quality of Life

CHAPTER 4 - QUALITY OF LIFE AND POPULATION DENSITY

Many countries and cities are overpopulated or have specific high density areas. But Neos, Veritor and Pragma do not intend to define population growth policy. They mean to study situations where depletion of non-renewable resources, impending potential conflicts and other people-induced conditions result from over-concentrations of population. These conditions portend severe reductions in quality of life.

Veritor is the first to address this. "We must keep our minds open when we survey prevailing conditions in the lands we visit. We have to be objective and try to discover fundamental conditions that need correction."

Pragma responds, "Yes, but we can only attempt a general survey and reach tentative conclusions. There are many variables that concern me. These involve dynamic population shifts and rapid changes that are brought about by economic, political and military events. New borders and divisions can be formed overnight. Conditions in one area may quickly affect another area despite man-made borders which are artificial and arbitrary."

Neos counters, "I think we must also project what is likely to result when such conditions prevail. Observing with open minds doesn't mean having blank ones."

Veritor points to a map and asks, "Where do people live and why? Is it a matter of geography, the lay of the land or availability of key resources? Latitude and altitude, hours of sunshine and climate will largely determine why people pursue specific occupations and activities, as will the presence of natural power and water resources. These will have a great influence on how much of the economy is likely to be based on agriculture, industry or commerce."

Neos concurs, "Certainly, favorable climate and available water make a significant difference in food production and how many crops per year can be grown. What, when and where food can be grown also depends, of course, on the nature of the land."

Pragma adds, "Another thing we must consider is vulnerability to random cataclysmic events. There must be constant vigilance and planned responses to disruptions and damage from hurricanes, tornadoes, hail, torrential rain, floods, heat waves and blizzards as well as earthquakes and volcanic eruptions. Coping with them requires special protection and avenues of escape. Extreme weather and natural disasters cause problems for all man-made environments."

Neos notes, "We have to pay attention to the dependency of forests and other plantlife on local ground water and precipitation. The presence of trees, shrubs and ground cover helps prevent soil erosion and slows down the rate of evaporation. This helps to refurbish and preserve the existing water table. Trees and shrubs are great climate makers. All green plantlife absorbs carbon dioxide and provides oxygen. This is particularly important in industrial countries where so much land is paved over or built on."

Veritor concludes, "There is one condition that is vital, the availability of natural resources and the means of producing energy in both rural and urban areas. Without sufficient electrical and mechanical energy, little can be done to effectively create new areas or improve heavily populated areas. Obviously, quality of life for all but the most primitive lifestyles is greatly affected by a lack of resources and energy insufficiencies. Even primitives need some level of natural resources."

Neos reflects. "Whatever humans produce must be in harmony with the natural environment. Abundant resources and a favorable natural environment are surely necessary, but what humans can modify or enhance will make an even more profound difference in the attainment of a high quality of life."

Veritor responds, "I think we must also observe how well societies have been planned and developed. I particularly refer to heavily populated countries and over-crowded cities where there may be an absence of facilities necessary to manage, change and grow."

Pragma adds, "Considering only the size of population of countries can be misleading. I think population over-concentrations are of more acute concern. It's a case of too many living too close together for harmony and freedom. Somehow there must be careful, gradual redistribution of population. Certainly, the preferences, lifestyles and habits of different cultures in the world must be considered in such redistributions."

Part I - Urgent Times & Crowded Places

CHAPTER 5 - HOW DENSE CAN WE AFFORD TO BECOME

The news is not good. Quality of life for people living in supercities does not improve when these cities simultaneously over-expand and increasingly compress. Look at what is happening all over the world! Mexico City has over 18.5 million people! Cairo's population exceeds 12.6 million! Shanghai is in excess of 12 million! Sān Paulo tops 10.1 million! Beijing has 9.3 million! Seoul, Calcutta, Tokyo, Bombay - it goes on and on! Many rapidly growing cities are headed in the same direction.

Questions arise. How densely packed can people live and work without sacrificing and losing more than can be gained? Are there benefits from overcrowding? Are humans content to live their lives in compressed quarters so intimately close with neighbors? How much privacy, peace and quiet do people need? On the sidewalks and streets, do people enjoy jostling each other, enduring noisy, smelly and frenetic conditions?

There are ominous symptoms of escalating problems in the supercities of the world. The incidences of violence are on the rise; homeless are everywhere. Hunger, illness and disease are commonplace, and the number of broken families is growing. More neighborhoods show greater physical decay and disunity.

Surely there must be attractions as well repulsions. Otherwise, why would people put up with it all? Is it because their home is there? Is it for their close friends? Is it for jobs, associations and affiliations? The attributes of the supercity warrant further discussion.

All the high population density areas of the world are potentially incendiary. People keep moving into and compressing areas already too dense. This stresses critical resources and the service capacities of the city's infrastructures. Without the presence of appropriate services, a semblance of order and relief from economic, social and spiritual deterioration, what prognosis is there for the future ? Chaos? Reliance on quick, desperate remedies or the acceptance of authoritarian rule?

Over-populated areas of the world imperil not only their own inhabitants but all the surrounding areas as well. Population compression of the supercities leaves population vacuums in the outer areas, devoid of most activity and utilization, leading to two concurrent extremes. For instance, the countryside around the supercity, Mexico City, has been neglected, and many have abandoned it. There are too few advocates available to remedy the situation. How can these extreme situations be resolved? The need for alternative solutions based on larger plans and concepts for living is obvious.

ANKARA 2.3 Million
/
BANKOK 5.2 Million
/
CANTON 5.7 Million
/
**MOSCOW
9 Million**

DHAKA 3.5 Million
/
SHENYANG 5.2 Million
/
TIENTSIN 7.9 Million
/
**CALCUTTA
9.2 Million**

TORONTO 3.3 Million
/
ISTANBUL 5.9 Million
/
JAKARTA 7.7 Million
/
**TOKYO
30.4 Million**

POPULATION OVER- CONCENTRATION

CHONGQING 6.5 Million
/
LIMA 5.3 Million
/
BOGOTA 5.7 Million
/
**MEXICO CITY
18.5 Million**

PARIS 8.5 Million
/
WENZHOU 6.0 Million
/
NEW YORK 7.3 Million
/
**CAIRO
12.6 Million**

MANILA 6.7 Million
/
KARACHI 5.2 Million
/
LOS ANGELES 7 Million
/
**SHANGHAI
12 Million**

SANTIAGO 4.4 Million
/
TEHRAN 6.1 Million
/
RIO DE JANEIRO 5.6 Million
/
**SÃO PAULO
18.4 Million**

NANJING 3.7 Million
/
LONDON 6.8 Million
/
BOMBAY 8.5 Million
/
**BEIJING
9.8 Million**

BAGHDAD 3.9 Million
/
N. DELHI 5.8 Million
/
BANDUNG 7.2 Million
/
**SEOUL
9.2 Million**

Figure I-5-A

CHAPTER 5 - HOW DENSE CAN WE AFFORD TO BECOME

Veritor asks, "Is it possible to have individual quality of life when there is an absence of a collective quality of life? "By a collective quality of life, I mean the vitality, cohesion and participation of members of a community or neighborhood. Like individual quality of life, emphasis is not only on surviving, but thriving. The welfare of all must be respected."

Neos immediately responds, "Collective and individual quality of life cannot be achieved by magic or voodoo or any other fragmentary or token efforts. Nor can they be achieved by diverting the populace's attention with the emotions of waging war. This is an old device to temporarily take people's minds off of their deficient quality of life."

Veritor adds, "People try to create, protect and control their immediate environment through extended families, social clubs, associations, religious groups and even local gangs. Television allows the enjoyment of communal events in the privacy of the home. Everywhere, human beings try to seek comfort and relief from the pressures, hardships or boredom of their lives. I suspect that people need to understand and appreciate what a better quality of life could mean to them individually and collectively."

Pragma answers, "Perhaps it is timely to present a list of statements that suggest what a collective quality of life entails. It seems to me there are so many lifestyles and cultures in the world that it would be impossible to satisfy everyone. There are numerous value judgements to be made. How can we hope to do this?"

Neos thinks about this for a moment ."The effort must be made. People can react to what is proposed and add or correct as they choose. What serious considerations of individual and collective quality of life could be made without initiating such lists for inspection and possible adoption?"

Pragma nods in the affirmative, "Concepts of quality of life must not remain an academic exercise. We need to question them and come to resolutions as to their merit in evaluating and correcting the problems of supercities. In this way new and better concepts for living can be created and implemented. Veritor, why don't you present such a list for evaluation?"

Collective Quality of Life

A community has an optimum quality of life when it promotes vitality and a spirit of cohesion and participation, when there is accommodation for different lifestyles and beliefs, and when there is respect for the welfare of all its inhabitants. As with individual quality of life, emphasis is not only on surviving but on thriving as well.

Collective Quality of Life occurs when there is/are:

- *effective means for distributing food, water, goods and other necessities.*
- *an environment free of pollution.*
- *appropriate housing facilities as a part of a community.*
- *adequate provisions for sanitation and health care.*
- *suitable employment for all who are able to work and care for those who aren't.*

- *a variety of industry, commerce and agriculture.*
- *local natural resources and skills available for sustenance and trade.*
- *adequate privacy, security and protection from criminal activity and harm.*
- *adequate provisions to face fires, floods and other natural disasters.*
- *alternate means for effective communication and transportation.*

- *local means for effectively generating, distributing and utilizing energy.*
- *networking of support and cooperation among communities.*
- *political diversity, participation and purpose and an effective government.*
- *multiple provisions for educating and training.*
- *sufficient recreational and cultural activities.*

- *community spirit and a feeling of belonging.*
- *multiple places for worship and association.*
- *adequate encouragement for each new generation to express itself and to participate in community service and development.*

Preliminary Survey - Selected Over-Populated Cities
(Multi-Source Ref.)
Collective Quality of Life

Sample Cities	Population	Approximate. Area- Sq. Mi.	Gen. Density Per Sq. Mi.	Local Density Per Sq. Mi.	Collect.Qual. of Life* Comp. Index 1- 18
Beijing	9,000,000	105	85.7K	>500K	8
Cairo	12,600,000	110	114.3K	>500K	6
Calcutta	9,200,000	300	30.6K	>500K	5
Istanbul	5,900,000	50	118.0K	>500K	7
London	6,800,000	500	13.6K	>100K	9
Los Angeles	7,000,000	460	15.2K	>100K	10
Mexico City	18,500,000	625	29.6K	>500K	7
Moscow	9,000,000	360	25.0K	>100K	9
New York	7,300,000	314	23.2K	>100K	9
Rio de Janeiro	9,500,000	150	63.3K	>100K	7
São Paulo	15,000,000	380	39.5K	>500K	9
Seoul	9,600,000	110	96.0K	>500K	9
Shanghai	12,000,000	110	109.1K	>500K	9
Tokyo	12,000,000	200	60.0K	>500K	10

* Index is based on criteria estimate, the higher numbers reflecting a comparative approximation of greater quality of life. All have increasing dependency on outside resources.

Table I-5-A

PART II
Justifying The Regional Concept

Part II - Justifying the Regional Concept

CHAPTER 1 - INITIAL JOURNEY

It is time to travel; it is time to learn. Veritor, Neos and Pragma prepare to visit the heavily populated areas of the world. During their journey, they will inspect sparsely populated areas as well as concentrate on population hot spots, those in a state of organized chaos. How can they hope to analyze such chaos when there is such a mad profusion of activity? It is a daunting task. Complex remedies to complex, perhaps undefinable problems may prove futile. Supercities seem to be bent on self-annihilation. There is a lack of positive direction. Perhaps the criteria of collective quality of life will prove helpful in understanding societal strain over-population.

Veritor, Neos and Pragma study a map of the world in order to select their destinations. They intend to pick highly populated cities on different continents because of their probable lower collective quality of life. There they expect to see many conditions that are highly deleterious to the cities' inhabitants with their multi-cultures and ethnocentricities.

Veritor begins, "We must note that there are at least seventy-two cities in the world with populations over two million, and there will be many more. We can expect them to follow similar growth patterns and have similar consequences as the target megalopolises we will be inspecting. I feel that these less populated, but very large and growing cities are already experiencing a diminished collective quality of life, particularly where there are population 'hot spots' or areas of extremely high density."

Pragma questions this. "What are these hot spots? Are you referring to high-rise apartment districts or slums and shanty towns? Not everyone who lives in high-density apartments has a severely diminished quality of life. Also, many parts of supercities have beautiful residential and cultural areas where there are theaters, museums, parks, recreation areas, local services and shopping. People who live there are able to create their own special environment. Even in less affluent areas people attempt to create their own unique ways of life."

Neos responds, "Of course such places exist, but people must still strive for a collective quality of life that includes all the supercity inhabitants. If the majority of people are ignored or neglected, quality of life cannot be considered collective, and as we have noted, any individual quality of life for a favored minority will be in jeopardy."

Veritor quickly agrees, "How can we hope to address the many adverse prevailing conditions by focusing exclusively on those minorities who suffer the least? Furthermore, most of the factors that must be considered affect all. Everyone is susceptible to crime, traffic congestion and collisions, air pollution, electric power failure, water shortages, fires and many other man-made disasters."

CHAPTER 1 - INITIAL JOURNEY

Neos adds, "Who is not vulnerable when resources become scarce and food and other necessities require rationing? Who will escape earthquakes, floods, severe storms and other catastrophies? Some who have the means may recover more quickly or escape, but individual quality of life would diminish for them also."

Pragma thinks about this for a moment and replies, "That makes sense. Collective quality of life is a challenge for everyone. But, now, what cities should we investigate?"

Veritor proceeds, "Let us pick the giant cities of the world to visit. I suggest that we go to Mexico City first. It has over 18.5 million people and has a number of high density hot spots. Then we should go to São Paulo in Brazil and compare the two. São Paulo has over 15 million people. Both are growing rapidly. I wonder how long they can continue to effectively cope with their continuing socio-economic problems? Such growth must be exacting a severe toll on their inhabitants' collective quality of life."

Neos concurs. "This sounds like a good approach for other supercities we visit as well. We should derive some valuable insights."

Veritor agrees. "Let's keep in mind what we are looking for in the first place. We cannot hope to make an exhaustive study of all variables for these ever-changing supercities. Many detailed investigations have already been made by highly qualified social scientists, city planners and other competent people interested in improving cities."

. . .

Mexico City, by far the most populated city in the world, sits at an altitude of over 7300 feet waiting for its fate. It is located mainly in what were former lake beds. Although it is ringed by the Sierra Mountains, the city's 18,500,000 inhabitants frequently cannot appreciate the beauty of their surroundings. Air pollution, a common affliction of cities that are traffic-ridden and industrially-oriented, obscures the view for the choking, water-eyed population.

Mexico City's population is unequally distributed over 625 sq. miles. New, unsupportable areas are continually being settled by a heavy influx of rural migrants as well as by the city's increasing number of local inhabitants. There are many shanty towns. During rush hours, the fearsome traffic becomes grid-locked. It is overwhelmingly noisy. Eight excellent, miraculously conceived and constructed rail lines are being extended outward in a vain attempt to meet the needs of over 5,000,000 travelers per day!

Perpetual early obsolescence dictates add-on and extended construction for buildings, bridges, roads, sewers and other installations without benefit and control of a new, integrated system master plan. Such is the case for water importation, storage and distribution. Acquisition of this key resource requires transportation and pumping from remote areas located at much lower altitudes and from distances of 60 to 120 miles away. Sewage and waste disposal remains an enormous nightmare and hazard. Electrical energy, from hydro-electric power, requires ever-increasing expenditures for greater generating capacity and for providing an extended, often difficult, complex distribution.

Much of the housing built by the poor is shabby. Due to expediency, construction ranges from fabrication using scrap material to buildings of questionable code adherence. This is characteristic of both the city's expanding areas and its internal poverty-stricken areas. The wealthy live in opulent enclaves surrounded by services and resources to meet their immediate needs and are insulated to some extent from the pandemonium around them.

Cultural and recreational activities abound. Mexicans are a people of spirit, and they can reflect on a long turbulent history. Such a history has produced archeological treasures, sites and museums which, along with numerous parks and gardens, are frequented and enjoyed by much of the population. Fiestas are also a way of life, despite the abject poverty. Earning a living remains a difficult feat for a great portion of the population. Perhaps it is the sense of family or extended family, in many cases matriarchal in structure, that allows the people to survive. There is a prevailing attitude of taking care of one's own. But with decreasing resources and opportunity, even family unity begins to suffer as more and more individual members are faced with over-competition. As a result, human values suffer.

CHAPTER 1 - INITIAL JOURNEY

MEXICO CITY SUPERCITY EXPANSION

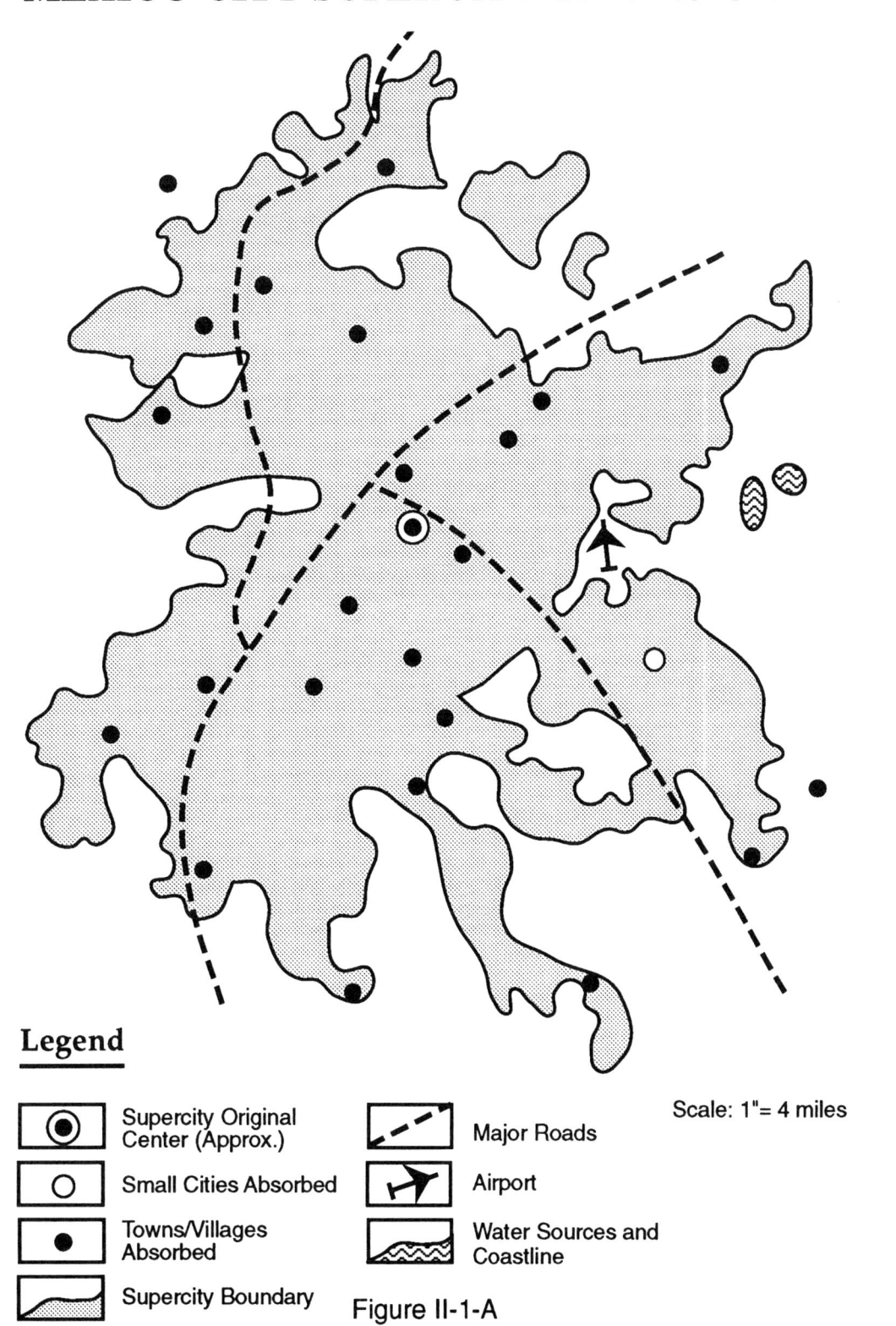

Legend

- ⊙ Supercity Original Center (Approx.)
- ○ Small Cities Absorbed
- • Towns/Villages Absorbed
- Supercity Boundary
- ---- Major Roads
- ✈ Airport
- 〰 Water Sources and Coastline

Scale: 1"= 4 miles

Figure II-1-A

37

In this setting Veritor, Pragma and Neos arrive and make their way through the city, taking notes and asking questions. The vast spectrum of humanity and human endeavor is bewildering. Under all of this tumult, however, are factors that change and motivate such activity.

"This is quite a display!" exclaims Neos. "I am struck with the number of contrasts. All my senses are assailed. It seems that everyone is wound up like a toy, each in single-minded pursuit. Some walk slowly as if in a daze, others are spectators and many move quickly and urgently to reach some destination."

Pragma responds, "It is always like this in big cities. The pace of everything quickens. The atmosphere is electric. But people who seem to be in a daze may be indifferent, bored or desensitized by the continuous daily bombardment of such frenetic activity. I see also that many Mexicans with different cultures do not have this time urgency. How else could they cope? Others who move in an extreme hurry may have developed highly tense personalities because of their working habits."

Neos asks, "I wonder how individuals in the supercity can closely relate to so many others? Do they become bold, brusque and indifferent to the plight of those about them? Aren't there frequent conflicts, cross-purposes and counter-demands? Do they react to others with cynicism, disrespect or arrogance? It seems an impersonal society."

Veritor listens carefully to these observations and answers, "You're right, but there are always people who remain compassionate and caring and form close-knit circles of families and friends. However, in the big cities, such attitudes towards others diminish. Less time seems to be available to listen and relate. The supercity becomes a society of strangers. It appears that the only time people interact is when common cause or grievance is involved. For instance, what happens when there is an earthquake or there is a sudden power blackout and everything comes to a standstill? Many realize their common dependency again and become human once more. It is a strange phenomenon."

Pragma disagrees, "Not everyone in a big city reacts to disaster this way. Sometimes people cooperate and are helpful, but all too frequently, others who have become so hardened, defensive, vengeful or self-indulgent, take advantage of the weak and helpless. The supercity is like a jungle. Roving gangs, looting, price gauging, deceptive advertising, etc. are but symptoms of a larger systemic problem."

"But what of Mexico City ?" Veritor asks. "There is in ever-present danger of disaster. This city has so many aggravating problems. I have the feeling that catastrophes are already happening. We can see that there is certainly severe competition for the same travel and living spaces and for available resources. Housing for most newcomers is practically non-existent, leaving millions in squalor. Who can manage such chaos?"

Pragma continues. "I think it is mad to import water from sources as far away as 120 miles and a mile lower in elevation. This is a desperate situation. How costly in labor and money this must be and only to sustain a worsening problem. Furthermore, much of this water has to be distributed to areas that don't even have piping or sewers."

Neos comments, "There can be no doubt that Mexico City's infrastructures have been over-stressed. Even though there are very many conscientious and talented administrators, planners, economists, architects and engineers who are making valiant efforts, corruption and political arrangements impede their efforts. How can these civil servants succeed in the face of willy-nilly development and indifference to building codes? Opportunism has replaced appropriateness. Compromise of principles and rationalization lead to more of the same."

Veritor turns the conversation to how Mexico City is expanding. "There is a growing influx of population from rural areas. These people, without homes or livelihood, become squatters who move into any vacant spaces that may belong to others or into green spaces that have been specially set aside. They are without resources and bring with them only the skills they had in rural areas, mainly farming. However, there are few areas to farm in the big city. To survive, they must form collective groups so that those finding employment can help feed the rest. Shanty towns grow into major slums, many existing in the very midst of highly developed and heavily-inhabited areas. Often, people in the towns set up their own quasi-governments in order to cope."

Pragma adds, "I also notice that these people live as close as possible to where work is likely to be. Because industry and other places of employment for them are dispersed throughout the city, their shanty towns are likewise dispersed."

Veritor asks, "What patterns of habitation are formed and how do people, the up-coming generations, as well as the rural arrivals, disperse themselves within a growing city? For many years, social scientists have been identifying such patterns. However, what happens today in the megalopolis is more erratic and unplanned. Mexico City appears to be in this category."

Patterns of City Growth

Cities grow with characteristic patterns. Usually a nucleus is formed for some purpose and this center radiates outward as population increases. Within these irregular radiating rings of growth both residential and non-residential functions take place, thereby segregating them. This growth is uneven, some areas growing at the expense or neglect of others. There is often a displacement of the nucleus as activities with different purposes crowd the center. Creators of a new center seek to retain easy proximity and access to the old. Examination of city growth patterns have been going on for very many years. Numerous attempts to design cities continue to take place. Concepts of a city, however, are not designed and planned to include future absorption of neighboring cities. As a result, incidences of congestion in living, traveling and working become common, and zoning becomes inconsistent and arbitrary.

Planned or not, the modern city is thought of as a single entity even when it expands without control to the status of a metropolitan area, metropolitan region(supercity), or megapolitan region (megalopolis)-Burgess, 1923. A region in this sense is ill-defined. It only refers to heavily populated areas and not to the outlying areas which contain necessary key resources for support.

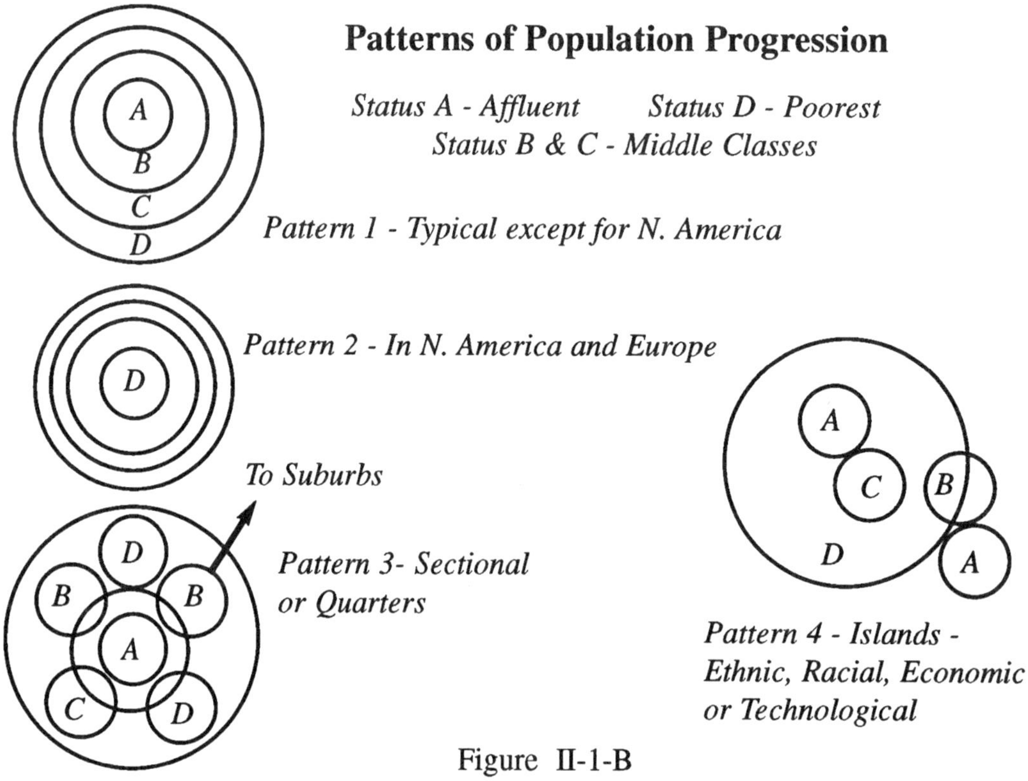

Patterns of Population Progression

Status A - Affluent   Status D - Poorest
Status B & C - Middle Classes

Pattern 1 - Typical except for N. America

Pattern 2 - In N. America and Europe

To Suburbs

Pattern 3 - Sectional or Quarters

Pattern 4 - Islands - Ethnic, Racial, Economic or Technological

Figure II-1-B

CHAPTER 1 - INITIAL JOURNEY

Patterns of Growth for the Metropolitan Area

<u>Metropolitan Area</u>

Initial Growth

<u>Metropolitan "Region" (Supercity)</u>

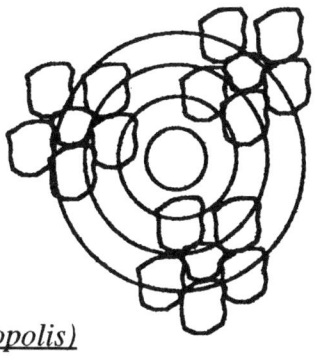

One giant center expanded to include small cities and their centers.

<u>Megapolitan "Region"(Megalopolis)</u>

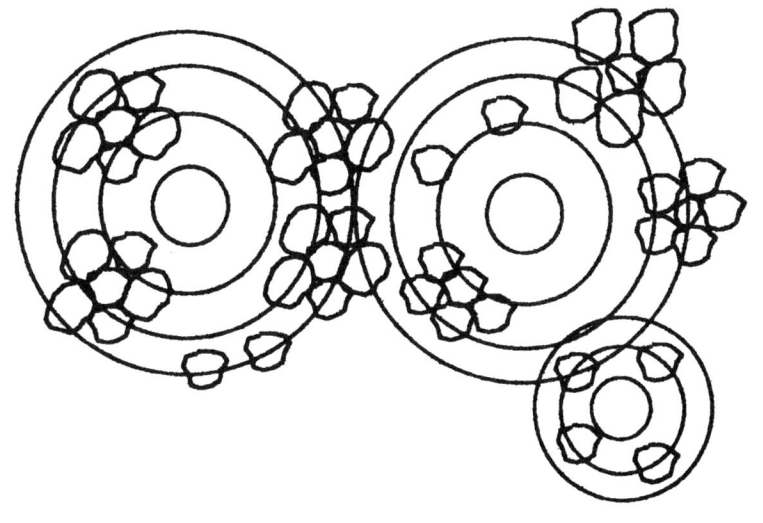

Two or more giant centers overlapping one another and absorbing or merging with smaller cities? towns, etc.

Many outlying areas have functional specializations like industrial, agriculture or air terminals which are gradually surrounded by residential and commercial areas. This mixture or mosaic usually produces zoning confusion and service anomalies.

Figure II-1-C

Neos is deeply curious, "I wonder if successive waves of newcomers make it impossible to plan effectively? For instance, when cities start, they often assign zoning for various purposes like light industry, commercial or residential and so forth. Retail establishments, educational facilities, police and fire stations, religious centers, recreation facilities and other services are usually located near the communities they are meant to serve. Cultural centers and major markets are located elsewhere. In other words, no regional concept or only a vague sense of it exists. There seems to be an obsessive focus on city institutional rigidity and not on how they may evolve when population growth explodes. Services like water supply, air traffic management and sewage treatment are not designed on a regional scale. Trying to plan and provide for them after adjoining communities have been absorbed is futile."

Pragma adds to this, "Mexico City seems to be undergoing evolutionary changes following the pattern of growth you have described. It has become a metropolitan 'region' or supercity, absorbing small peripheral cities in its expansion. Even neighboring Netzhuacoyotl with its 2,000,000 people has been enveped into Mexico City's sphere of growth."

Veritor acknowledges Pragma's statement and continues. "We can see that originally, the wealthy were in the center, the middle class next and the poor lived on the fringes without services. Then the affluent shifted the center for residential living. Eventually sections or quarters were formed according to economic status, commercial emphasis, occupational concentrations, the location of archeological sites and the need for cultural and religious centers, education centers, parks and recreational centers and government institutions. As Mexico City has grown, its sections and quarters have become islands in which people of like background and interests settled. Many areas of Mexico City have become specialized according to industry or other enterprises, but we can see that diverse areas have overlapped."

Neos is slightly agitated, "During all of this evolvement, the poor and the homeless have suffered most. So many live in such extremely dense areas. As I understand it, such density reaches as much as 500,000 people per square mile. This is like one person for every 55 square feet! In over-crowded situations the inhabitants have to make up their own rules for sharing, living, working, traveling and using space as we talked about earlier. This is not a good situation. Witness the thousands who sleep in the streets."

Veritor reflects, "I think that Mexico City's future will largely determine the destiny of Mexico, itself. This must be turned around. Mexico's future should determine Mexico City's destiny. A change in orientation is needed. We will think further about this, but now let us travel."

São Paulo, giant magnet of Brazil, draws people from miles around into its irresistible flux of activity. The city grows at a frenetic pace. It is almost as if there is

CHAPTER 1 - INITIAL JOURNEY

an unspoken challenge to make it become the largest population center in the world. What repercussions will there be from this madness?

São Paulo is favorably located on a coastal plateau near Santos, a port city. It's combined population with its vibrant neighbor, Rio de Janeiro, is about 25,000,000. It grew slowly until the coffee agribusiness took off. Its city planning was dominated by business interests which gave little thought to the quality of life of its inhabitants. The supercity has grown randomly and radially outward encompassing 88 municipalities. Its proximity to the port city, Santos, has facilitated an increase in São Paulo's involvement in import and export activities.

São Paulo has an underground railroad and surface transportation provides means for travel, but its vehicular traffic is overwhelming. This and extensive industry combine to produce extreme air pollution.

São Paulo's original center now has heavy congestion resulting from a population density of 500,000 per square mile. This has forced the upper class to create a new, adjoining center. The overall picture of São Paulo is one of unbridled growth with problems that will be, in many cases, unresolvable. Continuing influx of its rural population makes for more slums and many homeless people. Those who are employable take low-paying work, but unemployment, poverty and crime are increasing. In spite of this, there are well-attended park and recreational facilities as well as museums and other cultural activities for those who have the leisure and can afford them.

Despite a decrease in the collective quality of life for much of the population, there is a spirit of buoyancy, excitement and noise, characteristic of relatively young, booming cities. Stagnation and decay have not yet dominated the overall picture. Instead, there are valiant efforts by the governmental infrastructures to provide health and safety services and to meet transportation, communication and other service needs.

Unlike many other gigantic cities, São Paulo has key local resources. Besides abundant water and power, it is surrounded by agricultural lands and the raw materials necessary to sustain industrial and commercial growth. It remains immensely attractive to those in the poor rural areas around it. After all, this is where opportunity lies - in the big city. Birthrate is high, insuring a continuous supply of cheap labor for many generations, unless social discontent increases, as it invariably does over time, and political turmoil spoils all public and private plans.

SÃO PAULO (BRAZIL) SUPERCITY EXPANSION

ATLANTIC OCEAN

Legend

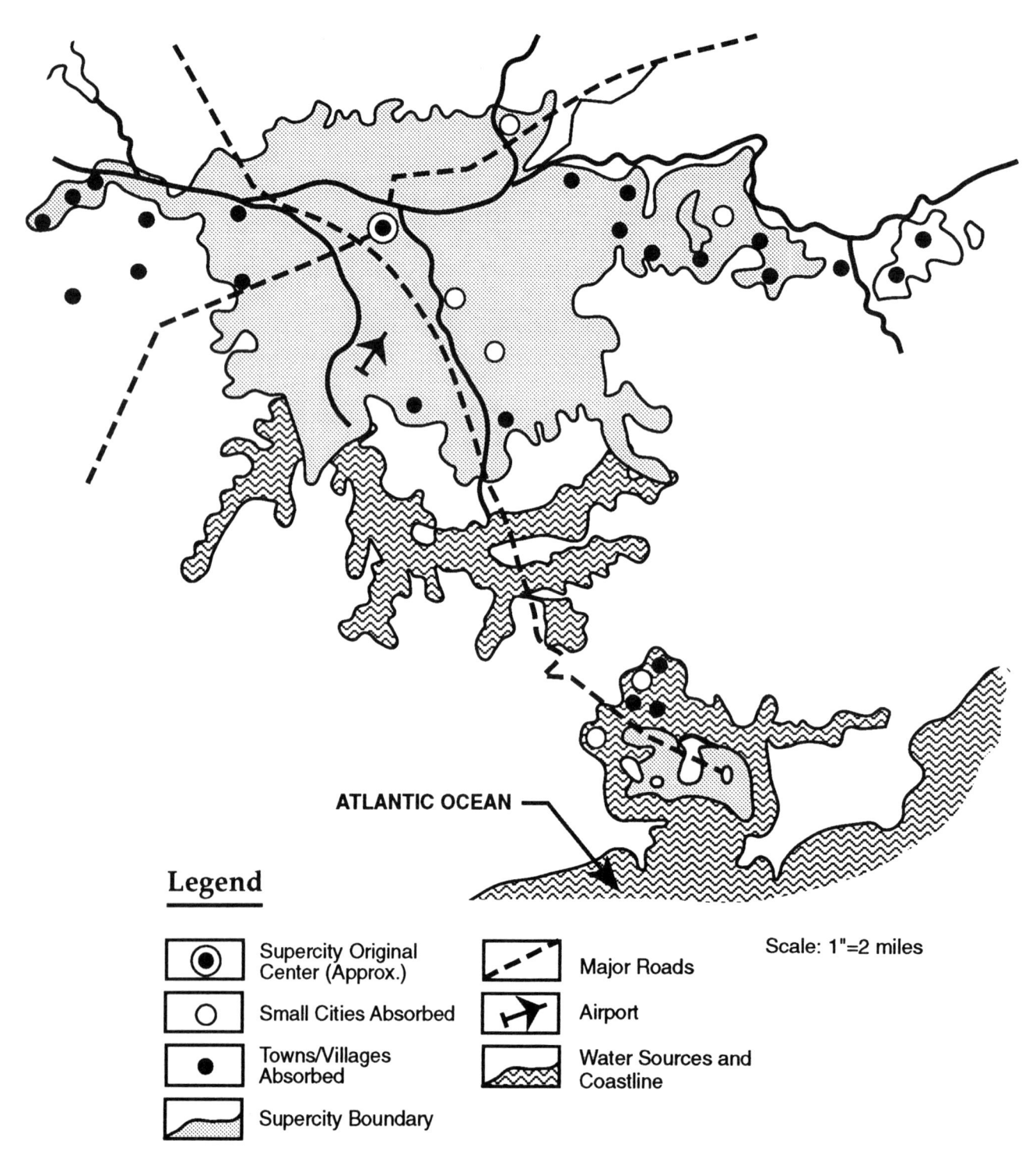

- ⦿ Supercity Original Center (Approx.)
- ○ Small Cities Absorbed
- ● Towns/Villages Absorbed
- Supercity Boundary
- ╌╌ Major Roads
- ✈ Airport
- 〰 Water Sources and Coastline

Scale: 1"=2 miles

Figure II-1-D

CHAPTER 1 - INITIAL JOURNEY

Veritor, Neos and Pragma are puzzled. There is a déjà vu quality to the scene before them.They feel that somehow it has all happened before, but yet there is something different. The expansion in population through growth and influx has been relatively rapid. The emergence of too large a population center often results in depersonalization of its inhabitants. Both rich and poor become numbers, mere statistics, subject to manipulation and deception. Furthermore, as those at the top seize more power, freedom diminishes. With absolute power, comes corruption, and the chance for for the multitudes to have a better life wanes.

Veritor is pensive. He finally speaks. "I see an interesting characteristic common to both Mexico City and São Paulo. Both are unstable and turbulent, yet dynamic. There are too many factions at cross-purposes, involved in intense rivalries and engaged in power struggles and corruption. With so much self-interest and so little common interest, it is extremely difficult to conceive, plan and implement small improvements to say nothing of the all-encompassing ones. There is little concern about what must take place to achieve a better collective quality of life."

Pragma adds,"I notice, too, that people are vulnerable not only to government malfeasance, but to the harm inflicted by large corporations and special interests. However, in the final analysis, specific people inflict suffering. One cannot blame only an impersonal institution for man-made actions. The systems that permit it are also culpable."

Neos observes. "When there are huge concentrations of population, it is as if the inhabitants are provoking the forces of nature. When concentrated so densely, more people feel the brunt of major catastrophes with greater intensity. Where can millions of people look for help at such times; can they hope to escape with their lives? Neither Mexico City nor São Paulo have the infrastructures to cope with natural or man-made catastrophes. And they are not alone. Size and congestion increase vulnerability; strategic deployment decreases it. There is not always safety in numbers. Schools of fish and other creatures may benefit from crowding together, but humans must repress this instinct. It gives a false sense of security, particularly in the supercity."

Veritor, Pragma and Neos have now visited two of the largest cities in the world. Two cities so different, yet so similar. São Paulo's locale and outlying resources may postpone major crises for its people.This is not true for Mexico City, which has overreached its limits.

There is a deep silence. The picture is building. Veritor, Pragma and Neos look over their maps again. It is time to make another quick survey of other kinds of overpopulated cities. From São Paulo they journey to Cairo, a city of over 12.6 million people, the largest in continental Africa.

Cairo, strategically located at the delta of the Nile River, has been in existence from antiquity. Approximately 48 million people live in the Cairo and delta areas.

Most of the other ninety-five percent of Egypt's land is arid and virtually unpopulated.

There has been no continuous planning of growth to the present, and it may not be possible to have it in the foreseeable future. Formed at different eras in history by many rulers, Cairo evolved with one civilization's pattern of growth overlaying the previous. The result has produced a multitude of archeological and historical sites as well as gardens, museums, universities and religious centers. Housing is in critical shortage throughout the metropolitan area with population density approaching 500,000 people per square mile in some areas. In crowded areas, nine people or more may occupy a single room. Many live in slums, dumps and cemeteries.

Transportation, including the railroads and Metro are antiquated. Roads are thronged with a diverse mixture of all kinds of vehicles, even animal drawn wagons. There is a steady bedlam of noise and traffic is engulfed in a constant state of gridlock. Naturally, the air is rife with pollution.

Egypt's federal government has developed industries to provide work for Cairo's burgeoning residential population as well as for the great influx of people from the rural areas. Massive housing projects are being built on the outskirts of the metropolitan area.

The federal government controls most of the heavy industry, petroleum, electrical power generation, water supply and major construction. Non-financial services and domestic markets are largely private. Unfortunately, there are few natural resources extracted other than petroleum, phosphate and iron ore.

Cairo dominates the socio-economic scene in Egypt. Development of Cairo as a supercity has been the main demanding focus to the neglect of the rest of the country.

"Is there hope for Cairo?" Veritor asks. "I notice that free education is available for students all the way through the university level. This is encouraging, but I wonder how many young people have to help their families make a living instead of going to school?"

Pragma adds, "The society seems to have good family and extended family structures. These are patriarchal and fairly stable. People seem to rely heavily on their authoritarian government, although, as in other supercities, subcultures abound and have their leaders."

CHAPTER 1 - INITIAL JOURNEY

CAIRO SUPERCITY EXPANSION

NILE RIVER DELTA

Scale: 1"=2 miles

Legend

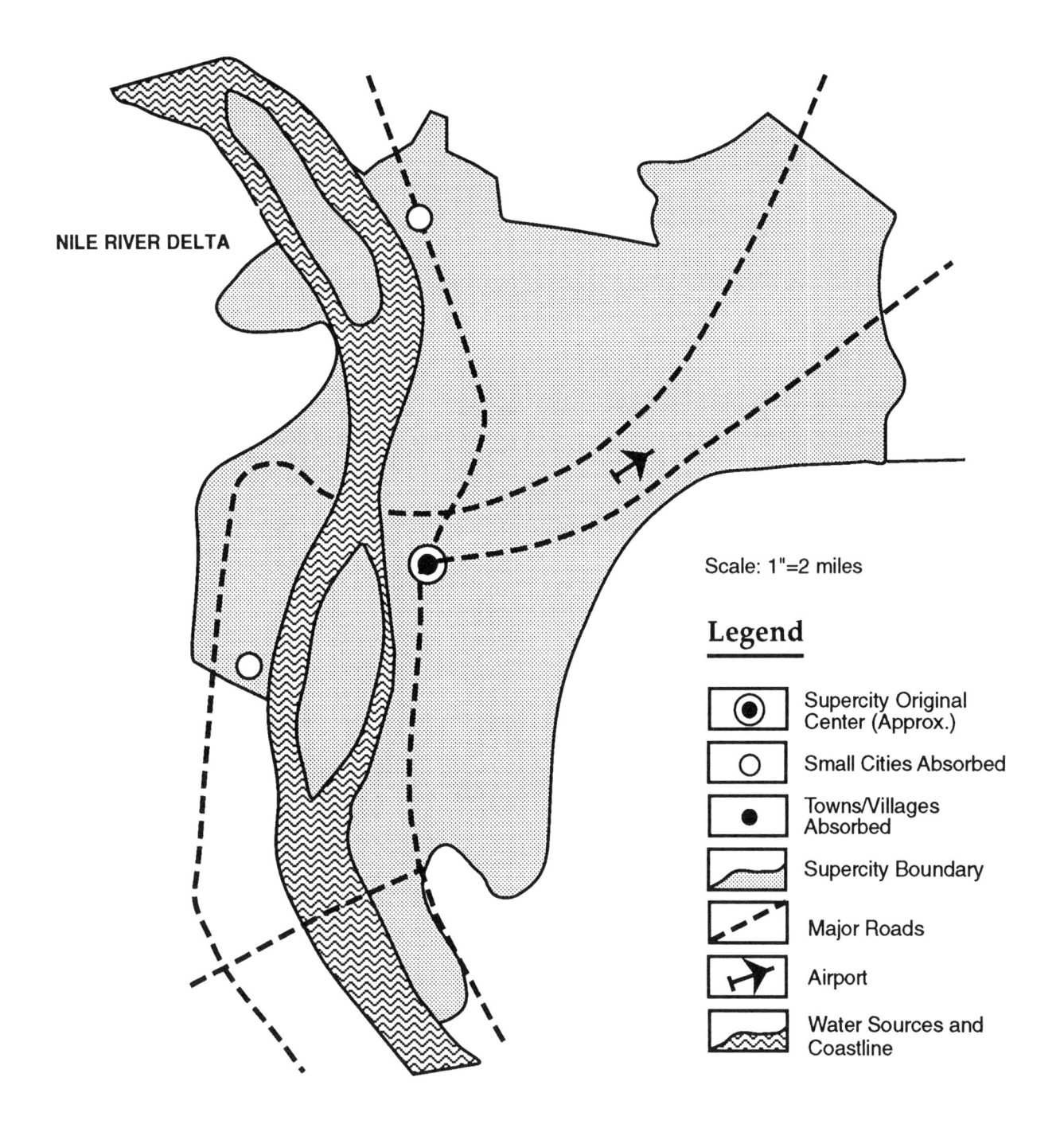

- ⊙ Supercity Original Center (Approx.)
- ○ Small Cities Absorbed
- ● Towns/Villages Absorbed
- Supercity Boundary
- – – – Major Roads
- ✈ Airport
- Water Sources and Coastline

Figure II-1-E

Neos notes, "I am impressed by how most of the people cope. Perhaps this is because there is a great deal of fatalism. People view the events of life as being in the hands of Allah. As a consequence, they have a 'don't rush, never mind' attitude toward crises. They have a friendly, easy-going manner."

Pragma responds, "This works fine for peace of mind, especially when people have to survive on a marginal basis. I'm not sure it is helpful for alleviating severe socio-economic conditions or for attaining a higher collective quality of life in the long run."

Veritor continues, "Egypt exemplifies the city concept with a typical urban sprawl pattern of growth we have seen so often. I am concerned about the conditions this generates and perpetuates. The government addresses major issues courageously, but unfortunately the problems that prevail are inherently systemic and linked to old concepts of social organization. For one thing, there is little control over key resources that are needed to sustain the population. The government is compelled to rely on exploiting surrounding areas without assuming the responsibility for caring for these areas and their inhabitants."

There is momentary silence as each reflects. Then Veritor points to another city on the map. "We need another supercity for comparison and contrast. I propose that we visit Shanghai. Like Cairo, it is controlled by its national government and depends for its very existence on the support of surrounding areas."

Neos and Pragma agree. "Pragma notes further, "We have a choice of many giant cities to evaluate. Each one of them could offer new insights into how problems are caused by high population density. Our visit to Shanghai may reveal what the Chinese government has done to remedy problems, and how people cope with the remedies."

Veritor, Pragma and Neos journey to China, the most populated country on earth. Shanghai is a key city of China, well-situated on the banks of the Huangpu River which is close by the Yangse River, a major transportation artery.

Shanghai has a population of 12,000,000 inhabitants. About seven million live in an area of 55 square miles; the most densely populated city in the world with up to 500,000 people per square mile. This jam-packed situation is the result of not only early Chinese government policies but also the past commercial and military dominance of foreign countries. Such dominance produced enclaves for the affluent as well as massive slums. Communist China eliminated the slums and redistributed its population. A major port handling one-half of China's exports, Shanghai is one of its three major cities and is controlled by the central government.

Typical of most cities, Shanghai has grown radially outward, but the location of functional areas is different. The shoreline provides port facilities for 35 miles as well as commercial houses and government agencies. The central area has a profusion of office buildings, shops and markets. Extending outward are highly industrialized areas

CHAPTER 1 - INITIAL JOURNEY

devoted to heavy industry and manufacturing . Many high rise blocks of apartments surround these industrial areas and house the workers. The first floors of the block buildings often contain shops for food, supplies, furnishings and other necessities. Air pollution and other contaminants permeate the environment. This juxtaposition of habitation with harmful toxic areas is unusual. Fringing the heavily populated areas are agricultural communes as well as special industrial complexes and their related communities. Parks, gardens, recreational and cultural centers and educational institutions are dispersed throughout the metropolitan area.

Taxis, bicycles, trucks, buses and trolley-buses are all heavily used means of transportation. Humanity fills the streets. Although there have been certain movements toward private enterprise, the central government controls society to ensure conformity and enforced sharing at all levels. Occupations are dictated as is birth control. How do people adjust to this? Have there been conditioned responses on a mass scale? Have people accepted such Draconian measures at a severe cost to individual quality of life in order to secure a low, but consistent collective quality of life?

These and other questions occupy Veritor, Pragma and Neos. They consider the experiment of communism, applied by an authoritarian government in its attempts to rectify severe socio-economic dysfunctions produced by over-population, particularly in the supercity of Shanghai. Non-communist governments have either been unsuccessful or have not even attempted radical changes on such a large scale. What methods, schemes and objectives would less authoritarian states employ to enhance individual and collective quality of life in the face of such population density?

SHANGHAI SUPERCITY EXPANSION

Legend

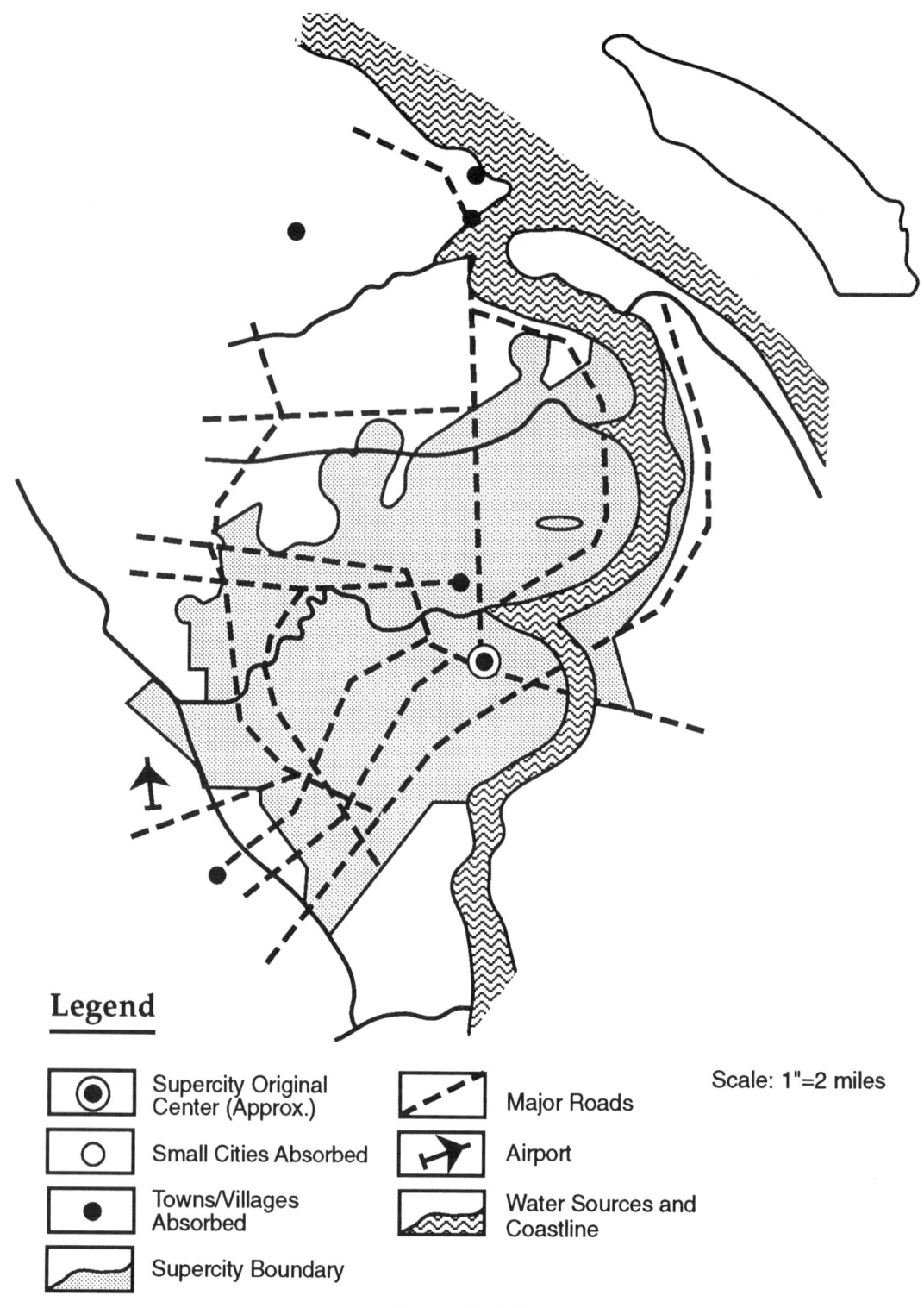

- ⊙ Supercity Original Center (Approx.)
- ○ Small Cities Absorbed
- ● Towns/Villages Absorbed
- Supercity Boundary
- -- Major Roads
- ✈ Airport
- Water Sources and Coastline

Scale: 1"=2 miles

Figure II-1-F

CHAPTER 1 - INITIAL JOURNEY

Veritor breaks the silence. "I think it would be premature to suggest, at this moment, alternatives to what China has done in addressing the problems of over-population in Shanghai. There has been great urgency in the search for solutions. Significant mistakes have been made, but they are inevitable when conducting a major experiment. I predict that there will be more experiments and more mistakes in the future."

Pragma questions this. "What does over-regimentation achieve? It seems to me that many leaders apply ruthless measures to solve problems. I believe that when humans are conditioned to accept an extremely low individual quality of life, there must be a great loss of self-expression and self-expectation."

Neos asserts, "It would certainly take persons of tremendous talent and drive to transcend such an environment. Even such exceptional individuals would probably be limited to a narrow band of excellence in an extremely restrictive system."

Pragma angrily notes, "Human beings are forced into subservience to the state as if it were an all-seeing god. Yet the leaders of the state are far from omniscient in their efforts to dictate concepts of ethics, morality and other behavior. Rules are made and enforced in an attempt to completely control hundreds of millions of lives. This is a monumental and ultimately futile task as I see it."

Veritor continues, "How do Shanghai's workers manage to exist in their tiny apartments? Surely there must be considerable friction and repression, not only within the family, but also with neighbors. Humans tend to store up grievances, and when a precipitous event occurs, pent up violence expresses itself. The ominous thing about all of this is that when there is mass complaint or rebellion, it must be immediately suppressed to protect the existing infrastructures and to avert total upheaval of the populace. Sudden relief from political oppression would not remove economic dependence on the state. Furthermore, anarchy, with freedom and no direction, would result in great chaos, and both individual and collective quality of life would suffer further."

Neos responds to this. "It seems to me that for Shanghai, as well as for all other supercities, there is an urgent need for alternative infrastructures to replace the old so as to prevent chaos and negative results. But, as you have stated, Veritor, alternatives are a subject for further exploration."

Pragma says, "I suspect that acceptable answers to most of the problems and conditions of the supercity cannot be found in the present makeup of their infrastructures unless their populations are sharply reduced. Somehow the influx of people must be diverted elsewhere."

Once again there is a pause in the conversation. Veritor, Pragma and Neos feel that they have uncovered valuable insights. Shanghai has offered an excellent example of the extreme steps employed to cope with exploding over-population and a radically deteriorating society. This example promises to be useful.

Veritor suggests, "Let us now go to Tokyo. It is a modern city with a long history. Its potential for accommodating its burgeoning population must now be considered."

Metropolitan Tokyo has extended outward to overlap the extremities of its neighbor, Yokohama, and continues to grow. Its pattern of expansion has made it a megalopolis that encompasses 23 central wards, 26 cities, 6 towns and 9 villages. With 12 million people, it has become an intensely overcrowded place to live and work. Dispersed in its midst are many, parks, shrines and temples and gardens including, of course, the gardens of the Imperial Palace, a symbol of Japanese solidarity. Major districts are given over to special functions like government, finance, commerce, industry, residential and entertainment. The patterns of these districts suggest random growth with some ingenious planning to accommodate the great influx of rural people as well as internal population, business and industrial growth. Massive blocks of buildings contain tiny apartments housing tens of thousands of people like bees in a hive.

Tokyo has the most sophisticated, advanced transportation system in the world, but even this has become over-stressed. Much of the population commutes up to two hours from scattered residences to places of employment. Despite its super achievements, Tokyo is falling prey to a common affliction - too many people and enterprises vying for the same time and space.

The capacity to endure and to survive tremendous socio-economic tension and compressed living is a result of Japanese culture. It takes early behavioral conditioning and stoicism to make individual quality of living totally subordinate to collective quality of living. For the individual, it is a matter of 'conform or perish'. The formulation and practice of cultural and social rules have long existed in Japan. These old formulations influence new rules made by industry and society. Although this overall system is ingrained, there are consequences. Authoritarianism is practiced not only by the government, but by peer groups and employers as well. Considering the severity of problems and conditions generated by over-population, strong discipline and control have been necessary. Although influenced mostly by pragmatic considerations, many adaptations that have been made are to Japan's credit.

CHAPTER 1 - INITIAL JOURNEY

TOKYO-YOKAHAMA, (JAPAN) SUPERCITY EXPANSION

YOKAHAMA

TOKYO WAN (BAY)

Scale: 1"= 8 miles

Legend

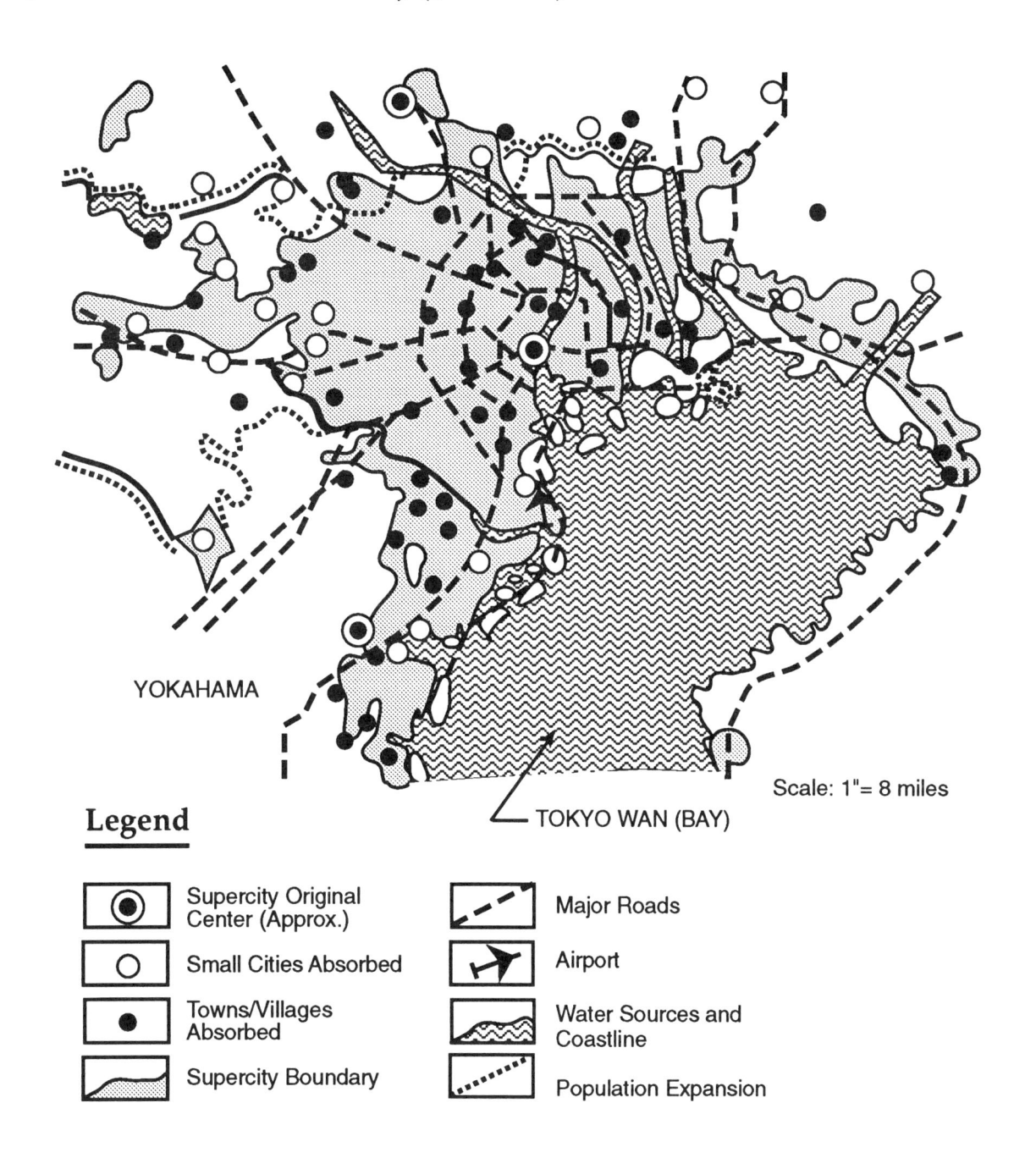

- ⊙ Supercity Original Center (Approx.)
- ○ Small Cities Absorbed
- ● Towns/Villages Absorbed
- Supercity Boundary
- Major Roads
- Airport
- Water Sources and Coastline
- Population Expansion

Figure II-1-G

The natural resources of Japan and Tokyo are sparse. Water, hydro-electric and geothermal electric power are available, but almost everything else must be imported. The great concentration of population in Tokyo makes distribution of resources and the disposition of wastes complicated and costly because more steps are needed to handle the irregular patterns of developing areas.

Veritor, Pragma and Neos are impressed with what they have seen, but are also wary of conditions which may not be correctable for Tokyo. After a pause, Veritor begins the discussion.

"It is evident that some cultures are able to adjust, compensate for crowded conditions or are able to undergo hardship and adversity more effectively than others. But it is also apparent that it takes a lifetime of conditioning and discipline for individuals to do so. People have emotions and feelings, and the Japanese are certainly no exception. They need outlets for these."

Pragma notes,"People are social animals; the Japanese culture emphasizes this. However, a sense of belonging and being a part of a social group can become obsessive. Group rejection of an individual in that kind of setting is devastating, even leading to suicide or crime. There are many cultures, like that of Japan, in which the worst thing that could happen to an individual would be to be ostracized."

Veritor observes, "As Tokyo becomes larger, more unmanageable and less cohesive, problems with crime are apt to increase. Subcultural groups will also grow. They evidently have always existed, but with acute competition in a crowded city, more and more people are left out and need to re-associate for support. Japanese who have not been successful see only poor prospects for further development or future acceptance. Without some direction, they are likely to become disgruntled, opportunistic and anti-social."

Neos responds, "Tokyo offers many forms of recreation assuaging people's need to escape and to seek relief. There is also a great reliance on holidays and festive occasions. In a male-dominated society, however, there are fewer outlets for women involved with children, home and social groups."

Pragma asks, "Have you noticed a great dependency on fate and chance in daily events? People in Shanghai also rely heavily on astrologically auspicious moments before doing things. It makes for a society that is increasingly fatalistic as well as materialistic."

Veritor nods. "I am more concerned with Tokyo's need to rely on resources from other countries. This reliance is exacerbated by the unsatiable demand for necessities, material goods, luxuries and distractions for its growing population."

Pragma sighs,"Materialism seems to be a tremendous motivating force not only for the people of Tokyo, but for other city dwellers everywhere. Hoping to increase individual quality of life, they seek quantity of life instead. By contrast, in Japan's rural areas, quality is still cherished."

CHAPTER 1 - INITIAL JOURNEY

Neos comments. "In most of Japan the imminent danger from natural forces such as earthquakes, fires and typhoons is considerable. The overcrowding of population makes the probability of enormous loss of lives and economic disaster a certainty. Tokyo is especially vulnerable to such catastrophes. Is it the immediacy of business as usual, the reliance on fate or a feeling of futility that prompts people and their leaders to continue along the same old paths of self-deception and potential self-destruction?"

Veritor, Pragma and Neos now cross Asia on their way to another giant city, Moscow, hub of Russia and the former Soviet Union. For many years it has been the focal point for the vast rural areas surrounding it. The city has steadily increased in size reaching a population of 9,000,000 and occupies an area of 360 square miles. Its nucleus is the Kremlin, seat of government, from which growth has radiated outward in a typical pattern absorbing small towns and villages, lakes and rivers. A highway encircles the city at its fringes.

Socio-economic upheaval and political turmoil continues in Moscow and the rest of Russia. Quasi-independent areas have emerged. A socio-economic vacuum has formed, and people, whose living depended wholly on Moscow and its narrowly defined programs for sixty years, now find themselves on their own, often jobless with critical shortages in what could be a land of plenty. This is the present.

Moscow is still a dominating presence. Like other giant cities it has expanded with factories and industry. It has built universities, converted palaces and churches into museums and has preserved many cultural activities. Recreation and sports are encouraged. Today there is a tremendous increase in freedom of expression after the darkness of oppression and secrecy.

MOSCOW SUPERCITY EXPANSION

Legend

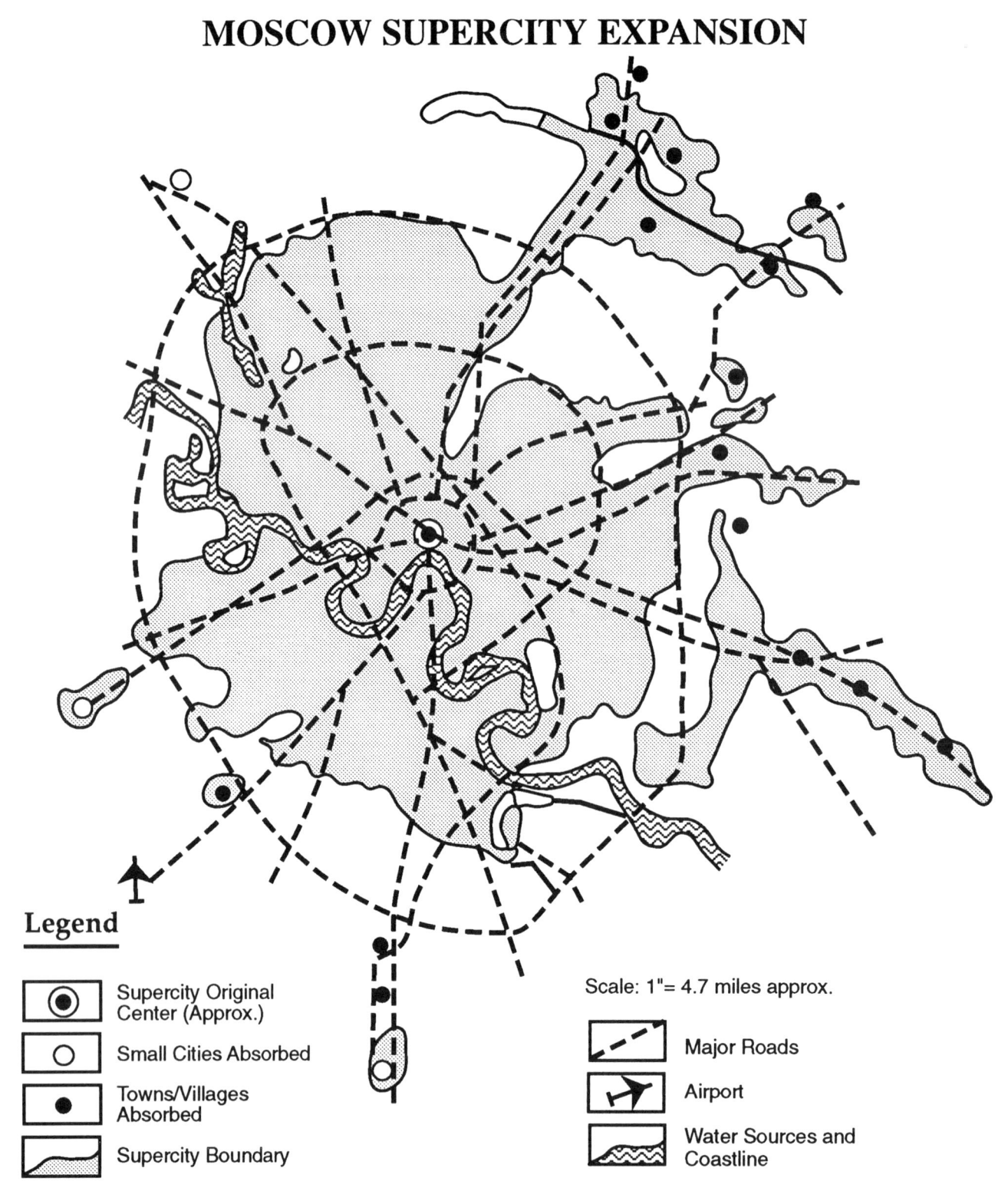

- ⊙ Supercity Original Center (Approx.)
- ○ Small Cities Absorbed
- • Towns/Villages Absorbed
- Supercity Boundary

Scale: 1" = 4.7 miles approx.

- Major Roads
- Airport
- Water Sources and Coastline

Figure II-1-H

CHAPTER 1 - INITIAL JOURNEY

Moscow has an unusually beautiful metro system as well as good public surface transportation. As with other supercities, transportation facilities are never enough. Housing is scarce in all parts of the city. As in other cities, huge, multi-storied apartment buildings appear everywhere. It is not uncommon for large families to occupy but a few rooms.

Crime, alcoholism, corruption and social restlessness have been increasing since the demise of the Soviet Union. Yet people are more open, less fearful and, as a result, often more friendly. There are signs of expectation mixed with frustration. With so many people striving for a better life and opportunity, can their expectations be realized in an overcrowded environment with greater competition and less resource control?

Veritor reflects on this and says, "New infrastructures and a socio-economic base are in critical need not only for Moscow but for the rest of Russia and the newly independent countries of the former Soviet Union. Moscow has been under the complete central control of a national government. Its people will have to gradually wean themselves from complete state dependency. Urgent needs like food, fuel, clothing and shelter can only be met by new systems. Employment opportunities must be created and responsibilities redefined."

Pragma contends, "Certainly there have been serious flaws in the overall system when not enough of the population had responsibility and could fully participate. Without having had a voice in government planning at lower levels and an effective way of resolving grievances, people had no incentive to participate."

Neos brightens and says, "I see great opportunity here for emerging infrastructures to avoid the turmoil other giant cities are going through, but there must be an openness to a larger range of ideas and population distribution. Otherwise, Moscow will be the last to benefit by whatever governmental and socio-economic experiments are derived and implemented."

Veritor responds, "I think most people are inherently afraid of the word 'experiment'. But experimentation is necessary because if we wish to improve conditions there will always be untried things to plan and do for the first time."

Pragma notes, "Moscow has abundant local and regional resources. In any revitalization, the government will have to use these wisely so as to avoid pollution of the environment and to not over-consume."

All three pause at this juncture for they must be on their way again. Veritor begins, "I think we should visit at least one more megalopolis before summing up our observations. I propose that we make the next city New York."

Pragma and Neos concur, for this promises to be a very revealing visit. New York has weathered several massive influxes of population from many lands, immigrants who came primarily because they sought greater opportunity and freedom. It has been the hope and dream of many deprived and poverty-stricken people seeking a better way of life. In their native lands these people were often mired in a life that offered few prospects for the future for them and their children. Congested, vibrant New York has been the first stop in America for millions of expectant newcomers. Can the supercity, New York, live up to their expectations?

New York is a city of skyscrapers, historic places, museums and many other cultural centers, universities and colleges, financial and business centers, small manufacturing and industry, entertainment and recreation. Many ethnic groups mix or concentrate in specific parts of the five boroughs: Manhattan, Brooklyn, Queens, The Bronx and Staten Island. New York is home to the United Nations and is a world center in many ways.

It is also a major example of city government infrastructures that are completely overloaded and in decline. The onslaught of so many people with their need for services has grown far beyond New York's capacity as a gateway city. There are insufficient local resources and employment opportunities. Many people are not adequately skilled, the basic educational systems are overloaded and blighted areas are spreading. Medical services are grossly inadequate. The situation has become desperate. Chronic crime, homelessness and deterioration of families and neighborhoods are on the increase especially in the more densely populated areas.

New York has more than 7.5 million people unevenly distributed over 300 square miles. During its history, New York has undergone a number of major changes in its pattern of growth, challenging successive city planners to cope not only with surface features like streets, bridges and buildings, but with underground systems as well, like subways, sewage, water and power. The original settlers expanded radially, but mainly to the east. Expansion since then has been random, expedient and based on compromise. Specific functional areas grew in an opportunistic manner. As the city deteriorated, many businesses and affluent people fled leaving numerous vacant, dilapidated buildings to form slums.

CHAPTER 1 - INITIAL JOURNEY

NEW YORK SUPERCITY EXPANSION

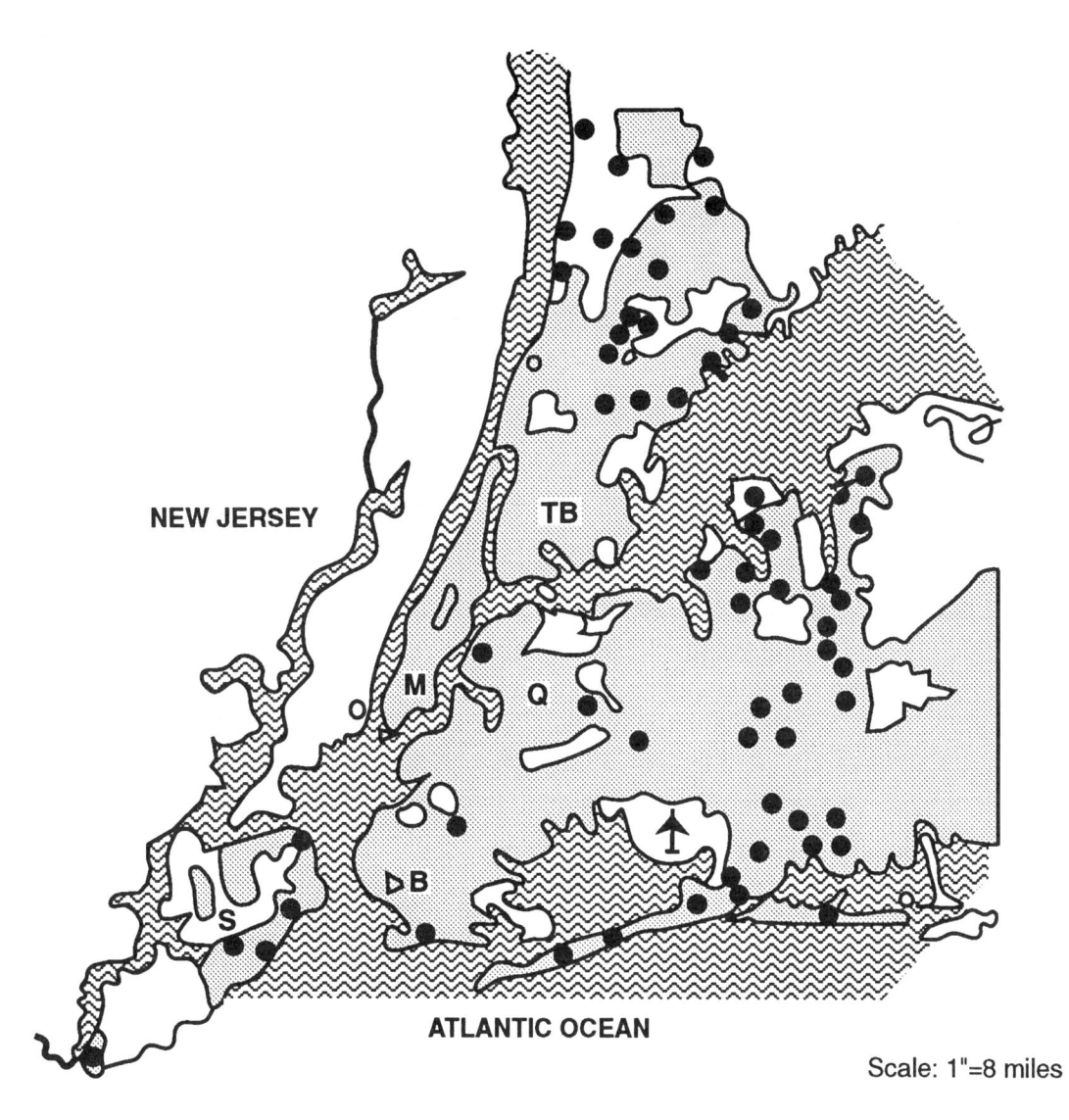

Scale: 1"=8 miles

Legend

- ⦿ Supercity Original Center (Approx.)
- ○ Small Cities Absorbed
- ● Towns/Villages Absorbed
- ⸺ Major Roads
- ✈ Airport
- Water Sources and Coastline

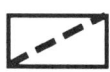

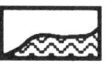

Boroughs

- **M** - Manhattan
- **TB** - The Bronx
- **Q** - Queens
- **B** - Brooklyn
- **S** - Staten Island

Figure II-1-I

A major problem that must be solved is the disposal of waste produced by such an enormous populace. The people of New York, as well as the rest of the United States, are avid consumers and are habituated to throw things away.

Veritor, Pragma and Neos are overwhelmed by the dynamism of New York. They are also apprehensive. There is much noise, confusion and disarray. Graffiti decorates or defiles every available surface, like the scent trails left by animals to mark their territories. Veritor speaks first."I sense a feeling of decay and deterioration in so many places. In block after block, buildings remain uncared for even when occupied. The homeless abound, tenements are jammed, and the streets are crime-ridden. All this contrasts with the city's massive skyscrapers, greater in number than anywhere else on earth, symbols of great power and wealth. Elsewhere, there are well-appointed dwellings where the very affluent live in virtual isolation. What is to become of this supercity of contrasts?"

Pragma adds, "In the past, New York has had planners of considerable talent like John Randel, Frederick Olmstead, Robert Moses and others. Randel introduced the street grid pattern for the future development of New York. This contrasts with a radial pattern of concentric circles of roadways superimposed on outlying areas."

Neos notes,"As New York's boroughs were forming, many people became involved in planning for future development. It seems that the modern concept of leaving more open spaces was not followed. However, some boroughs do have more parks. Because so many people have been trying to live in the big city, open land that had been planned has evaporated under political and developmental pressures."

Veritor sums up." I am not sure New York can survive without outside help. This may be true for all giant cities. They are no longer independent city-states with sufficient resources within their control. It is a daunting challenge to correct so many complex problems and to conceive and implement the many changes that are necessary just to prevent complete chaos. People with means have been gradually moving out, while people who are poverty stricken have been moving in. The tax base is disappearing. This is a losing proposition, a tremendous drain of capital and revenues as well as essential human resources."

Neos responds,"Perhaps it is possible to provide some relief to the giant cities of the world. National efforts could help provide relief from poverty and aid the recipients to become productive again. Not doing so will result in the prospect of individual and collective quality of life remaining but a remote dream. Cynicism, crime, isolationism and negativism will prevail."

"It is now time for a review of the cities we have visited, don't you think?" asks Veritor. " We need to retain the images and the knowledge we have gleaned. The reaction to major population increases is similar for all these cities. The solution to housing millions of people and many thousands of enterprises has been to build

CHAPTER 1 - INITIAL JOURNEY

upward, thereby increasing density per square area. The plan has been to build vertical communities and vertical business or manufacturing complexes. Presumably this has been to conserve ground area, shorten horizontal distribution distances between users and resources or services, improve communication and create 'communities'. Efficiency has become the by-word. But how effective have these plans been in practice? Humans have become faceless statistics. Any measure of effectiveness must include individual and collective quality of life. As we have noted, the compression of people creates greater rivalry for the same access space, availability of food, goods, recreation and cultural activities and privacy."

Pragma and Neos vigorously agree. Pragma states, "Many businesses, industries and services that try to expand upward have found more isolation, new restrictions and greater constraints than they expected. Furthermore, there is added complexity, like the need for elevators. There is also need for more energy to provide electricity, supply water, handle wastes, provide vertical and horizontal transportation, install structural additions and parking, install and maintain complex heating, ventilating and air-conditioning and so forth."

Neos joins in,"When there is increased competition for limited resources and services, cost goes up for everyone. Also, when systemic failures occur, everything may come to a halt. Many more people are affected, disrupting and diminishing the quality of their lives. There is greater dependency on others 'higher up' and a reliance on impersonal systems. Obviously, this situation cannot be improved by increasing population density."

Veritor proceeds further,"I have noticed that as more and more high-rise buildings are constructed, costs for purchase or rental go up. This is a deterrent to all people who need to keep their costs of living or their operating costs down. The tendency to repeat high-rise construction finds its way to the outskirts also, so that as the city expands, the same mistakes are repeated. To make things worse, skyscrapers increase and traffic becomes more congested as everyone tries to compensate for system design inadequacy."

Neos refers to the many notes they have accumulated while visiting the supercities and observes, "Managing supercities as they are appears to be a futile task because they are obsolete in design."

Veritor and Pragma acknowledge this, and Veritor continues,"We have learned that freedom of action and choice are threatened when the chaos in cities becomes unmanageable. Individuals must rely on the family or extended family in order to cope. Family unity is important, but what happens when the stresses of the environment become so great that families disintegrate? What happens when single parents or both parents must work for long hours, and children are left to their own devices, unsupervised or without schooling? The future is bleak for any society where this is common."

Pragma responds, "I think that a great number of people in the cities we have examined become accustomed to privation and a lower standard of living. This seems to continue from generation to generation for some. Others sacrifice so that their children will have a better life. For still others, the children rebel, are influenced by peer groups and drift through troubled lives."

Neos perks up, "I've noticed that people in some cultures and societies see life in a special way. They have simple, basic needs that are easily satisfied. What makes for a better quality of life for them may include many of those items we have listed, but to a lesser degree. Other people isolate or insulate themselves from much of what is going on around them. Maybe they are fearful, do not understand or do not care."

CHAPTER 1 - INITIAL JOURNEY

Conditions Within Some Supercities
(Derived From Multiple Sources)

Supercity	Infra-structure	Zoning	Housing	Employ. Opport.	Freedom	Crime	Resources	Coping
Mexico City	Federal Dominated Special Interest, Politic. Pwr. Oriented	Out of Control	Slums, Sub-Standard Housing Contrasts	Critical	Subverted By Poverty	Acute	Remote & Insufficient	Family Ties, Competitive, Fatalism, High Spirit
São Paulo	Regional Business Domination	Going out of Control	Slums High Density Contrasts	Poor Skill Matches	Open Society	Growing	Plentiful	Family Ties Competitive, High Spirit
Cairo	Federal Dominated Politically Powered Oriented	Non-Existing	Slums Desperate Shortage	Critical	Limited By Authoritative Government & Religion	Moderate	Very Insufficient Executive Power	Family Ties Competitive, Fatalism
Shanghai	State Control Central Plan, Min. Region Planning	Excess Control	High Density Buildings Apartments	Assigned Occup. & Enterprise	Very Restrictive & Social Conformity	Surpressed	Supplied By Central Government	Family Ties, Social & Sub-Servience
Tokyo	Federal & Business Dominated, Metro. Planned	Highly Structured	High Density Buildings Apartments	Highly Competitive, Organized	Social Conformity	Moderate & Growing	Very Depend.	Family Ties, Social Sub-Servience
Moscow	State Control, Central Planning (Changing)	Excess Control (Changing)	High Density Buildings Apartments	Assigned Occup. & Enterprise (Changing)	Restrictive (Changing)	Growing	Distribution Problem	Family Ties, Competitive (Changes)
New York	State Federal Dependent	Mixed & Inconsistent	Mostly High Density Slums	Critical	Open Society Subverted By Poverty	Severe	Needs More	Limited Family Ties & Acute Competition

Table II-1-A

Part II - Justifying the Regional Concept

CHAPTER 2 - ATTRIBUTES OF CITIES

Veritor, Pragma and Neos are once again in their mountain retreat. They are still thinking about the supercities they have visited, as well as about all cities of size. What are the attractions for those who live within the cities and for those who live in rural areas? Is it the prospect of greater opportunity, especially for those who are young? Certainly, people in rural areas compare what they have in their rural environment with what they imagine they would have in the big city.

According to projections, there will be hundreds of cities of at least 2,000,000 people by the year 2000. The concept of a city as a place to live, work and play remains an obsession. Although this concept has evolved through centuries, this is a relatively short period in the long history of mankind. As they have grown, cities have acquired both positive and negative attributes. How did this happen? Was it natural or induced? Was it random interaction of groups of people or special interests that gave the city positive and negative attributes? Was it rapid technological change, changes in standard of living expectations or converging economic purposes that brought more and more people to what initially was a more convenient common center? Did all of these factors create the city concept that is now evolving beyond its usefulness, especially when no longer manageable?

Veritor is the first to speak. "Cities are imprecise inventions created over a period of time by millions of people. These people had different interests, attitudes and ways of life as conditions and activities changed from generation to generation. This dynamic has perpetuated the city concept, making it the common way to live."

Pragma is aroused. "Of course, this has continued to happen. Isn't the evolvement of this concept a logical progression? Hasn't the city concept served humans well? When it works well, what better way is there to provide quality of life for people?"

Neos responds, "That is the crux of the matter. Surely, we need to recognize when cities can no longer provide quality of life, something has to change. The size, complexity and pace of city living must have limits. What was appropriate for one generation may not be for those who follow. But is mankind supposed to remodel, dismantle or rebuild its cities for each generation?"

Veritor continues, "I think mankind will continue to experiment through necessity, and something other than the city concept will evolve. After all, there are people in different cultures who achieve a comparatively higher individual and collective quality of life than the majority of those living in the cities. It might be wise at this time to review both positive and negative attributes of cities to see if we can determine whether there is a net benefit."

CHAPTER 2 - ATTRIBUTES OF CITIES

Pragma speaks, "This is a plausible course of action. I'm not sure we will be able to list and evaluate all of the positive and negative attributes that individuals may experience."

Neos proposes, "Let's look at the positive attributes first. I feel people must think they outweigh the negative."

Veritor notes,"The concept of a city has been to provide convenience, variety and necessities. Functions that provide them must be located where there will be abundant capital, services, labor, customers, users, transportation, communication and resources. It seems obvious that so many divergent interests would try to occupy the same prime space at the same time.

"Skyscrapers proliferate in an attempt to meet such need. Skyscrapers, however, are not appropriate facilities for most activities. Concentration of tall buildings radically inflates their operating costs and the costs of land and buildings. On the whole, their integration within the city is difficult and costly to others, bringing about a formidable systemic integration problem. Each skyscraper complex is dedicated to itself without regard to the load it imposes on surrounding areas."When this kind of self-interest is multiplied, it creates extensive dysfunctions throughout the city."

Neos asks,"How can any city government hope to deal with this? What rational zoning approach can be derived and implemented? How effective can any activity ultimately be in such a man-made environment? "

Pragma grimly responds,"To countless New Yorkers all the noise and excitement must represent the epitome of the 'good' life. How deceptive and superficial this all is."

Veritor sums up their thoughts. "There is no question that most city features, functions and activities could become more effective and appreciated in a regional setting, particularly when we examine the other side of the coin, namely the negative attributes of the city."

Pragma asserts, "There are so many negative attributes. Many are interrelated so that efforts to correct one affect another. For instance, if crime could be reduced, there would be less need for courts and jails."

Positive Attributes of the City

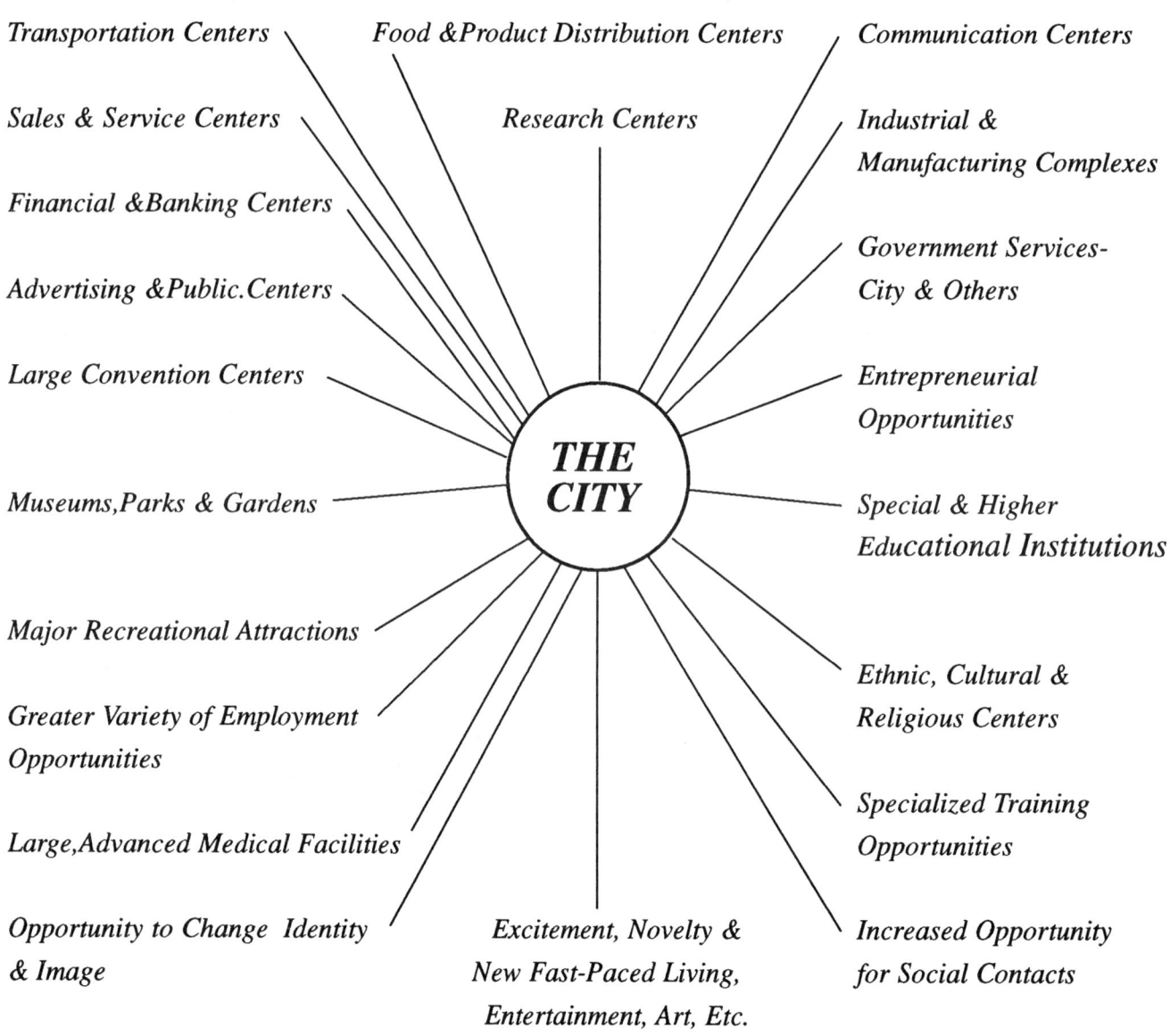

- Transportation Centers
- Sales & Service Centers
- Financial & Banking Centers
- Advertising & Public. Centers
- Large Convention Centers
- Museums, Parks & Gardens
- Major Recreational Attractions
- Greater Variety of Employment Opportunities
- Large, Advanced Medical Facilities
- Opportunity to Change Identity & Image
- Food & Product Distribution Centers
- Research Centers
- Excitement, Novelty & New Fast-Paced Living, Entertainment, Art, Etc.
- Communication Centers
- Industrial & Manufacturing Complexes
- Government Services- City & Others
- Entrepreneurial Opportunities
- Special & Higher Educational Institutions
- Ethnic, Cultural & Religious Centers
- Specialized Training Opportunities
- Increased Opportunity for Social Contacts

THE CITY

Figure II-2-A

CHAPTER 2 - ATTRIBUTES OF CITIES

Neos is more graphic in visualizing this. "I see the growing city with its increased problems as an inflating balloon that will burst if it continues to do so. If you probe it in one place, it will deform in another."

Veritor notes this and proceeds, "Apparently trying to correct single problems when they are related to others may prove to be futile and very costly. Solving the predicament of large cities requires comprehensive correction of complex, related problems which have common underlying conditions. It would be naive to think of solving them separately. But as a city grows, it is often very difficult to determine which conditions are causes and which are effects. One thing is certain; the supercity is destined for a profound breakdown of its political and socio-economic infrastructures. When this happens, the cures are likely to be more painful than the ailments. People often clamor for specific, quick temporary remedies but not long lasting cures. For instance, it is just and noble to provide an occasional meal for the poor and hungry, but this is a temporary expedient. What happens to their hunger on other days throughout the year? The conditions that allow this to happen remain the same."

Pragma brings up some other points, "It's obvious there are different kinds of competition in the city and elsewhere. Some forms are healthy when hard work and intelligent application are rewarded, individuals feel better about themselves. Competition may bring excellence in performance and innovation in approach when competitors follow the established rules. It motivates and stimulates, but when rules are not followed, it destroys others and their chance to compete. Only dominance and subservience are left. Fair competition is essential. The competition that the big city evokes results in success for those who already have money, power and influence. Rivals must often become arch-opportunists, sometimes cynical and often aggressive in behavior. Possessions and prestige become the premium goal in life."

Veritor and Neos nod vigorously. Neos states, "The city environment and excessive competition are likely to make a cooperative spirit difficult to achieve. Such a spirit would be a major accomplishment in itself. Then how can those in the city improve their condition? It will take considerable objectivity, comprehensive thinking and cooperative spirit to modify and correct city infrastructures."

All three agree that the positive attributes of a city can be better achieved with new alternative concepts of social organization. These approaches offer promise of enhancing the positive attributes while reducing the negative.

Negative Attributes of the City

Increased Traffic Complexity & Overload Problems

Increased Complexity & Cost of Communication

More Laws, Regulations, Restrictions & Problems

Increased Services Required

Extreme Housing Shortages & High Density

Increased Taxation

Shortages of Water

Increased Environ. Pollution

Increased Difficulty & Costs For Police/Fire Protection

Increased Zoning Difficulty

Increased Homelessness

Increased Family Break-ups

Increased Disease & Illness

Increased Vulnerability to Corruption

Increased Vulnerability/Exposure/ Massive Harm By Industrial & Traffic Wastes/Accidents;Epidemics, Earthquakes, Floods, Fires , Etc.

Increased Complexity & Costs of Government

Overload of Schools

High Costs of Living

Increased Complexity/Cost of Distrib./Shipping-Food, Material, Goods, Equip.

Increased Costs of Fuels, Water, Gas & Electricity

Increased Complexity/Cost -Sanitation & Waste Disp.

Increased Operating Costs for Industry & Manuf.

Insufficient Skilled Labor For Changing Technology

Insufficient/Unresponsive Emergency Services

Increased Complexity & Costs For Public Works

Overload of Courts & Jails

Increased Building Costs

Increased Crime & Gangs

Increased Substance Abuse

Chronic Unemployment

School Dropouts & Illiteracy

THE CITY

Figure II-2-B

Part II - Justifying the Regional Concept

CHAPTER 3 - RURAL AREAS AND OPEN SPACES

During their initial journey, Veritor, Pragma and Neos have observed more than high density populated areas. They have also been looking at rural areas and open spaces. They have seen how these areas and spaces are being utilized and how people manage to live there with whatever resources are available. They know much of the population influx to the cities originates in rural areas and open spaces.

Rural living, despite the absence of the amenities found in the cities, is still attractive to millions of people throughout the world. Most rural people need one or more occupations to subsist. Their main occupation may be in agriculture, animal husbandry, fishing or hunting, and extraction of resources. Handcrafted products may supplement the income they need to thrive or survive. Their incomes, however, are meager.

When critical resources become scarce, when the land becomes exhausted or when the weather becomes too extreme for too long, people are under pressure to move. Without assistance or encouragement to stay, they seek any relief, even the uncertainty of the city. They migrate to areas that seem more promising. This becomes very urgent when hunger, thirst, illness or loss of livelihood drive them from their homes. The city, however, is unable to use many farmers, fishermen, cattle raisers or miners. Prospective employers may be able to utilize a few people with mechanical or tactile skills, but to those without special training, only menial, low-paying work may be available. So rural people come, hopeful of employment and sell whatever they have in order to live.

Rural people have traditionally had large families to offset high infant and child mortality rates and ensure a sufficient number of workers to support the family. In some societies, having many children is considered to be an indication of ideal male virility and female fertility. But additional mouths require more food and other necessities. Poverty haunts these people who may be unable, unwilling or afraid to break with old customs and habits until it is too late.

Inhabitants of rural areas who form cooperatives may have better prospects. With enough working hands to meet peak demands and an improved capacity to borrow capital, they can purchase modern equipment and use modern techniques to produce more and to improve their lives. But cooperatives, themselves, do not have the scope and means to control the larger market and weather conditions or the depletion of their natural resources.

Occupations of Rural Areas

Rural people the world over characteristically make their living with whatever means and resources. They adjust, persevere, and exist, accepting whatever bounty that is received.

While resources remain plentiful, successive generations carry on the family occupation perpetuating local customs and habits. Tradition is the normal way of life.

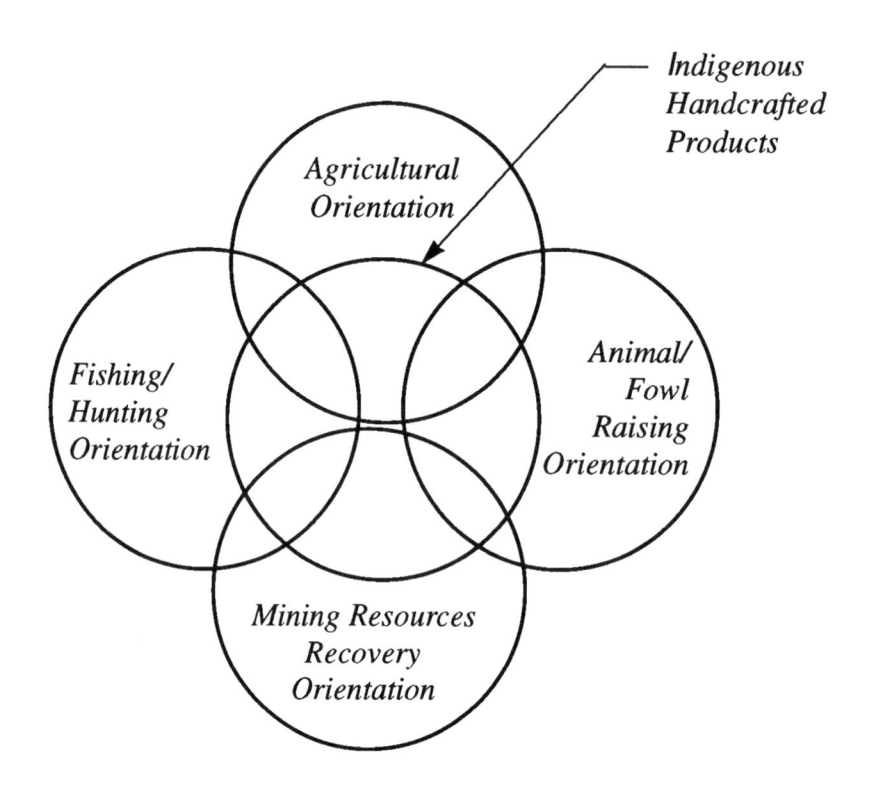

Agricultural Orientation

Fishing/ Hunting Orientation

Animal/ Fowl Raising Orientation

Mining Resources Recovery Orientation

Indigenous Handcrafted Products

Often more than one occupation is necessary over an extended period of time for rural populations to survive. Complete dependency on one occupation (and one resource) leads to high vulnerability from the extremes of weather and the variability of market conditions for whatever they sell or trade.

Figure II-3-A

CHAPTER 3 - RURAL AREAS AND OPEN SPACES

Veritor begins, "I am interested in people who settle new areas. What are they looking for? Why do they chance the prospect of hardship and suffering? Is this preferable to where they came from? How do they propose to sustain themselves in a new setting? Humans have always done this, it seems, but what motivates them?"

Pragma attempts to answer, "I think that people everywhere seek a better way of life, particularly when their quality of life is minimal. They have nothing to lose by moving on. When all that people have left is at risk or lost, they become survival-oriented. They may not have much choice, particularly when the 'enemy' is a hostile environment or a catastrophic event. People may try to anticipate and prepare for the future hoping they will somehow overcome hardships and perils when they occur. It takes bold imagination, keen insight and great resolve to look ahead."

Neos adds, "Interestingly enough, hardships and perils face rural people who move to the city as well as city people who escape to the suburbs, open spaces or other lands. It's a case of the grass being greener on the other side of the fence."

Veritor brightens in response to these observations. "We have more than just one problem of rural exodus to the city and how to stop it. We must also address how people can best be encouraged to leave the city to form new communities with new opportunities. History gives us many examples of this happening worldwide. For instance, many Americans left their familiar surroundings of eastern cities to cross the continent and pioneer the unknown west."

Pragma notes, "Perhaps rural people can be attracted to other open spaces. But what will happen if there are already people living there. There may be conflict or accommodation. For the latter to happen, there has to be preparation, communication and opportunity."

Neos asks, "What can be done to induce city people as well as rural people to move to specially prepared rural areas or open spaces? Can this be done before there is major turmoil, violence and disruption?"

Veritor responds, "There certainly needs to be major comprehensive planning by governments for population diversion and dispersion. But it takes much time and effort to bring about healthy changes. Most of the governments of the world are faced with this problem of diversion and dispersion. The question is what can they do if their habital land and primary resources are scarce?"

Population Dynamics of the Rural Area

- *Remotely located populations are compelled to become mostly self-sufficient. This often requires a different emphasis on individual or collective quality of life, particularly when isolation brings hardship without relief. To improve quality of life, such populations seek to associate with others and eventually to form common areas. Humans are basically social animals.*

- *Towns, settlements, villages, market centers, safe harbors, protected valleys and river junctions all provide common areas where there can be relief from isolation, support services can be acquired and critical necessities be obtained. These common areas grow in population as people who provide these things establish themselves and settle. As population grows, more needs can be met with schooling, medical help, spiritual comfort, social gatherings, equipment repair and maintenance and necessities not usually produced in the area.*

- *Certain favored common areas attract people from far and wide. What makes one place of focus more so than another without outside influence? Historically, trade routes, proximity to potable water and other natural resources, areas protected by natural barriers, sites considered sacred or having particular physical attraction all tend to increase population in an area. Surrounding populations converge there.*

- *Outside influence by government and private enterprise extensively modifies rate of growth, so that towns or villages eventually grow to become cities. These outside influences have special interests and bring government programs and business plans, money and technology to the area. Local resources, products and services increase, and more become exportable.*

- *The capacity of an area to grow in size depends largely on its ability to produce more than it needs and more of what others need. Even though people in these areas are mostly self-sufficient, they need to trade surpluses for what they lack in order to improve their standard of living and quality of life.*

- *The pattern of development for growing rural areas is erratic, reflecting local interests and possible development by outside interests. Overall community planning is beyond the scope of special interests which are associated with outside economic forces. Over a period of time a succession of special interests produce random development. Whatever infrastructure exists in the community is vulnerable and self-sufficiency begins to decline.*

- *The frailties of the rural infrastructure become more apparent when natural resources become depleted, when infusion of investment money disappears, when major catastrophes occur, and when any existing government programs are curtailed. The community's capacity to reorganize and stimulate internal enterprise is very limited. Occasionally, there is a local visionary with money and business acumen who shores up the economy, but this is an exception. Help from other communities and government jurisdictions is necessary if the community is to survive and thrive.*

CHAPTER 3 - RURAL AREAS AND OPEN SPACES

Pragma thinks about this last question. "It would be wise for combined government agencies to share mutually benefiting programs involving economic development, resource development and enhancement and community growth."

Neos adds, "I also think that how people resettle and grow is of prime importance so that the same excessive mistakes in development are not repeated."

Veritor shifts the emphasis of their conversation to another aspect of the overall problem of population dynamics, saying, "There are many combinations of problems in a world of contrasts. On one hand, we have extreme population density in so many places, while vast areas of the world remain sparsely populated or unpopulated."

Neos and Pragma agree with this observation. Pragma adds, "We have different situations for the open spaces of the world. Some are with people, some without; and some are with resources, some without."

Neos adds, "Then we have four combinations to that governments have to consider in order to attract people."

Pragma responds, "It's certainly difficult, if not impractical, to attempt development, except on the periphery of open spaces where there are no people and where no known resources exist. It would first be necessary to obtain water and power, and even then it would require an imaginative approach and considerable incentives to attract people. It's very hard to attract people to live on a moonscape."

Veritor looks askance, "Why would we want to have people living in such environments in the first place? Certainly polar regions and barren deserts are hostile enough and unsuitable for most."

Neos notes, "Of course, northern natives and desert nomads manage to survive. They couldn't do this without basic resources like food, water and fuel, however."

Pragma adds, "I think that is a key issue in all circumstances. For instance, there are often combinations of many people and insufficient resources in giant cities where key resources must be brought in from many miles away. At one time, these same cities probably had enough resources to meet their population demands until expansion strained them beyond their limits."

The Nature of Open Space

Much of the earth's land mass is barren, forbidding and devoid of human life. Resources do exist in these areas but how accessible and economically feasible and environmentally sound it would be to exploit them is questionable. Resources are rapidly being depleted in many places. Once productive, these areas have been abandoned because of attrition of their resources. This is cause for reflection. Water and energy, as resources, always remain key factors in allowing habitation, in the exploitation of other resources, and in the growing of trees, fiber and food. How should mankind treat the open spaces?

Utilization and Habitation Potential

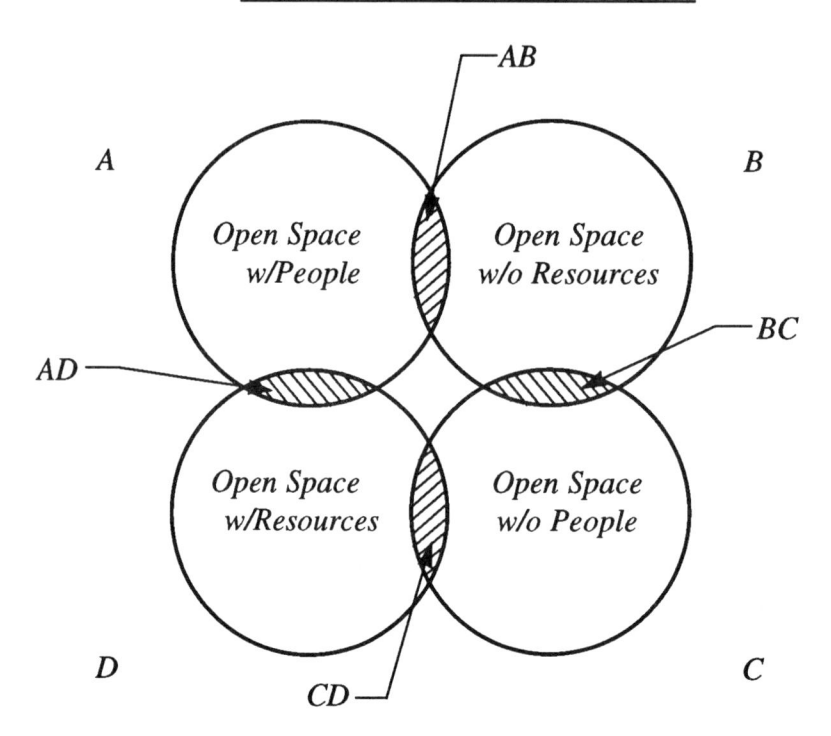

A — Open Space w/People
B — Open Space w/o Resources
D — Open Space w/Resources
C — Open Space w/o People

AB - *Needs water, electric power, conservation & restoration of resources & new infrastructures.*
BC - *Needs fringe area development & exploration of potential resources for utilization.*
CD - *Needs comprehensive regional planning, resource conservation, population redistribution.*
AD - *Needs comprehensive regional planning, resource conservation, population shifts.*

Figure II-3-B

CHAPTER 3 - RURAL AREAS AND OPEN SPACES

Veritor acknowledges this and says, "Very true, but perhaps this means that fringe areas of the open spaces must be made habitable someday, if only to extract resources that may lie in hostile environments."

Neos objects, "Wouldn't that tend to damage or threaten the fragile natural ecosystems of the environment? International acceptance, cooperation and caution must be part of such a prospect."

Pragma notes, "I am uncomfortable with the idea of humans trying to inhabit hostile areas that have resources. However, there are open spaces with considerable resources and with few people. Modern technology could provide special protection and other inducements for people who would work and live there. The resources would have to be very valuable, however."

Veritor is thoughtful, "I tend to agree that it is better to concentrate on environments that are not too severe for a good part of the year, provided, of course, that access to resources exists at such times. I believe humans are highly adaptable and can withstand many extremes of nature for limited periods of time. Beyond these time limits, psychological factors must be considered and above all, induced quality of life would have to be seriously considered."

Pragma adds, "Perhaps it would be helpful to define open spaces where potential living areas exist. Then we could decide which offer at least marginal living environments. Once this is done, resource abundance or minimum resources could be noted on a map that would show broad target areas for dynamic population shifts. Governments need such information because it is of international concern."

Neos answers, "I like this approach, and we and others should continue to pursue it."

Veritor concurs and says, "It is very important that governments tentatively select areas within their countries that could accept more population, and use new concepts of settling land. It is critical that they prepare and enhance the land and ensure needed resources before masses of population try to live and work there. It's also important that new appropriate government infrastructures be initiated in time for population moves."

Part II - Justifying the Regional Concept

CHAPTER 4 - OPEN BORDERS VS. TERRITORIAL IMPERATIVE

Following a territorial imperative reflects mankind's urgent need for security, abundant resources and a favorable environment. But what if the land of promise has already been fully or partially occupied by an indigenous people? Throughout history, local inhabitants have either resisted or accommodated intruders. Migrations and displacements have been a constant re-occurrence.

When desirable land was plentiful and people were sparsely distributed, borders were often defined by natural features. Few man-made barriers were needed except for local fortifications. The Great Wall of China is a notable exception. Eventually, population growth led to a rigid definition of property ownership and lines of demarcation. Extensive legal codes were created (British Common Law, Roman law, biblical injunctions, etc.) to reflect a more intense territorial imperative and, because of it, the need to settle ownership disputes.

Ownership implies the exclusive right to use the land and its resources in any way that does not conflict with the interests of owners of adjoining properties. In modern times, use of air space and subsurface have modified the concept of exclusive ownership which may now have to be 'shared' for specific uses.

However, when owners have exploited their properties without restraint, resources and environment have often been ravaged and destroyed. Many of their activities have polluted the environment and abused other people, at times threatening lives or compromising the rights of others. Obviously, ownership rights have to be coupled with responsibilities.

Cooperation must increase. All concerned parties must now consider the greater complexity of property interfaces. Properties have become a part of larger systemic socio-economic structures. Responsibilities have increased accordingly. Look at the increases in paperwork people with property must now handle. Rapid advances in technology and communications have greatly increased property interfaces.

Veritor, Neos and Pragma have been discussing these significant changes. Veritor begins," It's apparent that this pattern of evolutionary growth applies to national ownership as well. What one country does in its territory influences others. Nuclear radiation, chemical pollution, population pressure, resource attrition, economic dysfunction and others factors are not limited by man-made borders.

CHAPTER 4 - OPEN BORDERS VS. TERRITORIAL IMPERATIVE

Territorial Imperatives and Borders

From the perspective of space, the major features of the earth can be seen in their natural grace. There are no borders; there never have been. Mankind has created them. Man-made borders imply ownership; natural boundaries and features define relationships. Which shall it be for mankind? Borders and barriers block human cooperation and goodwill. Yet human need induces a territorial imperative, the seeking and establishment of a "homeland".

Individuals, as do tribes, ethnic groups and even entire nations, seek a place to survive and thrive. Countries do the same.
   - Quality of life is at stake.

Individuals, groups and nations attempt to protect what they already possess.
   - Material goods, acquired wealth, living space, property, land and resources and life-styles are at stake.

Individuals identify with others in a family setting, peer group, ethnic group, religious group, economic group, political group, or working group. Collectively they form nationalities and spheres of influence.
   - A sense of security, association and allegiance is at stake.

Individuals desire recognition and respect. Internationally, countries also seek recognition and respect.
   - Status in the competitive world is at stake.

These wants and needs appear to be natural inclinations, but when do they become disruptive and destructive? Are there ways to limit greed, waste, wanton destruction, malice, power and acts of crime resulting from these human inclinations? What will encourage humans to respect the needs of others?
   - The concept of networking links human endeavor and encourages participation. It modifies the meaning of the rights of ownership without responsibility, changing it to the rights of usership with responsibility.

"We have already discussed concepts of time and space as they apply to human needs. It seems to me that mankind must learn to share this world in a more rational and responsible way. Otherwise, reductions in quality of life are likely to happen at all levels of social organization. De-stabilization and its harmful consequences, in which more people will feel compelled to satisfy their territorial imperatives, are likely to follow. The rights of ownership will be challenged everywhere, often with violence. It would be far better to preempt this dire prospect through corrective action.

"First we must resolve the question of usership rights versus ownership rights in meeting human needs and sharing time and space. Population increases and compression will demand this. For instance, individuals need enough space for privacy as well as for sharing with friends or family. They also require exclusive or shared space to do specific work. A family needs a place to share as does a peer group to interact. People have to share roads and public spaces. Religious, recreational, cultural and other groups require special areas to carry out their activities."

Pragma nods in agreement, "Government services, industries, farmers and businesses certainly must have specific areas. How else could they function? But conflicts arise when these entities compete for the same space at the same time. I can see the concept of ownership will have to be altered; new arrangements and rules must be made."

Neos asks, "In the final analysis, isn't this why people form governments? Regulations are created not only to protect ownership and usership rights but to allocate time and space so that different functions can take place with minimum friction."

Veritor continues, "I think it is time for us to consider the concept of networking which I define as the linking of public and private functions by means of communication or energy transfer, exchange of tangible goods, products and services, the exchange of information and ideas and the direct physical interaction of people. Such networking is increasing in industrial countries and also in some emerging countries."

"We can identify international free markets and alliances, broadcasting systems, telephone systems, power distribution systems, industrial and production systems with international suppliers, transportation systems and public works systems as examples of networks. The concept of networking has obviously been around for many years."

Pragma quickly notes, "It seems to me all levels of government and their jurisdictions are incompatible with this. They have just not kept up with network development, so vital to the well-being of socio-economic organization. Major complications, duplications and additional costs are created by artificial boundaries or

CHAPTER 4 - OPEN BORDERS VS. TERRITORIAL IMPERATIVE

jurisdictions. When the key functions of a society have been networked, borders often become superficial or detrimental."

Neos responds, "That's a good observation, Pragma. Certainly, we must consider the networking concept when we design and plan new regional entities. It introduces a different approach to the formation and management of the modern society, as well as an exciting new approach for the undeveloped nations of the world."

Veritor adds,"The problem is that planning is often based on short term expediency and pressure from private interests without sufficient concern for the public. Look at the plight of cities where randomly developed space utilization has exacerbated problems. Governments lose touch with the societies they are supposed to be serving.

"Let's shift the discussion to another aspect of the territorial imperative involving population influx and internal population shifts as well as the partitioning and merging of countries. All are driven by socio-economics, political ideology, ethnicity or religious fervor."

Veritor notes, "Networking seems to be the last thing considered when people or countries are bent on exercising territorial imperatives. How often have countries attempted to lay claim to new borders without considering the needs of their neighbors? How foolish this is when both countries could have networked to their mutual socio-economic benefit. Some borders are more stable because of mutual respect, balance of power or because they are open in the first place."

Neos adds, "World maps are forever being redrawn; borders change and new countries emerge. Such changes are often attributable to ultra-nationalism, a step backward in development it seems to me."

Pragma looks askance, "I can't see ideological stances as being the most desirable stimulus of the territorial imperative. I think that new political ideologies are born in times of the poor socio-economic conditions. Past ideologies appear to have been insufficient for human development in which all people are encouraged to participate and grow."

Part II - Justifying the Regional Concept

CHAPTER 5 - ECONOMIC IMPERATIVE AND QUALITY OF LIFE

The economic imperative is one of scale and complexity in which production, distribution, exchange and consumption contribute or detract from economic well being. Means of production, management of distribution, regulation of trade, methods of exchange and patterns of consumption in the marketplace represent areas of study and research that have long been a challenge to economists, business and others. Veritor, Pragma and Neos recognize the utter folly of attempting to construct new theories or employ analysis in describing the economic imperative. They have a different purpose. Broad economic relationships linked with social implications are more likely to be helpful as they investigate a new form of society.

The economic imperative must be forever combined with the territorial and environmental imperatives in shaping the quality of life at all levels of society. Therefore, the global, national, regional, community, neighborhood and individual levels must all be considered in meeting these imperatives.

Veritor, Pragma and Neos are very concerned about life's inequities that often drive the economic imperative. The economic imperative reflects human need to survive and flourish. When people cannot make a living, quality of life is in jeopardy. War, crime and rebellion produce severe depredations, social decay and a reduction of self-esteem and productivity. When negative symptoms begin to appear, it is time to seriously reflect on how to meet the needs of the economic imperative.

"Let's consider the countries these people live in. Isn't it essential for these nations to carefully develop, enhance, renew, recycle and conserve resources as they plan and implement long term economic programs? How else can they hope to compete in world markets?" asks Veritor.

Neos answers, "I think they should also need to establish policies, programs and regulations at all levels of government based on some larger socio-economic vision, one that encourages participation and individual development."

CHAPTER 5 - ECONOMIC IMPERATIVE AND QUALITY OF LIFE

Levels of Economic Imperative

With few exceptions, all people and groups exhibit economic imperatives. This universal characteristic exists at all levels and is concerned with the need to produce, distribute, exchange and consume objects or services that are considered to have value. These functions involve producer and consumer, seller and buyer, giver and receiver relationships. Third party intermediaries, middlemen or brokers are often involved. Such duality exists within all economic systems in order for essential work to be done and supply and demand needs to be met. There are frequent inequities in all of these transactions. Sometimes, the transactions are made under duress or out of desperation when prevailing market conditions favor one party over another. Those who fall short of their economic imperatives are often faced with hardships and despair, and, as a result, they suffer losses in quality of life. Large economic differences between the poor and the affluent is of great concern as a destabilizer. Economic imperatives are related to other imperatives, and taken together contribute to quality of life in any society.

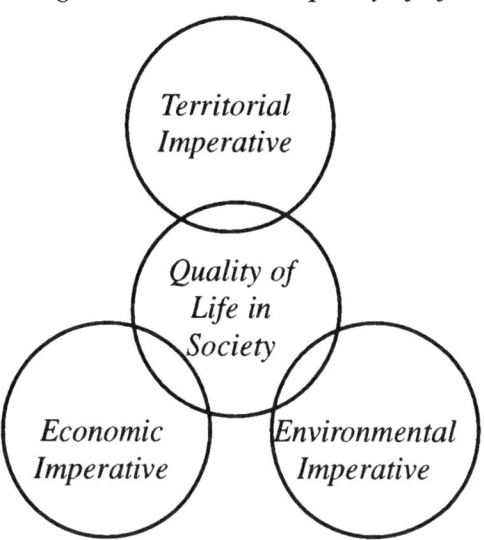

Territorial Imperative

Quality of Life in Society

Economic Imperative

Environmental Imperative

In order to improve quality of life without loss of territorial and environmental imperatives so as to enhance productivity, distribution, exchange and moderate consumption:
* *The nations of the world need to provide healthy economic environments on each continent.*
* *Nations need to provide inter-regional cooperation and networking.*
* *Regions need to provide a complete set of infrastructure networks that enhance the economic environment.*
* *Communities need to provide a mix of neighborhoods, services and commercial interests.*
* *Neighborhoods need to provide social settings for families and individuals to encourage voluntary efforts.*
* *Individuals need to be involved in mutually rewarding experiences that increase economic well-being.*

Pragma shifts the conversation to economic opportunity. "We know that many countries of the world lack all kinds of resources. They also lack capital and government programs to compensate for this dearth. The development of industry and business in such nations must emphasize value-added improvements to both imports and native resources in order to increase local income. For instance, they could enhance local products and imaginatively promote and increase local skills for competition in a world economy. If the natural environment offers potential interest to tourism, a new industry can be developed. This is especially relevant for under-developed economies."

Veritor adds to these observations. "Of course, industrialized countries already have an abundance of skilled labor, available capital, sophisticated economic infrastructures and the means for resource conversion and distribution even when they may have limited natural resources. They also have extensive experience in food and product processing, in the construction of different kinds of buildings, roads, bridges, terminals and in the installation of transportation and communication systems. Their economic advantages are decidedly greater than in under-developed countries."

Neos sums up this part of the trialogue. "Governments can help to stabilize and grow economies by initiating new programs and guidelines that will reduce risks and minimize excesses during economic development. Sustained regional programs with meaningful goals and properly managed infrastructures can lead the way by providing new, large scale economic opportunities. This would set an example for the rest of the country."

Veritor brings up a new concern. "The rate of consumption for products and services differs greatly from country to country. Certain everyday needs are basic to survival while others enhance quality of life. Many 'needs' are acquired; derived from imitation, custom and force of habit. Perhaps festive or religious occasions, ceremonies and celebrations and even the desire for social or economic status prompt people to acquire things. Many people consume excessively in order to satisfy a compulsion. Others surround themselves with luxuries beyond creature comfort. Are they compensating for some psychological privation?"

Pragma adds, "In the modern industrial state, conspicuous consumption seems to be the stimulus and yardstick for economic prosperity. Advertising and merchandising are major budget items for businesses and industries. Potential consumers are repeatedly bombarded by multi-media. It amazes me that so many people live so precariously beyond their economic means or prospects. Still others become involved in hoarding and accumulating more than they could ever possibly enjoy. This consumes a good part of their time and energy. It becomes the sole purpose of living even when it produces hardship and discomfort. How ironical!"

Part II - Justifying the Regional Concept

CHAPTER 6 - ENVIRONMENTAL IMPERATIVE AND SURVIVAL

The environmental imperative pertains to mankind's need to protect and augment natural surroundings, conserve natural resources and promote better living conditions. People have always sought ways to survive the changes and dangers of the natural environment. The environment has been the adversary. The goal of humans has been to conquer, overcome and outlast the climactic extremes, treachery of land, sea and rivers, and other natural calamities. Acquisition of earth's resources has been a part of this goal, whatever the cost. Other than major cataclysmic events, the most dangerous element in mankind's environment, however, has been other humans. The same situation exists today.

With great cleverness homo sapiens made tools, and over time, increasing their numbers and refinement. Some of the tools were for killing, others were for raising and preparing foods, some were for building and handling and still others for travel and communication.

Throughout history, humans have modified the environment to maximize their chances of survival and advancement. During all this experimenting, mankind has not been aware of or faced up to its abuse of nature. People needed trees and wasted the forests. People needed fish and depleted breeding stock. They needed minerals and coal and strip-mined, leaving pollution and erosion. They needed more of a certain crop and misused the top soil, letting it blow away. They burned fossil fuels, making the air dangerously toxic.

Countries became very proficient at wasteful warfare, employing collective cunning instead of wisdom. Crimes against people and property, the practice of coveting what others have, and the habits of hatred and distrust are constantly with the world today. Combativeness is characterized by both physical and verbal aggression. It is practiced by individuals and by groups of people. Countries attack their own minorities or their neighbors who may live or think differently. The tragedy of such combativeness is the repeated oppression and destruction of both latent human potential and natural and man-made environments.

We cannot accurately predict the long term future of the environment and resources. We can, however, attempt to create conditions that are more humane for as many generations as possible. With quality of life as a guide, with wisdom and with peace, mankind must continue to conduct noble experiments, learning to live in harmony and with respect for the earth.

Excessive and Improper Use of Resources and Environment

Combustion Wastes and Pollution

Illumination Energy Waste

Noise Pollution

Deforestation and Desertification

Weapons Buildup & Warfare Destruction & Pollution

Employment of Engineers, Scientists & Others for Waging Wars

Diversion of Human Resources & Money for Gambling

Diversion of Human Resources & Money Caused by Unaddressed Social Dysfunctions

Automotive Inefficiency & Over-Reliance

Mass Transportation Deficiencies

Construction Waste

All Commodities Waste & Over-Consumption

Increased Emphasis & Diversion of Human Resources on Marginal Services

Overfishing/ Overgrazing

Diversion of Human Resources & Money for Substance Abuse

Diversion of Human Resources & Money Due to Health Systems Dysfunctions

Food Waste and Over-Consumption

Water Waste and Over-Consumption

Agricultural Waste Pollution

Industrial Wastes & Pollution

Conflicting Uses of Land/Sea/Air Spaces

Diversion of Human Resources & Money Due to Crime

Diversion of Human Resources & Money & Family Breakdowns

Diversion of Human Resources & Money Due to Educational System Dysfunctions

CHAPTER 6 - ENVIRONMENTAL IMPERATIVE AND SURVIVAL

Veritor, Pragma and Neos feel drawn to the positive attributes of people. Although they sense that most of the world's population does not have thoughts beyond local survival, this will change. They anticipate that there will ultimately be greater efforts to create healthier environments. More people, especially leaders, will have to become more aware of the environmental imperative and network to achieve progress.

Veritor, who has been deep in thought, begins the discussion. "I am encouraged by the efforts of the many caring, knowledgeable and intelligent people who bring environmental problems and critical issues to the forefront. We can't possibly discuss all the global and regional issues they have presented, but we can review some key relationships that determine human approaches to both natural and man-made environments."

Pragma responds, "I think that a growing awareness of environmental issues by many more governments, corporations and the general public makes it increasingly possible to redefine the environmental imperative to show how mankind can and must live in order to thrive."

Neos asserts, "Some people have great respect for the natural environment; others don't. Some are more immediately dependent on all aspects of this environment while many others, like those living in industrialized countries, are apt to be more occupied with man-made environmental prospects and conditions."

Veritor listens closely and answers, "People must at least react to those environmental conditions that immediately affect them. I guess it's difficult for most people to become psychologically or physically involved in environmental crises happening to people who live far away, despite advances in modern communications. When people are more responsive to the travail of others, it is probably because they can identify with those who are afflicted and imperiled. Many consider it to be moral and socially responsible and concern themselves with the plight of others. But I think that the majority of people and their governments find that they have enough to cope with in their own countries. It is tragic because in many cases what is happening to others could happen to anyone and any country downstream. Many humanitarian organizations have been formed throughout the world for the service of humanity and to restore planet earth. Governments and multi-national corporations need to become increasingly involved, too, for practical as well as altruistic reasons."

Pragma notes, "Certainly, there are economic reasons for concern. One of them is the attrition of resources and the loss of access to them which we must discuss later."

Redefinition of the Environmental Imperative

- *It is imperative that mankind consider nature not as something to conquer, but as diverse variable elements to be understood and respected, to be utilized when feasible, and to be adapted to, when extreme, by man-made innovations.*

- *It is imperative that humans accept the fact that mankind, itself, is a part of the natural environment and is to be respected accordingly.*

- *It is imperative that mankind, involved with the creation of man-made environments, remember that cataclysmic events of nature are always impending.*

- *It is imperative that humans do not wantonly and deliberately destroy the ecospheres of the world.*

- *It is imperative that humans do not knowingly contribute to the extinction of helpful life forms in the environment.*

- *It is imperative that mankind create environments that are in consonance with nature so that harmony and security, along with uniqueness, may co-exist.*

- *It is imperative that mankind continue to pursue knowledge of the universe, including earth and every one of its regions, in order to more fully appreciate and understand mankind's place and destiny.*

- *It is imperative that mankind delve ever deeper into the internal mysteries of the human mind and body so that the inner environment can be made more compatible and in harmony with the external environment.*

- *It is imperative that humans in each generation work to protect and preserve the fragile, beautiful and beneficial wonders of nature as divine gifts.*

CHAPTER 6 - ENVIRONMENTAL IMPERATIVE AND SURVIVAL

Neos adds, "It's a long and arduous task to try to convince governments, cartels and corporations that it is in their best interests to protect endangered species, to protect the integrity of the land by giving up brute force approaches of extracting resources or to avoid developing resources to the extent that the environment will ultimately be destroyed. They deal in the present and near future, trying to respond to demanding constituents in the case of governments and to profit-minded investors and self-concerned consumers in the case of the corporations and cartels."

Pragma responds, "There are many conflicts of interest. Considering the wide range of confrontations that have been happening between environmentalists and certain government bureaucracies and business interests, it is amazing that any progress is being made to protect our planet."

Veritor nods in agreement. "It has taken years to develop national and international protective laws and to obtain compliance for even a relatively small number of critical situations. Whenever catastrophes occur, they prompt immediate reactions. Catastrophes are very tangible. Earthquakes, hurricanes and other natural events certainly command respect. Poisoning of air, food and water that results in sickness and death brings sharp responses. Climate changes, such as draught, that affect the growing of food are gradual until famine brings sickness and death as result of draught. The list is unending."

Pragma questions the others, "Can we expect further progress? It seems to me there is greater urgency than ever for governments to take collective action and provide far-reaching and enduring plans to contribute to the long-term preservation of the earth's environment."

Neos replies, "First it will take a much greater awareness and higher sense of purpose. People and their governments must modify their thinking. How can any meaningful progress be made without considering the long term survival of mankind? It means that new habits and practices in everyday living must be cultivated. New socio-economic and technological systems regions have to be conceived and developed with respect for earth and its resources."

Veritor says, "We need to better understand the relationships between the economic and environmental imperatives before trying to change the world. What is basic to future economic growth and human survival? Who should assume leadership responsibilities? How should they network?"

Part II - Justifying the Regional Concept

CHAPTER 7 - SHAPING THE FUTURE

Let us summarize before looking ahead to the future. The earth is bountiful, a magnificent planet that continues to nurture myriad forms of life and to provide abundant elemental resources and energy necessary for such life. Through the mutations and transitions of all things, the most consistent aspect of existence is change. Change in nature, with its many dimensions and manifestations occurs both as chaos and as repeatable patterns.

Mankind, a small part of creation and bound to its cycles of life and death, attempts to alter, manipulate, regulate and innovate within the natural environment by creating pseudo-environments. Ideally, these man-made experiments are intended to improve quality of life. Scientific and technological advances introduce new possibilities and problems. Rapid population growth, increased consumption, inability to manage transitions, growing system complexity and abuse of the natural environment and its resources have all contributed to the degradation of the modern world.

A major contributor to the decline of this world has been the growing obsolescence of the city concept that fails to meet even minimum expectations of quality of life. We have found both positive and negative attributes in cities, particularly large ones, and that the negatives far outweigh the positives. Can over-crowded population centers and cities be restructured and restored under prevailing conditions? Can the best features and functions of big cities be provided in different ways using other concepts of living?

Planners must come up with comprehensive answers to the chronic problems of big cities. Of all the glaring problems that must be faced, population density and increases are the most implacable. There are many unanswered questions. How can influx be sharply reduced, and how can those people who need to move find other places to live and work? How can those who remain in the cities flourish?

Do the infrastructures of the big cities have adequate capacities to serve a continuing increase in inhabitants? For that matter are the governments of over-populated countries able to provide for basic human needs when they have too many and more are coming? There are critical choices to be made. Making changes to meet needs depends on people's attitudes and their will to face the future.

Veritor asserts,"We've already discussed the supercities and other areas of dense population. Only so many people can exist in a given space, let alone have freedom and some mobility. People must have prospects for earning a livelihood and a chance to live the better life. But this is a matter of determination, not of vague and wishful thinking. Humans can produce a better world. They don't have to flounder and behave blindly and narrowly. They are able to gain a sense of vision, direction and responsibility. There is absolutely nothing that compels people to behave perversely, to

CHAPTER 6 - SHAPING THE FUTURE

act excessively and obsessively or to revert to brutality and wanton destruction. I think that mankind can at least exhibit the same magnitude of fervor to build a better world as it does to destroy it."

Pragma and Neos agree wholeheartedly with this appraisal. Pragma contributes,"I am convinced that mankind has the capacity to develop better ways of life. Humanity can and must meet the challenge of producing stable and progressive societies for a healthier environment."

Neos ventures,"New regional concepts offer people a choice. They can be desirable places to live, work, learn and enjoy. If they promote quality of life, they will attract people and enterprises to move from areas in which they cannot hope to flourish. Initial development is not likely to entice masses of people. Not everyone is a pioneer, ready for the adventures, risks and challenges of the new. There is apt to be a built-in caution for the untried, not yet existing or the unproven. Most folks stick with what is ' known', no matter how inadequate, confusing, frustrating and painful it may be. People are apt to decide to move only when another place appears to offer something better. People tend to imitate. If others are moving or buying in ever greater numbers, they figure it must then be the safe and profitable thing to do. It is sort of a trust in the 'collective wisdom' of many which may well turn into following the 'collective will' of many."

Pragma adds, "It takes persuasive leaders and many knowledgeable people in many disciplines to impart vision and faith in the future. They must communicate with people to show them that life can be made better when there is a goal, a plan and the will to carry it out."

Veritor asks,"Isn't it essential that people everywhere be encouraged to become involved? After all, cooperative efforts, as well as individual achievement, is essential for progress. Let's examine some attitudes that are necessary to shape the future."

Shaping the Future

Facing the future means visualizing what we would like to have happen and planning for contingencies. Optimum quality of life for all who seek it, requires sustained efforts, individually and collectively, to fulfill our visions and plans. These are multi-generational efforts and a legacy for all.

Mankind has the capability of shaping its future within the bounds of the natural environment and human physical, mental and psychological limitations. Humans can plan, prepare for and attempt to minimize adverse effects of inevitable cataclysmic events by providing necessary programs that define basic functions.

There is a Choice

Preferred Attitude	*Expression*
• *Positivism & Open Mindedness*	• *Facing the future and acceptance*
• *Future Goals & Purposes, New Objectives*	• *Tomorrow's events will affect us.*
	• *Everything changes; people have this potential.*
• *New Habits/Practices & Selective Change*	• *Necessity and curiosity induce human growth.*
	• *All governments reflect extent of public involvement.*
• *Awareness of Trends, Dangers & Opportunities*	• *Expect and encourage integrity.*
	• *Work and plan for what is needed.*
• *Changed Attitudes & Actions*	• *Participate and assume responsibility for self and the helpless.*

Non-Preferred Attitude	*Expression*
• *Negativism & Cynicism*	• *Resistance, escape and denial*
• *Fantasies, Illusions Wishful Thinking*	• *Tomorrow will take care of itself.*
	• *Things never change; people are basicly evil.*
• *Old Habits/Practices & Rigidity*	• *People are incapable of growing.*
	• *All governments are corrupt and inept.*
• *Uninformed Reaction To Current Events*	• *People are not to be trusted.*
	• *Take all that you can now; give very little.*
• *Rationalization of Actions*	• *Let someone else take responsibility.*

CHAPTER 6 - SHAPING THE FUTURE

Pragma shifts to another consideration, "I think many people are satisfied with where they live. They have become accustomed to living in overcrowded cities. They've adapted by creating their own special environments with friends and interests within the context of the larger environment."

Neos counters, "That's all well and good, but when big cities can no longer provide services, jobs and housing for millions of people, many others have the urge to escape. When people's basic needs cannot be met, where can they go? Can they afford the cost of going from city to city looking for employment, food, clothing and shelter? To me, regional development fills this vacuum. Its infrastructures will provide new, better places for people to live."

Veritor notes, "I agree. The dispersion of excess population has taken on a global urgency with the highest priority. Only random, catastrophic natural events could have a greater one. The question lingering in my mind is whether dispersion will only lead to the creation of more of the same adverse conditions that prevail in supercities? We already have many examples of flight to the suburbs of big cities by people and enterprises able to afford it. Randomly developed suburbs usually grow to become extensions of the old metropolises."

Neos brings up a related point, "I think the early planning and implementation of infrastructures to serve new communities in a timely, incremental manner will prove to be very cost effective. The argument that new infrastructures should be funded and installed after new enterprises and centers are already in place is seriously flawed. Without appropriate infrastructures in place, public and private developments will be haphazard. Many services and system interconnections are likely to be missing. Installing them later would incur major rework with exorbitant costs, higher risks, duplication and waste of resources."

Veritor reflects and says, "It's time to recapitulate. We have discussed the attributes of supercities. It's apparent that their over-population is likely to exceed available resources and the capacity of local leaders to govern. Timely assistance and investments are needed from outside sources. This is also true on a larger scale for countries that are overpopulated. So twin problems exist that involve population stabilization and shifts, but we will have to discuss this in greater detail when we address implementation."

Neos notes, "Obviously, new areas must be developed in a comprehensive way to alleviate overcrowding problems throughout the world. New options must be created."

Population Pressures - A Rationale for Dispersion

There is an analogy in physics. When a specific number of molecules are enclosed in a vessel with definite volume, the molecules (which are in motion) will collide. If more molecules are added, more collisions will occur. Increased collisions produce increased heat. Increased heat produces increased pressure.

There are ways to reduce this pressure:
- *Reduce the temperature and pressure by cooling and slowing down the molecular movement.*
- *Relieve the pressure by releasing molecules.*
- *Expand the size of the vessel, if possible.*
- *Continue to increase the temperature and pressure until the vessel explodes.*

People are the molecules. Cities with confining areas are the vessels. Conflicts, friction and collisions of people, vehicles and interests are the producers of heated exchange with attendant anger and pressure increases.

There are ways to minimize this pressure:
- *Expand the size of the vessel (build underground, build skyscrapers, build massive block dwellings of cities or communities).*
- *Within each vessel provide separations to channel movement of molecules to reduce friction and collisions and to allow freer flow (infrastructure development).*
- *Regulate temperatures and collision of molecules through exchanges using smaller interconnecting vessels (cooperative exchanges and networking).*
- *Limit the number of molecules in each vessel (zoning quotas on population influx and dispersion).*
- *Reduce the external temperature of the vessel for internal heat exchange (conservation and better utilization of resources and environmental protection).*

To complete the analogy we would think of humans as being composed of many molecules. Extending this analogy would be the grouping of humans like families and then collections of families into neighborhoods. These in turn would be combined to form communities and then networks of communities along with their centers. The analogy suggests a natural, safer, freer and functional concept of human interaction that has greater stability in the larger environment.

PART III
Regional Design & Concept

Part III - Regional Design & Scenarios

CHAPTER 1 - INTRODUCTION OF THE REGIONAL CONCEPT

Reflect on the perspectives and philosophies presented in previous chapters. What effective design for living would synthesize and represent them? The regional concept must be a candidate for consideration. This universal approach (with modifications) utilizes both the old and the new. It is comprehensive, innovative and attainable.

Veritor, Neos and Pragma are ready to discuss the general characteristics of the regional concept. Veritor takes the lead and says, "At last we have come to the essence of our search. We will expand on a description of regionalization in more detail later, but at this moment, let's talk about the region in general and define terms."

There is brief concurrence all around. But how can ideas and terms originating in different fields be expressed so they can be universally understood? In this modern age, names and expressions are frequently borrowed, invented or redefined in an attempt to communicate. Dictionaries undergo continuous revisions in an effort to keep up. Veritor, Pragma and Neos are aware of this as they proceed.

Neos says, "I think we can either define the region and its elements in terms of their physical makeup or we can define them in an operational sense to describe what they do or provide."

Veritor comments, "In our case, I think we will need to combine both kinds of definitions and hope that the mental pictures formed by them and their further use will enhance understanding."

Pragma reflects on the word "region" and looks at a world map. "Well, I can see many large areas, spaces or divisions that are called regions. The term region is also used for certain general locations like in the brain, parts of earth or space in the firmament. However, it's not very helpful to allude to a region in such a general way for our purposes. Neos, why don't you define the terms we will be using?"

CHAPTER 1 - INTRODUCTION OF THE REGIONAL CONCEPT

Definitions

Region - *A special area that provides a unique living environment and key resources dedicated to serving the public and private sectors. It consists of a network of infrastructures, communities, centers and support areas. These areas include arable and buildable lands and open spaces for conservation, resources and recreation. The total area of approximately 600 square miles is defined by natural boundaries, to the extent possible, and characterized by close proximity to such features as oceans, lakes, rivers, wetlands, valleys, mountains, hills, desert fringes or plainsland. The region's area must contain key resources sufficient to sustain an optimum population of approximately 1,500,000 people and a maximum of 2,000,000.*

Infrastructure - *One of a number of functional groups consisting of special systems necessary to develop, operate and maintain the activities of the region. Approximately thirteen groups apply their functions directly and through networking.*

Network - *Multi-faceted elements of a system that physically and functionally interconnect, integrate, coordinate and support communities, neighborhoods and special or dedicated centers of the infrastructures of a region. Regions are also networked to other regions and governmental entities. Networking involves the communication of information and ideas, the transfer of tangible items, and the physical interaction of people and people and machines.*

Community - *A subdivision of a region that provides for the needs of approximately 150,000 people grouped into neighborhoods. Public and private services in dedicated centers provide the civic, economic, educational, health and safety, cultural, recreational services and functions needed by residents and local enterprises.*

Centers - *Dedicated or special facilities and complexes within or near communities that focus on special functions of infrastructures at all levels of administration, legal and legislative, public safety, public and commercial utilities, public works, transportation, communication, industry, commerce, finance, agriculture, medical services, public health, scientific research, education, recreation, culture and religion. Centers of different size, scope and complexity are meant to serve the region, infrastructures, communities and neighborhoods.*

Neighborhood - *A subdivision of the community that involves a diversity of life styles and social, ethnic, religious and economic groupings. These provide for unique combinations of activities involving creativity and cooperative efforts for the mutual benefit and support of neighbors. Their immediate needs are met by close-by schools, medical clinics, recreational facilities and parks, religious facilities, local entertainment facilities, meeting halls for local affairs and events, emergency and safety services, commercial outlets and maintenance and repair services.*

Veritor notes, "It's apparent that without comprehensive, phased-in planning and design and timely networking of infrastructure implementation, there will be acute rivalry for access and resources in the development of infrastructures. Fierce opposition, conflicts of interest, obstructionism, exploitation, abuse of the environment and infringements on other's rights will ensue. Negative conditions and behavior might get out of control. The resulting chaos would be tragically wasteful. It seems to me modern systems management and planning in a regional context would make it possible to avoid such pitfalls."

Neos looks up and asks, "In contrast to the random, chaotic growth of cities, what could be more reasonable than the orderly progression of regionalization processes? Regional development would help create well-designed, viable communities. For instance, does it make sense to build homes in close proximity to hazardous industrial facilities? This has been done all along in big cities. On the other hand, it's judicious to locate communities so that they can benefit from regional infrastructure networking."

Veritor responds, "Those are important observations, Neos. We should avoid repeating old errors."

Pragma adds, "So much energy, time and so many resources are wasted just trying to compensate for random, sporadic, conflicting and out-of-phase growth. The regional network approach, however, promises the very opposite."

Veritor proceeds, "Let's look at the functional levels of a region. We can see that some inter-community networking functions must be carried out at the regional level where we would expect certain functional responsibilities to be. Regions are certainly necessary to integrate, coordinate and support the large scale requirements of the centers and communities. Regions must also interface with other regions and with existing government entities at different levels."

" For one thing, there has to be oversight and control over regional land, resources and space that extend well beyond the areas designated for special centers and community networks," Pragma notes.

Neos joins in. "I think this is an important and fundamental concern. Regions have to protect unspoiled natural areas as well as settled ones. These unspoiled areas provide another dimension in living and a chance for humans to experience nature's beauty and variety. Such areas need to continue to flourish unhindered by man-made projects or excessive modifications."

Veritor nods in agreement and continues. "Some regional areas will need restoration and development to enhance nature and to serve regional inhabitants. Projects will have to provide water and energy resources and special areas necessary for their servicing. We must show that regional areas have to be carefully designed and prepared to effectively provide an environment suitable for human habitation.

CHAPTER 1 - INTRODUCTION OF THE REGIONAL CONCEPT

"To my way of thinking, those who seek to exploit natural resources must use ingenious methods and new technologies to safely operate their facilities without causing harmful effects to the environment. Careless operations eventually become counter-productive. Regional governmental control is needed to regulate, coordinate and assist public and private center activities involved in developing regional resources.

"We need to specify what special centers are intended to do. I can see that infrastructure centers would be very large. At the regional level these large centers would provide services to benefit all networked communities as well as other centers. Major installations and operations would be designed to function for many years. Rapid obsolescence is too costly. Obviously, no community would be able to initiate and support the scope of these regional centers alone.

"One of the most important features of the region's networking capacity will be to effectively respond to emergencies such as catastrophic events. Modern and effective communication and transportation systems would enhance local survival rates and coping capabilities. Means for rapid emergency mass evacuation must be part of the overall system design. By contrast, there are few, if any, supercities with sufficiently developed infrastructures capable of effectively organizing, assisting, responding, and surviving major cataclysmic events."

After some reflection, Veritor adds."In order for centers to be effective, all-weather access must be available.This means more comprehensive, consistent and safe means for transporting people, products and raw materials must be provided. Furthermore, any movement of hazardous materials will require a separate transportation system."

Neos speaks up, "Certain sub-centers are also needed for all networked communities to extend services and benefits. They must be designed to meet the needs of each community and its neighborhoods. For instance, a sub-center may consist of a community college while a university with its larger capacity would provide educational services at the regional level."

Pragma responds, "I think a regional network center must also administer, plan, coordinate, integrate and support administrative sub-centers located in each community. This regional network center becomes a hub for cooperation and sharing of many inter-community activities."

Neos agrees,"Yes! That's a good point. It's also important to emphasize the dynamic relationships each community would have with its neighborhoods. By limiting population growth and by increasing community support, many problems that we see today could be resolved or avoided. Without the stress of too many people moving in, communities and their neighborhoods could readily accommodate diverse life styles and significantly improve quality of life. Of course, each community would self-administer, regulate and implement its local affairs. This contrasts sharply with big administer, regulate and implement its local affairs. This contrasts sharply with big cities."

Veritor and Pragma brighten. Veritor asserts, "Networked communities are likely to flourish and work together. They would become more aware of local deteriorating conditions. Isolation induced by the need for greater security would neither be necessary nor desirable. Local networking would help sustain the vitality of the community. These promising experiments should have universal appeal and suggest new basic designs for regions.

"The regional network experiment would also be significant in promoting international cooperation for regions within nations, for communities within regions, for neighborhoods within communities, for families within neighborhoods and finally for each personal relationship."

Pragma reacts to this, "This sounds like utopia, but I think quality of life must be fostered at all levels. No one should be ignored. The diminishment of quality of life for some means, in a larger sense, the diminishment of quality of life for all of society. Billions of people suffer because of poorly structured environments. Well-designed and developed regional infrastructures can improve the environment and promote quality of life for everyone."

Veritor continues, "The regional network of communities starts with various general premises, some of which may very well change as experience is gained. Of course, any knowledge derived from these regional experiments must be made readily available to other levels of government and outside cities and communities."

CHAPTER 1 - INTRODUCTION OF THE REGIONAL CONCEPT

Initial Community Development Premises

- *The population of a community is limited to approximately 150,000 in order to minimize societal problems such as crime, mental illness and others which tend to rapidly increase in per capita incidences beyond this number of people.*
- *The community is further subdivided into neighborhoods to form a mini-network.*
- *Each neighborhood is arranged to provide optimum privacy, yet offers social contact through common areas, malls, walkways, squares, parks, recreation areas, etc.*
- *Each neighborhood residential area is supported by local mini-centers and service entities.*
- *Each neighborhood is designed by public or private developers whose varied designs and arrangements encourage use of modern technology (i.e. solar energy electrical and space systems, waste processing into other usable forms, various communication satellites and systems, severe weather protection, central heating and cooling systems, etc.).*
- *Neighborhood residences are designed with a low profile (i.e. maximum of 2-3 stories).*
- *High rise buildings are located in relatively open areas with parking, augmented utilities, ready access, non-solar blockage to others and abundant foliage.*
- *Major transportation is mostly protected from the adverse weather conditions and adaptable to automation and other technological advances in traffic control.*
- *Neighborhood residential density of population (for a single level) is approximately 38 people per acre (14,000 sq.ft.) with an additional area of two acres of surrounding space. The average for two level dwellings is then 78 people per acre plus the two acres. (Western countries)*
- *Communities of 150,000 people use common areas that provide non-residential functions such as mini-centers, parks, schools, etc., utilizing approximately 25 sq. miles (including total residential space, road space, etc.).*
- *Regional areas contain not only the network of ten or more communities and internal centers, but the external centers needed for farming areas, air terminals with runways, etc. and wooded areas, bodies of water, mountains and uninhabitable land, etc., as well.*

although there are many semi-independent communities in the network, they can best flourish when there is full cooperation. The communities are expected to become mostly viable in their own right, but when it comes to providing public works, developing resources like water, power and agricultural sufficiency, effective distribution systems, effective mass transportation and communication systems and effective safety services, the pooled efforts and resources of the communities are needed, especially for large scale enterprises and investments for regional scope centers."

Veritor joins in. "The network approach is by far more reasonable than expecting each community to carry the burdens of such development and enterprise independently, often in conflict with each other. This problem is common everywhere. This is where a regional large scale design, planning and implementation capabilities are needed. Regional expenditures for community programs, services and activities would obviously be in the public's interest."

Pragma answers."Unfortunately, special interests often prevail at public cost. There will always be people who do not cooperate, do not contribute their efforts and insights to help any one else. Many will not want to share community responsibilities or costs. Their concern is limited and narrowly defined to satisfy only immediate personal gratification, giving no thought to long-term consequences that diminish the collective quality of life. Some people don't want to be taxed in any way, although they demand benefits from the society that serves them. This kind of social behavior exists at all economic levels and is not likely to disappear. We can only hope to minimize it."

Veritor notes,"This is one reason why regional infrastructures need early input during development from many of the interests who are participating. Comprehensive, reasonable and enduring planning and implementation should then take place. When planning and implementation is initiated early, infrastructures become operationally effective sooner, and most people will realize how much better life has become. Of course, creating a network of communities and centers will lead to clearer guidance, well-defined limits and coordinated support for developers, entrepreneurs, special center interests and public officials. Otherwise, without the existence of ground rules, zoning limits, safety codes, special environmental conditions and physical arrangement of the infrastructures, developers and investors would be faced with maximum risk, delays and conflict. This is hardly the way to attract people who are supposed to become actively involved in building and construction. I think they are likely to welcome the chance to participate, especially when cost overruns, civil suits and red tape can be minimized."

CHAPTER 1 - INTRODUCTION OF THE REGIONAL CONCEPT

Network Linking of Communities and Centers

The opportunity to participate in shaping the future so as to create a better living environment should be welcomed by those who think and act positively. The regional network concept offers such an opportunity.

<u>*Anticipated Benefits:*</u>

- *As the planned network is developed, new communities of different design can be built, all linked for mutual support and cooperation.*
- *People movers, commercial and industrial pre-planned transportation systems can be incrementally installed with more controllable costs.*
- *Public works for the whole network can be effectively designed, key basic structures and installations can be built and incremental installations provided as inhabitants need and can afford to complete them.*
- *A skilled work force can be retained that is stable and able to economically and readily reach places of employment.*
- *Communication systems can be effectively developed for both work and play that lend themselves to progressive installations with advanced technology.*
- *Dedicated distribution systems of all kinds can be simplified and made highly effective. This can also reduce operating costs.*
- *Special centers (i.e. air terminals, chemical processing plants, smelting and refining plants, etc.) that are hazardous to communities are placed and operated with safeguards in remote areas.*
- *Inter and intra-regional transportation separates commercial and industrial access from that designated for people moving.*
- *Emergency services can rapidly reach all the communities of the regional network. Community emergency services readily support each other.*
- *Dispersion of population within the network and alternate means of transportation allow rapid evacuation during major cataclysmic events, so more people can survive.*
- *Cultural, ethnic and recreational exchanges and events can be promoted, and major programs and centers can be supported by the network communities.*
- *The development of civic leadership, responsibility and participation can naturally take place and provide early training, experience and exposure for service in larger government entities.*
- *The educational system can be made more effective with cost, skill and facility-sharing.*
- *Public health and safety systems are closely integrated and interactive. All levels of medical care can be provided.*
- *Land use and zoning can be more consistent and less prone to improper use.*

Veritor responds, "Although we can see that there are many apparent advantages from networks, there are bound to be many more discovered as the regions develop. I think we also have to anticipate possible problems that may arise when developing regional networks of communities and centers. But I think many of these can be avoided with the approach we are proposing."

Neos and Pragma become a little apprehensive. Neos asks, "I wonder about the role of builders and developers in the private sector as well as those who become involved in the many public projects? Certainly, there needs to be strict fiscal and project accountability and public awareness as many activities unfold. In the regional network concept, effective management control will have to be exercised for all program phases."

Pragma answers, "Yes, that is true, but I am particularly concerned that developers and entrepreneurs have enough freedom and support to provide quality, innovation, efficiency and utility in their projects. They also need to make a profit. There have to be incentives and motivation to design and develop community neighborhoods."

Veritor adds, "Design and development for networks of communities and centers will naturally also include many innovations made possible by modern technology. Designs have to satisfy the special needs of different cultures and lifestyles. Innovation is certainly mandatory in many parts of the world where space and access are limited and where there are inadequate resources or harsh environmental conditions."

"What about the people who inhabit and work in networked communities?" Neos wonders. "If they are going to participate and be absorbed into the various communities, what training must be provided by the public and private sectors? It seems to me that this would be an excellent opportunity to upgrade the productivity, skills, competency and sense of direction for many people."

Veritor responds, "Of course. But it is necessary to convince both prospective employers and workers of this opportunity. How else can high quality, marketable and competitive products and services eventually be provided? We must propose expanded remedial efforts throughout the school systems at all levels. Modern skills require more, not less, educational preparation and training. I think the regional approach will help stimulate, focus, direct and motivate students and teachers as well as workers and employers."

CHAPTER 1 - INTRODUCTION OF THE REGIONAL CONCEPT

Community Network and Center Possible Disadvantages and Problems

- *Pressure and influence by developers may lead to plan deviation, resulting in over-development or out-of-phase development that is costly and detrimental to buyers in the long run.*
- *Private entities or public officials may ignore or abuse regional network guidelines and regulations for economic advantages.*
- *Power seekers without appropriate competence may attempt to control and exploit regional and network projects.*
- *People with extreme views may cause polarization which could delay or prevent network development .*
- *Special interests may acquire open and wooded areas or water and other resources of a region, thereby circumventing regionally planned population and resource development.*
- *Participating labor may not be given promised pre-training and educational opportunities in exchange for in-kind services during regional development.*
- *Incoming persons may not be helped to participate, grow, work and have the opportunity to invest in a place to live in one of the communities.*
- *Certain ethnic, racial or religious groups may be excluded from participating and belonging.*

Political, socio-economic and technological experiments are subject to weaknesses. Nothing that is man-made is perfect. Regional network concepts are expected to have flaws, but it is anticipated that these can be more readily remedied than those in city concepts.

Veritor proceeds,"Let's look at new regions. It makes sense that the growth of new centers and communities be limited in population size to match the capacity of regional resources and environment. We have also noted that the preparation and development of regions and networked infrastructures be progressive. This allows the communities to be gradually developed as they absorb people from rural or densely populated areas."

Neos is inspired and proposes,"Perhaps we should expand on what networks of communities and centers are intended to be. They can be designed to blend with various topographical and geographical environments. Also, we're not talking about one large governmental monolith with randomly developed infrastructures, but rather comprehensively and carefully developed regional networks of infrastructures that also conform to the immediate surroundings. This networking emphasis is intended to physically link the functions and facilities of many interests."

Veritor notes further,"I can see that the design and implementation of communities and special centers of the region can be quite varied but still retain similar relationships and functional emphases. Most of these functions are applicable universally, even though many can not be immediately applied or developed. The functions to be performed by the systems and institutions may have been given different names or may have been combined in different ways throughout the world. At this point let's refer to general regional physical and functional concepts."

Pragma agrees,"It's apparent that the needs of underdeveloped countries contrast greatly in sophistication with those of highly industrialized nations. Available resources and unusual environments are likely to impact designs; therefore, different scenarios must be developed for various areas."

Neos adds,"The networks of communities and infrastructure centers and systems have to be designed within the specific constraints of diverse environments, geographic locations, areas and climates normally addressed by extensive system integration. But for now let's concentrate on the regional basic design."

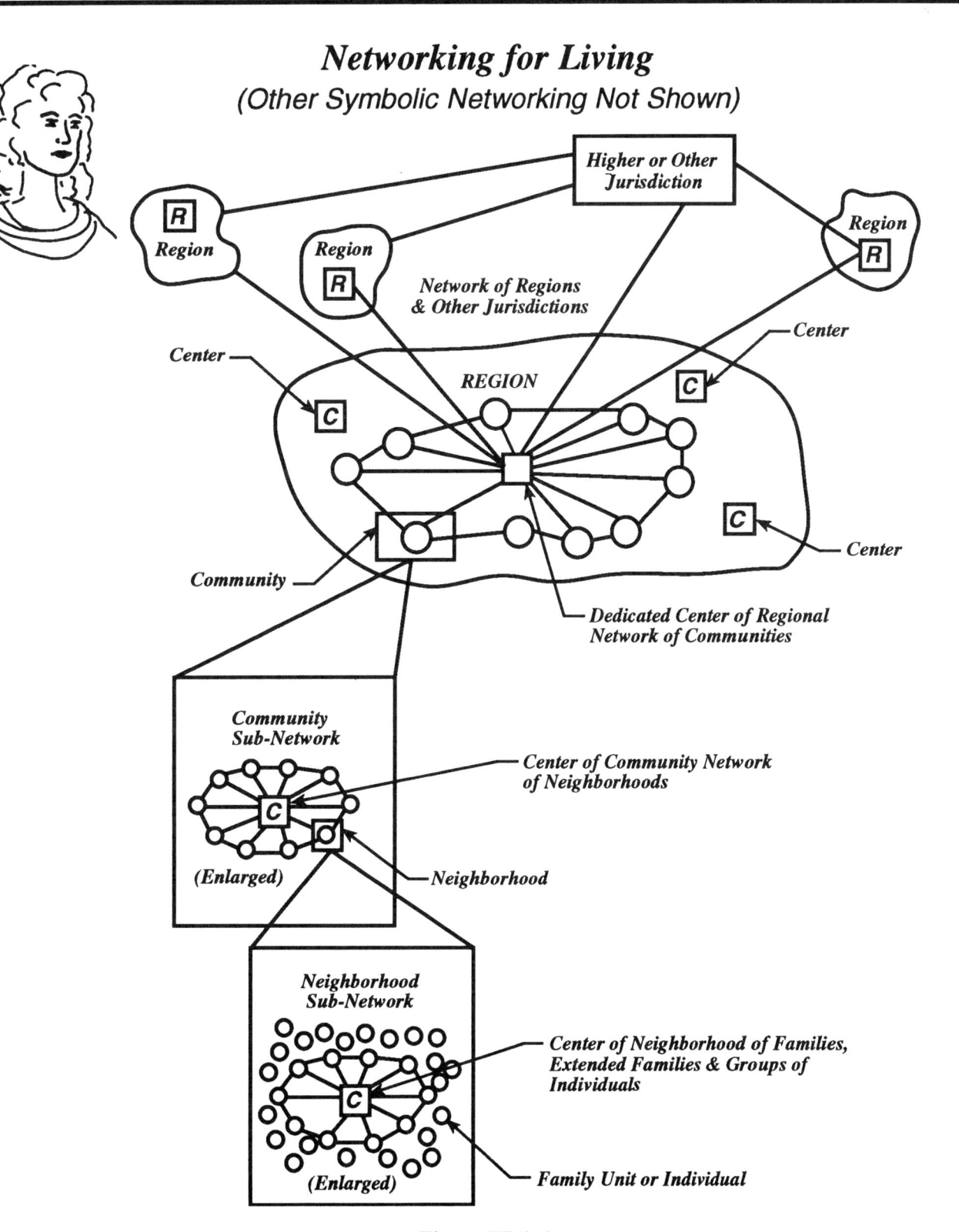

CHAPTER 1 - INTRODUCTION OF THE REGIONAL CONCEPT

Networking for Living
(Other Symbolic Networking Not Shown)

Figure III-1-A

Part III - Regional Design & Scenarios

CHAPTER 2 - FUNCTIONAL DESIGN OF THE REGION

One regional design cannot serve all cases. There are too many variables for that. What may be appropriate for one area, society or economy is not necessarily suitable for another. However, the regional concept provides fundamental functions, grouped and interconnected to allow for differences in design. These functions are necessary for human sustenance and growth in a stable and healthy environment.

Form follows function. This formula for design has long been espoused by many professionals in different fields. Regional design is predicated on this formula. Functions progress from the general to the more definitive. Functions are general actions taken or thought processes to perform certain types of work. There is a significantly large number of activities performed in a highly differentiated, industrial society; much fewer in a primitive society.

Functions are distinct but inter-dependent. They are part of a system, responsive to stimuli within an actual or perceived environment. For instance, there are numerous systems simultaneously active in the human body. We consider the system functions of a human being to be healthy when they respond appropriately and interact effectively.

Even as the classification of parts of the body does not define a living person, neither does the assembly of hundreds of thousands of elements or various institutional categories define a society. Likewise, a description of the physical characteristics or elements of a region also cannot fully define it.

Like the humans that form it, the corporate form of society has systems with distinct and inter-related functions. Closely related functions must be homogeneously grouped to effectively interact. When functions are missing or mismatched in such groupings, systems become ineffective.

When a society is dysfunctional, it is sick. Simple palliatives in the form of political slogans, scape-goating, token financial assistance or calls for the reduction or curtailment of vital functions are not corrective. Getting well requires a more comprehensive perspective and positive action. Inertia, ignorance, cynicism, negativism and fear stand in the way of healing.

The regional concept groups special system functions into recognizable infrastructures for close interaction and effective performance. Compare this with the chaos of over-crowded societies where it is apparent that infrastructures have become progressively ineffective and existing functions no longer perform well. Reliance on complicated, bureaucratic, hierarchical governmental structures leads people to deal with each other from positions of power rather than by networking. When institutional interfaces are poorly defined, omissions, conflicts, confusion, and frustration result.

CHAPTER 2 - FUNCTIONAL DESIGN OF THE REGION

The design, planning and implementation phases of new regional infrastructures offer millions of people the opportunity of a lifetime. The well-defined functions of these development phases will allow participants to identify and grow with their region. However, positive thinking, good will and hard work will be required to produce regions as well as to restore and remodel cities. Significant amounts of persistence and willingness to listen, observe, think and respond in ways that serve both the individual and the common good are necessary.

Functional deficiencies crop up at every level of operation. Incompetence or failure to perform functions according to expectations is far too common and make matters worse. People may lack motivation, have inadequate training, be mentally or physically inhibited or be faced with trying to perform functions that are ill-defined or appropriate for a different level. However, most deficiencies can be remedied.

Neos, Veritor and Pragma take up the trialogue again. Neos notes, "Competency to perform at each level is a serious problem. If expected functions are not performed well or avoided at the neighborhood level, a higher level may need to fill the void. We find this repeated for the community, the region, inter-region and higher. Functions usually break down in networking because people fail to communicate. Failure to perform, often leads to a loss of local control and benefits. Someone at a higher level may be forced to take over lower level functions, sometimes without sufficient knowledge of what is required. I would like to provide further observations on this subject."

Pragma answers, "It's important that not just government but all large corporations carefully regroup their activities according to functional emphasis and relatedness. Personnel, when organized into such teams, often work more efficiently and effectively together, and fewer people are usually required for each job."

Expectation of Functional Competency For Regionalization

How can we recognize appropriate competency at different levels? An individual may be able to demonstrate functional competency at more than one level, but not at all levels at one time. Evaluation of functional competency at any level may be based on established requirements or expectations in society and the workplace. It is important that such expectations be realistic. Each individual or group of individuals differ in how well they perform. In the individual, the functions of body and mind develop together as an integrated system. As each individual matures, he or she attain successive levels of functional skills. Unless there is a breakdown in physical or mental development, the individual gradually becomes competent enough to perform necessary functions.

Many functions of an individual interface with those of others persons as well as with the general environment. Two people (like husband and wife),who share common functions, form a unique relationship recognized by society. In family dynamics there is an extension of shared functions and interactions, and no external person or agency should be competent to act for the family unless there is disintegration of its functional well-being.

Groups of individuals combine their efforts to perform thousands of functions. A functional group that is already involved in some activity, agenda or specialization should be responsible for and capable of performing its own assigned or assumed functions. Only a malfunctioning group would require outside help or interference (by the law, social services or medical help).

Networking functions begin when two or more people have a common purpose. When networks are successful, it is because they are functionally compatible and have well-established interfaces. It seems irrational that functional incompatibility would be deliberately introduced into a network relationship, but this happens frequently. Sometimes it is a matter of personality (how people behave in performing assigned functions). At other times it is a matter of mismatched skills and knowledge.

At the community level, infrastructure networking includes neighborhood interrelationships. Correction of functional incompatibility or neglect at the neighborhood level requires coordination and other common efforts which can best be provided at the community level. Organization, coordination, arbitration and regulation of common events, resources, space and time are provided at the community level. Ordinarily, individual neighborhoods would be responsible for handling these functions.

Both the regional and community levels have special centers with a concentration of functions that require certain kinds of skills, background, capabilities and organization necessary to meet public or private needs. People with compatible

CHAPTER 2 - FUNCTIONAL DESIGN OF THE REGION

functional capabilities and purposes are likely to work competently together in their unique areas of specialization. Separating their closely related functions and arbitrarily assigning them to unrelated or pseudo-organizations and activities would be counter-productive. This may happen when people interested in gaining "political" control or status dictate assignments.

The wide range of activities at the regional level becomes chaotic and ineffectual without the implementation of infrastructure development and networking. In their absence, functional duplication, misapplication and a squandering of skills proliferates. This waste of human, natural and fiscal resources only aggravates the problem. Chaos produces enough unnecessary complexity, obstructing the possibility of management control and accomplishment. This is what we see in larger cities today.

It is apparent that closely-related functions must be grouped or linked in order to organize the infrastructures of a region. This may be accomplished by grouping infrastructure networks that have the most frequent common interfaces, allowing better communication and closer interfaces to exist. The infrastructures remain semi-autonomous, but they are able to share resources and costs whenever there is common cause.

Closely-related groups of infrastructure networks on a regional level are basic to the overall organization. Some networks, like communications, influence all others at every level. Others are highly dedicated. But infrastructure networks are not the only ones that exist. There are thousands of networks continuously being formed, formally and informally, to provide human exchange and cooperation. These independent and private networks exist at all levels. They are directly or indirectly affected by the directions governmental infrastructures take and the limits that are imposed. Regional infrastructure linkage-type networks are particularly important in predicting how all other networks will ultimately perform.

Part III - Regional Design & Scenarios

CHAPTER 3 - REGIONAL INFRASTRUCTURES & NETWORKS

The term infrastructure, as it is used here, means functional groups or agencies with facilities, systems and operational capabilities that must exist within a society to effectively serve regional public and private interests. More than one infrastructure provide both the organizational arrangements and the glue that hold a society together. They enable, further and support the collective purposes of its inhabitants. They do this by enhancing and conserving resources and by promoting interactions.

Infrastructures and their networks are more extensive and complex for highly evolved societies. Those for simpler societies with limited technological development are far less complicated. If these societies are going to progress more rapidly, it will be essential to design and define new infrastructures for them .

The big picture must show the relationships of all primary functions. This is a networking process which links areas of common functional emphasis. If systems are not explicitly linked, they will work poorly or not at all. This has long been an axiom of science, technology and management.

The process of relating things is also one of discovery. An association has been used many times in different fields to reveal, understand and define related problems more completely. Once this has been done, problem definition can be expanded, isolated and addressed.

Because of their complexity, major functions are usually described with diagrams and notations for all levels of networking. The expansion of functional definition may become so extensive as to require computer assistance. In view of this, it's apparent that a preliminary effort must be made to describe the infrastructures of a regional concept.

Functional groups are networked to exchange information and tangible items in the pursuit of common purposes or goals. Networking takes place both vertically and horizontally in a direct manner and continues through all program phases, including operations. This contrasts with the activities of hierarchal bureaucratic institutions which tend to network internally as a pyramid in vertical manner while having limited networking with other institutions and the public.

At the regional level, there are subordinate functions, derived and expanded from the major ones, to identify kinds of work and extent of responsibility. People assigned to these functional levels must be sufficiently competent to perform their duties effectively. Sub-level responsibilities for communities and neighborhoods are more specialized and explicit than those of higher levels. People assigned to or assuming these sub-levels carry out most of the networking. The network concept and functions extend to all centers. The functions of a center are managed by leaders with special technical skills and competence; the functions of a community are managed by leaders who can meet the needs of the community. Neighborhood functions have to be implemented by competent people willing to assume local responsibilities, expending time and energy to carry out the common affairs

CHAPTER 3 - REGIONAL INFRASTRUCTURES & NETWORKS

of neighbors. Sharing multi-level responsibilities is particularly important during emergencies.

Neos, Pragma and Veritor become deeply engrossed in the subject of infrastructures and their networks. Neos has been preparing general concepts for each. Pragma is somewhat skeptical about shared control of networks at various levels and especially on a non-regional scale,"We can only speculate on whether competency and a sense of responsibility will exist at any level. There is no absolute guarantee. In all likelihood, participation and competency will be encouraged in a regional setting, but the pursuit of private agendas and gain will probably continue."

Neos returns to the subject. "What should comprise regional infrastructures and networks, and how should their functions be grouped? We are talking about experimental re-organization to improve functional compatibility and effectiveness. Once we combine functions, how must they interface within each regional group and with communities, neighborhoods and centers? The creation of new organizations has always been experimental."

Pragma answers, "Many infrastructure networks are already linked, like power networks, water systems, waste disposal systems, and re-cycling systems. Other related infrastructure networks could be linked with these. It's important to note that communication system networks and sub-networks, which may be already highly developed technologically and functionally, will be difficult to integrate with other kinds of infrastructures that are less developed or neglected.

"Transportation system networks and sub-networks often consist of a mixture of over-developed and under-developed systems. Under regionalization, they should undergo a remarkable metamorphosis as they are made more compatible."

Veritor agrees, "Let's determine what each infrastructure emphasizes. In doing this, we need to demonstrate how each is meant to enhance quality of life."

Neos adds, "I can see that every cluster of primary functions will have sub-functions that are performed throughout the region. Some special sub-functions would be performed in facilities located in centers, communities or open areas of the region where they are more effective. Local facilities for emergency services would obviously have to be strategically placed so as to be convenient for all. We must realize that many local services like trash pick-up and water delivery are now necessities in developed societies."

Veritor suggests, "Let's now show an overview of regional infrastructure functional groupings. As we have mentioned, extent of development will depend on the responsiveness and existing capabilities of host countries."

Neos concludes,"When we finish examining these basic regional infrastructure clusters, we will then need to examine each of them to describe their various levels of networking. Regional Network-Group A , an infrastructure concerned with regional administration and management, will be our first exploration."

Overview - Building the Infrastructures

Grouping of regional networks is essential. It allows closely related functions to interface and not be isolated, duplicated or omitted. Such groupings are further identified by whether people, themselves, are the prime object for service and treatment or whether the environmental and operational conditions are the prime object or a combination of both.

Regional Groups

A — Administrative:
- Administrative Management Network
- Budgeting Allocation Network
- Extra-Region, Coordination Network
- Public Finance & Taxation Network
- Inter-Region. Coordination Network
- Operational Planning Network

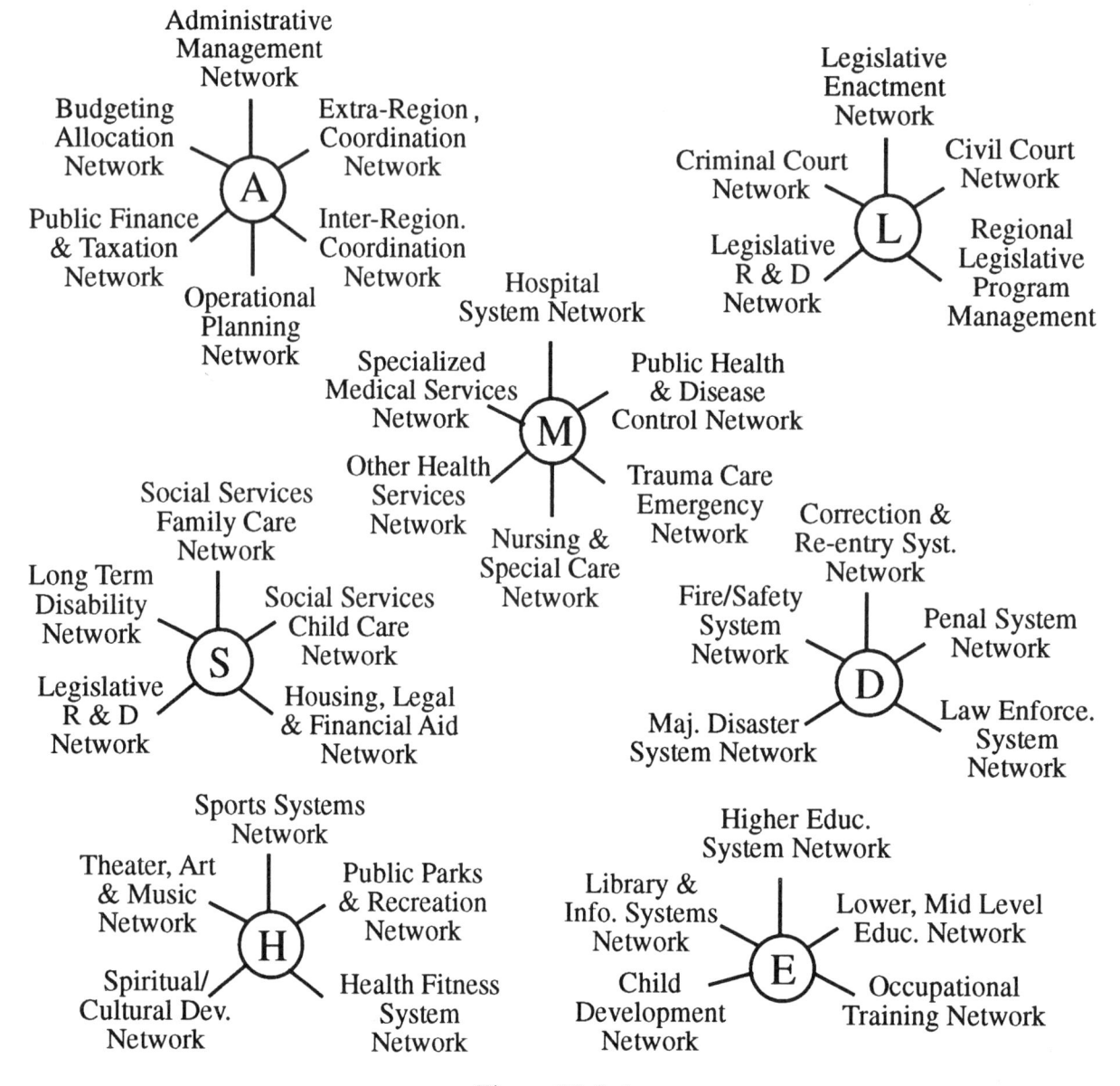

L — Legislative:
- Legislative Enactment Network
- Criminal Court Network
- Civil Court Network
- Legislative R & D Network
- Regional Legislative Program Management

M — Medical:
- Hospital System Network
- Specialized Medical Services Network
- Public Health & Disease Control Network
- Other Health Services Network
- Trauma Care Emergency Network
- Nursing & Special Care Network

S — Social Services:
- Social Services Family Care Network
- Long Term Disability Network
- Social Services Child Care Network
- Legislative R & D Network
- Housing, Legal & Financial Aid Network

D — Defense/Safety:
- Correction & Re-entry Syst. Network
- Fire/Safety System Network
- Penal System Network
- Maj. Disaster System Network
- Law Enforce. System Network

H — Health/Recreation:
- Sports Systems Network
- Theater, Art & Music Network
- Public Parks & Recreation Network
- Spiritual/Cultural Dev. Network
- Health Fitness System Network

E — Education:
- Higher Educ. System Network
- Library & Info. Systems Network
- Lower, Mid Level Educ. Network
- Child Development Network
- Occupational Training Network

Figure III-3-A

CHAPTER 3 - REGIONAL INFRASTRUCTURES & NETWORKS

Overview - Building the Infrastructures (Continued)

Grouping of regional networks does not include myriad others that are non-governmental or private. Groups A and L relate to the groups below but are not repeated here for clarity.

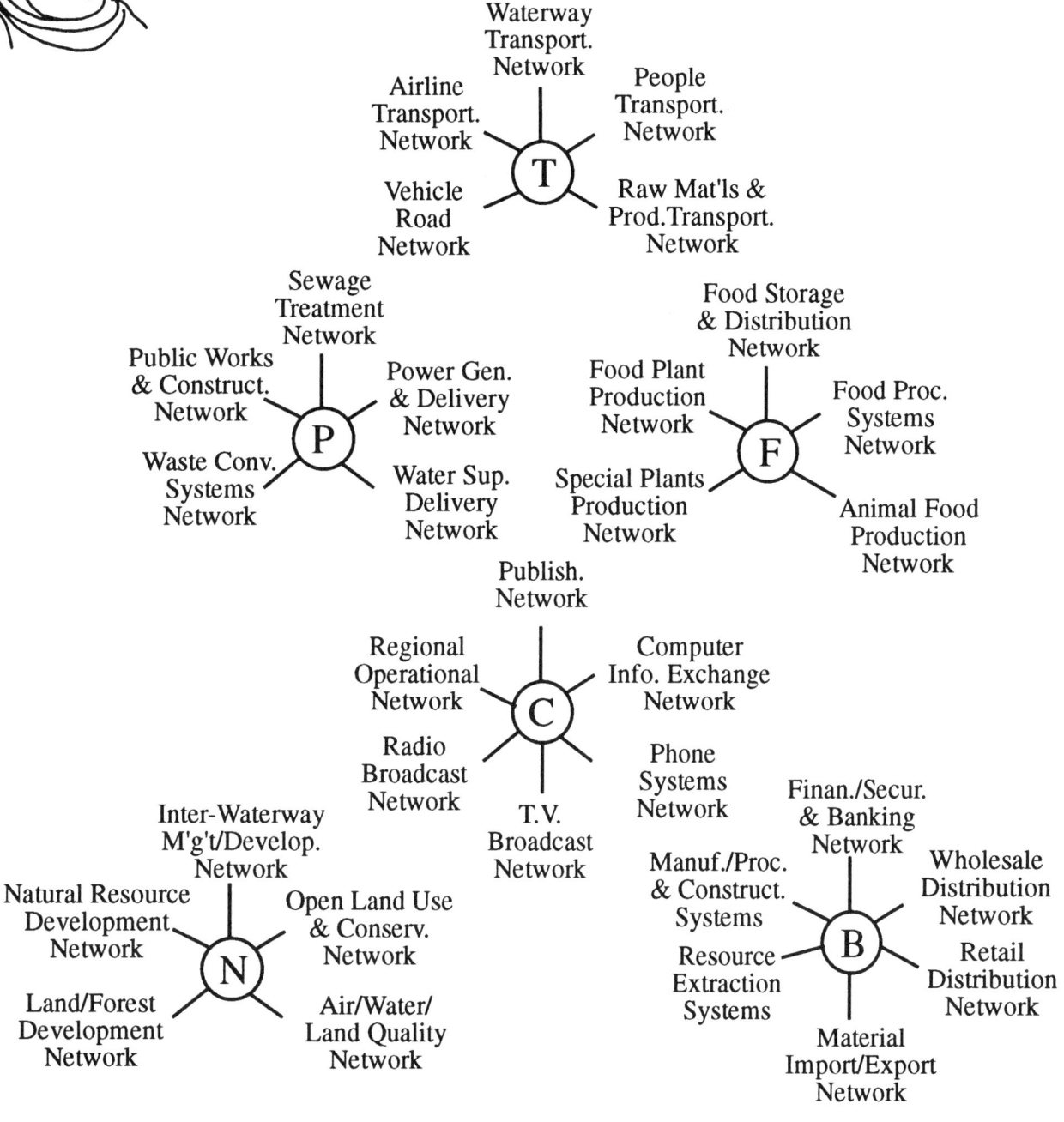

T (Transport):
- Waterway Transport. Network
- Airline Transport. Network
- People Transport. Network
- Vehicle Road Network
- Raw Mat'ls & Prod. Transport. Network

P (Public/Power):
- Sewage Treatment Network
- Public Works & Construct. Network
- Power Gen. & Delivery Network
- Waste Conv. Systems Network
- Water Sup. Delivery Network

F (Food):
- Food Storage & Distribution Network
- Food Plant Production Network
- Food Proc. Systems Network
- Special Plants Production Network
- Animal Food Production Network

C (Communication):
- Publish. Network
- Regional Operational Network
- Computer Info. Exchange Network
- Radio Broadcast Network
- T.V. Broadcast Network
- Phone Systems Network

N (Natural):
- Inter-Waterway M'g't/Develop. Network
- Natural Resource Development Network
- Open Land Use & Conserv. Network
- Land/Forest Development Network
- Air/Water/Land Quality Network

B (Business):
- Finan./Secur. & Banking Network
- Wholesale Distribution Network
- Manuf./Proc. & Construct. Systems
- Retail Distribution Network
- Resource Extraction Systems
- Material Import/Export Network

Figure III-3-A (Continued)

113

Regional Network - Group A

The regional network functions of Group A involve administration, management, budgeting, public financing, taxation, regional planning, and intra and inter-regional coordination. Administrative functions are required to monitor, control and direct regional activities at all levels. This is made possible by budget networking. The administrators follow policy decisions to determine how developmental and operational programs and projects are to be funded, implemented and monitored. Particular attention is paid to the optimum utilization of human and natural resources.

Closely allied with such efforts are the preparation of yearly and multi-year budget projections. These are developed with the participation of other relevant infrastructure groups. It also includes participation by community and center administrations based on their anticipated needs and planned activities.

General planning information (prevailing demographic data, legalities, social, business and environmental conditions and trends) is necessary for establishing policy, budget projections and appropriate resource utilization.

Inter-regional coordination involves all governmental and quasi-governmental activities of the region. It brings together often disparate interests by establishing common agendas, clarifying issues and obtaining agreements and consensus among the communities, special centers, regional level entities and private interests.

Extra-regional coordination involves similar coordination functions with other regions, contiguous jurisdictions and higher levels of government where common interests (or conflicts) exist.

The regional concept recognizes administrative and management functions as fundamental. They must be performed with a goal of meeting the needs of as many people as possible. Therefore, functions such as comprehensive planning and development, monitoring of operational conditions, and early remedial action are essential.

Finally, during the implementation of the Group A infrastructure, the opportunity will exist for developing future leaders; helping them to think comprehensively, act with resolution and principle and cultivate a sense of humanity. This maturation process is urgently needed.

CHAPTER 3 - REGIONAL INFRASTRUCTURES & NETWORKS

Regional Network Group A & Center, Community and Neighborhood Levels

General Interfaces

SPECIAL CENTER (Regional or Community Levels)

Customers, Clients or General Public

- Policy Making System M'g't
- Budgeting & Acc't'g
- Regional Interf. Coord.
- Services, Transactions Main Activity
- SC
- Internal Operations Network
- Maint. & Support Serv.

REGIONAL LEVEL

- Admin. Management Network
- Budgeting Allocations Network
- Extra-Region Coord. Network
- Public Fin. & Taxation Network
- A
- Inter-Region Coord. Network
- Regional Planning Network

→ Other Government Counterparts

→ All Other Network Groupings

COMMUNITY LEVEL

- Admin. Network
- Budgeting Allocations Network
- Regional Interface Network
- CO
- Public Fin. & Taxation Assess.
- Commun. Interface Coordin.
- Planning, Zoning

NEIGHBORHOOD LEVEL

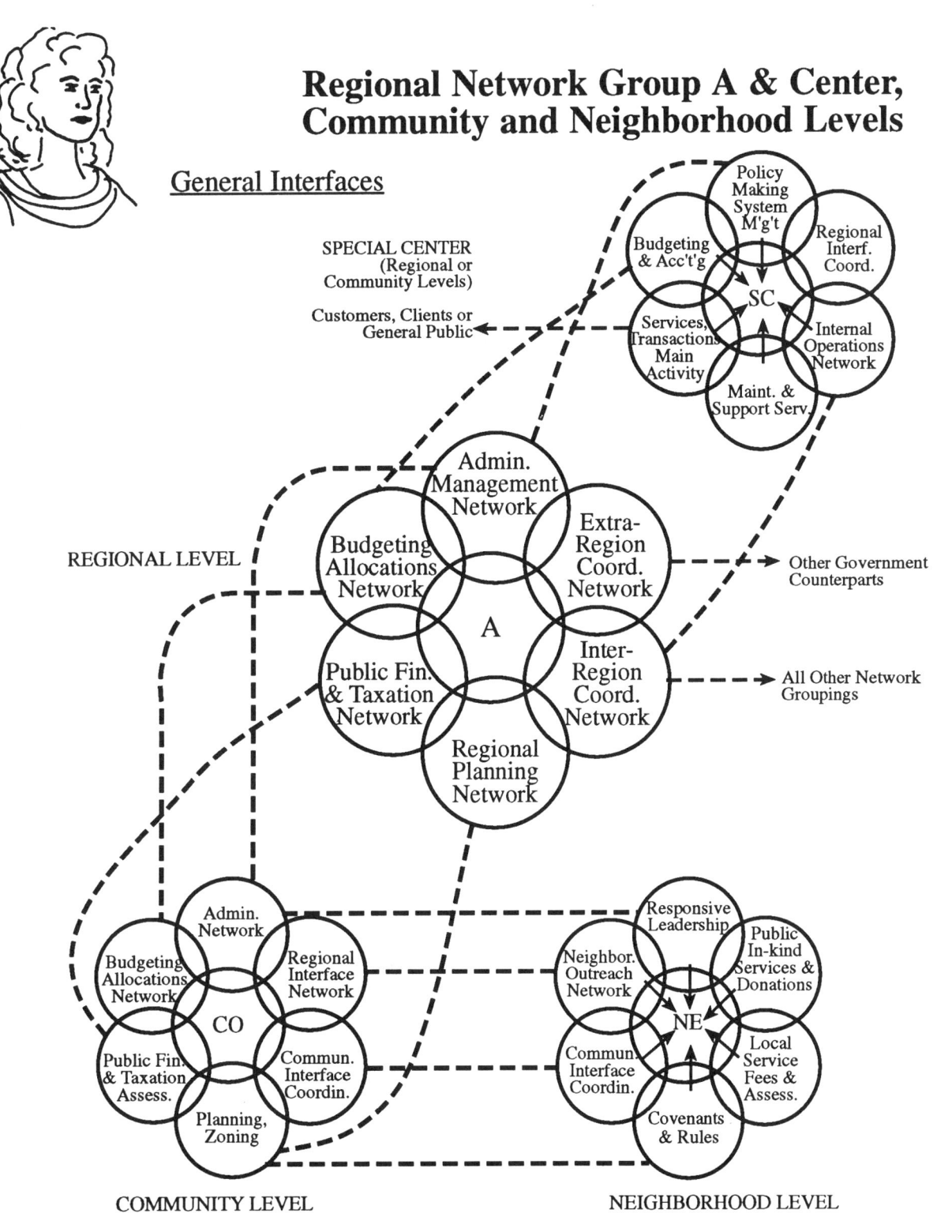

- Responsive Leadership
- Neighbor. Outreach Network
- Public In-kind Services & Donations
- NE
- Commun. Interface Coordin.
- Local Service Fees & Assess.
- Covenants & Rules

Figure III-3-B

115

Neos introduces the second infrastructure group, Regional Network-Group L, legislative and judicial, which directly affects people and the environment and operations of the region. " Every society has to have rules that govern behavior, limit excesses, establish priorities and define and resolve conflicts. The more complex a society and the more compact its population, the more rules are necessary. Obviously each person cannot make up self-serving rules; there would be chaos and law of the gun. Self-imposed rules and restraints, household rules, neighborhood covenants, regulations and restrictions, school codes, religious doctrines, game rules, criminal codes, traffic regulations, commercial and workplace laws are but a fraction of the consciously imposed societal laws that guide human behavior. Natural laws superimpose the greatest constraints and restrictions.

"Regions must exact well-conceived, unambiguous laws. Revisions to improve and simplify them would be a continuous process in an emerging society. Legislative research and development functions would provide clarifications and modifications, especially with the participation and support of other regional infrastructure networks. The making of laws has been purposely linked with the deliberation functions of the court, encouraging timely changes to poorly written laws that cannot be properly enforced. Law-making and judicial functions for the region would be performed by elected representatives at the regional and community levels. Courts would be upgraded to be more effective and timely, using new communication systems and up-to-date logistical control."

Pragma answers, "I agree regional research and development could markedly improve quality of legislation. Certainly, networking with the other infrastructures would always be helpful. What often happens is that law-making becomes so overly focused, fragmentary and arbitrary, it excludes consideration of relevant and underlying conditions. This may result in conflicting or contradictory laws, more problems for the courts and injustice for society."

Veritor notes, "That is very perceptive. The functions of other activities can and must contribute specialized information necessary to make laws effective. People's respect for laws is the ultimate test of such effectiveness. Poorly written, unjust and ill-conceived laws evoke disdain, distrust, manipulation and evasion. They become counter-productive and undermine and obstruct justice."

Neos suggests, "Perhaps the use of functional flow logic diagrams would be of help to legislative analysts and others who create and modify laws. This analytical tool provides paths of logic, discloses loopholes and considers all relevant conditions. It is a well-established technique often used in industry and computer sciences. It helps to pinpoint fragmentary thinking."

Veritor notes, "It seems to me the overburdening of criminal and civil courts in many industrial countries is the result of the systemic breakdown of society. Using

CHAPTER 3 - REGIONAL INFRASTRUCTURES & NETWORKS

new system analysis approaches, many conflicts could be defined, arbitrated and resolved early at the inter-personal neighborhood, and at special center levels, long before costly litigation becomes necessary. The idea is to recognize and address problems before they fester into severe conflicts or criminal activity."

Pragma completes this part of the discussion. "Legislation enacted at the regional level needs to be implemented by competent, socially and politically aware people so that a wide range of programs involving regional needs can be implemented. In order to be effective, these programs must have the strong participation of both the centers and the communities. Costs may be reduced because many functional capabilities to carry out detailed aspects of the programs would already exist within the centers and communities . Of course, if the programs involve major changes, cost-sharing might then be necessary."

Neos now refers to another presentation. "Here is a diagram of Group L infrastructure which generally expresses what we have been discussing."

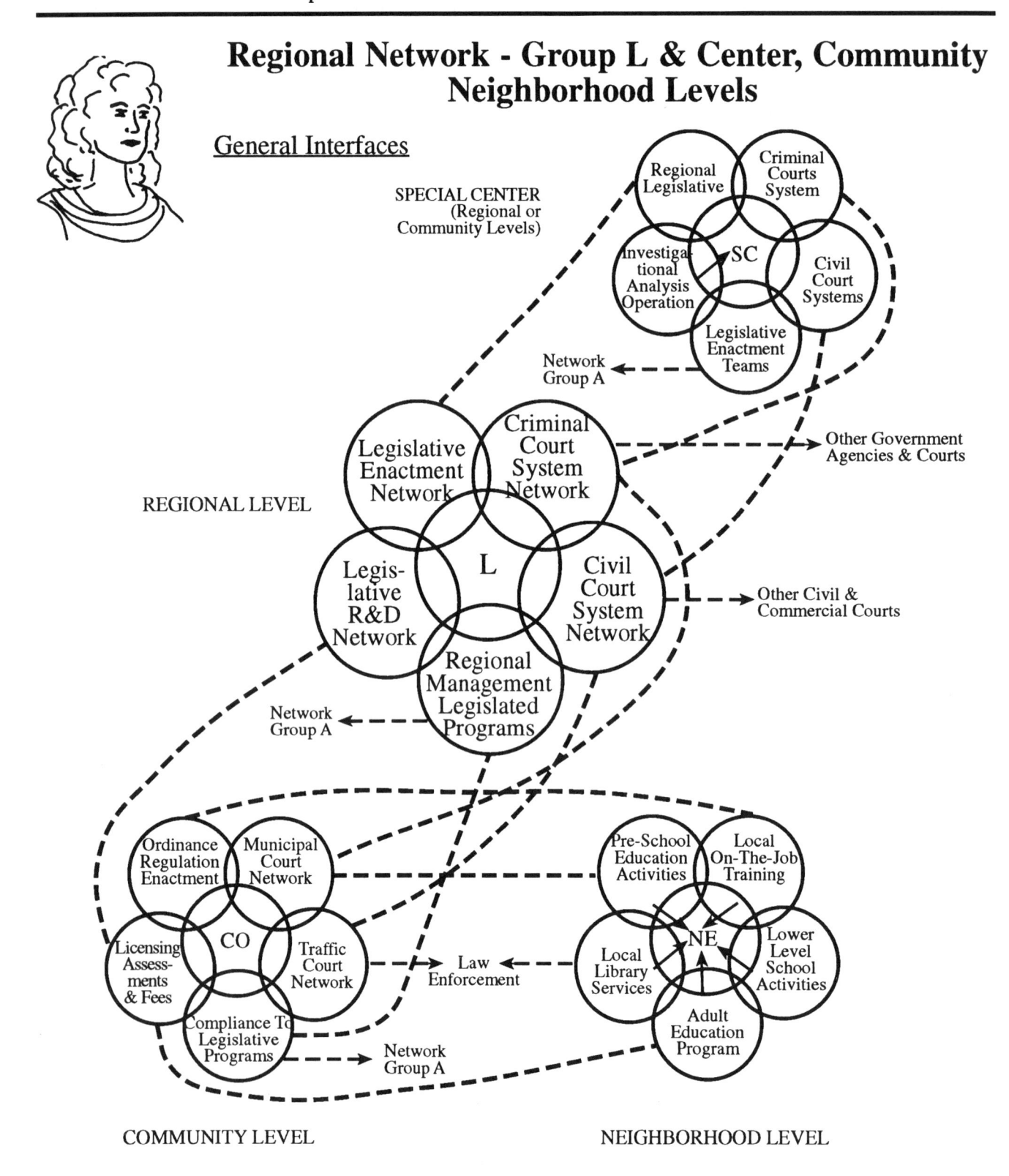

Explorers of the Mind: In Search of a Better World

Regional Network - Group L & Center, Community Neighborhood Levels

General Interfaces

SPECIAL CENTER
(Regional or Community Levels)
- Regional Legislative
- Criminal Courts System
- Investigational Analysis Operation
- SC
- Civil Court Systems
- Legislative Enactment Teams

→ Network Group A

REGIONAL LEVEL
- Legislative Enactment Network
- Criminal Court System Network
- Legislative R&D Network
- L
- Civil Court System Network
- Regional Management Legislated Programs

→ Other Government Agencies & Courts
→ Other Civil & Commercial Courts
→ Network Group A

COMMUNITY LEVEL
- Ordinance Regulation Enactment
- Municipal Court Network
- Licensing Assessments & Fees
- CO
- Traffic Court Network
- Compliance To Legislative Programs

→ Law Enforcement
→ Network Group A

NEIGHBORHOOD LEVEL
- Pre-School Education Activities
- Local On-The-Job Training
- Local Library Services
- NE
- Lower Level School Activities
- Adult Education Program

Figure III-3-C

CHAPTER 3 - REGIONAL INFRASTRUCTURES & NETWORKS

Neos has been examining another infrastructure functional network grouping that provides direct services to people in the region. "Many of the functions of Network Group L relate to those of Network Group D which has to do with public safety. We deliberately include police, fire and other emergency functions in this group because a change in focus is indicated.

"Officers of the law must become more closely involved at the neighborhood level, with crime prevention and victim assistance increasingly emphasized. We have already broached the subject of anti-social behavior. When people become so hostile, violent and aggressive that they seriously harm themselves and others, then society must apprehend and constrain them or redirect their attention and energies. Both offending individuals and the attitudes of society must be held responsible. At least both bear the consequences. More effective treatment must be devised for those exhibiting anti-social behavior."

Veritor agrees, "Much crime can be eliminated or prevented through regionalization. We must create an environment that minimizes harmful incidences and friction and redirects or rehabilitates lives. Of course, it's difficult to show compassion for those who have victimized others. But, as it so often happens in decaying societies, victims and abusers begin to consider anti-social behavior as the norm."

Neos answers, "You're right. In a regional setting there would be less congestion, less anonymity, greater neighborhood cohesion and stability and, therefore, a greater chance to observe and respond to negative activities and aberrant behavior. Neighborhood designs must ensure privacy within homes yet encourage interaction and a sense of belonging. Police communication and networking techniques have become fairly well advanced in some big cities. Such networking would be utilized at all levels. Regional peace-keeping functions would have well-defined networks that dovetail with other private and public agencies and extend to communities and their neighborhoods. But it's at the neighborhood level that significant benefits would be realized."

Veritor notes, "Police have a dual role in the regional concept. One is to enforce the law and keep the peace and the other is to aid those in distress or those who are about to become victims. Peace officers have other functions, but these are the most significant ones. By establishing distinct and accessible neighborhoods, the police will be able to serve more effectively in preventing crime, in apprehending criminals, providing assistance to victims and reducing neighborhood tensions. In order to accomplish this, general proliferation of weapons in a neighborhood must be curtailed or controlled. When weapons are too easily obtained, there is likelihood for their greater use. Peace officers should not have to face potential violence alone. Regionalization with its networking emphasis must help remove this serious risk to officers and to the public."

Pragma responds, "Prevention of criminal activity would greatly reduce overload on the penal system. Building bigger jails is necessary when neighborhoods and families disintegrate, job opportunities diminish and crime increases. Disrespect for law, the environment, property, other humans and self are perpetuated unless regional networking and neighborhood participation in crime prevention are initiated."

Neos offers some further insight. "Once individuals are convicted and sent to prison, they are bound to be influenced by others in their new environment. They may already have become hardened criminals from juvenile experiences but, once incarcerated, it is almost certain they will remain or become hardened criminals. It also seems to me that frequent inter-regional rotation of incorrigible prisoners would help discourage prison gang formation."

Veritor notes, "This is a good idea. Then the process of correction or rehabilitation must become more effective. Inmates should receive remedial education and undergo medical and mental health treatment. Prisoners, depending on how much risk is involved, could be given work furloughs to support dependents. I think that, as a condition of release, a long period of public service should be made mandatory so as to modify the individual's behavior and encourage community responsibility."

Pragma responds, "This is certainly necessary, but criminals should not be pampered. When prisoners are paroled, they must not return to their old neighborhoods where the same negative conditions and influences may prevail. Halfway houses and employment to pay for their keep would be needed. These approaches are not new, but they can be greatly improved in a regional setting to make them more effective."

Veritor says, "I'd like to bring up public safety and vulnerability which are different aspects of this network group. We have previously discussed the probability of both man-made and natural catastrophes occurring. A regional multi-level preparatory system that begins at the local level must provide easy escape routes when needed. At the neighborhood level, organizational plans and procedures would be established to fit the local environment. Almost all public services, including the police and fire departments would be involved, and neighborhood preparedness would be linked to and supported by the network at all levels of the region."

CHAPTER 3 - REGIONAL INFRASTRUCTURES & NETWORKS

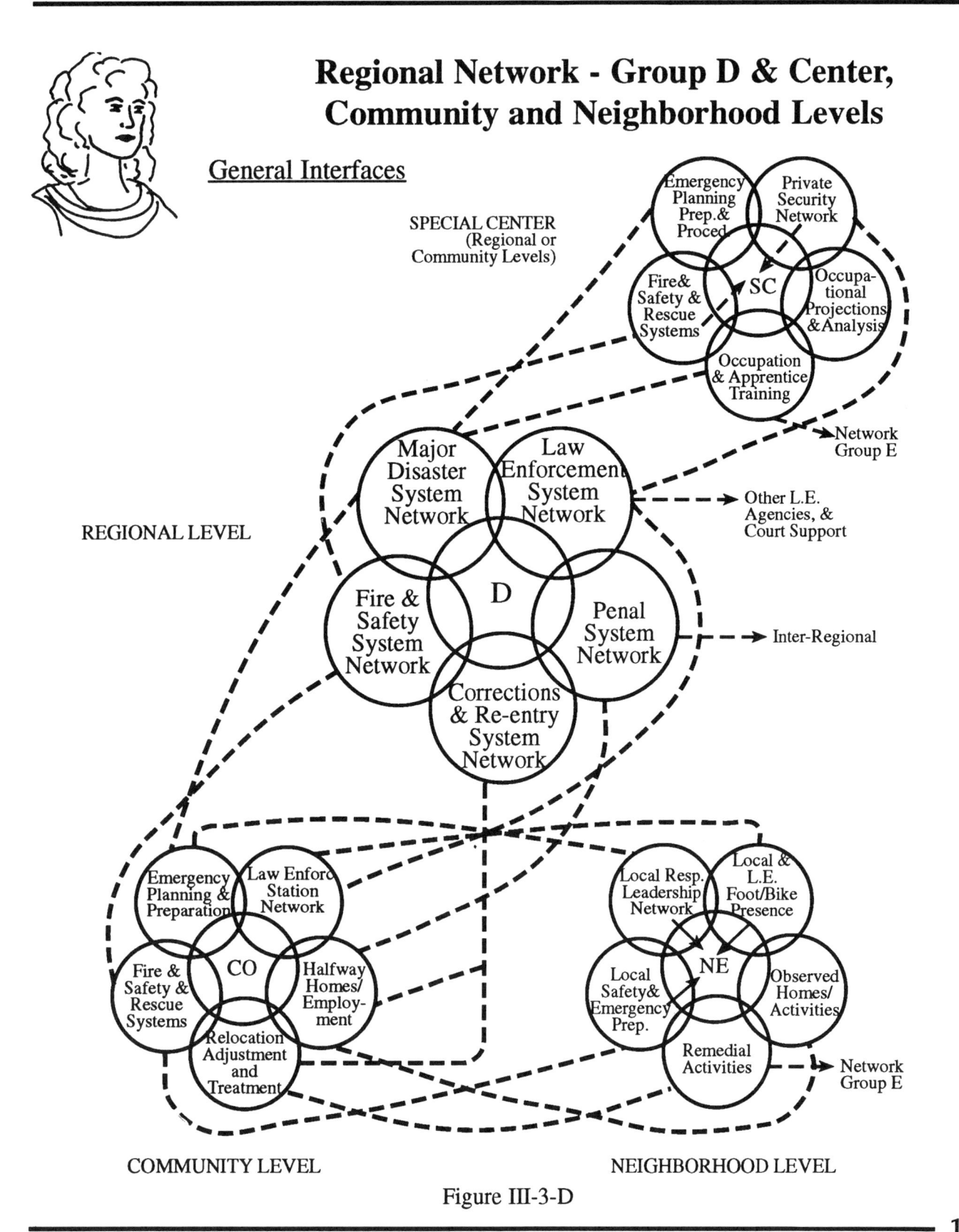

Regional Network - Group D & Center, Community and Neighborhood Levels

General Interfaces

SPECIAL CENTER (Regional or Community Levels)

- Emergency Planning Prep. & Proced.
- Private Security Network
- Fire & Safety & Rescue Systems
- SC
- Occupational Projections & Analysis
- Occupation & Apprentice Training

→ Network Group E

REGIONAL LEVEL

- Major Disaster System Network
- Law Enforcement System Network
- Fire & Safety System Network
- D
- Penal System Network
- Corrections & Re-entry System Network

→ Other L.E. Agencies, & Court Support

→ Inter-Regional

COMMUNITY LEVEL

- Emergency Planning & Preparation
- Law Enforc. Station Network
- Fire & Safety & Rescue Systems
- CO
- Halfway Homes/Employment
- Relocation Adjustment and Treatment

NEIGHBORHOOD LEVEL

- Local Resp. Leadership Network
- Local & L.E. Foot/Bike Presence
- Local Safety & Emergency Prep.
- NE
- Observed Homes/Activities
- Remedial Activities

→ Network Group E

Figure III-3-D

"Local leaders must assume new responsibilities. If they do not, then others at higher community or regional levels will need to take over. Responsibilities passed on to others carry a price. Either taxes increase or people pay for services privately. Freedom has its price."

Pragma notes, "Local fire departments and rescue teams provide professional assistance and services for local emergencies. But for major catastrophes, the network functions at all regional levels must be mobilized. This takes comprehensive preparation and well-designed procedures to effectively cope with catastrophic events, provide evacuation and allow outside agencies to assist and accelerate recovery. "

Neos realizes that emergency medical facilities must be made available as well as rescue teams for triage and treatment of seriously injured or sick people. "I think that this is the appropriate time to discuss other aspects of the regional network group designated as 'M'. Regionalization is an ideal concept for defining the various kinds and levels of functions required for comprehensive health care. Group M functions are necessary for preventing illness, improving human health, caring for the sick and improving quality of life for those in pain."

Pragma notes, "The regional concept has the appropriate size of population and scale of activities to afford advanced, high technology equipment, improved medical procedures and practices and all kinds of specialized and general health care."

Veritor adds, "You're right. The region offers networking of functions at all levels of care. It represents a rational way to provide for everyone and to accommodate both public and private types of care. When carefully designed and developed, a new regional infrastructure for health care would be more effective, substantially reduce medical and hospital costs and prevent rapid, uncontrollable inflation in health costs by increasing efficiency and reducing waste."

Neos states, "For one thing, there have to be changes in attitude about the way services are rendered. Institutions and their operations exist to serve humanity and not the other way around. This order is reversed when excess profit-making dictates the level and quality of services. When alleviation of human pain and suffering and remedial services are thought of as a business and a means of making profit, then an inherent conflict exists. How can such seemingly opposite goals be reconciled? Let me present what regionalization proposes."

CHAPTER 3 - REGIONAL INFRASTRUCTURES & NETWORKS

Towards Universal Health Care

Regionalization takes an enlightened view of universal health care through the design, development and operation of network systems that function primarily to improve the human condition. This means preventing the spread of contagion and disease, alleviating pain and suffering, restoring people to healthy, productive lives, correcting or compensating for physical and mental defects, assisting the sick and disabled, promoting mental and physical health through improved habits and practices, and assisting in the provision of lifetime health care services. It does not emphasize profits.

To pursue the above stated goal requires investments in time, effort and resources. It takes research, special training, dedication, innovation and effective allocation of resources.

In order to appropriately and wisely apply and utilize such investments, an infrastructure design must include the creation of environments that are conducive to providing health care for all.

If a society ignores the need for a universal health care infrastructure:
- *Inflation of medical costs will continue to increase.*
- *Fewer people will be able to afford or have access to quality health care.*
- *Insurance rates will continue to climb as costs of medical care escalate.*
- *The costs of processing paper and performing record-keeping functions will often exceed the cost of direct health treatment.*
- *Room costs in hospitals will often exceed the cost of renting a five star hotel room.*
- *Liability and malpractice insurance and lawsuits will continue to increase and add to non-productive health care costs.*
- *Advanced medical technology, equipment and procedures will only be available to a limited number of people. Buying and using such advances will become too costly.*
- *Existing health care systems will not reach out to the many who need services. This will result in greater losses of productive work time, increased severity of medical and psychological illnesses through neglect and greater vulnerability to contagious diseases.*
- *There will be continued neglect of pre-natal and infant care in many cases.*
- *Elderly and other fixed income people may face impoverishment from overwhelming medical costs .*

The organization or re-organization of medical functional networks is an urgent need throughout the world. Regional concepts provide medical infrastructures that offer greater hope of enhancing quality of life and would set an example of what could be accomplished.

Pragma contributes, "There are workable health care systems in most industrial countries. We have to consider making quality health care and advanced medical technology available to all. This is a goal. It may be unrealistic, but we must try. In Third World countries millions of people receive little or no health care and are often subjected to severe diseases, malnutrition and poor sanitary conditions. Of course, the extremely high birth rates in such areas are a major inhibiting factor in providing adequate health care."

Neos answers, "We ought to generally outline how this regional infrastructure is to be established. Obviously, the physical activities and facilities of the regional infrastructure networks must be placed where they will do the most good. Some infrastructure functions must be centrally located while others must be dispersed or mobile so as to be readily accessible to users."

Pragma adds, "Regional Network Group M, as with all others, is meant to clarify and integrate operational and support functions so that less administration will be necessary. The networking approach is used to routinely interface related operational functions. Planning, supporting and overseeing operations, of course, are basic administrative functions that must be applied without duplication for all activities."

Neos notes, "Regionalization, with its larger planning functions, is essential to the development of Network Group M's efforts to serve the public. We have to recognize that this infrastructure is immensely complex. Because of this, it is even more important to have smoothly interacting functions. There must be major functions at special centers that support the region's communities and neighborhoods by providing advanced medical treatment, research and quality control. The emphasis is to provide public and some private means for complete public health needs down to the neighborhood level."

Veritor responds, "Yes, that's true. It is also important for infrastructure group M to encourage in-home nursing and medical services for shut-in patients. Local clinics for emergencies and minor complaints would also be established on the neighborhood level. Physicians who work for the health care network, of course, would also be given time for private consultations during off hours."

CHAPTER 3 - REGIONAL INFRASTRUCTURES & NETWORKS

Regional Network - Group M & Center, Community and Neighborhood Level

General Interfaces

SPECIAL CENTER
(Regional or Community Levels)

- Specialized Hospital Facility
- Specialized Medical Treatment
- Specialized Med. Educ. Services
- Special Facil. & Equip. Maint. Network
- Specialized Trauma Center
- Specialized Nursing Care
- SC

REGIONAL LEVEL

- Hospital System Network
- Public Health & Disease Control Net
- Specialized Medical Network
- Other Health Services Network
- Trauma Care Emergency Network
- Nursing & Special Care Network
- M

→ Universities & Others

COMMUNITY LEVEL

- General Hospital Care
- Prevent. Medicine Network
- Triage & Trauma Services
- Facility Maint./Sup. Network
- Non-Med. Health Services
- Mobile Spec. Diag. Services
- CO

NEIGHBORHOOD LEVEL

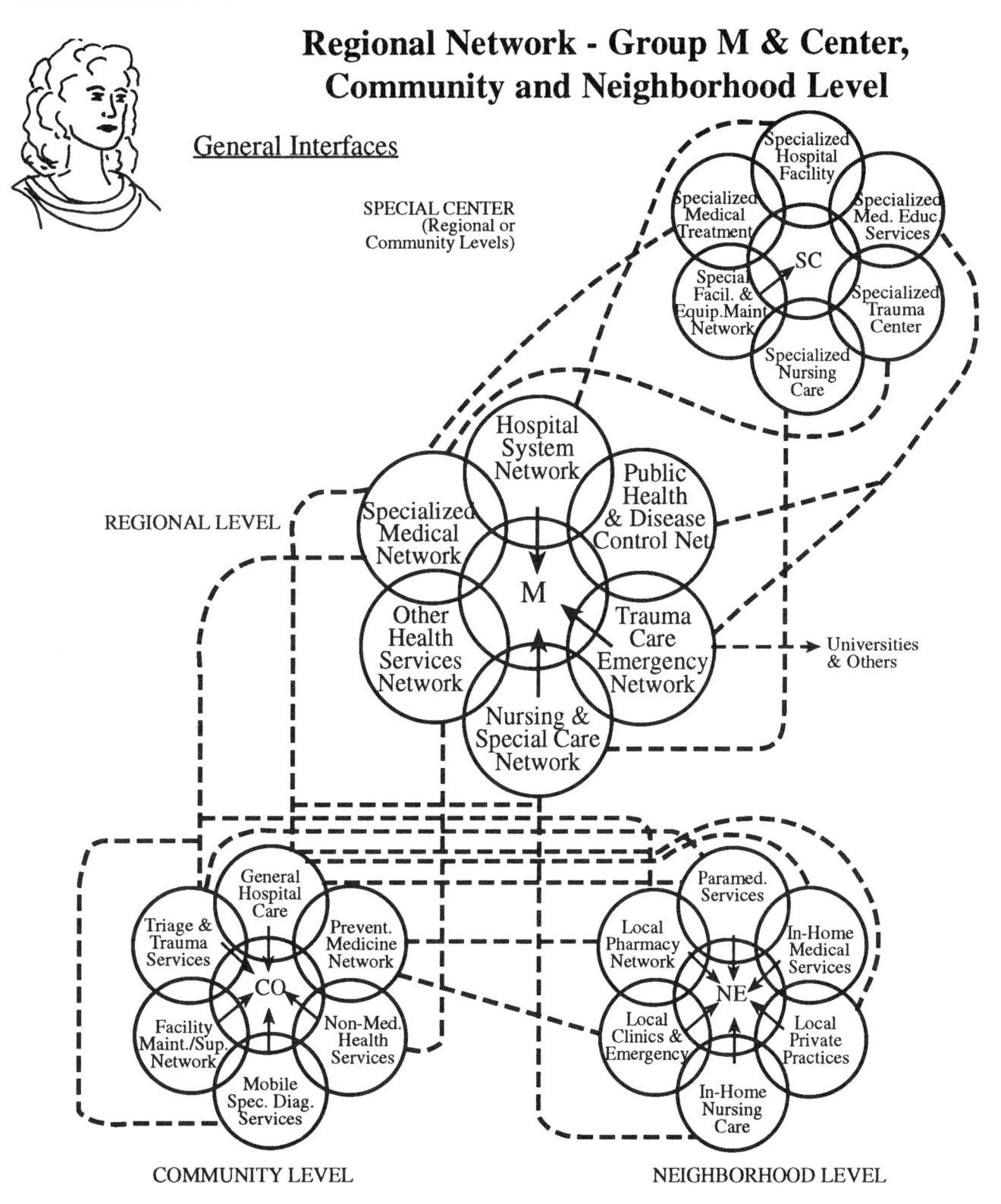

- Paramed. Services
- Local Pharmacy Network
- In-Home Medical Services
- Local Clinics & Emergency
- Local Private Practices
- In-Home Nursing Care
- NE

Figure III-3-E

125

Neos comments. "Major capital expenditure for facilities and advanced, high-tech equipment ought to be made by the regional level government to benefit everyone in need. The public should take the responsibility for this investment in exchange for lower cost, high quality health care services. The people of each region are in the best position to do this for themselves. Cooperative efforts with other regions would also be of great benefit. Initial financial help from a higher governmental entity or private sector may be necessary to rapidly build facilities."

Pragma adds, "There are other areas in which costs can be reduced. For example, eliminating irrelevant details, billing and much of the paperwork that plague health care systems. For instance, many such systems, like those in the provinces of Canada, eliminate most of the detailed paperwork in their health plans. Patients pay for services rendered, not paper and profit. What is saved in paperwork, ostensibly needed for private insurance claims, statistics and cost effectiveness analysis, is put into direct health care and treatment. The public subscribes to a plan which is a non-profit, publicly owned insurance. So in the regional concept, people would be collectively insuring themselves and reducing their costs for rendered services. Private insurance would still be available but no longer necessary to most."

Veritor agrees. "There are many other areas of major cost saving or cost-sharing. New pharmaceuticals are expensive because of the risk and time involved in research, testing and gaining government approval and in promotional costs. These costs plus profits boost selling prices. Public taxes would provide development cost-sharing or grants to drug companies to reduce risk, share profits and lower prescription costs. This method of underwriting would also be used to increase competition to further reduce costs to the consumer."

Neos notes, "We have already mentioned the high cost of hospitalization where room use cost is likely to remain high, especially when occupancy rate is too low. Overbuilding of fixed rather than variable capacity hospitals leads to this. Under-building for any capacity is the usual case worldwide, however. The tendency of the regional infrastructure design would be to emphasize variable capacity hospitals and the transfer of patients to their own homes as soon as they are able to move safely. Patients would be supplied with monitoring equipment and hookups to be used during convalescence. Periodically or on request, house calls would be made by network doctors and nurses or by contracted local neighborhood physicians. Neighbors could be hired, if necessary, to look after or bring food to people living alone and needing help."

Pragma says, "We have only covered a small fraction of what Network Group M is about, but I think we have some idea of how powerful the integrating process of regionalization can be."

Veritor adds, " We gain insight by showing the different levels of infrastructure functional design. Poverty-stricken countries would especially benefit from such an approach. Their infrastructure designs may be far from ideal, but they would at least be developing in a positive direction."

After a pause, Neos begins. "Network Group S provides direct personal services to needy people as its primary purpose. Societies throughout the world contrast by either confronting or ignoring the problems of their people. In the latter case there are teeming millions who suffer intensely from a wide range of deprivations, passively accepting their lot in life. Social responsibility is deficient for much of the world's population. But anyone in any country can become a victim of circumstances and have a need for assistance. Who is immune?"

Pragma counters, "Well, aren't people responsible for their own welfare? In many cases, don't they bring misery on themselves and, therefore, have to pay the consequences? When people behave irresponsibly, must others pay?"

Veritor is disturbed by this. "Yes, it is true that many people cause or contribute to their own problems. It happens everywhere, and it is sad to witness. They act as if they don't care what the consequences of their actions will be. But it may be a case of ignorance or helplessness to change their circumstances. The issue before us is to learn how to cope with not only anti-social consequences, but how to create a society that functions more effectively in minimizing ignorance, indifference, hostility and cynicism. The regional concept is meant to advance civilized behavior and discourage barbarism."

Neos reflects and nods in agreement. "The issue is one of assuming responsibility. Of course, it begins with the individual, but how can those who are helpless like the young, the incapacitated, the aged and the disabled help themselves? Who is responsible for their care, and who is competent enough to meet their needs? It would be normal to expect that some members of a family would be competent enough to take care of others in the family. But families often flounder and struggle; their members find themselves in turmoil, inept, helpless or harmful to each other. Who is to blame? This is a non-question with no good answer. Responsibility for coping with disabilities and distress may ultimately belong to various levels of society?"

Social Responsibility

- *Who should be responsible for social services to the needy? There are many functionally competent organizations at all levels of society to serve the needy. In a civilized, just and humane society, the responsibility lies with all such entities in some way.*
- *Certain entities are better able to address different kinds of deprivation than others.*
- *Coping with social problems begins with the individual. If unable to cope, higher levels of competency are necessary.*

Social Problem	Individ.	Family	Neighbor	Community	Spec.Center	Region	Nation
1. Natural disaster	•	•		•	•	•	•
2. Economic downturn	•	•		•	•	•	•
3. Genetic affliction		•			•	•	•
4. Abandoned child/aged		•		•	•	•	
5. Chronic illness	•	•	•	•	•	•	
6. Terminal illness		•	•		•	•	
7. Accidental disability	•	•		•	•	•	
8. Criminal injury/abuse	•	•		•	•	•	•
9. Inflated living costs				•	•	•	•
10. Homeless	•	•	•	•	•	•	•
11. Hunger/malnutrition				•	•	•	•
12. Lack of jobs	•	•		•	•	•	•
13. Lack of educ.prep.	•	•		•	•	•	
14. Insufficient livelihood	•	•			•	•	•
15. Sociopaths	•	•	•	•	•	•	
16. Unjust laws re: poor				•	•	•	•
17. Victim of theft			•	•	•	•	
18. Family breakdown	•	•		•	•	•	
19. Severe mental illness		•		•	•	•	
20. Very low I.Q.		•		•	•	•	
21. Parental child neglect		•	•	•	•	•	
22. Unwed minor mothers	•	•	•	•	•	•	
23. Harmful peer influence	•	•		•	•	•	
24. Substance abuse	•	•	•	•	•	•	•
25. Spousal abuse	•	•	•	•	•	•	

If the above are not adequately addressed, who pays the consequences of criminal and social violence and the harm that follows? From which of the above social problems is anyone immune?

Table III-3-A

CHAPTER 3 - REGIONAL INFRASTRUCTURES & NETWORKS

Pragma ponders these rhetorical questions and notes, "Somehow, we have to confront social problems on the premise that people ought to correct or at least manage their own problems to the extent they are able to. I agree that many problems cannot be resolved, only compensated for."

Veritor responds, "We can see in Regional Network Group S (social services) a general approach for mobilizing resources and performing functions at different levels that could make a great difference in society. But social problems cannot just be handed over to some 'higher' all-knowing authority for total responsibility. It also takes increased responsibilities and direct action at the lower levels."

Neos continues the discussion, "Social services, as they now exist, attempt to identify problems, bring resources together and help individuals and families cope with adversity. It has taken many years of progress to be able to get to this point. But functions meant to alleviate problems seem very difficult to carry out. Compensation is more likely to be employed than correction. In other words, efforts expended for individuals and families tend to be reactive and after the fact, a characteristic we also see in law enforcement. Regionalization emphasizes prevention of many kinds of social problems by confronting conditions at all levels that contribute to social breakdown."

Pragma asks, "Well, where do we start? It is an enormous and never-ending effort. I think a shift in responsibilities may help, but who can guarantee that people will assume them?"

Veritor answers, "There is no guarantee, only a strategy and re-structuring that encourages competency. I notice that there are some natural subgroupings at the regional, special center, community and neighborhood levels where competency and resource availability would be likely to be found."

Neos observes, "We can readily identify senior care, care for minors and family care at the regional level. Various laws encourage this. Appropriate functions must serve each of these groups. For example, many elderly people become disoriented and need special attention. Geriatric medical services and both public and private facilities must be provided for such care.

"At the community level, facilities, programs and transportation are needed to assist senior citizens with personal problems, recreation, adequate diets and in getting about. Such functions are closely linked with the recreational, cultural and spiritual functions of Network Group H.

Explorers of the Mind: In Search of a Better World

Regional Network - Group S & Center, Community and Neighborhood Levels

General Interfaces

SPECIAL CENTER (Regional or Community Levels)

- Acute Disability Services
- Advanced Elderly Care
- Homeless Remedial Services
- SC
- Child Crisis Network
- Family Crisis Services

REGIONAL LEVEL

- Long Term Disability Network
- Soc. Serv. Senior Care Network
- Housing Legal & Financial Network
- S
- Social Services Minor Care Network → Juvenile Courts
- Social Services Family Care Network → Domestic Courts

COMMUNITY LEVEL

- Disa. Ther. & Adjustment Services
- Senior Transport & Assist Network
- Relo./Rehab. & Employ. Network
- CO
- Child Protec. & Foster Care → Courts, Mental Health
- Adult Protec. & Assist. Network → Courts, Mental Health
- → Potential Employers

NEIGHBORHOOD LEVEL

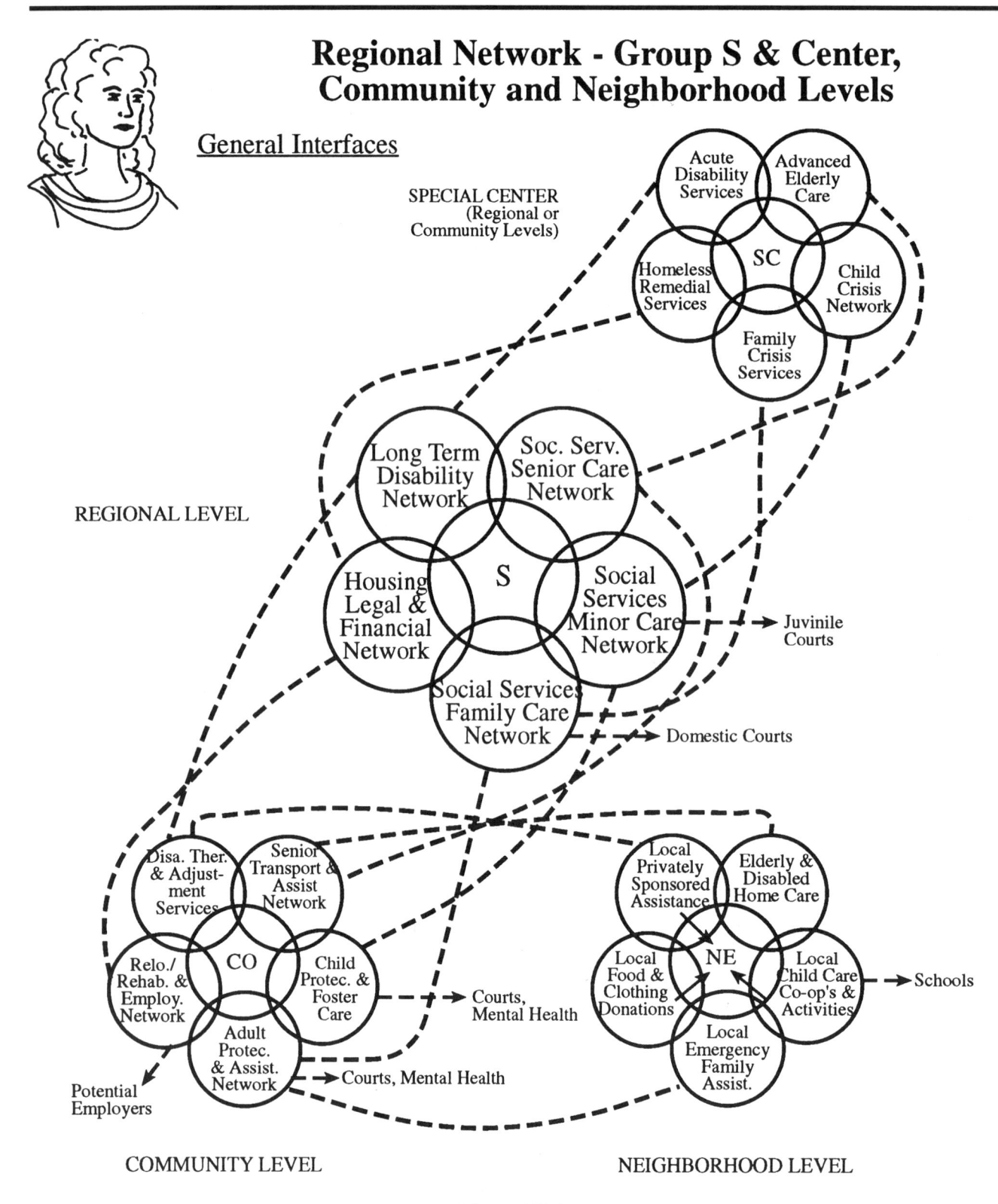

- Local Privately Sponsored Assistance
- Elderly & Disabled Home Care
- Local Food & Clothing Donations
- NE
- Local Child Care Co-op's & Activities → Schools
- Local Emergency Family Assist.

Figure III-3-F

"In-home help must be provided by both public and private means at the neighborhood level, especially for house-bound elderly. This function is primarily a family responsibility. If no help materializes, special services, the community and the neighborhood must help."

Pragma reacts, "But there are times when many seniors can be very useful in volunteer roles, for instance, in classrooms as teacher aids or tutors. A symbiotic relationship often develops between older people and small children. Older people still have much to give and receive."

Veritor adds, "The care of minors, of course, includes more than small children. Social service functions at the regional level must network with others in the communities. It is essential that children who are troubled be evaluated and receive early remedial help. Often a deficient home life or hazardous neighborhood environment puts children at risk. Without love and guidance they become children in crisis. Special centers and resource networking are required to help them."

Neos asserts, "Children of all ages must be supervised during all out-of-school activities, especially when parents are working. Special teachers or adult leaders are needed for supervising their play and for helping them to learn better work/study habits. This is an opportunity for children to develop their reasoning skills, physical abilities and creative expression so that they have a chance to grow and be productive."

Veritor notes, "There is another problem area. The family unit represents the last bastion of defense when a society is in trouble. When families break down in great numbers, the time is long overdue for action. Individuals become more vulnerable. It is often necessary to protect abused spouses and children. So the regional network reaches out into the communities and their neighborhoods when traumatic events occur that are beyond self help."

Pragma adds, "There are other key areas of networking required at the regional and other levels. A major contributing factor in stabilizing home life is sustained economic security. Lingering economic crises can heavily stress family relationships. But society, itself, pays a price when this situation is widespread and prolonged. Financial depletions and physical and mental disabilities create homeless people. Regional centers would provide major assistance in their relocation."

Neos agrees and adds, "This will call for legal and financial advice and aid, along with low cost housing, in order to rectify the problems. Both the region and the community must provide such functions. A society cannot just release the disabled into the streets where they are likely to be abused. Nor should they assign them to questionable non-care giving facilities. At the community level, both therapy and adjustment strategies for survival, recreation and learning would also be provided for those who are able to partially sustain themselves."

Pragma nods in agreement and says, "Of course, the private sector and many charitable organizations continue to augment public efforts by encouraging voluntary help. More religious and social organizations must be encouraged to become increasingly involved in helping those who are incapacitated and those who are downtrodden, but able to become self-sustaining once again."

Neos introduces the infrastructure design for Network Group H (recreational, cultural and spiritual), "This infrastructure emphasizes functions meant to enrich lives and to bring out the best in people. The idea is to divert human interest and energy from that which is harmful, destructive or wasteful and to channel such interest and energy into beneficial, productive, creative activities. Therefore, increased efforts would be expended on sports and other recreation, and cultural events like art, theater, festivals, music and the spiritual. Such activities stimulate greater awareness and develop mind, body and spirit for everyone in the region. When opportunities are missing in a society, quality of life is significantly reduced. It is important in a society that during non-working hours people become involved in their communities and neighborhoods. It is necessary for people to live life beyond basic survival, and it is essential for a society to create a healthy living environment in which all have a chance to grow and thrive."

Veritor smiles, "I like your comments, Neos. Group H brings together activities and a multitude of interests suitable for all ages. People need a chance to participate and express themselves, to emulate those who are talented and skilled, to develop that which is latent within themselves, and to stop long enough to appreciate and cherish our magnificent world of beauty, diversity and spirit. We, too, are a part of creation, and we ought to respect this in thought and deed. We need to encourage people to seek, enjoy and appreciate the new, the revitalized old and an enriched shared environment."

Neos continues, "Network Group H has many levels of special centers meant for different purposes. Some require support from the region as a whole and are of broad interest. Some hold special interest for specific segments of the population. Still others are of local interest and are mainly for communities and their neighborhood sub-cultures and activities. But large centers are also a part of the picture. Some activities would take place in public forums, places of worship, recreation areas, arenas, schools, parks, halls, malls, streets and assembly areas. The activities could be formal or informal and accommodate a wide range of interests."

CHAPTER 3 - REGIONAL INFRASTRUCTURES & NETWORKS

Regional Network - Group H & Center, Community and Neighborhood Levels

General Interfaces

SPECIAL CENTER (Regional or Community Levels)

SC
- Major Multi-Culture Presentations
- Public & Priv. Health Centers
- Development Recreation Activities
- Major Center Events-Art, Theater, Music
- Stadium Multi-Sport Activities

→ Inter-Regional

REGIONAL LEVEL

H
- Spiritual Culture/Devel. Network
- Health Development Network
- Public Parks & Recreation Network
- Theater, Art & Music Network
- Sport Activities Network

→ Inter-Regional, International

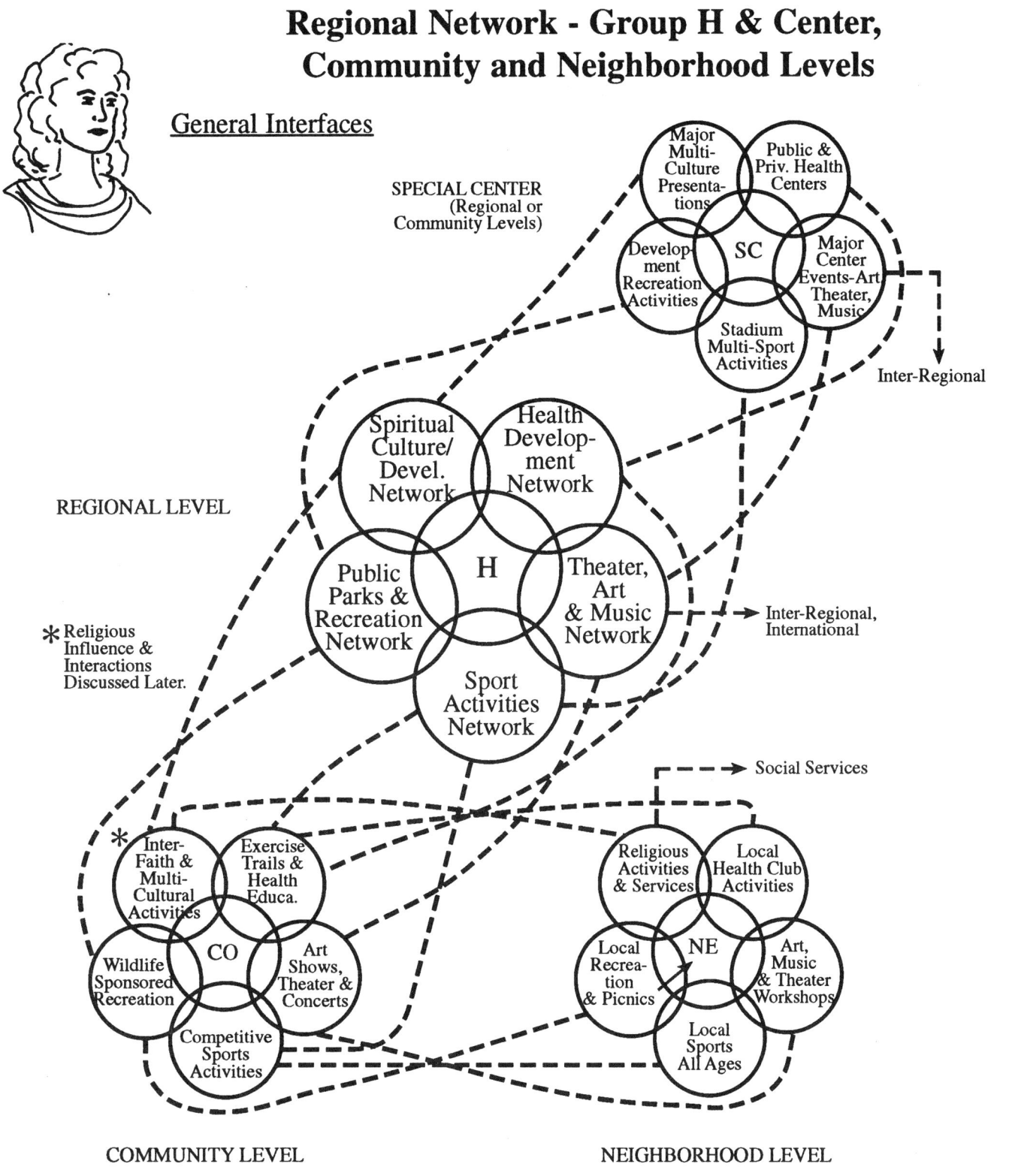

* Religious Influence & Interactions Discussed Later.

→ Social Services

CO
- * Inter-Faith & Multi-Cultural Activities
- Exercise Trails & Health Educa.
- Wildlife Sponsored Recreation
- Art Shows, Theater & Concerts
- Competitive Sports Activities

NE
- Religious Activities & Services
- Local Health Club Activities
- Local Recreation & Picnics
- Art, Music & Theater Workshops
- Local Sports All Ages

COMMUNITY LEVEL   NEIGHBORHOOD LEVEL

Figure III-3-G

133

Veritor continues, "The world of theater, art and music is all-embracing, and this strengthens the argument for its functional meaningfulness. Also, it is apparent that all religions and cultures of the world employ the arts in various forms and expressions that help shape human minds and behavior. History provides arguments for their continued functional utility in regionalization."

Pragma asserts, "Early regional development of all of the functional networks of Group H by public and private entities must be emphasized. Certainly, when youth become involved in such activities as theater, art, music, sports and recreation that promote healthy living, it will leave very little remaining time for them to become involved in anti-social and self-destructive activities. The idea is not to destroy the natural exuberance and spirit of people but to introduce alternative, positive activities as outlets. They would then feel that they are accepted in the main stream of society without loss of individuality. It seems to me that when people are continuously idle and accept no responsibilities, they become susceptible to anything that eases their boredom."

Veritor responds, "You are entirely right. How can people attain quality of life when they are subjected to harmful stimulations? Society loses not only potential human resources, but other resources during its attempts to cope with criminal activities as well as compensating for broken lives."

As planned, Neos, Pragma and Veritor do not attempt to expand on the functional interfaces and subjects of the Regional Network Group H. They only mean to indicate the kind of infrastructure groupings that are needed. This is also true for another Regional Network Group E which is concerned with education.

Neos notes, "This regional network grouping utilizes experience gained from existing educational systems. Its main goal is to encourage individuals to think independently and to develop skills necessary for personal growth, understanding, coping and contributing to society in a rapidly changing world. Motivation for learning is a key factor in achieving effective education."

Veritor adds,"The true measure of how effective any educational system performs may be found in how well people eventually function, individually and collectively, in society and the workplace. We need to ask how well do people demonstrate positive attributes in behavior, how well do they perform their jobs and how well do they participate and interact in their homes, neighborhood and community environments. How well do they prepare for emergencies and participate in activities that provide continuous growth? We may also need to look at how other network functions perform in the measurement of educational effectiveness."

Pragma responds, "I think your observations of the true measures of educational effectiveness are valid. When individuals are ill-prepared to work, we witness continuous, intractable unemployment and a scarcity of essential skills needed by

CHAPTER 3 - REGIONAL INFRASTRUCTURES & NETWORKS

industry, science, technology and in many other fields. When individuals feel left out, we see more health problems and suicides, more substance abuse and an increase in violence and gangs. The non-participation of members of a society results in their lack of awareness of issues that could affect their lives. Also, when employed in menial, repetitive jobs, people may try to compensate for them by spending non-working hours in idleness or as spectators living vicariously in the lives of sport heroes or other idols. They watch life and the world go by, unfulfilled and easily manipulated by emotional events. The measures of educational effectiveness are everywhere, but they can only indicate what has happened in the past. Regional attempts must be made to do better for present and future generations. The remedies for improving skills, broadening knowledge and increasing awareness of people are difficult and costly. However, such remedies must be enacted now and continuously monitored."

Veritor nods in agreement."It seems to me that the regional concept with its infrastructure network is ideal for ensuring such support for the educational system. It is also ideal for establishing stable and supportive communities and neighborhoods in which families can thrive. Unfortunately, although voluntary and spontaneous public support for every family and every child in need is required, haranging people to act responsibly has often proven to be futile."

Regional Educational Development

People seek knowledge in order to grow, understand and cope. This is a constant of life. There are fundamental reasons why people, especially young people, pursue knowledge, understanding and basic skills. Yet millions of people think of this investment in life as a luxury, an ordeal, as boring or an unnecessary effort. This attitude can only leave them unprepared for a full, productive and meaningful life. The educational infrastructure of the regional concept offers the means for inducing motivation in students and helping them derive a sense of direction.

It promotes education at all levels so that people will have a chance to achieve self-realization. What must any regional concept of education be predicated on? It must encourage all people to:

1. *Grow to reach full potential.*
2. *Become aware of self and others.*
3. *Develop specific skills for employment.*
4. *Become more aware of the immediate environment.*
5. *Learn to work with others.*
6. *Understand issues and current events.*
7. *Continue to develop in order to be able to adapt.*
8. *Learn how to help others in need.*
9. *Learn how to lead and follow.*
10. *Learn how to listen fully.*
11. *Learn how to concentrate and focus.*
12. *Develop a value system.*
13. *Learn how to make decisions.*
14. *Gain knowledge from past events.*
15. *Learn how to form goals for the future.*
16. *Learn how to plan and compute.*
17. *Learn how to deal with adversity.*
18. *Become creative and productive.*
19. *Become aware of the wonders of nature.*
20. *Sustain a lifelong curiosity.*
21. *Learn how to share ideas, feelings and insights.*
22. *Gain knowledge about other people, their environments, values and customs.*
23. *Learn how to recognize harmful and hazardous situations.*
24. *Learn about basic science and our physical world.*

CHAPTER 3 - REGIONAL INFRASTRUCTURES & NETWORKS

Neos states, "In Regional Network Group E (education) we have already mentioned child development and the need for greater parent-teacher cooperation on the community level. We have also discussed pre-school education on the neighborhood level where child care and supervision must be sustained. The means for assisting exceptional children must also be ensured in special centers."

Pragma answers, "It is unwise to advance unprepared, below grade level students to higher grades. This can only guarantee failure and lifetime problems for these individuals and society. Remedial help must be greatly increased. This approach is by far more cost-effective to individuals and society as a whole. At higher levels of learning, remedial tutoring and counseling allow individuals to correct poor learning habits and increase comprehension. All students need to acquire multiple skills for employment and for participation as citizens. This is an investment that must be made. There are no shortcuts. Of course, when it comes to full occupational readiness, special instruction is required. This may be provided in special schools or on-the-job training."

Veritor concludes, "There are now many more learning tools that can be used for teaching. Computers and visual aids have become common and valuable tools both in the school and the workplace in industrial countries. But for now, let us present an infrastructure diagram for Regional Network Group E."

Explorers of the Mind: In Search of a Better World

Regional Network - Group E & Center, Community and Neighborhood Level

General Interfaces

SPECIAL CENTER (Regional or Community Levels)

- Excpect. Child Develop. Activities
- Remedial Educ./Train Activities
- Development Recreation Activities
- SC
- Remedial Lower/Mid-Level Educ
- Remedial Higher Educ. Tutoring

REGIONAL LEVEL

- Child Development Network
- Occupational Training Network
- Library & Info. Systems Network
- E
- Lower, Mid-Level Educ. Network
- Higher /Educ. System Level

→ National Regional, Business & Industrial Plans

← Other Educ. Institutions & Research

COMMUNITY LEVEL

- Child Dev. Teach./Parent Workshop
- Gov./Indust. Sponsored Job Prep.
- Info. Storage & Retrieval Storage
- CO
- Mid-Level School Activities
- Community College & Work Prep.

NEIGHBORHOOD LEVEL

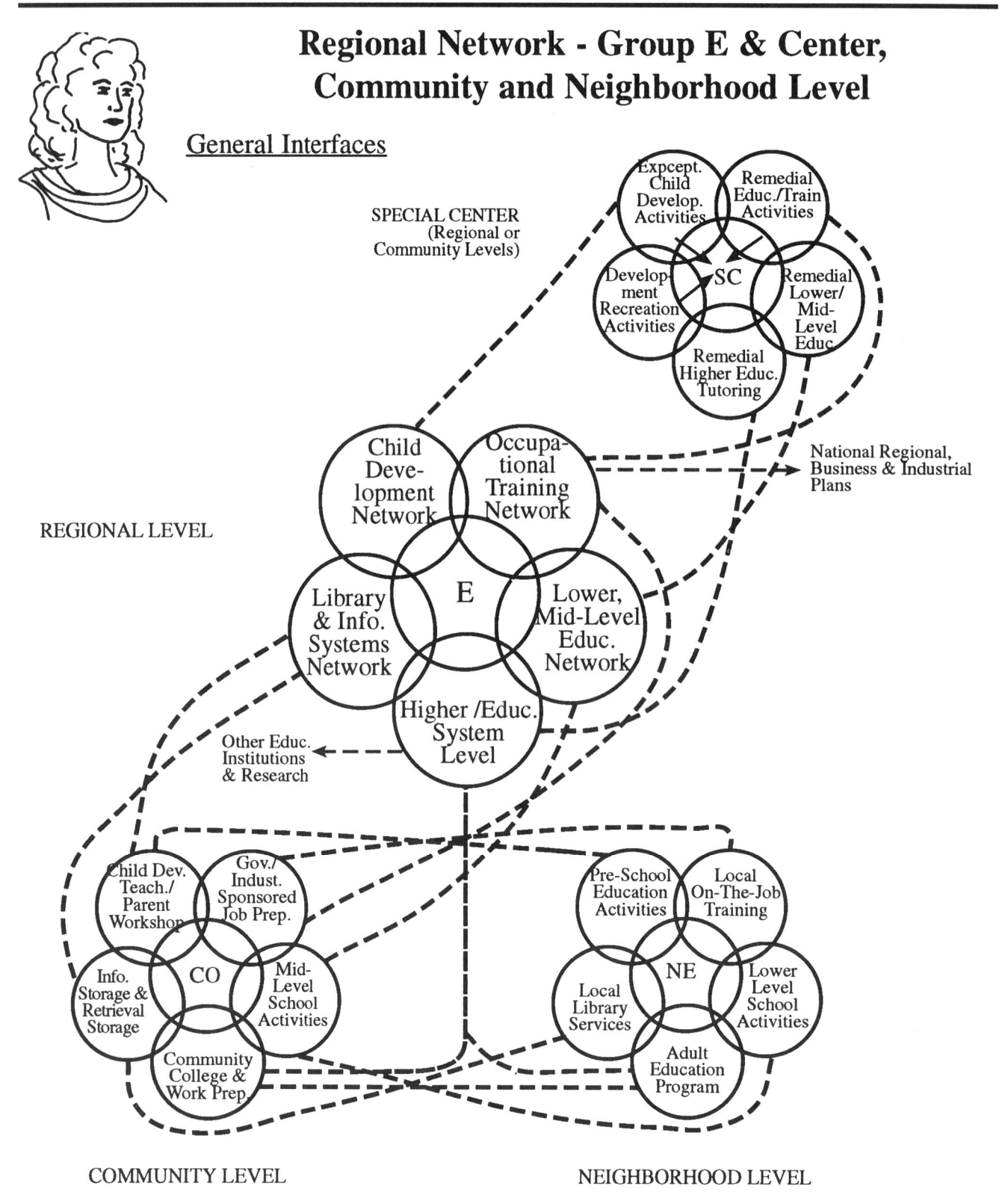

- Pre-School Education Activities
- Local On-The-Job Training
- Local Library Services
- NE
- Lower Level School Activities
- Adult Education Program

Figure III-3-H

138

CHAPTER 3 - REGIONAL INFRASTRUCTURES & NETWORKS

Regional Network Group C is involved with communication systems applicable to all fields. It is the most complex of regional infrastructures, involving both the means and methods of communication. Although multi-faceted and too extensive for presentation here, its relevance to other regional infrastructures must be articulated. The design of all infrastructures, centers, communities and neighborhoods should incorporate appropriate communication technology and approaches, allowing for further growth and improvements. Communication sophistication must match the existing or projected capacity of the region.

Communication techniques are capable of both subtle and powerful persuasion and can serve to entertain, educate, sell, coordinate or control in many positive ways. Unfortunately, repetition, cameo shots, contrived associations, fragmentary or distorted data and opportunistic communications can and do mislead. Poorly informed, biased or unthinking audiences are particularly susceptible to mis-information. This is the dark and ominous side of communication, dangerous to humanity.

The proliferation of information poses another dilemma. People in affluent industrial countries are faced with a multi-media bombardment of persuasive information. How does one separate the wheat from the chaff? The sheer volume of it cannot be totally ignored or quickly categorized. How does valuable information get through? "Attention-getters" are carefully and cleverly designed and packaged. The trivial and the significant are sold with equal gusto or finesse. It is difficult to avoid assaults on individual privacy. Although the public needs to be informed with timely, meaningful and complete information, especially when it pertains to public issues, too much information at one time or the repetition of the same material is likely to exceed human capacity and tolerance. Controlling the quality of content is a serious responsibility. Those who manage and program the mass media must bear this in mind.

Neos, Pragma and Veritor have been discussing the various ramifications of communication. Again they are concerned with individual and collective quality of life. Neos begins, "Much of advertising stresses consumption on the premise that the more variety is offered, the larger, faster, louder or flashier something is and the younger and newer it is, the better quality of life will be. To have more means the 'good life'. In affluent countries, luxuries are confused with necessities. Wants are confused with needs and quality of life is confused with quantity."

Pragma responds, "There is so much waste. Companies or special advertising interests say that they must produce what the public wants in order to make more profits and to provide more jobs. Therefore, they must sell in quantity. But I wonder about the squandering of valuable natural and human resources used to produce short-lived goods that may actually detract from quality of life because they distort needs."

Veritor agrees, "Yes, I think there is a lot in what you are saying. It has to do with materialism, sensationalism and profit-making.The subject of ethical, constructive communication is a complex one. It includes the freedoms of speech and of trade.

However, these are principles and not absolute concepts. So we are not likely to resolve them as issues for now. We need to stress what the regional concept does to create an effective communication infrastructure. Looking at the positive aspects of communication, we can see how vital and important it is for all activities in the region. So it is essential to put modern methods and resources of communication to useful and beneficial purposes."

Neos continues, "At the hub of Regional Network Group C are public and private general communications networks of all kinds. Another regional network, involving telephone systems, provides a primary means of direct exchange. Computer systems continue to become increasingly valuable, performing many functions routinely and accurately. The use of regional, special center and satellite computers also allows for the continuous monitoring, control and management of programs, processes and day-to-day operations of activities in the region. They are a significant adjunct to planning, estimating and decision-making and allow for management visibility of a large variety of public and private operations and interfaces.

"Technology varies, and we need only mention a few things for our purposes. All of these are available in affluent countries. Information signals may be transmitted by electrical wire, glass fiber light conduits, radio airways, microwaves, cellular relay stations, and satellites. Video/telephone networking is a new technology that shows great promise. Rapid advances in computer technology provide linkage with telephone systems, and access to vast information storage and retrieval systems for home and workplace. The region would make good use of such advances in technology."

CHAPTER 3 - REGIONAL INFRASTRUCTURES & NETWORKS

Regional Network - Group C & Center, Community and Neighborhood Levels

General Interfaces

SPECIAL CENTER
(Regional or Community Levels)

- Agric., Indust., Labor.
- Inter-Region
- National & Regional

Special Center nodes: Finance Exch. Commun. Center, Resource Management Center, Traffic Control Center, Postal Deliv. System Center, Weather & Environ. Center, Emergency Center — SC

REGIONAL LEVEL

Regional nodes: Computer Info. System Networks, Regional Operational Network, Radio Broadcast Networks, Publishing Networks, Telephone System Networks, T.V. Broadcast Networks — C

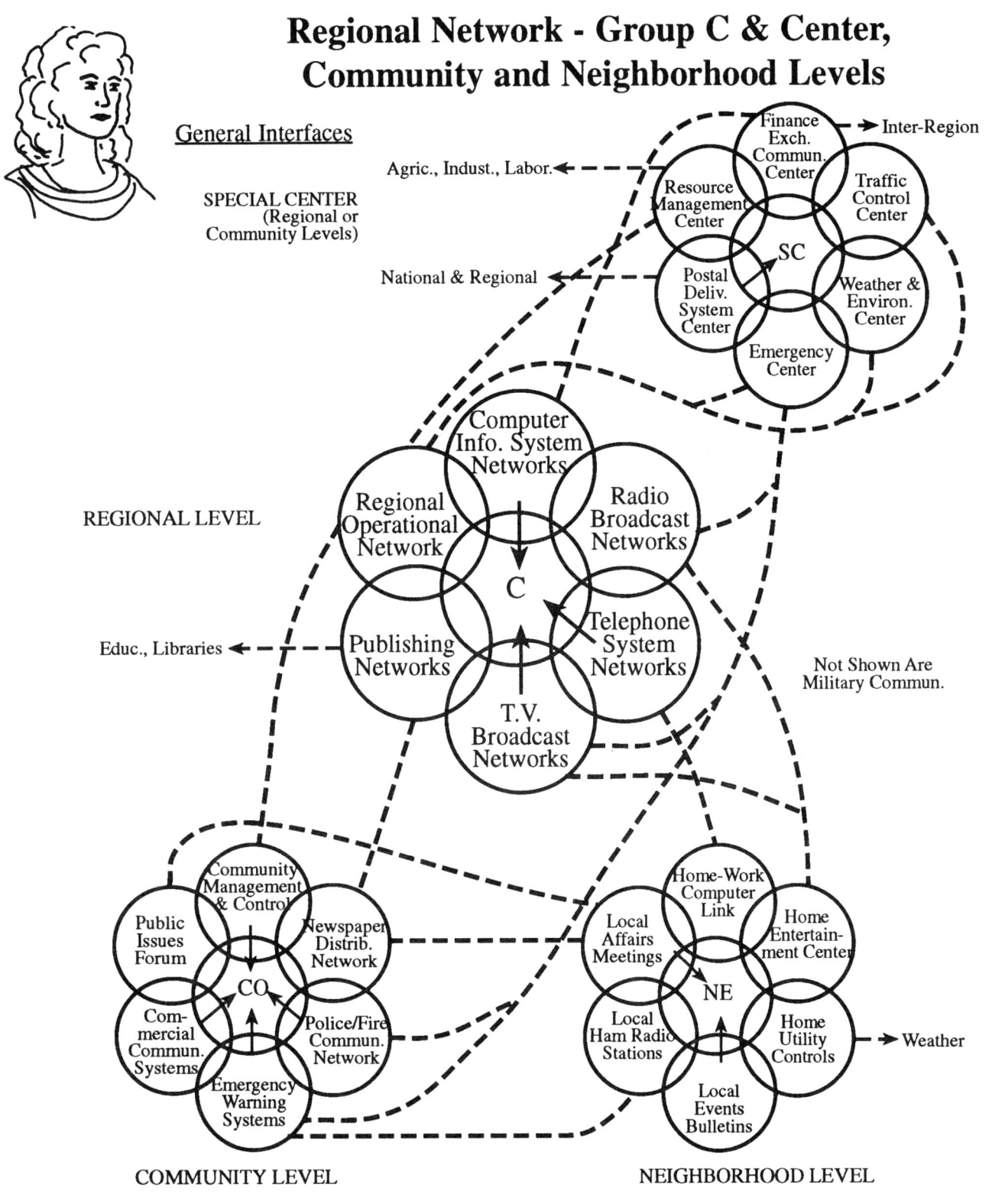

- Educ., Libraries
- Not Shown Are Military Commun.

COMMUNITY LEVEL

Community nodes: Community Management & Control, Public Issues Forum, Newspaper Distrib. Network, Commercial Commun. Systems, Police/Fire Commun. Network, Emergency Warning Systems — CO

NEIGHBORHOOD LEVEL

Neighborhood nodes: Home-Work Computer Link, Local Affairs Meetings, Home Entertainment Center, Local Ham Radio Stations, Home Utility Controls, Local Events Bulletins — NE

- Weather

Figure III-3-I

Pragma responds, "I can see how communication would be vital for all of the special regional centers. Traffic control, weather and environmental services and emergency services require substantial communication support. Another special communication center would be established to serve commerce, industry and agriculture infrastructures and the marketplace. Banking and commodity exchange functions would be included. This would be invaluable for trade and the arrangement of private and public financing for necessary enterprises because the center would also be interacting with inter-regional, national and international financial entities."

Neos adds another prospect. "In an industrial region, it would be feasible to link the workplace and home by computer. Travel could be minimized when work could be produced independently in the home with minimum supervision. Voice with visual monitors and phone transmission of copy would allow many distantly located people to work closely together. Only periodic visits to main places of work would be needed. This is happening today to some extent. Increasing the prospects of these arrangements would depend on the kind of enterprises that are developed in the region."

Neos continues, "There is an important issue concerning communication system vulnerability, the problem of a prolonged electrical power failure caused by major catastrophic events. Imagine what happens when power fails, especially in industrial countries, and all computers and control systems shut down. Paralysis of all critical functions follows. Regional infrastructures must provide backup power generating facilities at all levels."

Veritor notes, "You're right. The region must provide emergency communication measures. Obviously, emergency warning and services are closely linked with fire and police activities, utilities, regional operations and community management and control, especially in times of crisis."

Neos ventures, "We need to discuss another key infrastructure, Regional Network Group T, which has to do with transportation networks, their progressive expansion, system improvements and integration for regionalization. First of all, when selecting functional areas of activity during the planning phase of regional development, planners must indicate where centers, industry, commerce, habitation and agriculture will be located. Planning and zoning would help define capacity requirements for the design and selection of transportation systems. The lay of the land would be assessed to ensure environmental conditions are thoroughly considered before actual development."

Pragma notes, "I can see three possible strategies for implementing transportation systems. One approach would be to let the demands of random growth of population and other concentrations accumulate to justify investment. Another is to zone and plan for the needs of a given size and distribution of population and to install the trans-

CHAPTER 3 - REGIONAL INFRASTRUCTURES & NETWORKS

portation system ahead of time so that it is fully available for early convenient use. A third way is a variation of the second in which planning and zoning of key areas in the whole region would be determined and then transportation would be incrementally built as demand increases and investments allow."

Veritor responds, "In my opinion, the third approach is the most feasible for developing regions. The first approach is actually the most difficult, time-consuming, disruptive and costly because much of the region would have to be developed with temporary, make-shift roads. These would become quickly obsolete. Building new transportation systems could involve extensive reconstruction, condemnations, displacements, legal conflicts and major political obstacles. Preparations would, therefore, take a considerable and uncontrollable amount of time and money. In the meantime, with so much uncertainty, people in such developing areas would begin to heavily rely on some other less effective means of transportation, often permanently. They would have to be 'sold' when new systems are proposed. Such an approach would highly inflate investment costs, produce much waste, raise taxes and increase opposition. It is a backward way to get things done."

Neos adds, "The second approach is better than the first because all of the major pitfalls are avoided. Costs are more controllable, and usefulness of the transportation systems would be immediate. The systems could be expanded as the population grows and areas become more developed. They could also be conveniently located. Any initial or interim development, however, still requires consideration of environmental conditions and compliance with a regional master plan."

Pragma sternly asks, "This is all well and good, but who would pay for the investments? There would be no revenue income from taxes and bonds. Also, would the people who move into the region have any say about the new transportation system's design and development? Who would do the original planning, and who would be making the early decisions?"

Veritor reflects on this and responds, "For one thing, a great majority are never involved in planning and development. However, they might have a say in any development that may directly affect them by increasing their taxes. But basic decision-making and comparative system planning and design or trade-offs would have to be done prior to the major influx of inhabitants and participants in the region. It is analogous to buying a house. The house's location and features have already been established when it is bought. Few eventual owners plan and control the original construction of their homes. They chose and buy what developers have designed and built.

"In the case of regional planning, design and development, the major infrastructures require specialists in many fields and the early initiative and participation of higher levels of government. Developers and eventual operators of centers must become closely involved early to make known their special requirements. Developers must also obtain clearly defined infrastructures and guidelines to avoid extra cost burdens and over runs. As development progresses and the infrastructures begin to take shape, developers become increasingly involved at the community and neighborhood levels.

"The third approach seems the most feasible of the three approaches because planning and zoning would be done early, and development would increase incrementally as outside investments and regional income are received. Of course, this does not imply a 'pay as you go' basis. Large amounts of funds have to be raised before infrastructures of regional magnitude can be developed. Initial funding would come from higher government levels. This expenditure is justified because the overcrowded conditions of the supercities would be partly alleviated and continued population growth would demand it. The prospect of creating new designs to improve communities and neighborhoods would also warrant it. Private investments would be made at the regional level by large companies such as utilities to ensure compatibility with their own technologies, facility designs and networks. Incremental investments must also come from many other sources in the form of bonds to ensure that the development of major works is started and continued in a timely manner. This type of investment would be of considerable interest to companies and private citizens who plan to become part of the region. All major investment plans must become public knowledge to avoid conflicts of interest and abuse of public funds."

With this general discussion completed, Neos begins to probe functional networks at the regional level. "Regionalization offers a tremendous opportunity to plan and develop transportation systems that are safer, more economical, less polluting and less space-consuming. Management and control of speed for different zones of activity would be initiated. This would have a positive impact on the the environment. Safe and effective transportation must be designed and built into systems. It is not a matter of wishful thinking or whim. Effective transportation is accomplished by introducing new kinds of systems that are designed to best serve specific regional needs."

Pragma nods in agreement. "For example, it makes no sense to have heavy trucks vie for the same road space as compact passenger vehicles. Trucks may have greater visibility but poorer maneuverability and control at high speeds; compact vehicles are just the opposite. To the extent possible, there should be two arterial road systems within the region itself. Regional design puts centers, industries, manufacturing and some commerce in locations that encourage the construction of separate roads and access for trucks, trains or ships at ports. Commercial and industrial transportation involves the carrying of special cargo, some of it dangerous. Industry and commerce may be engaged in the import or export of raw materials or manufactured products and, therefore, have unique transportation requirements. It is hazardous and inefficient to have road networks and transportation systems meant to primarily carry people in competition with heavy industrial and commercial vehicles."

Neos and Veritor concur. Neos says, "I would like to present a diagram of the infrastructure of Regional Network Group T. It shows various levels of transportation including the special functions of control centers. Degrees of sophistication and need will vary from country to country according to existing access, extent of development and availability of capital. The principal functions shown are, therefore, generally applicable to systems of different sophistication."

Pragma notes, "Community leaders are often concerned that the traffic on high speed highways will by-pass their commercial facilities. In the regional concept, no community has a particular disadvantage because of fast moving traffic. When higher speed highways are built, they would allow easy access to and from commercial centers. However, there would need to be built-in regulation of movement upon entering or exiting."

Veritor adds, "This brings us to the subject of high speed, automated vehicle control centers and their regional network systems. There is an implied need for regions with much industry and heavy traffic to have safe, rapid movement of vehicles and people to and from various key locations. People who have one or more vehicles are reluctant to give up their freedom of movement. Yet how much freedom is there when roads are too congested and jammed with traffic. Are over-stressed drivers free? Just think about the unsafe conditions, time loss and energy waste. Accidents and vehicle breakdowns contribute to highway congestion and slowdown. With an over-burden of traffic, the incidences of lane-switching, tail-gating, repeated braking, hazardous leaving, entering and passing make a uniform speed of travel impossible. Building more lanes or highways as a solution to the problem is very costly and represents an increased risk to human lives. More lanes increase the prospect of more lane-changing whenever automobiles try to enter or exit, and this leads to more, fast, dangerous maneuvers. Band-aid solutions don't solve the problem and sometimes worsen it."

Explorers of the Mind: In Search of a Better World

Regional Network - Group T & Center, Community and Neighborhood Levels

General Interfaces

SPECIAL CENTER

- Bus./Rail Terminal Center
- Automated Vehicle Contr. Center
- Air Terminal and Traffic Contr.
- SC
- Truck/Rail Industrial Terminal
- Dock/Port Control Center

Inter-Reg.
National/Inter-Regional Weather Info, Etc.

REGIONAL LEVEL

- People Transport Network
- Vehicular Road Network
- Airline Transport Network
- T
- Material/Product Transport Network
- Waterway Transport Network

COMMUNITY LEVEL

- Bus and Rail Stop Network
- Main Road Arteries & Exits
- High Speed Automated Exits/Net.
- CO
- Commercial Delivery Network
- Canals, River & Lake Traffic

NEIGHBORHOOD LEVEL

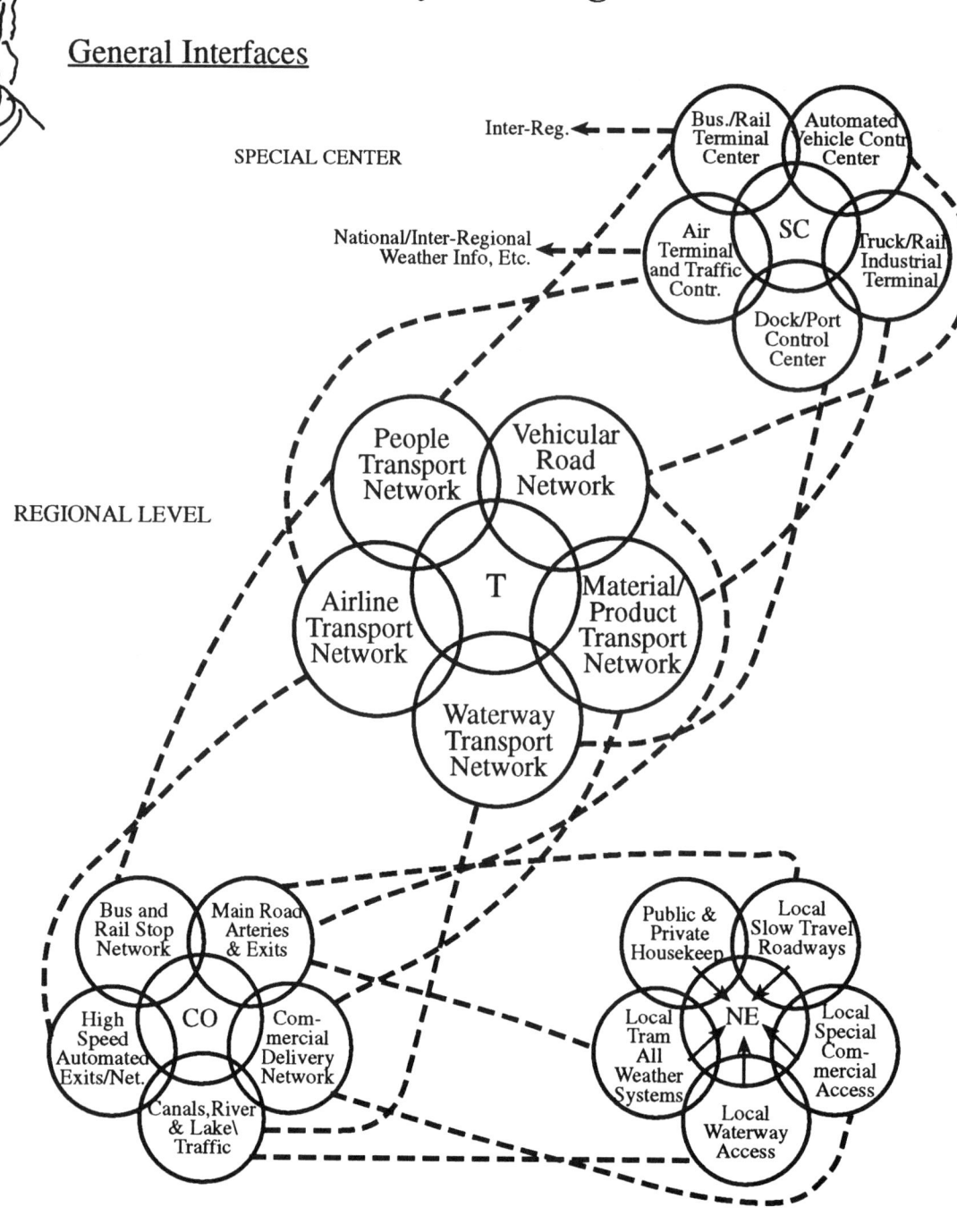

- Public & Private Housekeep.
- Local Slow Travel Roadways
- Local Tram All Weather Systems
- NE
- Local Special Commercial Access
- Local Waterway Access

Figure III-3-J

146

CHAPTER 3 - REGIONAL INFRASTRUCTURES & NETWORKS

Neos responds, "Your observations are thought-provoking. Let's consider better means for travelling where speeds can be made more uniform, yet safe. This requires special designs to transport people either with or without vehicles. What I have in mind is a type of electro-magnetic levitation system that employs special, programmable, self-propelled carriers. The carriers have radar sensors that automatically activate braking when approaching another carrier that is either stopped or going at a slower speed. Special rails provide guidance and levitation. There are two kinds of carriers. The first carries vehicles with their passengers. The second type is a people carrier. Vehicle carriers are pre-programmed for a specific terminal destination by the driver of the vehicle and can be interrupted or over-ridden by a central control terminal for emergency exiting. People carriers stop at pre-determined stations similar to various existing subways and elevated systems.

"The region would investigate and analyze various people-moving and vehicular transport systems for effectiveness and compatibility within the regional design concept. There are a number of schemes already in operation. Incidently, new designs are also needed for air transportation and waterway transportation."

Pragma and Veritor are receptive to Neos's ideas. Veritor remarks, "I can see some distinct advantages to what you have described. The vehicle carrier system would eliminate most problems having to do with the non-uniformity of vehicles. Someday, all passenger vehicles may have to have certain size limits, but we can't count on this. In the meantime, however, oversized vehicles must be automatically diverted from automated systems to existing conventional roadways."

Pragma adds, "There are some other apparent advantages to the piggy-back transport of automobiles. While being carried, a vehicle would not be using its own fuel, and propulsion and braking would be entirely more efficient. Average speeds would be higher and acceleration and deceleration smoother. Safety could be greatly improved. Special, self-propelled, and radar braked carriers enable all traffic to flow at uniform speeds."

Neos has another remark about this subject. "The electrification of the rail for such systems is amenable to even greater improvements in the future. For instance, the discoveries and developments being made in superconductivity are likely to have a tremendous impact."

Two Automated Carrier Systems

Increased safety, economy, convenience and time-saving are provided by the introduction of new regional, automated systems. It is important that there are no delays to their installation.

Passenger Vehicle Carrier

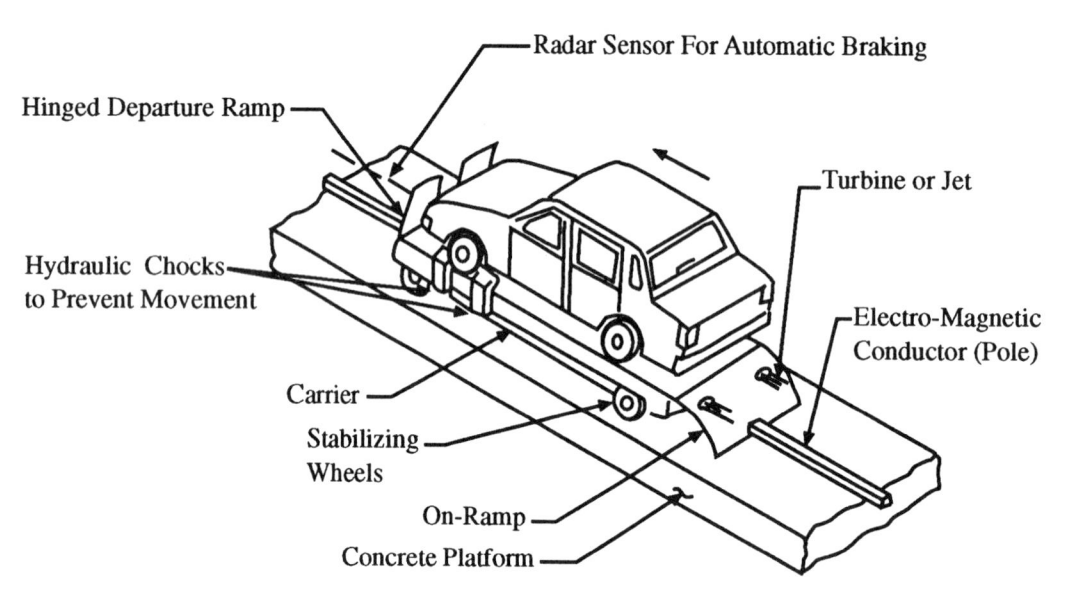

Labels:
- Radar Sensor For Automatic Braking
- Hinged Departure Ramp
- Turbine or Jet
- Hydraulic Chocks to Prevent Movement
- Electro-Magnetic Conductor (Pole)
- Carrier
- Stabilizing Wheels
- On-Ramp
- Concrete Platform

PASSENGER CARRIER

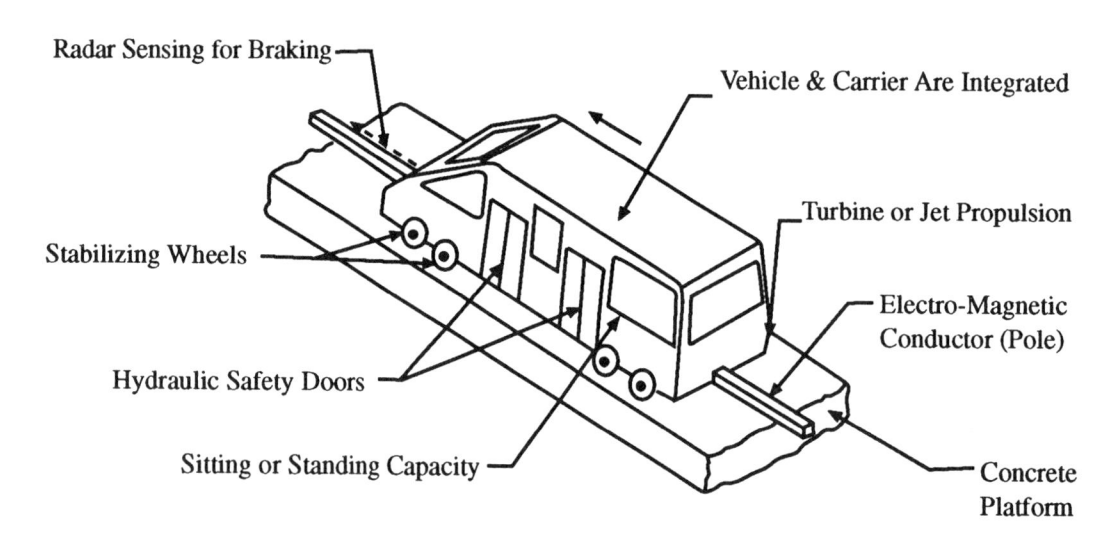

Labels:
- Radar Sensing for Braking
- Vehicle & Carrier Are Integrated
- Stabilizing Wheels
- Turbine or Jet Propulsion
- Hydraulic Safety Doors
- Electro-Magnetic Conductor (Pole)
- Sitting or Standing Capacity
- Concrete Platform

Braking is directly or remotely activated if needing to stop at a specific or programmed terminal.

Figure III-3-K

CHAPTER 3 - REGIONAL INFRASTRUCTURES & NETWORKS

If there is a need to exit at a specific terminal, braking is either activated directly or automatically from a remotely located control center.

Pragma adds, "We must not forget that people require better ways to travel to their places of work. If these are located a considerable distance away, then safer and more rapid forms of transportation systems are important. Terminals, conveniently placed in central and outlying locations of the communities and their neighborhoods, would encourage people to use vehicle and passenger carrier systems. These systems must reach out to remote, but highly utilized, places like air terminals, industrial centers and others."

Veritor notes, "It's also important that there be free, convenient places for people to park so that they can use the passenger carriers. Low cost rental vehicles, buses and taxis at the terminals would complete the system. If people want to use the vehicle carrier system, then there must be safe means for embarking and disembarking their vehicles at these terminals."

Neos excitedly responds, "I can envision such terminals for doing this. Vehicles would drive up a loading ramp and on to a waiting carrier. Special terminals would allow loading and carrier acceleration for merging at main line carrier speeds. The carrier would be pre-programmed for disembarking at a specific terminal and would automatically enter the main line at a controlled, constant line speed. The driver or central terminal would have over-ride control to allow alternate points of disembarkation in emergencies. Upon reaching a destination, the carrier would automatically leave the main line, slow down and exit. Leaving the main line requires deceleration and diversion to an off-loading line at a terminal destination. One such scheme is shown for doing this. Carriers are repositioned for continued use both at the terminals and at a center where programmed redeployment of empty carriers meets queuing peak demands. Surplus carriers at exits re-enter the system to avoid stacking.

Pragma listens intently and says, "It seems to me that the design you describe is feasible and should work quite well. Systems with terminals like this must be developed to meet the needs of a modern industrial society."

Veritor nods in agreement. "This would be an important opportunity for businesses involved in manufacturing, fabrication and automation. For instance, the aerospace and automobile industries must shift their focus. They must design and develop new products compatible with such mass transit systems. Of course, new approaches will become increasingly feasible when regionalization is introduced. Many companies worldwide are becoming more aware of this opportunity and show willingness to seize the initiative and invest."

Terminal Embarking & Disembarking Concept

There are many unique designs for terminal loading and unloading for both kinds of carriers I've mentioned. Of course, such designs must also have special provisions for carrier maintenance and storage. I would like to present a terminal embarking and disembarking concept. This terminal design is shown by itself, but is suitable for use in all communities and outlying centers.

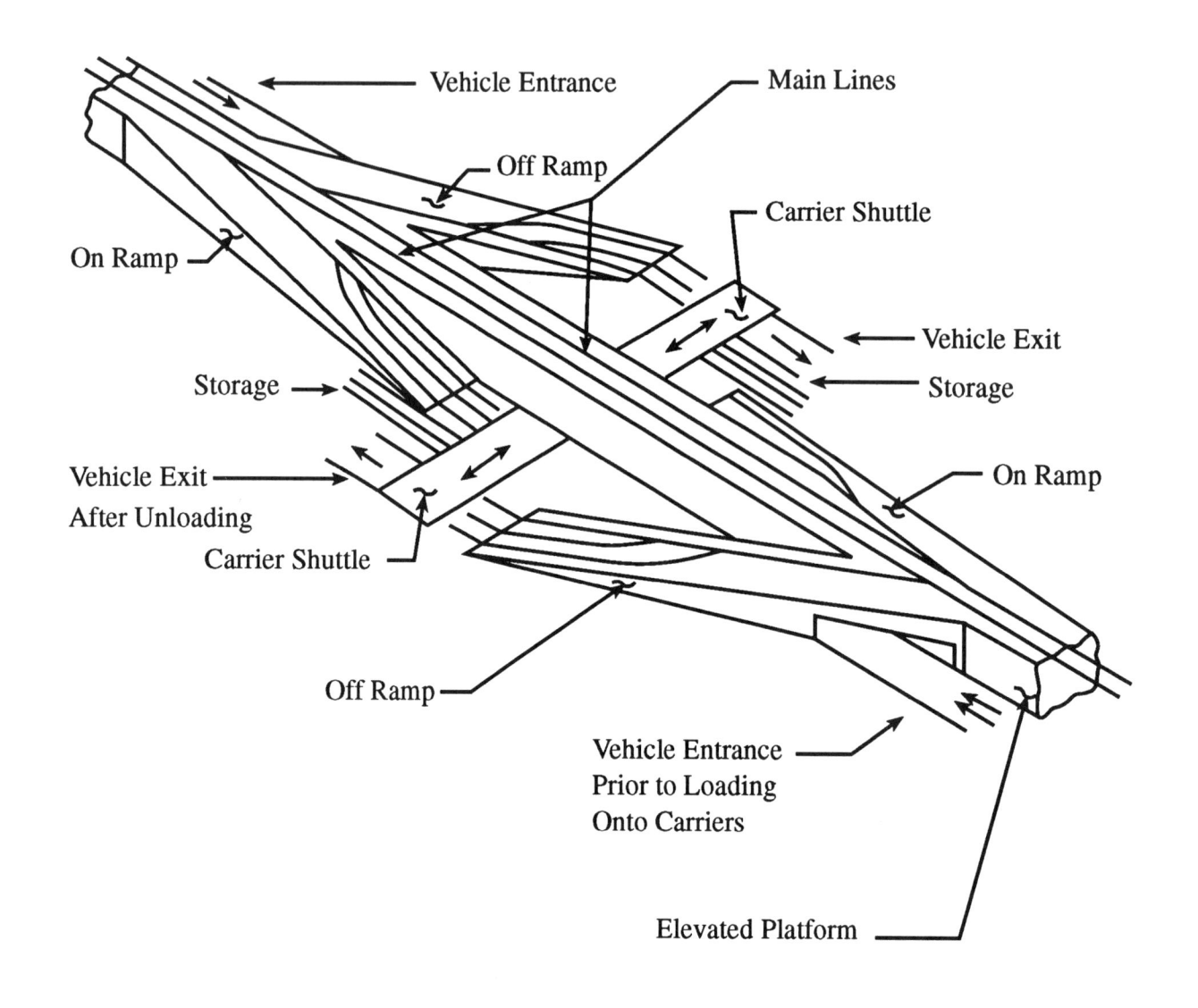

Figure III-3-L

Pragma adds, "I think that many such companies are well aware that a mass transportation market has still not been developed. There has to be implementation of a transportation infrastructure capable of accommodating advanced designs. Otherwise, it becomes very difficult to convince governments and the public of the practicability and affordability of such modern mass transit systems."

Neos brings up a different aspect. "Traffic speed must be reduced within the community. The idea is to design traffic to flow smoothly with a minimum need for signal lights and with complete separation from pedestrian traffic. More overpasses and underpasses are indicated."

Veritor notes, "A number of changes have already been initiated in cities of industrial countries. So we have some precedence. Vehicular traffic is excluded from designated shopping and service areas except for special entry for commercial delivery or maintenance purposes. Some cities have automated people movers in malls or centers. The regional concept would foster this feature of having malls and centers in new community and neighborhood designs that exclude main traffic from specific areas."

Neos pursues the subject. "I see vibrant, but peaceful neighborhoods where travel is leisurely, a pace that reflects a new social setting and an appreciation of the immediate surroundings. The roadways and utilities would be partly concealed or underground. If waterways are nearby, then public access and docks would be provided for recreation and for getting about.

"There would be all weather access to local mini-centers for shopping and for other personal needs. Trams would be introduced into neighborhoods, and over and underpasses would minimize traffic that is hazardous to pedestrians. The development and arrangement of homes would be based on an integrated neighborhood concept that promotes harmony and close neighborhood support. This may not always happen, but this option must be provided by creating specific environments for this purpose. It is a challenge for builders and developers to be in accord with the larger needs of the community and region."

Pragma concurs, "Transportation and communication are essential to the well being of people. They permit an impressive number of events to take place that can improve quality of life. Of course, there are other tangible things involved. Regional neighborhoods offer an excellent opportunity for builders and developers to go beyond their need to make a legitimate profit. It gives them a chance to not only build houses, but to create the physical arrangements that make for cohesive neighborhoods."

Veritor adds, "Some major builders and developers have already ventured to do this. Their efforts deserve recognition and emulation, especially so during the development of regionalization."

Neos, Veritor and Pragma are aware that other kinds of transportation are required for the movement of raw materials, manufactured products and agricultural produce. Pragma begins, "We have mentioned industrial materials that may be hazardous and require special handling. Obviously, these will be moved by a dedicated transportation network including rail, highway, air and waterway systems. During shipment, some materials being transported require refrigeration, shock protection, pressurization, vacuum, extra insulation or isolation, etc. Regional design and zoning would place related terminals and special centers far removed from population concentrations. Complete protection of the environment and regional resources would be a requirement. However, such remote operations within the region must still be readily accessible to employees living in populated areas."

After a pause, Neos notes, "There is another infrastructure called Regional Network Group P that provides functions for basic public works like power, water, sewage and waste systems. The planning and installation of public works requires the close cooperation of builders and developers with government entities. A long term view is essential for the infrastructure of Group P because when public works become obsolete or outgrown too quickly, major rebuilding and new system design and development must take place. This can place a major burden on tax payers."

Pragma answers, "To contain their costs, developers and builders emphasize only those codes and regulations necessary to get the job done. However, this often proves to be difficult when infrastructures are not yet in place or plans are continually changing."

Veritor proposes, "It would be much better to have prospective builders and developers present their planning needs while infrastructure design and development and environmental factors are being considered. This approach would stress cooperation and reduce risk. Environmental conditions could be carefully evaluated and resources would be conserved because regional planners could devise timely rules and regulations and provide guidance."

CHAPTER 3 - REGIONAL INFRASTRUCTURES & NETWORKS

Regional Network- Group P & Center, Community & Neighborhood Levels

General Interfaces

SPECIAL CENTER
(Regional or Community Levels)

SC
- Civil Eng'g Planning & Analysis
- Main Water Resources & Treatment
- Air Terminal & Traffic Control
- Main Power Production System
- Sewer Treat. & Utilization System

REGIONAL LEVEL

P
- Public Works & Construct. Network
- Water Delivery Network
- Waste Convers. System Network
- Power Gener. & Delivery Network
- Sewage Treat. System Network

CO
- Public Works Construct. & Maint.
- District Water Resources & Reserves
- Waste Convers. & Separation System
- Electric Power Sub-Station Network
- Sewage Treat. Sub-Station Network

NE
- Local Public Works Devel. & Maint.
- Local Recycling Systems
- Local Waste Separation Co-ops
- Local Solar Power Gen. Co-ops
- Home Recycl. & Disposal Systems

COMMUNITY LEVEL   NEIGHBORHOOD LEVEL

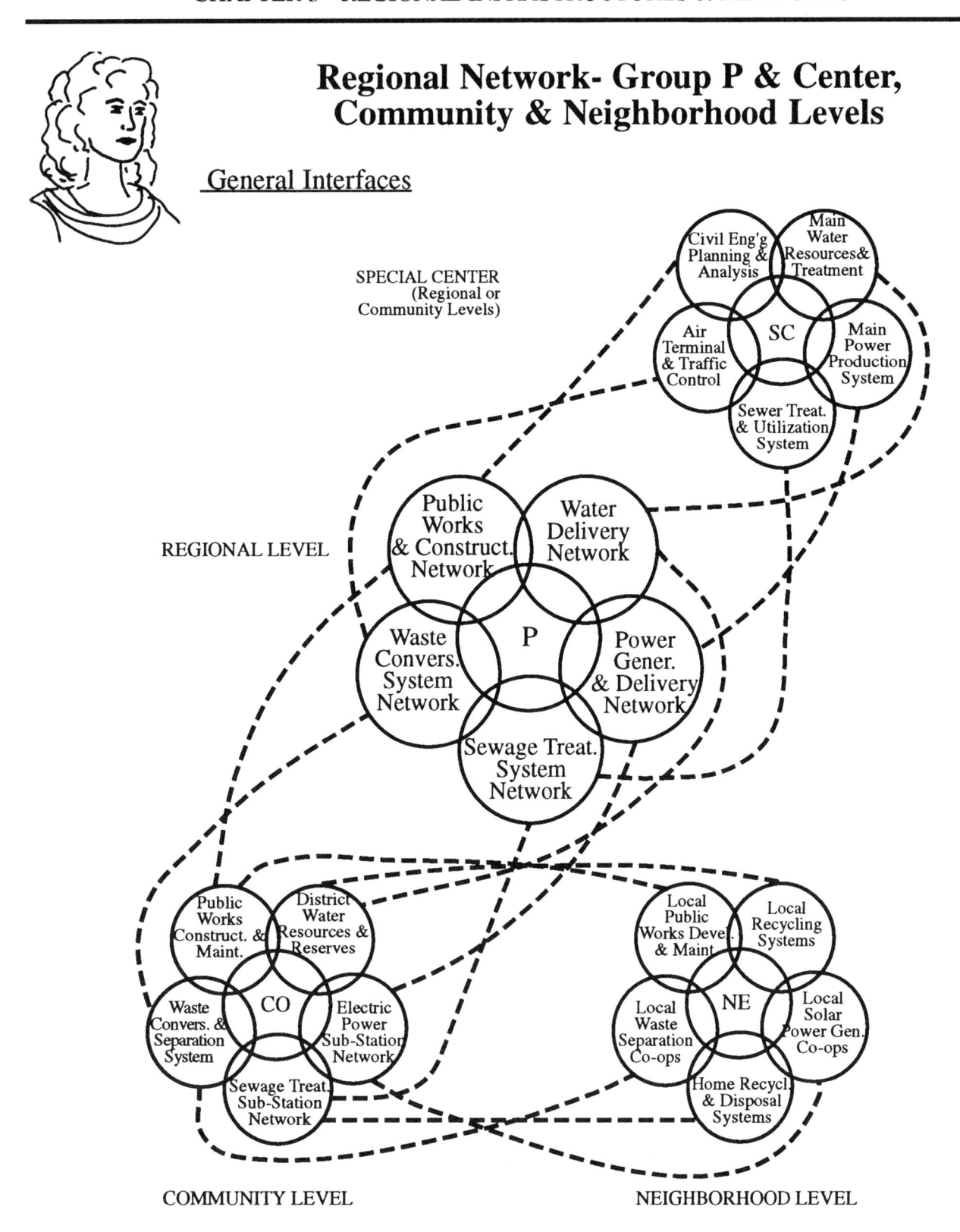

Figure III-3-M

153

Neos refers to Group P. "This infrastructure for water and power, waste disposal, sewage and associated special centers is shown on the regional level. However, it is also necessary to consider network functions at the community and neighborhood levels. People are mostly effected at these levels by basic infrastructure deficiencies and want something done about them."

Pragma concurs, "Of course, when water and power are cut off, waste and sewage accumulate, flooding and landslides occur and bridges collapse, people immediately react to what may have been gradually impending for some time."

Neos notes, "By carefully designing and installing utility systems and preparing the terrain without destroying the environment, new effective, secure, accessible, maintainable communities and neighborhoods can be developed. The regional network pattern of distribution of water, power, communication, drainage, sewers and so forth would be greatly simplified and standardized. Builders and developers would know where and how neighborhood utilities will be provided in order to design their own portions of development. Developers are expected to provide housing and other buildings with lower profile area for less exposure to extreme wind and weather. Lower and more uniform buildings would avoid obstructing sunlight for home or neighborhood solar energy systems. Greater energy savings would result. "In the design of regional communities and their neighborhoods, embankments would partly surround areas of habitation. These embankments would be landscaped with shrubs and trees and provide open space for activities, hiking and bicycling. When practicable, there would be strategic and unobtrusive placement of solar energy panels and collectors, fuel cell systems and wind turbines on portions of the embankments. The idea is to give character to the land, yet provide greater utility. Living would be enhanced by the creation of more natural surroundings."

Pragma and Veritor are in full accord with the promise of such experiments. Pragma notes, "The layout of embankments need not be rectangular. In some cases they would follow the lay of the land or coastline or be circular. The idea is to create networked havens for living and still have everything associated."

Neos proposes, "There have been a number of experiments in creating such safe havens and closer societies. The regional concept, of course, brings together many such arrangements. Society would then be integrated but allow for privacy. Let's present some tentative neighborhood and housing patterns and perspectives."

CHAPTER 3 - REGIONAL INFRASTRUCTURES & NETWORKS

Community & Neighborhood Patterns & Perspectives

There are many variations of patterns and profiles for communities and their neighborhoods. A few are shown here. The arrangements and sense of neighborhood are emphasized within the larger context of the region where networking and support are more likely to exist. People want close proximity to shopping, schools, services, spiritual and civic activities. They especially need readily available emergency services, transportation, hospitals and appropriate local auxiliary utilities. Balance must be struck between private, uncrowded living space and common spaces set aside for the good of the neighborhood.

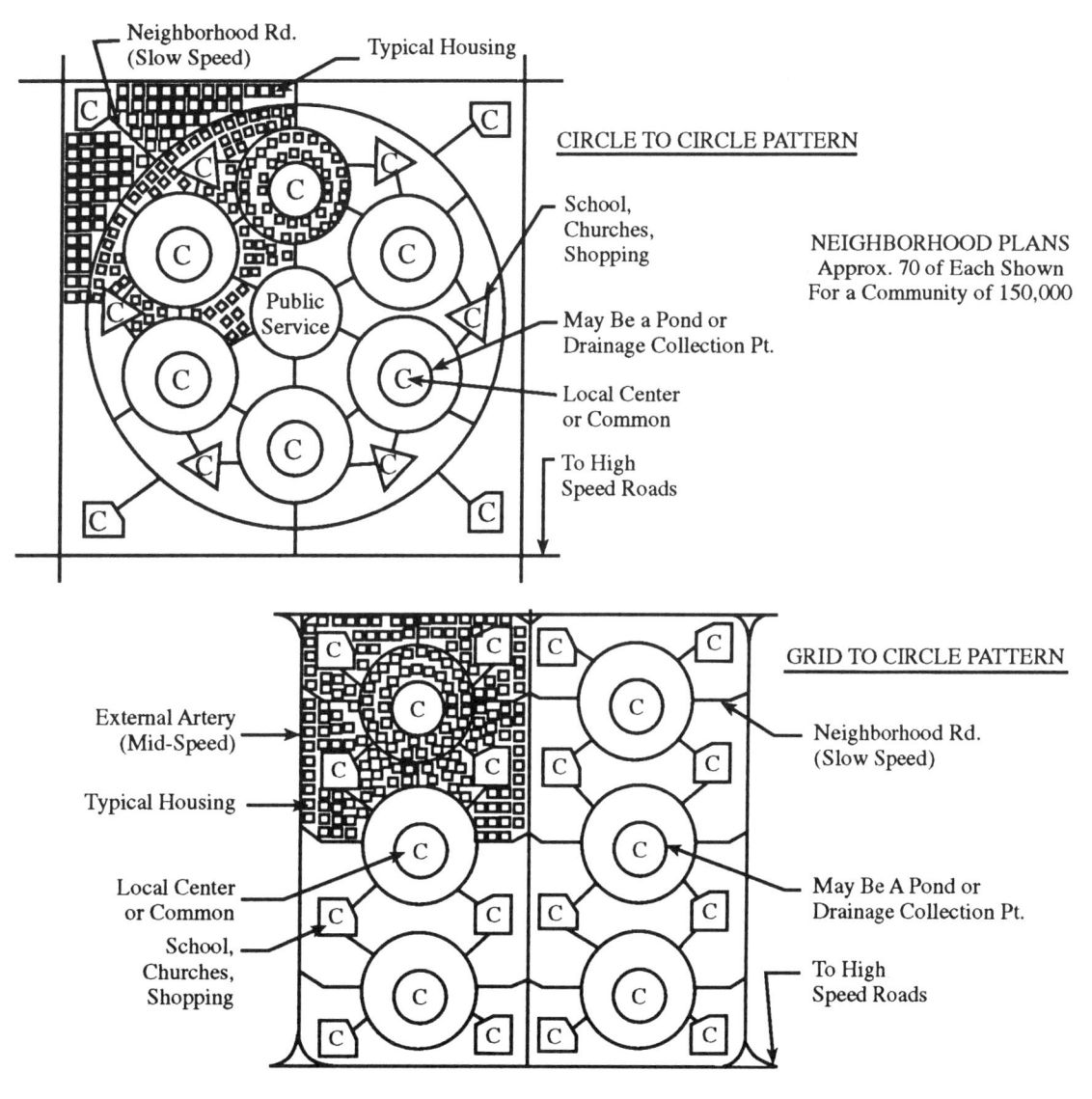

CIRCLE TO CIRCLE PATTERN

- Neighborhood Rd. (Slow Speed)
- Typical Housing
- Public Service
- School, Churches, Shopping
- May Be a Pond or Drainage Collection Pt.
- Local Center or Common
- To High Speed Roads

NEIGHBORHOOD PLANS
Approx. 70 of Each Shown
For a Community of 150,000

GRID TO CIRCLE PATTERN

- External Artery (Mid-Speed)
- Typical Housing
- Local Center or Common
- School, Churches, Shopping
- Neighborhood Rd. (Slow Speed)
- May Be A Pond or Drainage Collection Pt.
- To High Speed Roads

Figure III-3-N

Neighborhood Housing

- Neighborhoods should comprise different kinds of housing to accommodate the requirements and economic means of the inhabitants. Neighborhoods benefit by having mixes of housing that are grouped into single and multiple dwelling clusters with variations in design. The housing sites must be carefully located for optimum livability. The surrounding area must be carefully selected to ensure that adverse conditions are not present.
- Neighborhood buildings should include sub-ground level construction on sites that are located well above existing water tables.
- Except for very slow traffic areas, neighborhood housing must have pedestrian overpasses at busy intersections (which are kept to a minimum by design). This may sometimes be accomplished in conjunction with artificial or natural embankments that add character to the local terrain.
- Embankments are also intended to be used for walking and bicycle trails, solar collector placements, fuel cell power systems, wind turbines, and foliage that help to buffer weather.
- Neighborhood pedestrian and activity zones would be free of automobiles.
- Underground placement of networks for communications and power, water supply lines and sewer lines would be characteristic in neighborhood development.
- Neighborhood drainage ponds and outflow channels would be provided to contain and divert excess water from places of habitation and centers.
- As mentioned above, a great variety of housing cluster patterns exist. A few are shown for multiple unit dwellings that offer privacy, yet introduce a sense of belonging to a neighborhood:

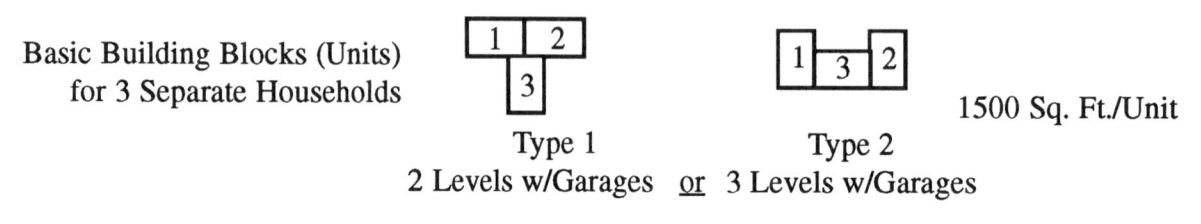

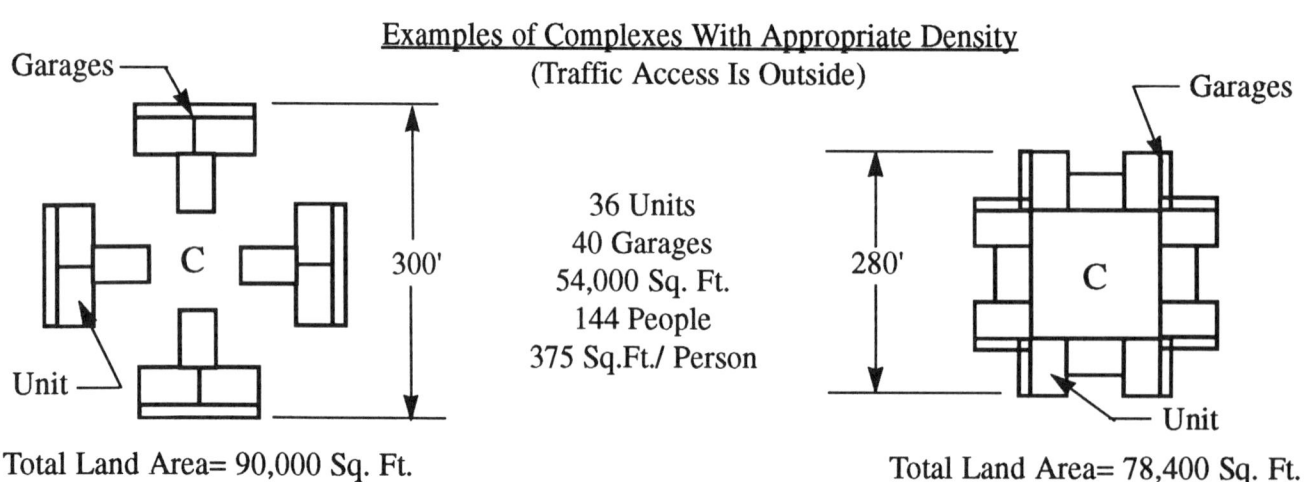

Basic Building Blocks (Units) for 3 Separate Households

Type 1
2 Levels w/Garages

Type 2
3 Levels w/Garages

1500 Sq. Ft./Unit

Examples of Complexes With Appropriate Density
(Traffic Access Is Outside)

36 Units
40 Garages
54,000 Sq. Ft.
144 People
375 Sq.Ft./ Person

300'

Total Land Area= 90,000 Sq. Ft.

280'

Total Land Area= 78,400 Sq. Ft.

Figure III-4-O

CHAPTER 3 - REGIONAL INFRASTRUCTURES & NETWORKS

Veritor reflects on what has been presented." It seems to me that the early initiation of basic regional infrastructures and networks encourages cooperation and new concepts on a local scale. Many cooperative efforts do not have to be formal, standard or rigid. It is neither sensible nor realistic to make neighborhoods all alike and sterile. It is a matter of neighborhoods doing things with imagination within their own human scale using local available resources and obtaining special assistance from the community or region, when necessary."

Pragma notes, "When neighborhoods become successful because of outside support, they must also reciprocate by helping other less developed neighborhoods. This is important because when great economic disparities, poorer living conditions and poverty infest neighborhoods, there is a potential threat to the community as a whole and especially to the affluent areas. The latter become targets for criminal activity. It is not a matter of saying, 'We have ours, now you get your own'. Hopefully, economic disparities will not lead to a proliferation of isolated, heavily guarded, affluent neighborhoods."

Veritor responds, "I think that more people need to participate in the development of the total infrastructure as well as in their newly emerging neighborhoods. If people in each neighborhood pass on their knowledge, time and special resources to others, what a better world this would become."

Neos nods enthusiastically and proceeds, "There are many new things that can be accomplished in individual homes and neighborhoods. We have already mentioned local auxiliary energy systems. Special local installation apparatuses for recycling water and waste may become feasible. For instance, waste water can be salvaged, treated and used for gardens."

Pragma adds, "Perhaps neighborhoods could do this to conserve water. It may be too expensive to provide drinkable water this way, however. Other neighborhood or community cooperative enterprises such as recycling trash have proven to be feasible. Money obtained from this could be held in reserve for neighborhood emergencies and projects."

"Of course, we have already mentioned solar energy, wind turbines and fuel cell systems," says Veritor. "These local systems could be neighborhood enterprises that complement main energy supply sources, and this could bring reductions in the cost of electrical energy and home heating or cooling. Also, they would provide backup, interim supplies following catastrophes."

Neos broaches a different subject. "There must be an infrastructure to develop, monitor, conserve and protect the environment and natural resources. We will call this infrastructure Regional Network Group N. Although the main functions are performed at the regional level, much must be done at the community and neighborhood levels as well. For instance, environmental concerns include quality assurance of the air, water and land in the region. This is best handled at the regional and inter-regional levels with agreements, standards and enforced compliance. At the community level, ordinances must protect waterways and the air from local polluters. In neighborhoods, mutual pride could engender good housekeeping practices and special handling of household toxic substances. This is important because everyone is responsible for maintaining environmental quality. It cannot be passed on as solely a government or other person's problem and ignored."

Pragma asks, "What about land use? Open spaces must continue to be protected in the regional setting. When people and companies show no concern for the public and the natural environment, doesn't this require strong legislation and strict law enforcement?"

Veritor answers, "Yes, laws are necessary here. We also need special centers with functions that protect land, air and water resources and others to repair damage to the environment. If necessary, punitive fines and clean up costs must be assessed. The unique functions of the centers would require people who are technologically competent in water, waste and sewage treatment and land management. They must understand the ecology, geography, hydrology, climatology and history of the region. How else can land be properly set aside for development or conservation?"

Pragma adds, "Special centers are also required to wisely manage the natural resources of the region. Infrastructure Group N is designed to perform management functions during implementation and operation of the region. These functions require people with mining, forestry, engineering and other technological disciplines "

Veritor notes, "Communities and neighborhoods have a basic responsibility for the conservation of resources and environmental protection. There are common areas at all levels. This calls for a sharing of responsibilities and neighborhood functions. Communities need to enact ordinances that define, protect against and discourage destructive behavior in order to ensure the well-being of each neighborhood."

CHAPTER 3 - REGIONAL INFRASTRUCTURES & NETWORKS

Regional Network - Group N & Center, Community & Neighborhood Levels

General Interfaces

SPECIAL CENTER
(Regional or Community Levels)

- Water Treat./Air Monitor. Center
- Hydrology/Land Stabil. Center
- Tree & Shrub Nurseries
- SC
- Natural Res. Devel. Center
- Eng'g Des. Inter. Dev. Center

REGIONAL LEVEL

- Air/Water/Land Quality Assur. Network
- Land/Water Forest Devel. Network
- Open Land Use/Conservation Network
- N
- Natural Res. Development Network
- Inter-Waterway M'g't/Develop Network

COMMUNITY LEVEL

- Water/Waste Ordinance & Control
- Public Tree Planting Services
- Zoning Ordinance Enforce.
- CO
- Natural Resource Conserv.
- Waterway Ordinance Enforce.

NEIGHBORHOOD LEVEL

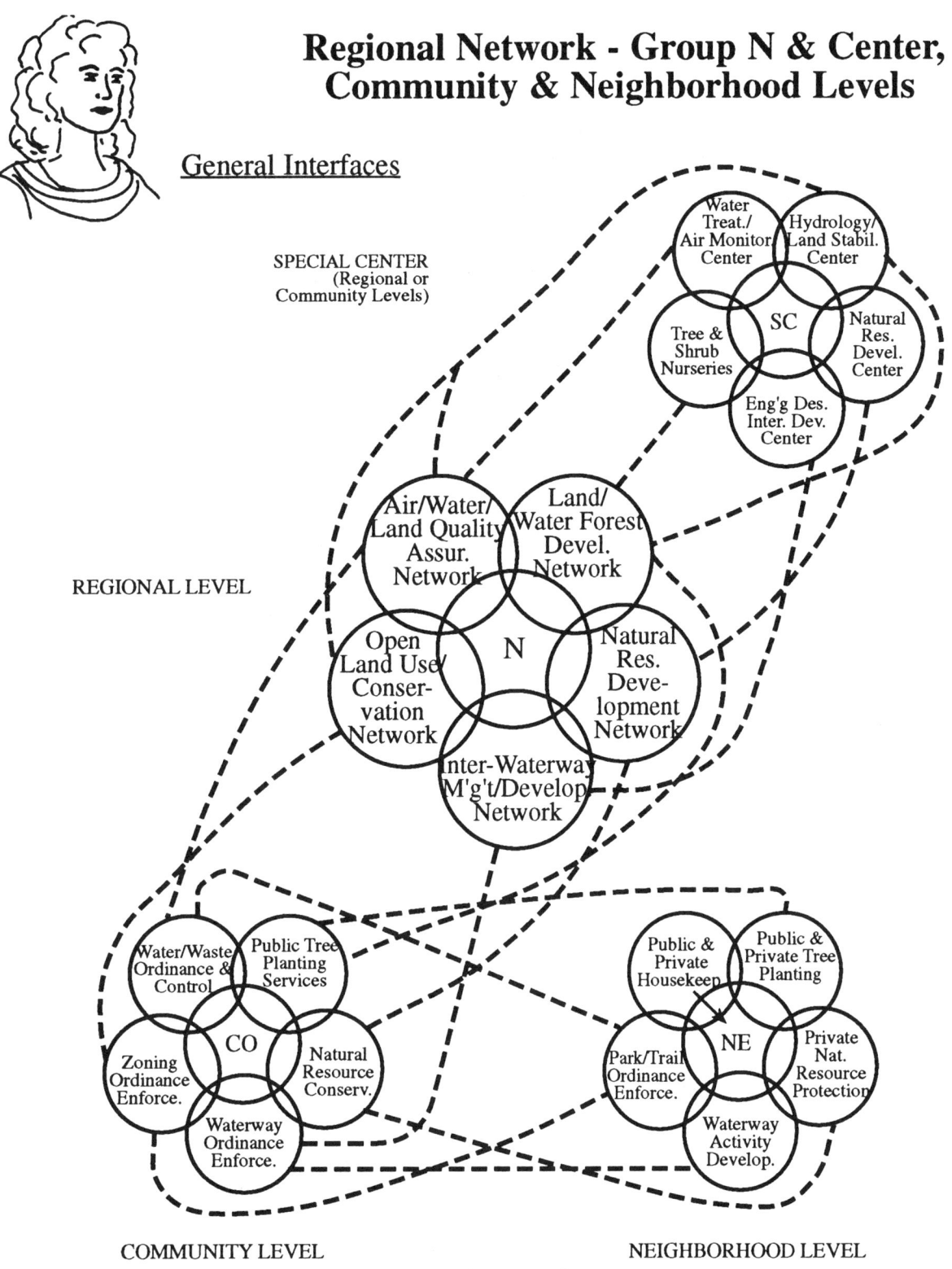

- Public & Private Housekeep
- Public & Private Tree Planting
- Park/Trail Ordinance Enforce.
- NE
- Private Nat. Resource Protection
- Waterway Activity Develop.

Figure III-3-P

159

Neos expresses thoughts on another subject. "We have not yet discussed the enhancement of food and plant growing for regional development. Now it is time to emphasize the need for an infrastructure with functions that facilitate food growing, processing and distribution. Regional Network Group F is meant to do this.

"As with other infrastructures, this one involves the whole region, special centers, communities and neighborhoods. All contribute. The majority of food comes from regional level farms and food processing centers. The farms produce food from both crops and animals. Some also grow trees, plants and flowers for various purposes.

Food processing, packaging and shipping are done on a regional scale. Some of the products produced would be intended for export, the rest for regional consumption. The processing centers would be dispersed throughout the farming areas of the region, close to spurs for transportation."

Pragma asks, "What about distribution? It seems to me that the regional network concept would provide an ideal way of distributing food to the communities and their neighborhoods. Industrial countries already have distribution systems that are quite efficient. People are able to buy food from specialty food shops, restaurants and fresh produce markets. These are often under one roof in supermarkets. The regional approach includes and is meant to enhance many of these modern approaches to merchandizing and distribution."

Veritor notes, "In many affluent industrial countries people are given many choices of fresh and processed foods far beyond their needs or even their wants. Doesn't this lead to flagrant waste? Of course, abundance is far better than scarcity. But I wonder about lost resources and over-indulgence? The regional concept would be concerned with ensuring sufficient nutrition for all within the region. No one must go hungry, and no one would be denied survival through system neglect. Every civilized society subscribes to this, but still the contrasts between hunger and plenty are clearly present worldwide."

Neos concludes by adding, "The regional approach would encourage enterprises in food growing at the neighborhood level as well. There is a certain amount of independence and self-reliance that needs to be encouraged in individuals and in cooperatives. Accordingly, land would be set aside in the region for such purposes. This would contribute to those in need or provide occupation or recreation to people of all ages. Planting and growing things would be a particularly beneficial activity for teenagers, turning their energies into accomplishments and self-development."

CHAPTER 3 - REGIONAL INFRASTRUCTURES & NETWORKS

Regional Network - Group F & Center, Community & Neighborhood Levels

General Interfaces

SPECIAL CENTER (Regional or Community Levels)
- Food Storage & Distrib. Centers
- Food Processing Centers
- Special Plant Production Farms
- SC
- Animal Food Production Farms
- Plant Food Production Farms

REGIONAL LEVEL
- Food Storage & Distribution Network
- Food Process. Systems Network
- Other Plant Production Networks
- F
- Animal/Fish Production Network
- Food Plants Production Network

COMMUNITY LEVEL
- Specialty Food Distrib.
- Super-Markets
- Gardens & Parks
- CO
- Meat & Fish M'k'ts
- Fresh Produce Markets

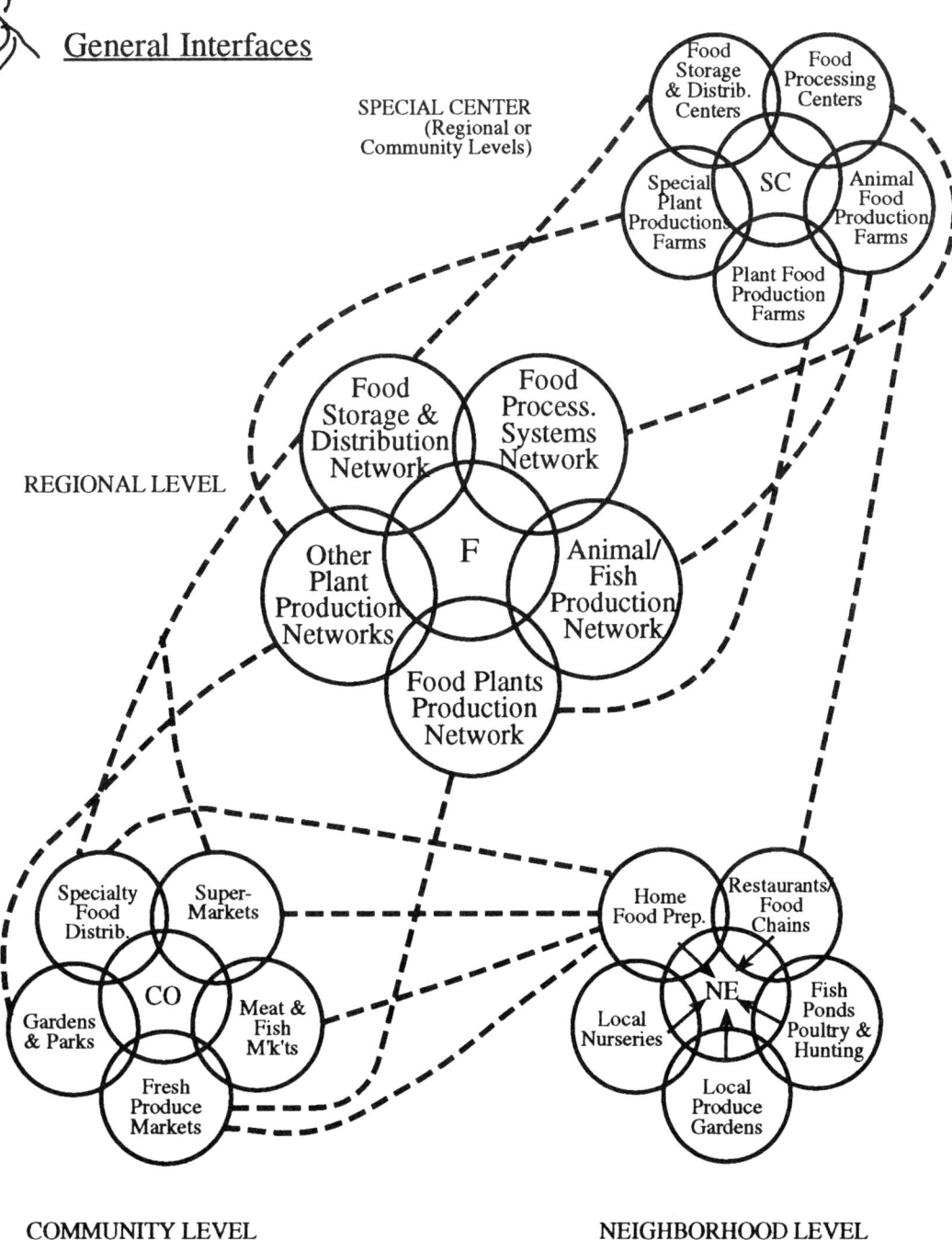

NEIGHBORHOOD LEVEL
- Home Food Prep.
- Restaurants/Food Chains
- Local Nurseries
- NE
- Fish Ponds Poultry & Hunting
- Local Produce Gardens

Figure III-3-Q

161

Pragma and Veritor like this idea. Veritor says, "Activities such as these make for closer knit neighborhoods. Even though members of a neighborhood may be different in some ways, they can all share common land and ideas in creativity. This would bring people together in a positive way. I recognize that this specific project may attract only a fraction of the population, but there are many other possibilities as well."

Pragma responds, "Although each neighborhood may wish for some autonomy, the fact remains there must still be working relationships and social interactions within the community and the region. This is particularly apparent in the dependency on food services and other necessities. In a world filled with a growing number of people with limited resources and shared environments, inter-dependencies are becoming increasingly part of life."

Neos listens carefully to these observations. "Your statement on inter-dependence is very pertinent. It leads us to this infrastructure, Network Group B, with its functions that pertain to commerce, business and industry. Societies have always had some arrangements for bartering, buying and selling and a multitude of ways to make a living. In the regional concept, all infrastructure levels would be highly developed and networked to effectively carry out Group B functions."

Veritor answers, "This is important. If any one level is ignored or neglected, it could bring about severe repercussions. At each level there would be different sets of functions for production, economic exchanges and distribution. Obviously, distribution and import/export would be critical.

"Let us examine the special centers where trade takes place, large scale business headquarters are located and capital resources are gathered and made available for development and growth. Other centers provide for storage and distribution of many kinds of goods and materials. Without these essentials in an infrastructure, how could a modern society flourish or survive?"

Neos agree, "I have prepared another diagram for this infrastructure. Its functional levels are all critical for industrial societies. It would be somewhat simplified for many Third World countries and would not be appropriate for communist regimes as they are presently constituted. However, many of the general functions may still apply."

CHAPTER 3 - REGIONAL INFRASTRUCTURES & NETWORKS

Regional Network - Group B & Center, Community & Neighborhood Levels

General Interfaces

SPECIAL CENTER (Regional or Community Levels)

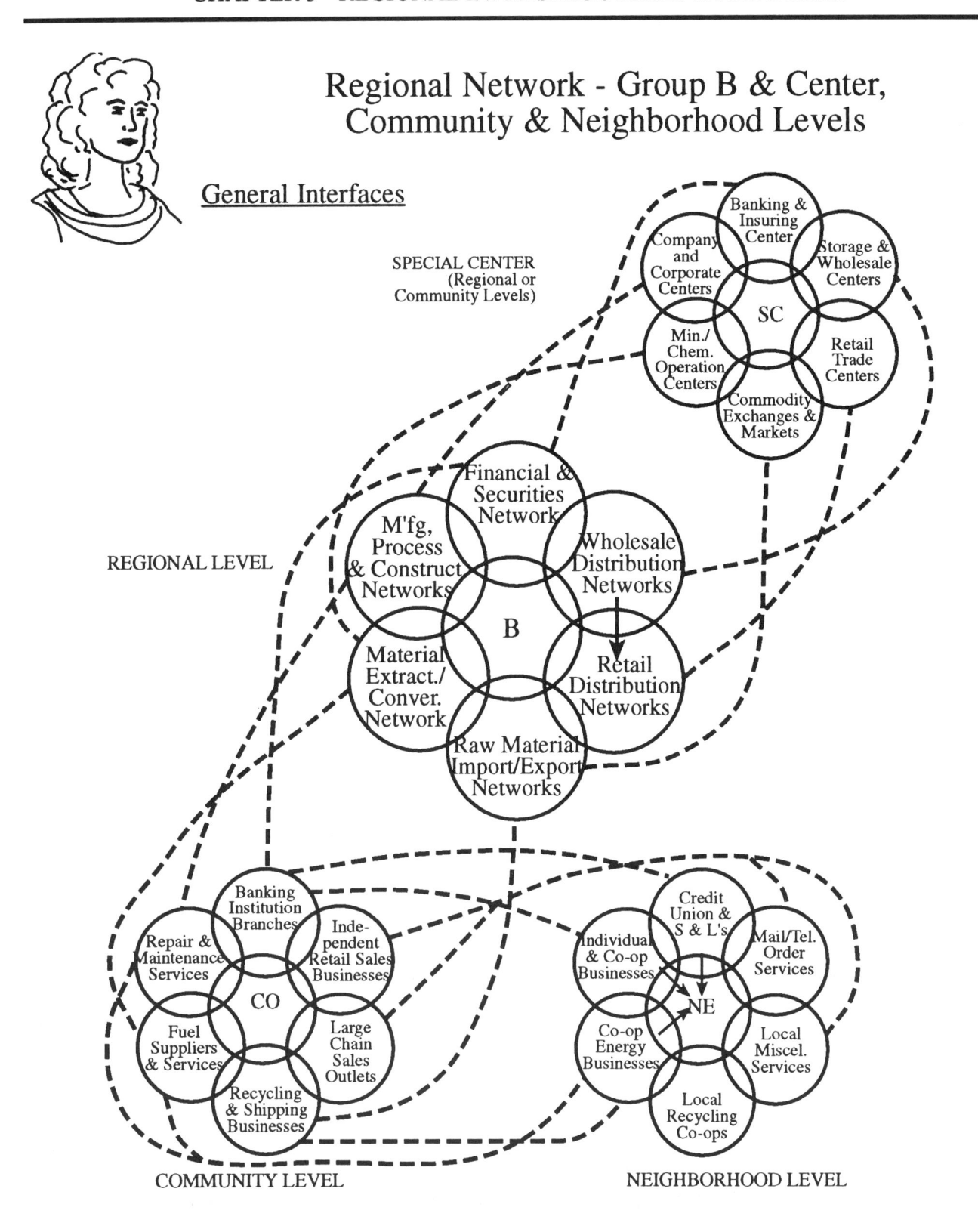

SC:
- Banking & Insuring Center
- Company and Corporate Centers
- Storage & Wholesale Centers
- Min./Chem. Operation Centers
- Retail Trade Centers
- Commodity Exchanges & Markets

REGIONAL LEVEL

B:
- Financial & Securities Network
- M'fg, Process & Construct Networks
- Wholesale Distribution Networks
- Material Extract./Conver. Network
- Retail Distribution Networks
- Raw Material Import/Export Networks

COMMUNITY LEVEL

CO:
- Banking Institution Branches
- Repair & Maintenance Services
- Independent Retail Sales Businesses
- Fuel Suppliers & Services
- Large Chain Sales Outlets
- Recycling & Shipping Businesses

NEIGHBORHOOD LEVEL

NE:
- Credit Union & S & L's
- Individual & Co-op Businesses
- Mail/Tel. Order Services
- Co-op Energy Businesses
- Local Miscel. Services
- Local Recycling Co-ops

Figure III-3-R

163

Pragma asserts, "A region cannot remain totally independent if it is to reach its full potential. There have to be economic inter-regional exchanges and support within the context of larger markets. This would bring about greater import and export trade."

Veritor adds, "This becomes very apparent when we consider possible regional vulnerability. All societies need to help each other especially when there are natural or man-made catastrophic events. We have briefly mentioned this earlier."

Pragma continues, "Let's examine the special centers. It is easy to recognize their inter and intra-area dependencies. Most aspects of these are well-known, and they are applicable to regionalization. For instance, products, large and small, must be stored in quantity to meet anticipated market demand. Most manufacturers, fabricators and producers require a middleman function to free up their capital and to distribute their products. Manufactured goods need to be produced long before they are ever bought and utilized. Some manufacturers establish their own retail outlets in order to be more competitive and to make more profit. Large retail chain stores may also attempt to replace the functions of the wholesaler and buy directly from the manufacturers. In many cases the wholesaler functions would be indispensable in the distribution system.

"Some products to be marketed would still be in the raw state. If they are mining, timber or agricultural products, they would be very susceptible to current and future market fluctuations. So commodity exchanges would be needed to buy them, assume future market risks and allow for capitalization of further production. However, farmers, mining companies or lumber mills may attempt to sell directly at the local level and take the risk themselves, but they must sell in volume.

"Capital for enterprises could come from sources inside or outside the region. Banks would handle this function and lend start-up or operating capital to those who are beginning or already involved in enterprises. They would also lend to those who need to purchase homes, vehicles and others major items. Some capital would come from large insurers and from other private investors.

"As in any free market, many companies would raise capital by selling part interests in their enterprises to investors in the form of stocks and bonds. Investors would be paid dividends and/or capital gains for their portion of stock investment in the marketplace. Companies could incorporate and expand far beyond the confines of the region. They may also become conglomerates and hold many kinds of businesses. However, it is important that private corporations become concerned and actively involved with regional well-being.

"A region may have mineral, chemical or oil deposits. Obviously, communities must be located a sufficient distance from areas where resources are being extracted and processed. Fortunately, these resources are usually be found in areas that are

CHAPTER 3 - REGIONAL INFRASTRUCTURES & NETWORKS

remote from communities. During resource extraction and processing, environmental protection is mandatory no matter what the short term employment effects and economic impact may be. Loss of environment means loss of quality of life in the region's communities, and this exacts too high a cost, sometimes in lives lost."

Neos and Veritor have been listening carefully, and Veritor begins to talk about another aspect of the infrastructure."Effective distribution means ensuring that goods and services are made available to people at the community and neighborhood levels. In the regional concept, shopping centers with retail outlets and services would be designed to be integral with neighborhoods. Economy, accessibility and convenience are all prime considerations.

Services are especially essential in communities of industrial societies. There is a greater need for a variety of them because modern technology involves installation, maintenance and repair and a plethora of professional and technical services. The more affluent and complex a society, the more services are required. This means that any significant changes in such societies must be comprehensive because there would be a large amount of service inter-dependency."

Pragma notes, "Other vital services should be mentioned. Delivery of fuel, electricity and water are essential. People do not usually appreciate such services until they attempt to independently provide them. This often happens in third world countries, and it becomes very time and energy- consuming. Community or neighborhood collection and disposal of trash and waste are also essential. Imagine people in a modern society trying to individually dispose of or convert waste instead of working collectively to efficiently handle the problem. The greatest waste of all would be human resources."

Of all the infrastructures of the region there is a special one which must eventually exist in a society so that it will flourish and progress. This infrastructure has to do with the integration of advanced research and development in all fields. In the regional concept, networking is particularly relevant in such an infrastructure. Although this infrastructure is an integral part of the region, its scope transcends it. This scope includes direct interfaces with counterparts in other regions and countries.

It is critically important that government sponsor and support advanced research and development. Through its government, the public must be willing to assume the financial cost and risk of such research and development in order to grow, prosper and increase quality of life.

The direction is clear. Haphazard, highly fragmented, counter-productive and overly-secretive research and development must be replaced by a greater openness and a sharing of both information and credit for accomplishments. Of course, there may be monetary rewards involved, but these can also be shared by prior agreement. The important thing for humanity is to emphasize cooperation, rather than exploitation.

Neos, Pragma and Veritor are deeply immersed in this subject because it spells the difference in mankind's preparedness to cope with certain future major cataclysmic events. They realize that while some competitive spirit is highly beneficial, destructive rivalry is not.

Neos notes, "In my opinion, there are considerably more unsung heroes in research and development than Nobel prize winners. The latter reflect major accomplishments and deserved recognition. In the meantime, many hundreds of thousands continue to work long hours for humanity. Why not encourage them with greater support and reward them for what they give and we receive?"

"The idea of creating a massive research center in which universities, business, agriculture, industry and various government agencies would contribute, exchange information and derive knowledge is not without pitfalls," Pragma retorts." There are dangers in forming an all-powerful elite who are accountable to no one and who exclude the public's input. After all, they would be using public funds."

Veritor responds, "There is always that danger, but we are not talking about a dictatorship or a privileged elite who are aloof to the human condition around them. Foremost in any research and development must be the desire to serve mankind, to help people grow in a healthy, safe and relatively secure environment and to protect that environment in which we must all live. The noble search for higher knowledge must be uninhibited and open to reason, intuition and curiosity. The dynamic characteristics of the regional concept will provide the appropriate environment for this."

CHAPTER 3 - REGIONAL INFRASTRUCTURES & NETWORKS

Advanced Research and Development

The regional concept includes the advancement of research and development in many fields. It is not enough to limit such efforts to the private sector. The private sector, if motivated primarily by profit, is apt to remain isolated and protective in its research and development work.

There is a need for an inter-disciplinary regional research and development center with satellites whereby information, techniques and expensive equipment can be shared. It makes for cross-stimulation of ideas and saving in time, money and effort. It makes for the earlier introduction of findings for applied research in both the public and private sectors. Regionalization, in its integrating role, brings together and sponsors advanced research and development in conjunction with and in support of international, national and interregional like-minded entities.

No attempt to fully define these relationships can be made here, for only an indication of different areas of emphasis can be expressed. Neither can the complex linkages with the academic community be defined, only implied.

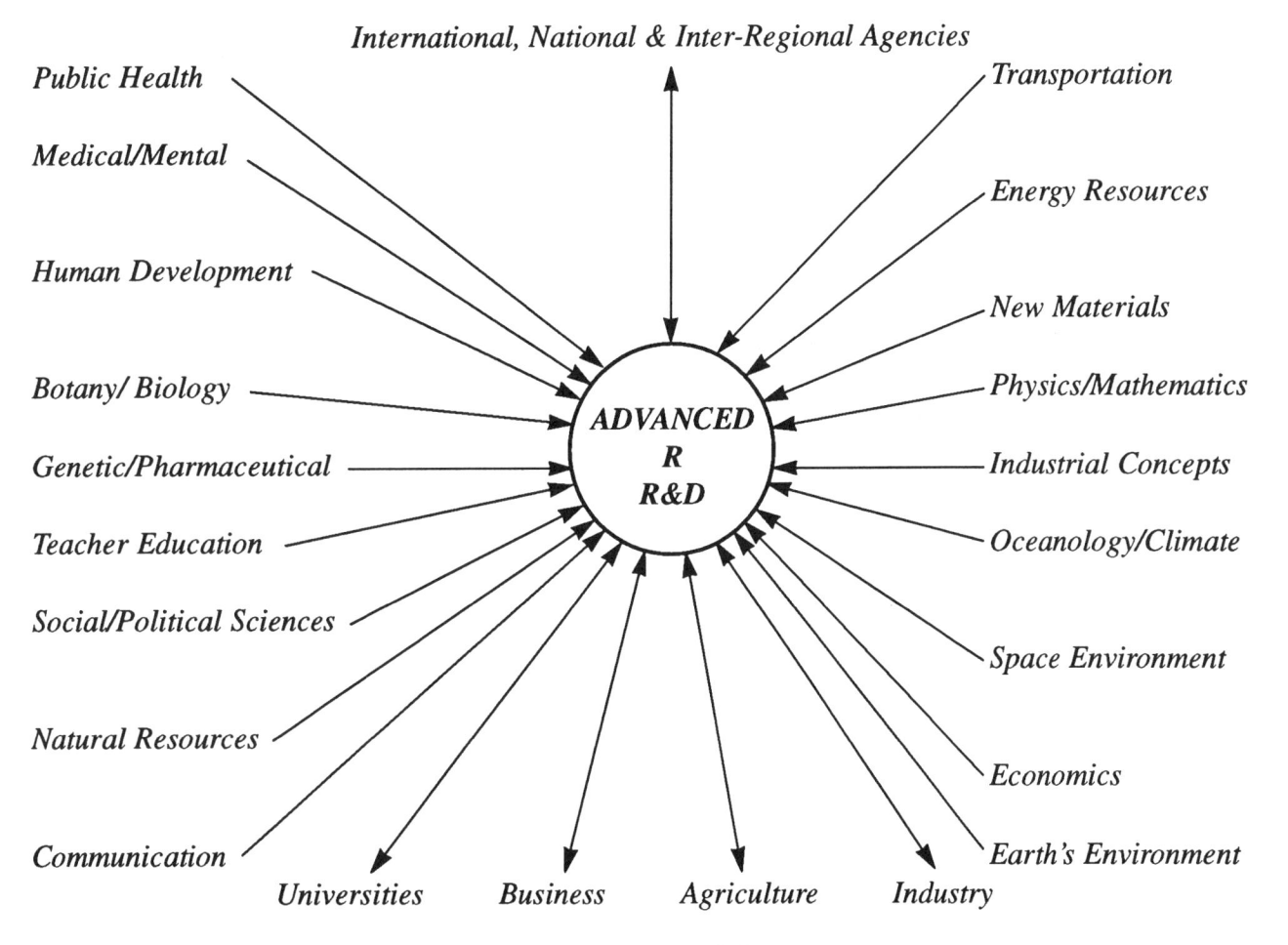

Figure III-3-S

Neos, Pragma and Veritor are silent for a moment. Veritor speaks, "There is something that we have glossed over in our discussion of infrastructures. We have not addressed relationships that have prevailed throughout history, that of humans and their belief systems. It includes organized and unorganized religions and those who profess no religion but are still ethical humanists.

An infrastructure that includes multi-religious aspects is Regional Network Group H which briefly mentions spiritual and cultural emphases and development in a society. Functionally and organizationally, religious groups often identify with each other, adhere to a common concept of God and express certain values, attitudes or doctrines of what human relationships ought to be. So, depending upon individual adherence and interpretation, spiritual and cultural considerations may positively influence behavior and participation in all aspects of living."

Pragma responds, "As it stands, there is a challenge to all religions to advocate and persuade, but not to impose their theological doctrines or perspectives on others. Regionalization not only accommodates more than one spiritual belief system, but also cultural mores and scientific findings in promoting openness, ethical behavior and a search for greater awareness. There are many facets to moral, productive and creative living."

Neos asserts, "The key to religions rests in what they have to offer and how people act on their beliefs. It seems to me that there are significant roles for religious groups to assume not only for the sake of their fellow religionists, but for society as a whole. It would be inconsistent and perhaps hypocritical to espouse social justice and humanitarianism and not pursue them in life's activities. For instance, will religious feelings carry over to alleviate suffering or to correct conditions that produce homelessness and hunger? Are the disabled and pain-ridden ignored and are spouses, the elderly and children cared for and not abused?"

Veritor nods in agreement and adds, "Ethical and moral behavior, rectitude and respect are needed in all walks of life. Neos, why don't you describe this further in a diagram?"

CHAPTER 3 - REGIONAL INFRASTRUCTURES & NETWORKS

Regional Multi-Belief Impact

The regional concept encourages ethical and moral concepts in the formation and operation of the infrastructures of the region. Different religious perspectives and beliefs add to the eclectic composition of a regional society. Religions can have a positive effect, but, by simple inspection, they cannot expect to control or direct the multiple, complex make-up of the infrastructure networks in a region or any other society. The impact of multiple religious application on major issues must be objective, not subjective. Therefore, the separation of church and state reflects greater wisdom. But any positive influence from religions indicates that they need to grow beyond ritualism, dogma, mysticism, beyond social isolation and beyond xenophobia. Religions can define and serve some larger purpose, and this is what counts.

EFFECT ON INFRASTRUCTURE NETWORKS

Social Acceptance ←

Social Harmony ←

Theater, Art & Music ←

Medicine ←

Mental Health ←

Family Development ←

Care of Homeless, Poor and Hungry ←

Care of Disabled & Pain-Ridden ←

Care of Elderly & Children ←

REGIONAL MULTI-BELIEF APPLICATIONS
* Social Justice
* Humanity
* Love
* Concern for Self & Others
* Morality
* Ethics
* Rectitude
* Universal Spirit

→ In Government

→ In the Courts

→ In the Legislature

→ In Law Enforcement

→ In Business and Commerce

→ In Communication

→ In Industry

→ In Education

→ In Occupational Selection

↓ In Promoting the Goals for Quality of Life

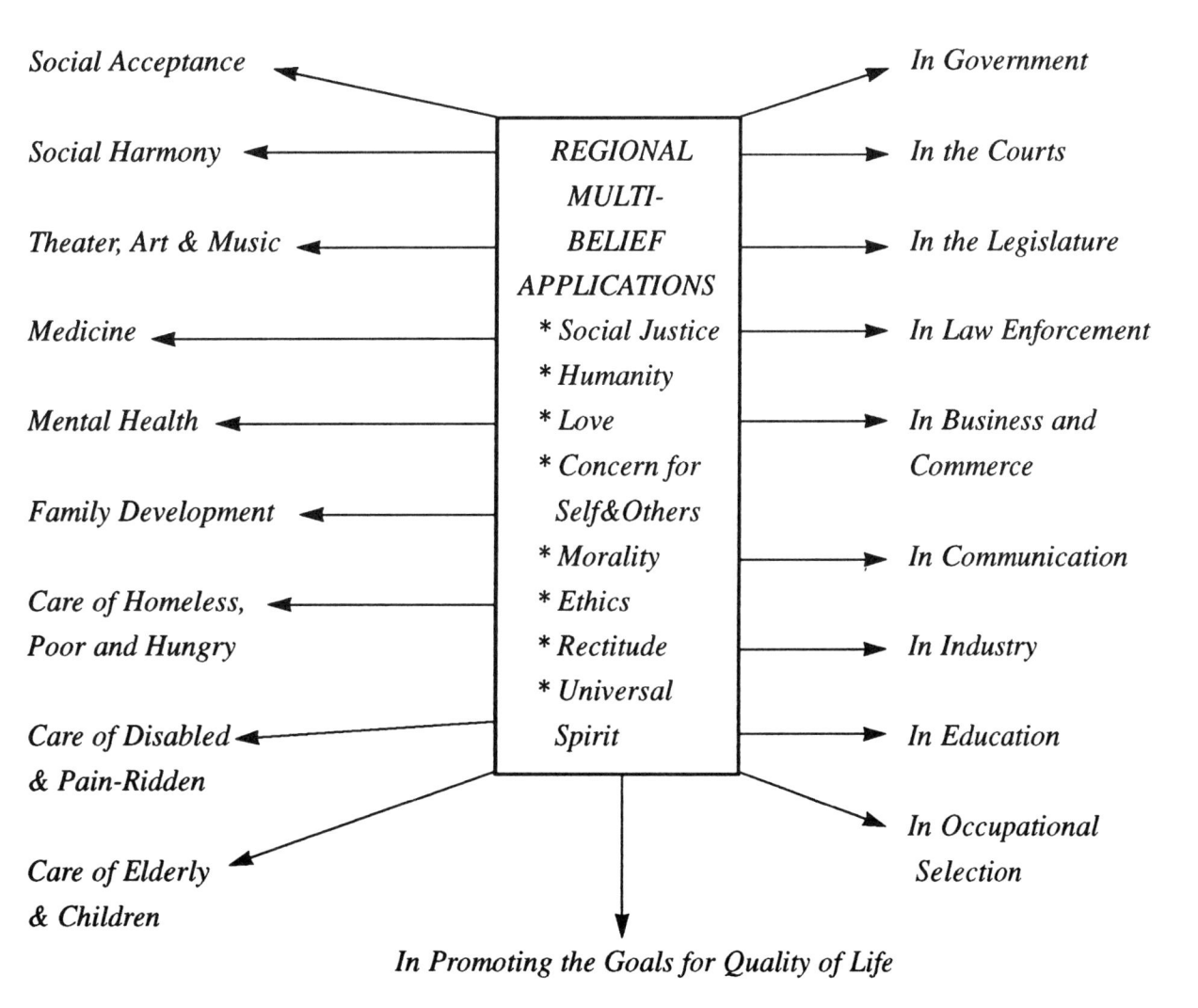

Figure III-3-T

The political aspects of the regional concept intrigue Neos, Pragma and Veritor. They cannot conceive of regionalization as a new political ideology although one could attempt to brand it. As such, the regional concept is an eclectic approach that encompasses diverse points of view and methods, political or otherwise, that contribute to a better quality of life. It is open to both dissimilar and congruent points of view because what constitutes a better quality of life may vary. Multifarious as it may be, regionalization emphasizes functional improvements to the infrastructures of societies so that they may flourish.

Neos begins, "The designs of regional infrastructures are undeniably based on the principles, organization and methods of government. It seems to me that this would qualify a region to be a political entity in the static sense of the word.

"In a dynamic or operational sense, the region includes many public and private institutions within infrastructure network groupings that have very many functional interfaces. As these functions are carried out, there are bound to be different political viewpoints and positions taken in making choices and taking actions. Some will advocate different kinds of changes, and others will oppose them. Some will say go faster, use more resources to achieve objectives, and others will say the opposite. Some will seek positions of control, and others will try to protect them. This is inevitable even in a philosophical, scientific or technological world."

Pragma responds, "It seems to me that the regional concept, itself, transcends a politicized approach which may swing from one extreme of total, absolute central control to the other extreme of anarchy or unconstrained individuality. I doubt that extremes of any kind will lead to a better collective quality of life for all humanity. How can regionalization, which advocates no extremes, account for those who would keep the status quo when their support is needed for vital changes? How can the transcendency of the region deal with hidden agendas, special interests and entrenchments within, near or above it ? Who knows how far fear of change and common growth will perversely undermine all good intentions?"

Veritor notes, "That scenario is possible, but the regional concept is our best hope. Maybe enough of these resisting elements will see personal gain in the emergence of the regional entity. Maybe it will take a crisis or series of natural, economic or social catastrophies to convince enough people that corrective changes are urgently imperative. Will timely foresight and actions be taken? Will hasty changes be made in a wasteful, fragmentary fashion? One thing is clear. The realities of harsh events will modify political perceptions."

Part III - Regional Design & Scenarios

CHAPTER 4 - THIRD WORLD INFRASTRUCTURES

The subject of regional infrastructures has been revolving about industrial, sometimes affluent countries. But much of the world and most of the regions to be developed are in Third World countries where lifestyles and beliefs are different. However, countries have much in common in terms of relief from human suffering and privation that are aggravated by the absence of adequate infrastructures.

Pragma is the first to speak. "Life is much less complex in many ways for people in Third World countries. Making a living and enduring hardship can be harsh and unforgiving, especially in hostile environments. There is greater reliance on the family or extended family. People are particularly vulnerable to the whims of both nature and other people. When they are adversely affected, they usually tolerate their lot in life with a sense of fatalism, grim humor and stoicism."

Veritor notes, "Religious, extremely wealthy, political elite or military leaders usually dominate Third World countries. These leaders serve as judges and jury and dictate how people must live according to the often limited codes of religious doctrine, economic expediency, ideological dogma or physical force. Such leaders vary in intelligence and skill, but are usually very decisive in such settings. Any existing governmental infrastructures involved are shaped and skewed to satisfy this dominance. However, there are severe limitations to the range of functions that can be performed by purely economic, theocratic or totalitarian governments. Therefore, much needed infrastructures shrink in scope or are absent. The functions of men, women and children are usually sharply defined in such societies. The full scope of quality of life, however, is missing."

Neos adds, "It seems to me that if regions are to be formed in such countries, the infrastructure networks would have to be regrouped because of existing political conditions. Otherwise, it would be very difficult to get their leaders to accept the regional concept. These countries have various patterns of social organization and established customs and rules ingrained in the population. There are severe peer limits placed on individual expression and development. So people in some of the Third World countries may have a natural reluctance to change."

"The infrastructures in some Third World countries are highly centralized and break down in hierarchal fashion to lower levels of control. When they are theocratic or totalitarian countries, conformity to authority is paramount. There are distinct, proscribed cooperative relationships and expectations. Life is lived by formulas, ritual and everyday occupational disciplines. Deviationists are severely punished."

Pragma notes, "As we examine both the theocratic and the totalitarian forms of government in many of the countries, we see that they have many things in common. Both can be militant and undemocratic. This is noticeable in their existing educational infrastructures and the way they govern. So regionalization has to consider that for theocracies, governmental functions pertaining to religious studies will have to be included because religious practice is mandatory. In totalitarian states, governmental functions are rigidly formulated, and in order to maintain power and control, military force is used. People are conditioned to protect the state from dissenters within and from enemies without. We can see that members of their legislative bodies and their courts follow the dictates of the ruling party."

Veritor reflects on this. "The communication infrastructure is a key area that is controlled by the leadership to manipulate information and to retain power. Freedom of expression in both forms of government is restricted, and this extends to what is taught in their schools and what is found in their libraries."

Neos adds, "We can see that if regional concepts are eventually incorporated, many changes would have to take place. There would have to be much greater emphasis on social services to help disadvantaged and disabled people. Extensive improvements in the delivery of health care and medical treatment would also be necessary, especially in efforts to reach out to the many who are neglected and ignored."

Pragma notes, "It is apparent that most of the infrastructures we have discussed are suitable in any country. Administrative functions, public works, medical services, law enforcement, communications and transportation are fundamental."

Veritor adds, "Of course, the environmental infrastructure would be an added responsibility in new regional development in these countries. The development and protection of land, air and water and conservation of existing resources are in the best interests of any country. This also goes for the upgrading of technology, manufacturing, processing and the appropriate handling of resources."

Neos concludes the discussion. "It would be interesting to see how responsive these non-democratic countries would be to the changes mandated by regionalization. If they did accept them, I suspect that many of them would eventually evolve into pluralistic societies and become democracies."

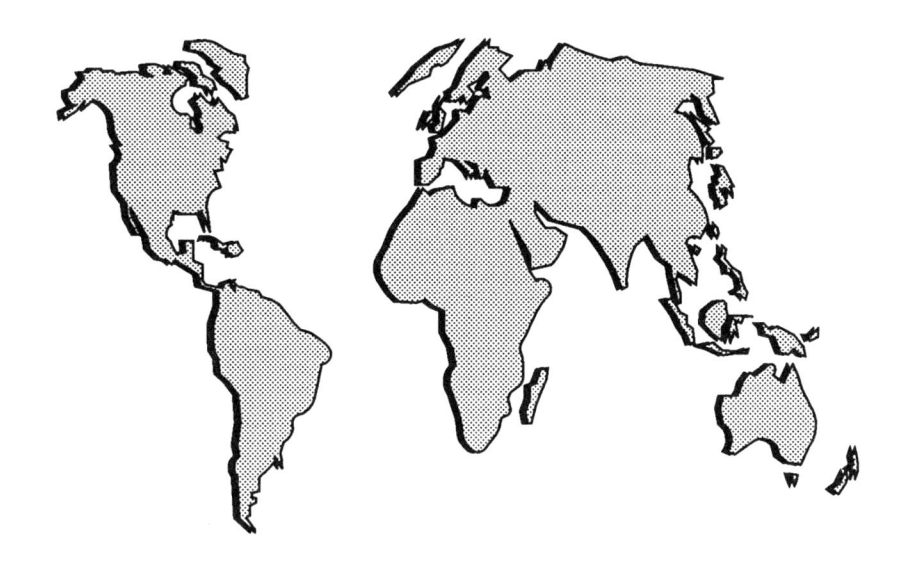

PART IV
Preparation For Tomorrow

Part IV - Preparation For Tomorrow

CHAPTER 1 - REGIONAL PREPARATIONS

There are compelling reasons for addressing global resources and environmental conditions in a comprehensive way. One is that non-renewable resources are finite and must be managed prudently without reckless exploitation. Another is that the natural environment will be called upon to support an ever-increasing population and accommodate regional resettlement. It must be restored in general and prepared to meet that demand.

World wide implementation of regionalization will necessitate extensive design and planning as well as raising billions of dollar in funds. Fund raising must be accomplished over an extended period as regionalization is implemented worldwide. As assets accumulate to develop selected regions, implementation phases must be expeditiously initiated. Countries with the greatest assets would be expected to rapidly take the lead.

The progressive and successful implementation of regions will serve as a model to encourage and accelerate efforts worldwide. If there is sufficient vision and will power, the rate of completions should match projected population increases by the year 2020 when 7.7 billion people are expected to inhabit the earth! If the countries of the world are indifferent, unthinkable human suffering, resource scarcities and environmental devastation are predicted. These severe problems would require draconian measures to compensate for human profligacy.

If world population projections prove to be reliable, 5,000 regions, including modifications of existing cities, must be implemented by the year 2020. This is a formidable undertaking, but what other acceptable alternatives exist? Would they not be many times more overwhelming and costly? Should mankind wait and see?

Although regionalization is targeted for both urban and rural areas, large, sparsely populated areas must first be enhanced and developed to improve conditions at potential sites that are candidates for selection. Fringes of barren areas must receive attention to correct land and water resource waste and to prevent the spread of desertification. Trees and shrubs must be introduced for climate modification, soil stabilization and as renewable resources. Long range development and general restoration of areas contiguous to possible regional sites is necessary. The rate of preparation and implementation of regionalization must be greater for specific areas of each continent where prevailing population pressures are more acute.

Regional designs for specific areas on each continent must also be compatible with local geographical features, physical anomalies, level of technological development, natural and human resources, cultures and customs, climate and, of course, political systems.

The basis for estimating required regions are provided in Table IV-1-A, Proposed Apportionment of Regions; Table IV-1-B, Regional Development Rate; and a presentation sheet, Estimate of Regional Needs Worldwide on the following pages.

. . .

Neos is particularly eager to face the challenges of regionalization and notes,"Fortunately, many competent people have been addressing all aspects of world resources utilization and environmental conditions. An increasing number of public and private entities have been defining and discussing critical world problems in such areas, and they have been gradually accumulating abundant, persuasive information. Their scientific findings and observations must be taken seriously, and new innovations like regionalization must be initiated to reflect them. It's time to make changes, correct harmful practices and curb excesses. If the nations of the world wait too long, all they will be able to do is record a history of ignored opportunities."

Proposed Apportionment of Regions

Continents

	Africa	So. America	No. America	Europe	Asia	Australia	Other	Total
Pop.1990	646,389,000	290,014,000	416,664,000	715,233,800	3,132,638,000	16,820,000	-	5.3 Bil.
2020	1,131,200,000	435,000,000	521,000,000	894,000,000	4,700,000,000	21,025,000	-	7.7 Bil.
1995	2	1	2	2	3	1	1	Intially
2000	6	2	4	6	10	2	2	Accrued
2005	24	6	10	24	60	3	4	Accrued
2010	96	32	48	72	300	5	10	Accrued
2015	288	90	144	216	1500	8	24	Accrued
2020	700	280	335	580	3050	14	41	Accrued

1995A total of 5000 regions is the goal by the year 2020

Table IV-1-A

Regional Development Evolvement

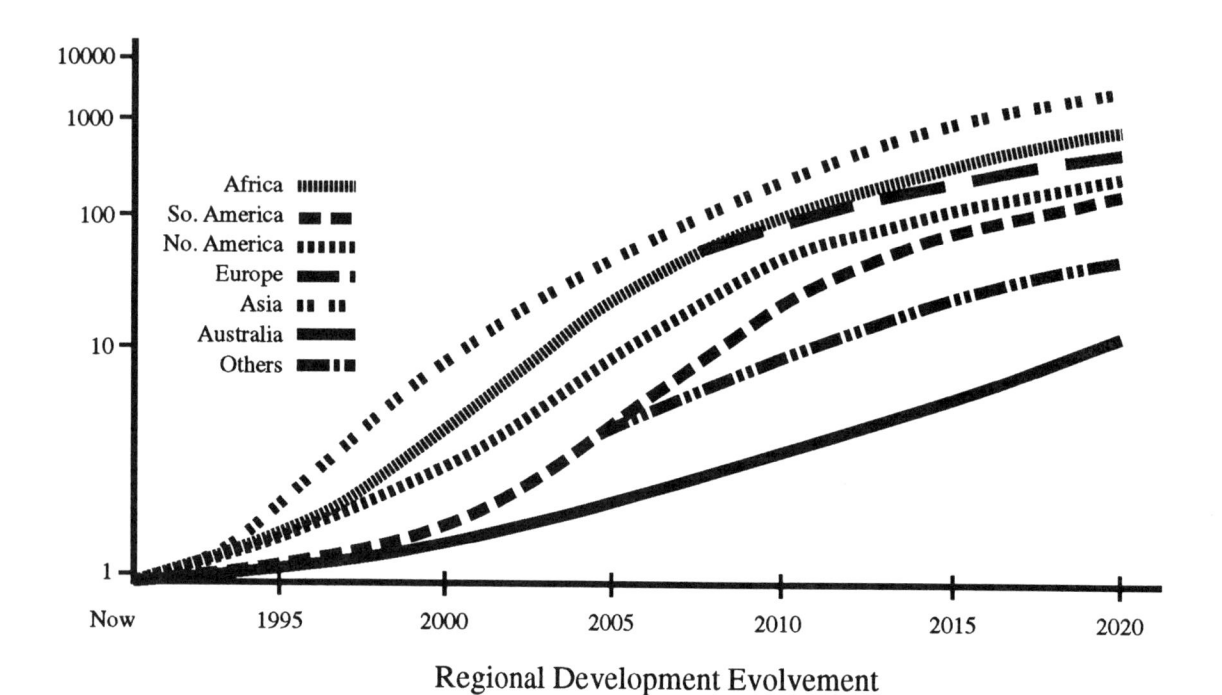

Table IV-1-B

CHAPTER 1 - REGIONAL PREPARATIONS

Estimate of Regional Needs World Wide
(Initial Computations)

Will there be enough potential land to establish regional sites in the 21st century?

- Each region accommodates a community network and various centers for a tentative population of about 1.5 million people living within approximately 600 square miles. This area offers the prospect of sufficient key resources, a favorable environment and arable land for agriculture to support the network of communities and special centers within each region.
- The maximum arable land existing worldwide is 3.1 billion hectares or 12 million square miles (derived from Figure IV 2-A). Only a portion of this arable land is appropriate for regional site selection. The rest would remain open range and some crop land.
- Selected sites are likely to encompass rivers, lakes, coastal areas and certain interior areas where ample aquifers exist. Earth's rivers alone, according to estimates, have an influence on 1.1 billion hectares or 4.3 million square miles of land.
- Loss of potentially habitable lands through desertification seriously limits site selection options unless restoration is undertaken. Another 10% of the 1.1 billion hectares of currently usable land may be lost through desertification, leaving a net area of only 1.0 billion hectares or 3.8 million square miles. *
- Number of regions ultimately available in the 21st century worldwide is: 3.8 million sq.miles / 600 sq. miles per region or 6450 regions.
- Total number of people ultimately accommodated worldwide would be: 6450 regions x 1.5 million people per region or 9.7 billion people. (This population may be reached by 2050.)
- Approximately 5000 regions involving 7.7 billion people by the year 2020 are assumed to be the target for planning purposes in an effort to reduce the adverse effects of long-term global over-population and over-concentrations.

Food and Population, Roger Revelle, Scientific American, Sept.1974
**Desertification of Arid Lands*, H.E. Dregne, Harvard Academic Publishers, N.Y. 1983

Part IV - Preparation for Tomorrow

CHAPTER 2 - FEEDING THE WORLD

Veritor begins the conversation. "I am concerned with world prospects for feeding a vast number of people. Will there actually be enough arable land and productive seas to provide food for 7.7 billion people by the year 2020? What about the likelihood of even more people in subsequent years? Even today, with 5.3 billion people on earth, millions die of famine, dehydration and malnutrition. We are faced with not only the need to grow and harvest more food, but to create new means for protecting, storing, processing and distributing it. Distribution will be particularly critical as the population densities of many more supercities increase."

Neos adds, "Some people have a great abundance of food, while others know only the bitter pangs of hunger and starvation. I have heard that 15 million people die from hunger each year and another 300 million barely exist, unable to help themselves. Disparities can be witnessed even within individual countries. I anticipate further increases in population, mostly concentrated in food-scarce areas, where catastrophes of much greater magnitude than today will take place. It's a vicious cycle. Weak from hunger and riddled with disease, malnourished people become ineffectual in producing food. Outsiders who attempt to help them are faced with daunting problems. Helping such people to eventually help themselves is a universal challenge. I believe that now is the time to act, long before crises of great magnitude happen."

Pragma asks, "How much potential arable land is there in the world? How many people can it sustain? Will there be enough arable land to not only support 7.7 billion people by the year 2020 but 9.7 billion by the year 2050? Even if the land and its resources could be eventually developed to provide for 40 billion people, what would our world be like then? Would there be any quality of life left? Wouldn't there be the need for extreme regimentation and constraints, people living elbow to elbow. Would people live in a world that has become a prison and then a grave?"

Neos responds, "Your questions are very troubling, Pragma. This may be an appropriate time to briefly review the status of arable land in the world."

CHAPTER 2 - FEEDING THE WORLD

World Land Cultivation
(Quick Summary of Arable Land)

<u>Utilization</u>
- Total arable land is 24% of the earth's total land mass of 57.3 million square miles.
- Cultivation potential of arable land:

				Available per person:
For Africa	32.0%	500 million hectares	*	1.0 hectares
So. America	21.6%	370	*	.9
No. America	53.3%	450		1.4
Europe	88.2%	170		.3
Asia (w/Russia, etc.)	85.8%	315		.2
Australia	16.6%	120		4.8

Total Potential = 2,425 million hectares or 9.37 million square miles
* Can be increased several times with increased irrigation.

- About 20% (640 million hectares) of non-arable land is in the Humid Tropics.
- Another 10% (240 million hectares) of arable land needs irrigation.
- An additional 26% (630 million hectares with water) remains uncultivated because of economic, institutional and socio-political constraints.
- The presently available 2,426 million hectares can be possibly increased by 26% to 3.1 billion hectares or 12 million square miles.
- Efficiency of farming can be greatly improved by irrigation and by use of fertilizers. (approx. 50%). Other contributions come from crop rotation, insect/rodent/disease control, improved storage and improved distribution to market.
- World food banks are needed in the short run, and modern agriculture and intensification of food research are necessary for the long run.(R.Revelle)
- Relatively inexpensive fertilizers as well as fuels for running pumps, machine operation and food processing are needed, probably from petroleum refining or oil producing algae.
- There is a strong correlation between increased nutrition per capita and a reduction in human fertility. Could this be that human need to over-propagate is a natural or perceived response to compensate for high death rates, especially among children?

- References:
  1. Atlas of the World, 6th Edition , National Geographic Society.
  2. Food and Population , Roger Revelle, Scientific American, Sept.1974.
  3. State of the World , 1989,1990,1991, World Watch Institute Report on Progress Toward a Sustainable Society.
  4. The World Food Problem , 1967 Report, Pres. Johnson's Science Advisory Committee

Figure IV-2-A

Veritor listens and says, "A great deal of land on each continent is primarily used for grazing. During prolonged droughts, grazing animals like sheep and goats closely crop the grass causing top soil to become exposed to drying conditions and to be easily blown away."

Neos also notes, "Millions of people live marginal existences partly because they are heavily reliant on such grazing animals for food as well as other basic uses. In Africa's sub-Sahara, rapid desertification is taking place because of overgrazing and land misuse. It seems to me it would be wise for these people to try to change from a dependency on grazing animals to the production of poultry, fish and other protein foods."

Pragma counters, "That may not be easy. Getting people of different cultures to alter their eating habits and food preferences can be a difficult thing to accomplish. Even though they may be hungry, some people need to be weaned before they are able to tolerate certain new kinds of food. These people are also reluctant to give up other benefits that come from raising sheep, goats and cattle, such as wool, leather and milk."

Veritor observes, "Perhaps adaptation is the key factor. In order to survive, people must learn about and try new ways of living. A number of dedicated international agencies have been trying to introduce new products, methods and approaches for growing food and other necessities in Third World countries with varying success."

"How people utilize land reflects their adaptability," Neos offers. "Mixing and rotating different kinds of crops and controlled grazing and feeding of livestock remove much of the risk. Farmers would realize greater independence and security. It seems to me that when land is only put to a single use, the farmer's crop becomes more vulnerable to certain diseases and variables in weather like drought, hail, high winds and heavy, prolonged rains. Growing only limited kinds of food depletes the land, top soil disappears and fertility is lost. All of this has been known to agriculturists for a long time."

Pragma adds, "Confronted with harshness in their lives, many people become fatalistic and accept all that happens to them as pre-ordained. They fail to appreciate their own potential for making decisions and creating new opportunities necessary to improve their lives."

Neos asks, "I wonder why more people don't begin to develop fish ponds, raise fowl and grow other edible things? This can be done in small areas. Raising pigs is also advantageous in crowded areas. China and other countries have been doing this for years. Although some cultures and religions prohibit the raising of pigs for food, there are many advantages to the barnyard approach because less energy is used in producing a greater variety of nutritional foods. Wastes can also become fertilizer to enhance soil and improve yields of nearby crops. This arrangement has been proven to

CHAPTER 2 - FEEDING THE WORLD

be both necessary and effective."

Veritor observes some other factors. "We have only briefly alluded to fish farming, but the development of fish stocks, as an alternative way to obtain protein food, can take place in nearby rivers and lakes as well as in man-made fish ponds. Hatcheries, however, are probably required for special experimental studies on the growing of different species that show economic promise by rapidly multiplying and increasing in size. There has been considerable development in fish farming worldwide, especially on the Pacific rim. Aquaculture produces about 10% of fishery products."

Pragma notes,"People who inhabit islands and coastlines have been catching fish by a variety of methods, many highly innovative and practicable. However, overfishing, diminishing supplies of ocean nutrients, changing water salinity and temperature and polluted conditions have forced some fishermen to range far out to sea because local waters are no longer productive. This also discourages small operations because the type of fishing gear required and boats required are too expensive."

Neos returns to the subject of regional preparation. "Naturally, a region must have the capacity to supply its own population with enough food. If there are surpluses to sell, trade or store, so much the better. In many parts of the world growing enough food to feed the local population is a full time occupation and little energy is left over to do much else. But let's go on to another aspect of regional preparation, that of the management of water in agriculture. Although much has already been learned about hydrology and soil composition, in many areas of the world, salt left in the ground after flooding is a severe problem."

Pragma responds, "Yes, good soil composition and water resources are both essential. Fertile soil can be ruined by improper irrigation and drainage causing salts to accumulate at the surface. For one thing, it is best to use a drip feed method or to flood only the narrow furrows between plants. There is no value in watering weeds. Water must be directed to the plant roots and allowed to percolate and drain. The condition of the subsurface soil and slope of the land must also be considered. Earth-moving equipment provided by the region would help prepare the land for proper drainage and distribution channels."

Veritor observes, "Although different types of cooperative arrangements already exist in many countries, an improved regional agricultural infrastructure would provide planning, help resolve problems and improve coordination of farming activities in the region."

Pragma answers, "Many individual farmers have limited knowledge and options in agronomy and would benefit considerably from a regional agricultural infrastructure. Skilled, hard-working farmers laboring alone may suffer losses from such things as plant pestilence, disease and water shortages. With regional development, water catchments would be developed to store water or to recycle run-off water. Large area coverage for pestilence and disease control would be possible and provide an effective way to reduce agricultural risks."

Veritor thinks about farmers who live in arid and desert-like countries and asks,"What happens to good intentions and hard work when persistent dust storms inundate crops? Many countries, even non-arid ones, are subject to droughts. The usual efforts to irrigate or utilize other watering methods under such conditions often become futile. Where and how do these dust storms originate? Can anything be done for these susceptible areas?"

Pragma quickly responds,"Unfortunately, the origin of many such dust storms are hundreds of miles away. Seasonal heat creates convection winds. They whip up dust and sand which penetrate good farm land and smother fields along the way. Crops perish, and millions of lives are imperiled. Also, the continued loss of trees and vegetation aggravates the situation. Poor agricultural practices also contribute to desertification and reflect a long term abuse of the land. Without ground cover the remaining top soil dries out and is carried away."

Neos nods and asserts, "New methods must be attempted on a grand scale to deal with dust bowls and desertification. The problems are both regional and inter-regional. large multi-national approaches are the only way to solve them or at least reduce their severity. It's quite evident many countries must learn to collaborate in common efforts to stem the desertification tide.

"Particularly high convection winds prevail for many large areas. High wind velocities near the surface of the ground cause dry particulates to become airborne. These areas could be sprayed with waste petroleum or other binding materials to make the material heavier and resistant. This would help stabilize some of the vast surfaces where dust storms originate. A second thing that could be done would be to reduce the velocity of the generating winds by erecting intermittent barriers like wire mesh and deflectors, especially where dunes are forming and drifting to endanger habitations. A third approach would be to strategically locate sand traps (mesh, fences, etc.) to slow down dune growth. If sand intrusion has been sufficiently slowed, another method could be to plant hardy grasses and shrubs followed by appropriate trees in an attempt to recapture land."

CHAPTER 2 - FEEDING THE WORLD

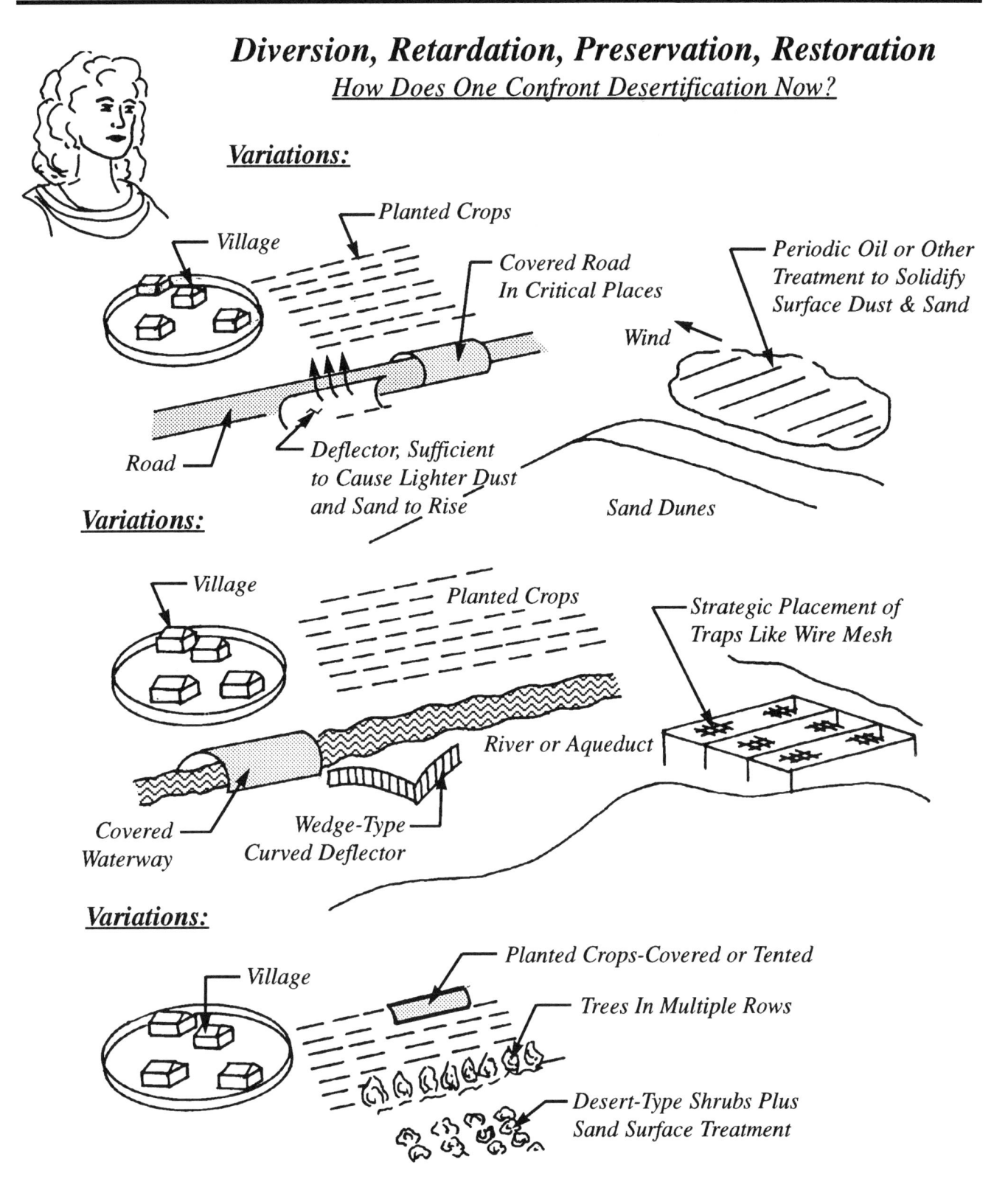

Diversion, Retardation, Preservation, Restoration
How Does One Confront Desertification Now?

Variations:

- Village
- Planted Crops
- Covered Road In Critical Places
- Periodic Oil or Other Treatment to Solidify Surface Dust & Sand
- Wind
- Road
- Deflector, Sufficient to Cause Lighter Dust and Sand to Rise
- Sand Dunes

Variations:

- Village
- Planted Crops
- Strategic Placement of Traps Like Wire Mesh
- Covered Waterway
- Wedge-Type Curved Deflector
- River or Aqueduct

Variations:

- Village
- Planted Crops-Covered or Tented
- Trees In Multiple Rows
- Desert-Type Shrubs Plus Sand Surface Treatment

Figure IV-2-B

Pragma reacts, "These sound like major undertakings. Would they be worth it? Much capital and a great expenditure of human resources would be needed. Who would be likely to attempt such enterprises?"

Veritor responds to this. "Of course it has to be worth it. Think of the valuable arable land that is threatened when the desertification process is allowed to go on? What areas would be left for people to grow food? It's a matter of survival. It is apparent that many nations and their regions must continue to try new experiments to control desertification."

Pragma changes the subject. "Mankind faces many other land preservation problems which also warrant our consideration. The Amazon comes to mind. Hundreds of thousands of farmers and cattlemen are cutting down enormous sections of rainforest. New dirt roads continuously penetrate the interior. Bulldozing and a slash and burn process are used to claim more land to raise food. Unfortunately, the soil only remains fertile for a few years, and then its nutrients play out and people are forced to move on. Rainforests are abundant in nutrient mainly in their tree canopies far above the forest floor. Materials drop from the canopies to supply ground nutrients in a fragile eco-system. Receding water from seasonal floods and myriad streams and tributaries carries many of these nutrients and top soil to the Amazon river to be held in suspension or become part of its sediment."

Veritor notes, "I think that the silted bottom of this enormous river holds what could become material for new top soil for redistribution over spent farmland. However, as sediment, it is depleted of oxygen and larger particulates to prevent it from caking under the hot tropical sun. Perhaps it's also deficient in certain necessary nutrients to make the land fertile once more."

CHAPTER 2 - FEEDING THE WORLD

Top Soil Replacement for Cleared Tropical Lands

Depletion of the top soil of land cleared from rainforests is rapid. Its fertility is but a few years, prompting further burn and slash destruction of this world resource. Replacement of the top soil with balanced, enriched dredgings creates a new, much needed industry of considerable potential to better the lives of the inhabitants.

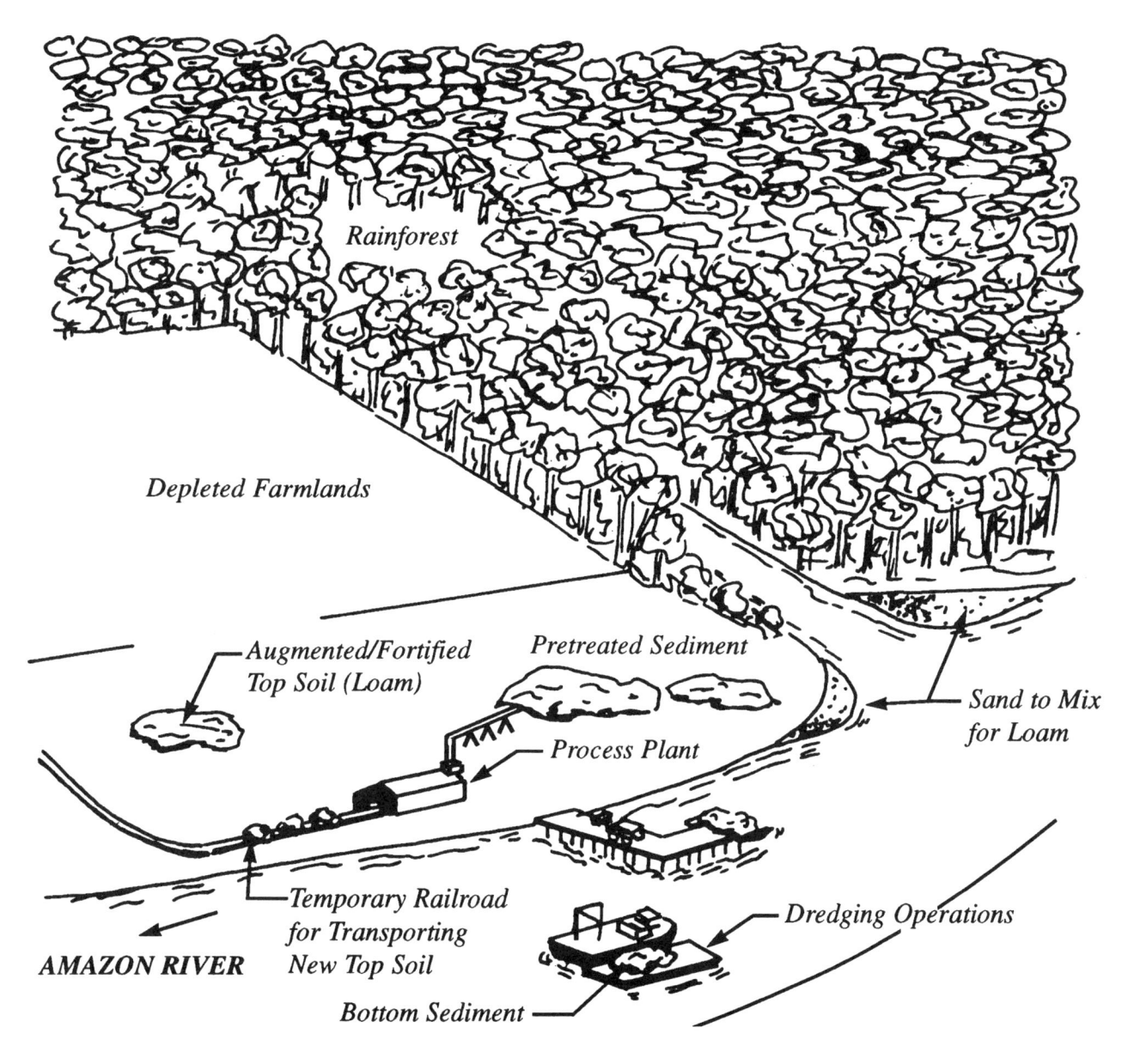

Figure IV-2-C

Neos responds, "I don't see this as a major problem. The sediment is abundant, and its excavation could provide a balanced growing medium by adding amendments. To promote restoration of the land, a number of new industries could be formed under the aegis of the regions. It is a value-added process that would involve the participation of a great workforce and result in considerable benefit to the regional inhabitants."

Pragma adds, "This process could also spawn a number of related enterprises. I can see such activities organized on a regional and inter-regional basis. This would most likely impel related infrastructures to develop special new operations and provide community network development."

Veritor brightens. "I would not be surprised to find that during the continuous dredging operations, precious metals and other valuable by-products would be recovered. Also, sand banks and bars would be removed as navigational obstructions and provide materials for subsequent mixing with sediment to produce loam. Disturbing the bottom may even expose food to attract fish."

Neos answers, "I like the idea. Dredging operations and fishing operations would co-exist. This kind of thinking is consistent with a comprehensive systems approach that is part of the regional concept."

Pragma also nods approval. "Enterprises often attempt to produce a single product or accomplish a single task which may then make them market sensitive or environmentally unsound. When a systems approach is not used, capital investments are apt to be poorly utilized. I think major expenditures should be made for installations designed to accommodate more than one use, if possible."

Veritor adds, "We need to mention another major benefit that could accrue from land restoration. The remaining rainforests should be conserved as a valuable asset and protected from those who would continue despoiling them. The argument is stronger for the inhabitants to preserve the Amazon for its eco-systems in meeting long term local and global needs. Long term thinking must prevail."

Both Pragma and Neos enthusiastically agree. Neos states, "When many different interests are involved, a regional approach is the best way to provide coordination, integration and regulation for the common good. A regional entity would allow its inhabitants to have a voice in making commitments and would encourage more people to assume responsibilities."

Pragma is pensive. "I think reckless and greedy mining and lumber operations will still despoil the rain forests. Such operations must be controlled and better use given to the forest. Rainforest eco-systems contain myriad, potentially valuable and life-saving plants and other living things found nowhere else. Why destroy them? Their diversity is essential for mankind and the world's future."

CHAPTER 2 - FEEDING THE WORLD

Veritor also reacts to this. "The Amazon tropical rainforests are a treasure trove of biological diversity. Scientists derive knowledge from the wealth of botanical varieties and the multitude of creatures that subsist on them. Mankind is still learning about the evolutionary processes of extremely valuable and diverse biota in place. Even as ignorance, arrogance and greed continue to destroy the forests, ways must be found to impress on hundreds of thousands of people living in the Amazon that there are better ways to not only earn a living but to have a better life. They will need much assistance, however."

Neos notes, "It's been suggested that people should be more involved in the profitable management and utilization of the forest. Science-related surveys, special cultivation of crops for new foods and medicinals must also be undertaken. Special aerial tramways and walkways could be installed for tourism which would provide employment for many people."

Veritor suggests, "Our discussion of the Amazon can only introduce some of the critical agricultural aspects that are involved. Obviously, population pressures are a major issue. People need land for farming, and the rainforest is there for the taking as long as it lasts. Regionalization with its comprehensiveness and openness to new ideas and ventures would offer hope for the future of the Amazon and all other biospheres in the world where population increases and unplanned development invite environmental and social destruction."

A Different View of the Amazon
(An Alternative or Complement to Agricultural Dependency)

Operation of rain forest-related enterprises that respects and enhances the Amazon's environment offers far better alternatives to the slash and burn clearing of land, heavy indiscriminate logging, open pit river-clogging and polluting mining operations and other single-minded profit-driven activities that currently prevail. Brazil has the jurisdiction and prime responsibility for the development, conservation and protection of the Amazon. Brazil alone, however, cannot bear the full burden of economic pressure and social decay that drives its people to seek woefully short-sighted remedies. Exploiting and destroying a treasure so important to the world is an enormous crime against all humanity. Access to the Amazon must be controlled to allow preservation and the assurance of future benefits and productivity. When a policy of ceaseless road building began to "open up" the rainforests, it encouraged greed, desperate hope, and escape from over-crowded cities. A second look must be given to this policy because it is bankrupt and prevents many other things that are more valuable from taking place. Preferable uses of the Amazon do not require intrusive road building and destruction.

The preferred use of the Amazon is in the development of:
- *enterprises involving botanical research for agriculture and medical purposes.*
- *facilities and programs for tourism.*
- *highly regulated logging industries for local use in the manufacture of products like furniture and building products.*
- *scientific programs involving eco-systems and employing local inhabitants.*
- *fish farming cooperatives utilizing native fish of commercial value.*
- *cottage industries to make use of miscellaneous forest products.*
- *highly regulated mining operations on a scale that allows cooperatives to be formed, licensed and held responsible for environmental protection.*
- *small farming cooperatives that make use of scientific methods without reverting to slash and burn procedures.*

Access to the forest for all development would be limited to :
- *waterways using powered and non-powered shallow-bottomed vessels.*
- *self-propelling carriers above the forest floor using aerial cables.*
- *limited, all weather roads to specific permanent sites (if abandoned, roads must allow forests to regain natural status) and for law enforcement..*
- *Helicopter travel to pads strategically located for specific, legitimate purposes.*
- *Small aircraft flights to airstrips strategically located for safety stops.*
- *Limited, light weight "walkways" above the forest canopy for research and special harvesting.*
- *Small foot paths on special pontoon boardwalks that float during flooding season.*

CHAPTER 2 - FEEDING THE WORLD

"Preservation of topsoil is a major problem throughout the world," states Pragma. "When this is due to to poor farming practices, it may be because there is a reluctance to expend the extra effort to create soil banks or to practice methods that prevent erosion. Nutrients are lost with such erosion, requiring greater efforts to raise food."

Veritor answers, "Recent significant discoveries in agriculture offer alternative ways to improve nutrients in the soil. One method has been to plant legume seeds that have been treated with Rhizobium bacteria. This increases the plant's capacity to fix nitrogen. Approaches like this have proven highly effective. Also, by rotating crops with those usually planted, nitrogen and other nutrients can replenish the soil and foods can be produced with greater yields. Of course, wiser use of the land means conserving water as well."

Neos volunteers, "It is amazing to see how much has been done to make plants resistant to insects and diseases. Genetically altered crops can even be made to flourish in briny water. The Third World, in particular, has a great deal of saline land that can be used for growing hardy, salt-tolerant plants called halophytes."

Veritor adds, "Also, many arid parts of the world could benefit from genetic research. Knowledge gained from such research could become invaluable in reducing famine and malnutrition, especially during periods of drought or disease. Genetic research is an essential investment for economic and humanitarian reasons."

Neos responds, "I would like to mention some successful experiments in the use of halophytes that have taken place in different areas of the world."

Growing Crops With Salt Water *

The halophytes or salt-water-tolerant plants offer promise for the 21st century. New sources of food supplies, increased employment and a contribution to soil reclamation and anti-desertification are prospective benefits. Some halophytes have been used in ancient cultures; others are the result of genetic research in bio-technology. The following are some examples:

Distichlis Salicornia Sporobolis	- Flora of southwestern United States; seeds are pounded into flour and oil extract.
Zostera marina	- Seeds pounded into flour by Seri Indians
Palmer's salt grass	- Used in the California Gulf by Cocopa Indians; pounded into flour for bread.
Others	- Salt water leaf protein extracted for seawater candy and to improve traditional foods in Sri Lanka.
Tomatoes, melons, cotton	- Specially grown in Israel **
Kalar grass	- Foodstuff for livestock in Pakistan
Salicornia	- Produces safflower-type oil in Mexico
Quandong tree	- Produces cherry-like fruit in Australia
Derived halophytes	- Application of genes for enhancing asparagus and some strains of wheat, with tolerance for barley and rice.
Conventional crops Galapogas tomato derivations	- Cross-breeding with conventional tomato to grow in salt water.

Thirty nations are currently involved in saline agriculture!

* *Research News,* Science Magazine, Vol. 248, May 25, 1990
** *Also barley, rye, Italian millet, alfalfa, ladino clover, tramira field mustard, sugar cane, some reedsand rushes, Burmuda grass, dropseed, saltgrass, etc. show good salt tolerance. Sandy or gravelly soils are needed. -"Salt Water Agriculture", H. Boyko, Scientific American, Mar.1967*

CHAPTER 2 - FEEDING THE WORLD

Pragma continues the conversation. "Aren't great quantities of food spoiled, lost, and wasted because of distribution difficulties?"

Neos responds, "Yes, there are many problems involved in the harvesting, preservation, processing and delivery of produce. Harvesting may be too slow, allowing greater exposure of crops to destructive elements such as heavy rains, hail, floods, hot dry winds before they can be stored and protected. Also, insects, rodents, birds, livestock and wild animals have a greater chance to consume part of the exposed harvest.

"Expediting the safe storage of harvested crops doesn't necessarily require sophisticated equipment, just imagination. For instance, crops can be placed in safe, short term storage in the field or they can be moved by temporary aerial or ground conveyors to special areas for quick transfer to trucks or bins as harvesting progresses. This is important as many parts of the world do not have an abundance of good roads. Smaller, simpler and more manageable systems would be a practical alternative to large machinery. Of course, there are other ways available to transport food. Those who live near lakes, rivers, canals or ocean shorelines have been using boats, rafts and other means since earliest times. Regionalization, incidentally, would provide canals for multiple use as a part of an overall scheme."

Veritor notes, "People cling to long established habits of harvesting. Therefore, new effective approaches should be easy to demonstrate. A major concern of mine is the spoilage that occurs during storage and transportation to market. In hot climates, refrigeration is not likely to be available for individual farmers, but farm collectives may be able to buy and maintain freezers and refrigerators."

Neos answers, "There are many ways to preserve food such as curing, freeze drying, wax coating, vacuum packing, sealing, pickling, cold storage, radiation as well as additives like salt, sugar and many different chemicals. The wealthier, more developed countries have modern storage and food processing plants. Unfortunately, the machinery and equipment for many of these processes are beyond the financial means of many people."

Veritor reflects for a moment and says, "During our discussion on food, I have been thinking about how advantageous solar energy applications could be in this area. I think solar equipment will increasingly provide converted energy for not only growing food, but for harvesting, processing, shipping, consuming and converting waste. Even now solar energy panels have been used to provide refrigeration needed for shipping. The possibilities are numerous."

Neos suggests, "Perhaps simple solar energy ovens could be used for drying, roasting, curing or pre-cooking the fresh produce in Third World countries. Such ovens already exist in some Asiatic countries for this purpose. Do you think that even this uncomplicated method may still cost too much for many farmers and processors of food in poor countries?"

Pragma nods in agreement and adds, "Regional infrastructures, in particular, would provide mutual assistance and cooperation. This would go a long way toward upgrading all processes for harvesting, storing, converting and delivering food products."

Veritor reflects, "We have described a handful of ideas that show promise. We can only begin to introduce such new possibilities. For many years, farmers have employed innovative practices such as land terracing, irrigation distribution systems and underground or covered water ducts even before piping was developed. Also, we have only broached the subject of hybrid plant development which allow certain crops to survive drought and pestilence."

Neos adds, "Emphasis has long been on the increase of crop yields. Improvements in giant food-producing reduces labor while increasing production. Ingenious methods of processing crops have also evolved rapidly in the industrial world. However, I think some major countries have produced dust bowls through improper and over-intense farming practices like growing only single crops. The use of pesticides and chemical fertilizers that has so greatly increased crop yields has also poisoned farm workers. Artificial means of preserving foods during processing have sometimes proven harmful. It seems to me that in such cases mankind has been out of balance and discordant with nature. But the learning process goes on."

Part IV - Preparation for Tomorrow

CHAPTER 3 - WATER RESOURCES & CRISIS MANAGEMENT

Living things are composed of mostly water and, of course, are completely dependent on its continued availability. It is no wonder that there is great concern for this most precious of earth's resources. Some portions of the world are blessed with water in abundance, and people who inhabit such areas are not motivated to conserve it.

There are many areas of the world, however, that have very limited water resources. Severe conflicts arise when it becomes critically scarce. When populations converge in specific areas, we need to consider their water resources. Is water close and accessible enough to be tapped for consumption? At what cost? If scarce, how can the inevitable rationing be made equitable? What if there are prolonged droughts caused by major climate shifts, something that has happened many times in the past? Have enough reservoirs been built? Regional site selection must consider the availability of this key resource.

There is more. Where there is ground water, it may be contaminated by agricultural run-off that contains pesticides and fertilizers. Such runoff may enter rivers, lakes or the sea or percolate down to existing aquifers. The effluents of neighboring industries, refineries and manufacturing may contain toxic wastes that do likewise. Furthermore, airborne chemical wastes may produce acid rain that eventually affects potential water resources. Critical draw-down of water levels in local aquifers and catchment areas may lead to salt water intrusion, if located near coastlines. Also, there may be depletion of ancient inland aquifers that cannot be readily replenished.

Dependency on the vicissitudes of weather for life-giving rain affects most of the world's population, and regional design and development must attempt to compensate for weather extremes in meeting human need. Most weather conditions fall well within human tolerance and acceptability. Occasionally, however, hurricanes, howling blizzards, blinding and choking dust storms, persistently driving rains and the like disrupt and threaten life. People are driven to action when the need to cope becomes apparent. In some major catastrophes, ways of life may be irreversibly altered.

How much attention is paid to prevailing weather conditions in far away lands? Unless people are traveling there or they know someone who lives there, such conditions might as well be on the moon. However, global weather ultimately affects local conditions. Global warming, coastal tides and storm effects, river flooding and their consequences are not just someone else's problem. Major natural episodes can disrupt the supply of a key resource, like water, which may originate elsewhere. Local dependency may also result in local scarcity, and a socio-economic chain reaction sets in. Humans must become mutually supportive in order to effectively adjust and compensate for weather extremes. This suggests the need for a social organization that encourages cooperation.

Weather, of course, affects water supplies. Multiple uses and demands for water call for careful distribution, conservation, replenishment and recycling. Distribution is made extremely difficult when people inhabit areas far removed from supplies. Poorly planned land use may also lead to an overlapping checkerboard configuration with great differences in water need and utilization. Under these circumstances, engineering becomes a difficult challenge, and planning becomes very costly to users. As the complexity of a system increases, priorities of distribution become a major issue and the solutions satisfy few. If water for the farmers becomes heavily rationed or they are charged more for it, food prices go up for the consumer. If industry and manufacturing water supplies are overly restrictive, some companies may have to curtail production or move away. If fire-fighting services are rationed, they may become less effective, and insurance rates might go up. If the population at large is denied sufficient water, property values might go down. Long term planning and management of water is essential. Appropriate regional infrastructures would provide workable ways to do this through better zoning and land use.

Many requirements can be met by water of less than pristine quality. Reclaimed water, such as from runoff and recycled waste, is usable for some kinds of agriculture, industrial processes and landscaping. Drinkable water requires purification either on a large scale prior to distribution or subsequently by the eventual user. In any case, the value of reclaimed water is easy to see when fresh water becomes scarce.

Agriculture has the greatest need for water. It may also waste the most. Permitting rapid evaporation before plant roots can benefit, watering of unplanted areas, allowing water-logging and saline buildup in the soil, applying water at the wrong time of the day and improper selection of crops are all misuses that must be corrected. It is estimated that more than half of the water used in the world is wasted. Improved techniques in irrigation are called for. Initial capital costs and techniques may exceed the capacities of individual farmers because special piping and pumps are usually required. Local collective improvisations could prove effective.

CHAPTER 3 - WATER RESOURCES & CRISIS MANAGEMENT

Irrigation
(Derived From Multiple Water Sources)

- *Irrigation for crops must be considered when selecting sites for new regions.*
- *Irrigation is essential when rainfall is inadequate to grow sufficient crops to sustain a region.*
- *Providing irrigation on a large scale is limited by the distance from supplies like runoff from rivers and by the water level of local lakes and aquifers. If the ocean is nearby, desalination of sea water may augment available water supplies.*
- *Only about 4% of river runoff is diverted to the world's farms.* As populations have grown, so has the need for increased irrigation.*
- *Advances in technology have radically changed irrigation techniques in agriculture, and this has led to significant economies in water utilization. Primitive types of irrigation like slucing and ditch-digging, used for thousands of years to distribute water, are still common. Modern technological approaches, advocated by regionalization, would employ drip irrigation both above and below ground. Precise metering of water would ensure that only desirable plants grow; evaporation losses and weed watering would be kept to a minimum.*
- *In any case, when there is scarcity, the first priority of water resources must be for direct human consumption before agricultural use. Reclaimed water may then be utilized for irrigation.*
- *Concurrent with extensive water conservation and scientifically managed irrigation in controlled environments comes the requirement for growing crops that have draught resistance.*
- *Furthermore, irrigation must avoid improper drainage that leads to waterlogging and saline deposit buildup. Such accumulations occur mostly in arid areas where arable land is at a premium.*
- *Increased irrigation also necessitates the construction of small dams, reservoirs, pumping and piping facilities, catchment areas and the building of aqueducts and networks of canals.*

* *Food and Population,* Roger Ravelle, Scientific American, September, 1974

As they reflect on this subject, Neos, Pragma and Veritor consider the availability of water in eventual site selection. Regionalization will be dependent on prevailing weather and water supply conditions in various parts of the world.

Neos attempts to clarify. "Environmental concerns influence the design of regions. In addition to natural or man-made conditions, there are geographical factors that may concern regions that share contiguous coastlines, rivers, lakes, mountains, latitudes and terrain."

Pragma agrees, "Yes, it's also important to remember that regions cannot be totally independent because of external influences and interactions. Even so, plans must be developed so each region will become largely self-reliant."

Veritor asserts, "Major benefits can be obtained by establishing networks of regions for mutual support and interaction of functions. Networking is very essential because major natural disasters or shortages could happen to any single region at any time."

Neos returns to the subject of providing water for regions. "It's apparent that the initial regional sites should be located in areas with relatively low population density where fresh or salt water is present within the immediate environment. The amount of water available for collecting, processing, treating and distributing will largely determine the optimum mixes of enterprises, activities and growth for its future inhabitants. I assume that water supplies will not be uniformly available throughout a regional site. The presence of underground aquifers would be of great help in distribution."

Pragma responds, "I expect regionalization would develop plentiful water reserves for times of drought. When water supplies are abundant, they could also be used to help meet emergency inter-regional needs during times of severe scarcity or natural catastrophe. Water exchange arrangements call for a high degree of cooperation and responsible, long term planning."

Neos shifts the conversation, "This brings us to the topic of reservoirs and dams. It would be better to build smaller reservoirs and dams rather than larger ones. Small ones are apt to have less impact on the environment, can be more quickly capitalized and built and would avoid delays, inflationary costs and overruns. Also, I think such projects would be more technologically and operationally manageable."

Veritor agrees. "Smaller units can be more conveniently and economically placed. More natural habitats could be kept intact. Water and power would supply prospective users with shorter, simpler, smaller and less costly pipeline systems and more direct power delivery of electricity."

Pragma brings up another point. "The regional concept advances the design of well-conceived systems with effective networks for distribution. The idea is to build in controllable increments compatible with the requirements of other regional infrastructures."

CHAPTER 3 - WATER RESOURCES & CRISIS MANAGEMENT

Neos adds, "When installations are smaller and more direct, the upgrading of technology should be easier to phase in. Besides improved water systems, we have to look towards the time when superconductivity and microwave transmission of electrical power will be feasible. Hydroelectric plants at the dams and other power systems must be designed to accommodate them. Allowing for new technology and growth is good practice in engineering and technological planning."

Veritor has been very thoughtful. "It seems to me that there is more than economics involved. We must be concerned with building a healthy, aware and productive society in which human potential and needs are respected. The cost of not developing wisely and comprehensively will be by far greater than any initial capital outlay for projects not system designed and integrated."

Pragma nods in agreement."Before we continue to discuss other regional preparation needs, we ought to remember the need for water recycling. We've learned much from space programs about such recycling. Such water is already being used by some industries and agriculture where the climate is arid and water is scarce. Regional development must consider and encourage recycling enterprises."

Veritor adds, "You have brought up an important point. There will be many opportunities for entrepreneurs because regionalization will encourage new enterprises and the reduction of investment risks. However, new guidelines, limits, safety precautions and liability must be considered before entrepreneurs can proceed prudently."

Neos ventures into a different area of water acquisition. "Most of the world's water resources are in the ocean with its 317,000,000 cubic miles of salt water. I believe it is this enormous volume that must be considered for innovation in order to meet fresh water needs."

Veritor answers, "Regions built near coastlines with deep off-shore waters would have the opportunity to economically utilize and convert sea water without having to incur very high pumping costs. However, the delivery of such fresh water to remote inland users will be costly."

Neos suggests, "Processed water could be imported from coastal regions to be mixed with water in interior reservoirs or for recharging existing underground aquifers. The idea is to create alternative sources. It's also important to define the quality of water most suitable for a variety of users. For instance, some industries, chemical processes and medical applications have stringent requirements for zero parts of salt per million of water. This may be obtained by secondary desalination processes on a small scale to meet specific needs. Drinking water quality does not have to be provided for agriculture, but it is needed for human or animal consumption. This means that highly purified water does not have to be delivered in great bulk for every purpose. Cheaper water processing can be provided for many purposes."

Veritor agrees and says, " In our discussion of agriculture we've noted some crops may even use brackish water when soils are sandy or gravelly. Most of the other croplands require desalting. So it seems to me that farmers could benefit by having available technology for different kinds of purifying systems according to what they are growing. Canals could be used to divert water to meet such needs. They could even introduce fertilizers this way if the canals were lined or special pipelines shared their space."

Pragma is skeptical about this. "It is true that treating high quality bulk water using large systems requires more costly equipment, but the systems are far less labor intensive, considering the large amounts of water that are being processed. Also, many consumers demand and need high purity water. Recycled water for farming must not contain harmful organisms or contaminants. Perhaps, as you have noted, the regional network design would provide appropriate processing and distribution schemes to meet well-defined functional irrigation and other needs."

CHAPTER 3 - WATER RESOURCES & CRISIS MANAGEMENT

World's Water Supply

Distribution of All Water: *

Location	Water Volume (In Cubic Miles)	Percent of Total Water
Fresh water lakes	30,000	0.009
Saline lakes and inland seas	25,000	0.008
Average in rivers and streams	300	0.0001
Soil moisture and near-surface ground water	16,000	0.005
Deeper ground water	2,000,000	0.61
Icecaps and glaciers	7,000,000	2.15
Atmosphere	3,000	0.0001
Oceans	317,000,000	97.2

Salt Content of Different Kinds of Water and Use: **

Deionized & distilled industrial water	- 0 ppm
Drinking water	- 500 ppm
Fresh water	< 1000 ppm
Brackish water	- 1,000 ppm - 35,000 ppm
Sea water	> 35,000 ppm
Great Salt Lake & Dead Sea	~ 250,000 ppm

 * U.S. Geological Survey estimates
 ** Desalination: "Water for the World's Future", R. Popkin, Frederick A. Praeger, N.Y., 1968

Table IV-3-A

Removing Salt *

*There are at least thirteen methods of removing salt from water. The methods provide for various degrees of purity. Combinations of processes and improved materials and techniques have been increasing the practicality of desalination worldwide. 4,000 plants are presently involved in scores of countries producing a total of about 3.4 billion gallons of potable water per day.***

Processing

    Methods (Distillation)
        Long-tube Vertical (Multiple Effect)
        Multi-stage Flash Distillation
        Multi-effect, Multi-stage Distillation
        Vapor Compression Distillation

The following group of methods involves membrane technology used extensively for brackish water desalting. This technology has been advancing rapidly and holds promise for use with sea water as well.

Processing

    Methods (Membrane)
        Electrodialysis
        Transport Depletion
        Reverse Osmosis

The following three groups of methods involve humidification, freezing and chemical separation as the means for obtaining fresh water.

Processing

    Methods (Humidification)
        Solar Humidification
        Diffusion Humidification
    Methods (Freezing)
        Direct Freezing
        Secondary Refrigerant Freezing
    Methods (Chemical)
        Ion Exchange
        Hydrate

* *"Desalination: Water for the World's Future"*, R. Popkin, Frederick A. Praeger, N.Y., 1968

** *"Desalination of Brackish and Marine Waters"*, P.H. Abelson, Science Mag., Mar.15, 1991

Figure IV-3-A

CHAPTER 3 - WATER RESOURCES & CRISIS MANAGEMENT

Neos states, "I would like to suggest a few schemes that could be targeted for regional use in the interior of a hot, arid country in one instance, and in another, a coastal area where the water immediately off-shore is at least 800 feet deep. Like many new ideas, however, they are best portrayed and their value made more apparent when they are presented in the context of a larger scheme or plan. It is important to recognize the intrinsic value of new ideas without having to first resort to rigorous proofs and dissertations. Of course, it would take a leap in faith to expect people to appreciate and accept such ideas without clear introduction to the subject."

Pragma asks, "Why don't you present the interior scheme for hot, arid lands first? What would be the elevation of an interior area with respect to the coastline or ocean? Would we pick places in the interior that already have salt water or are barren? I can see that when there is a difference in elevation, a connecting canal could be built to a dam with a hydro-electric power plant for generating electricity."

"When we begin to talk about a canal in a hot climate, evaporation water losses must be considered," Veritor adds. "Even though it usually amounts to only about five percent, it does contribute to unnecessary waste. If a canal is used for transporting water, then it ought to also be covered to reduce evaporation and to keep out silting dust. We must conserve as much water as possible. Of course, a very large pipeline instead of a canal could also be used to transport water to the interior and avoid evaporation losses."

Neos reacts enthusiastically to this turn in the conversation. "If a pipeline is used to transport sea water for driving a turbine to generate hydro-electric power, it would only serve a single purpose and bear the total capital cost. However, a canal could also be used for surface transportation. A lake created at the end could be used for desalinating purposes and solar thermal systems. As we mentioned earlier, once capital and major efforts are invested to build canals, pipelines and their facilities, other compatible functions would also become feasible."

Pragma concurs. "In other words, you mean an integrated system with multiple purposes would provide many side benefits. There is no doubt in my mind that a regional approach with its infrastructure design would encourage this kind of system development."

Neos begins anew, " Let me go back to the first scheme I proposed for a canal or combination of canal and pipeline that allows sea water to flow mostly through gravity from the ocean to some large catchment area or dry lake region in the interior. If the elevation differences are large enough, small dams and hydro-electric generating plants could be included wherever steep gradients occur. "There are a number of places where this can be done such as in Israel, starting from the Mediterranean Sea to the Dead Sea where there is a 1300 feet change in elevation within 50 miles. Most of this elevation change occurs abruptly near the inland sea. In Egypt, there is a large drop in elevation from the Mediterranean to the Qattara Depression, in Ethiopia from the Red Sea to the depression of Denark, and in Algeria from the Mediterannean Sea to the Chatt Melrhir, to name four of them. Many of these areas would benefit greatly from a multi-purpose design which could then go hand in hand with regional development."

"But first let us consider what such a multi-purpose system would be like in the Negev of Israel. We note that the canal and some pipeline would be located where there are many days of solar input. Covering a major portion of the canal with a curved roof enclosure would exclude blowing sand. The cover would be made of a greenhouse-type plastic material so that solar heating would take place for evaporating some of the flowing sea water. Fresh water condensate would form and be collected at night as run-off. Within the covered space, above and spanning the canal for much of its length, would be support racks for growing food hydroponically. A variety of plants would utilize either fresh or salt water. High vapor content of air within the enclosure would enhance plant growth."

"Periodically, smaller canals would branch off to feed solar ponds for the production of electricity and for growing special algae for fuel. Other branch-offs would then be used either for aqueducts or pipelines for irrigation purposes. The irrigated farmland would be used for growing appropriate plants from partially fresh water. There would need to be many more design and planning details as well as ancillary development, but this is the general concept of the system."

Pragma comments on this description. "It makes sense to me that evaporation for desalination is accomplished with solar energy which, of course, is free. The approximate area of solar exposure for a 30 foot wide canal, fifty miles long, would amount to about 7,900,000 square feet! This would be a significant growing area for various types of agriculture."

CHAPTER 3 - WATER RESOURCES & CRISIS MANAGEMENT

Multiple Uses of Sea Water Under the Aegis of Regional and Inter-regional Development

Combined Applications of Integrated Innovations:

Major capital expenditures of the basic system are shared in this multiple venture which also allows off-shoot enterprises to flourish.

Ocean or Sea

Irrigated Land for Agriculture

Evaporation/Condensation Provides Fresh Water

Gravity Flow

Covered Canal

Agriculture Practiced Under Plastic Roof Produces High Vapor Requiring Less Root Feeding

Canal Bottom is Blackened for Greater Solar Absorption

To Lower Elevation Hydro-electric Power Plant

Solar Salt Water Pond

Solar Pond Provides Electricity And Fuel-yielding Algae

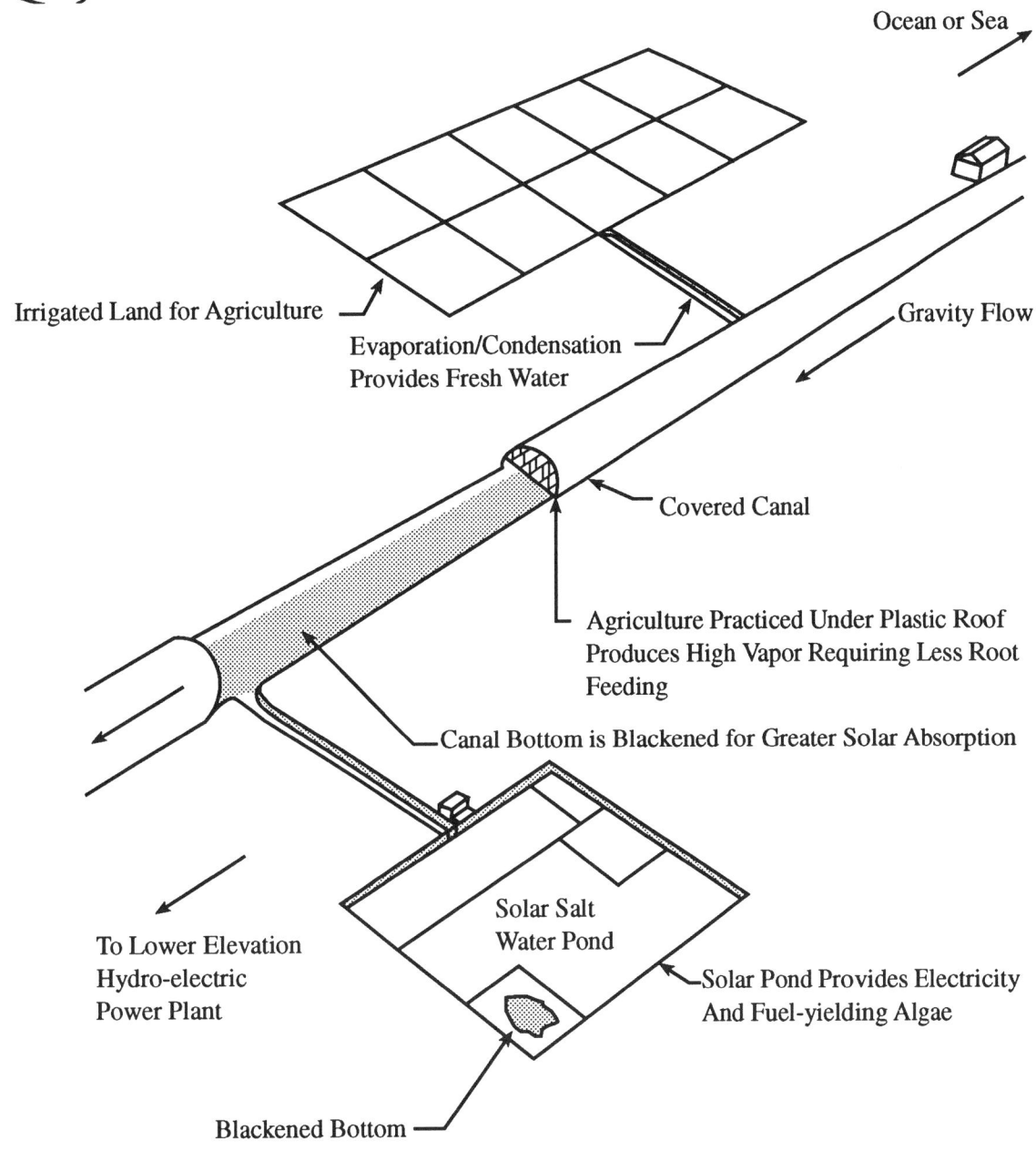

Blackened Bottom

Figure IV-3-B

Veritor then asks, "What about the second water scheme you mentioned? Does it have multiple purposes also?"

Neos answers, "In this case I will only describe a general system that provides fresh water directly from the ocean. Such a scheme could be used for existing coastal areas as part of new regional development. There are other schemes for ocean-oriented industrial municipalities that have many enterprises in conjunction with this system, but that is not what I am presenting here.

"The proposed method is for desalting ocean water using reverse osmosis undersea at a depth of at least 800 feet. At this depth the pressure is approximately 25 atmospheres which is enough to induce the osmotic process separating salt from sea water through a membrane. This is accomplished without need of additional energy although pumping of fresh water would increase the rate of processing. Note that the fresh water produced has less specific gravity than sea water and must, therefore, rise to fill some kind of vented storage.

"I would like to present a picture of such a system. Its separation and collection apparatus lies on the ocean floor. Double cylindrical structures made of a rigid, permeable outer cylinder of considerable diameter and an inner cylinder that is semi-permeable provide for osmotic exchange, preventing salt from passing through the membrane. The outer cylinder protects the inner one and is strong enough to allow back-flushing to remove contaminants.

"Fresh water is collected on a continuous basis from numerous configurations that help fill one or more large, submerged storage bladders. Pumping can also occur at the surface from an ocean terminal or directed to shore for further distribution. During pumping, the pressure in the bladder is reduced, allowing the osmotic process to speed up and improve efficiency."

Veritor reacts favorably to this description and states, "This is the kind of innovation that we need! I think the idea deserves further investigation. If desalting can take place in the ocean and fresh water stored there, it would represent a significant improvement over processing and storing water on shore where land is at a premium. However, we ought to emphasize that deep water is necessary near the shore in order to process water to exact greater economy."

CHAPTER 3 - WATER RESOURCES & CRISIS MANAGEMENT

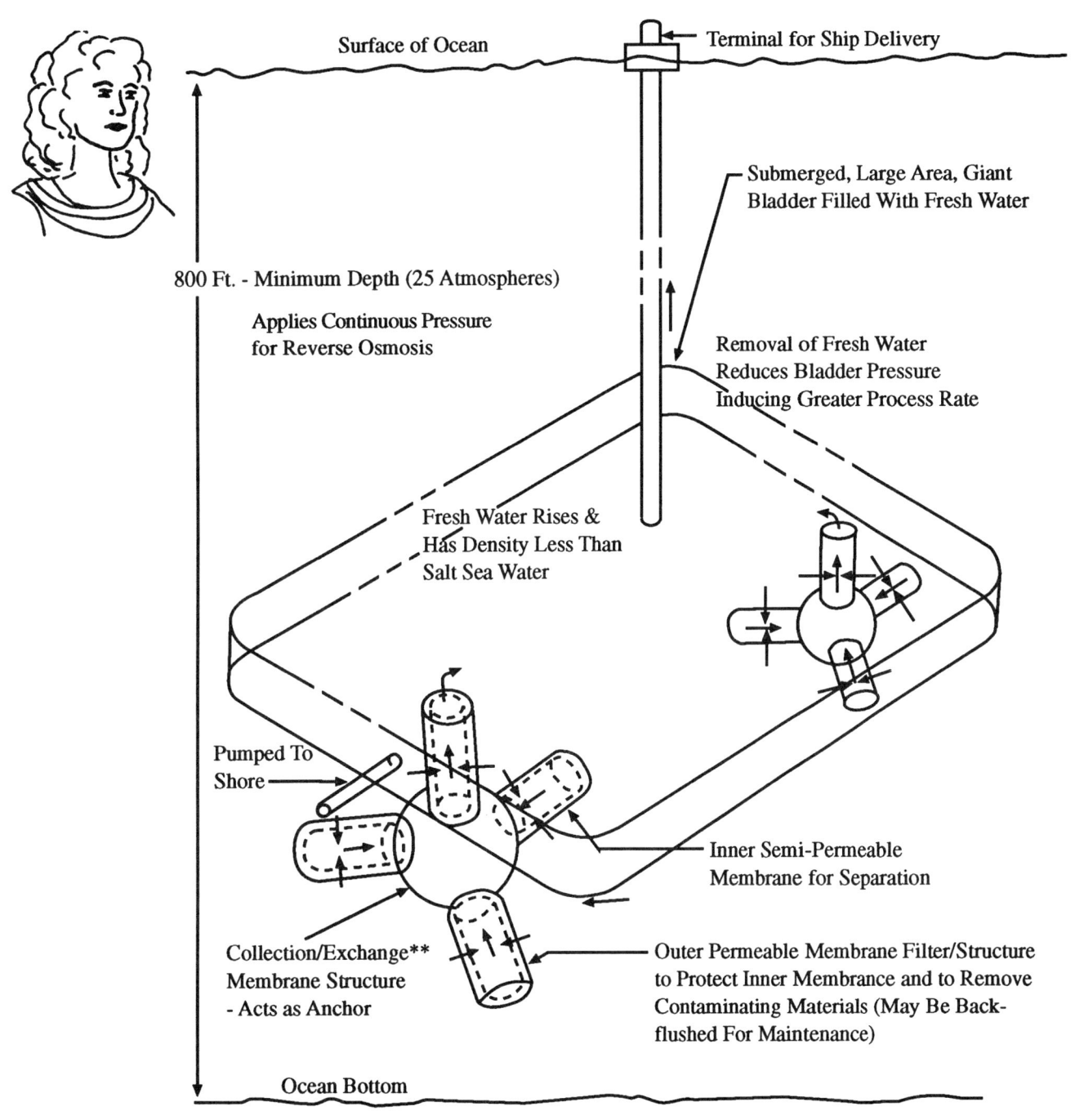

Surface of Ocean

Terminal for Ship Delivery

Submerged, Large Area, Giant Bladder Filled With Fresh Water

800 Ft. - Minimum Depth (25 Atmospheres)

Applies Continuous Pressure for Reverse Osmosis

Removal of Fresh Water Reduces Bladder Pressure Inducing Greater Process Rate

Fresh Water Rises & Has Density Less Than Salt Sea Water

Pumped To Shore

Inner Semi-Permeable Membrane for Separation

Collection/Exchange** Membrane Structure - Acts as Anchor

Outer Permeable Membrane Filter/Structure to Protect Inner Membrane and to Remove Contaminating Materials (May Be Back-flushed For Maintenance)

Ocean Bottom

Scheme Showing Reverse Osmosis/Force Method*

* Vision & Venture For the Continental Shelf, G. Siegel, West Coast University, L.A., 1969
** Undersea Storage and Distribution System, G. Siegel, U.S. Patent #3,610,194, Oct. 5, 1971

Figure IV-3-C

Part IV - Preparation for Tomorrow

CHAPTER 4 - ENERGY: DEPENDENCIES & ALTERNATIVES

Neos, Pragma and Veritor pause and then proceed to another key resource, that of energy. Their interest at this point is to present a background of global non-fossil and fossil energy resources, particularly as they may apply to regional selection, design and development. Like water resources, there is considerable concern for the availability, conservation and utility of energy resources.

Some kinds of energy resources are abundant. Others exist, but they have to be made available. Availability of energy resources means that they can be accessed, recovered, converted, processed and delivered in a usable form. To do so requires many different kinds of natural and man-made systems that utilize heat, electricity, illumination, mechanical devices, radiation, hydraulics, chemical processes, combustion, monitoring and controls. It takes energy to provide energy.

We know that energy is not always prudently used. It may even be used to destroy (i.e. nuclear energy, chemical energy, mechanical energy as employed in weapon systems). Mankind has a responsibility for the appropriate and constructive utilization of energy.

The above statements appear to be deceptively obvious, but most people consume energy excessively, wasting much of it. Some of this is unavoidable because energy systems are not inherently 100% efficient. The industrial world over-consumes various forms of resources like fossil fuels as if they were in infinite supply. This is a major misconception. Increased populations, greater industrialization, expanded transportation and modern agriculture will ensure the rapid depletion of all kinds of energy resources.

The responsibility of mankind should be to at least develop regional infrastructures for the early introduction and integration of energy conservation and alternate energy sources. This is not likely to be cost-effective without regionalization. As today's infrastructures and population concentrations evolved, relatively few conceived of the emergence of new non-fossil energy systems. Now, however, notable achievements in alternative energy and energy saving systems have been introduced. They are being applied to transportation, power generation and communication in most industrialized countries. There has also been a growing awareness of new energy technologies waiting in the wings.

CHAPTER 4 - ENERGY DEPENDENCIES & ALTERNATIVES

Inevitable Move to Alternative Energy Resources

- In the past, resources have been readily accessible but, today, underground resources are as yet undiscovered, are increasingly inaccessible, are often low grade or remain undeliverable because of rising costs.
- Variety and abundance of energy resources are not uniformly distributed worldwide.
- Technological development and economic opportunities in areas of abundance attracted greater numbers of people, resulting in an accelerated demand for resources.
- These areas have developed rapidly because abundant resources were readily locally accessible for exploitation.
- Higher demand brought about improved means for exploitation and utility but with increasing costs and rates of attrition of resources and environmental conditions.
- Undeveloped areas of the world became more attractive with lower costs to exploit energy resources.
- Lower initial costs of these far away energy resources caused increased industrial nation dependency. High consumption became addictive, and costs began to rise.
- Other forms of local energy resources, increasingly competitive in cost, began to be developed within the industrial nations. Little regard was given to adverse effects on human health and environmental pollution.
- Many industrial countries introduced greater efficiency and conservation of energy, but addiction to over-consumption remained.
- Technological and economic development began to exceed infrastructure capacity; high consumption was built into prevailing systems. Planning was dictated by the captains of industry and other private development. Governmental infrastructures tried to compensate but with minimum effectiveness and higher operational costs.
- Alternative energy resources and technologies have gradually gained attention. However, attempts to introduce and integrate some of them into existing infrastructures have led to greatly distorted estimates of projected costs, net efficiency, feasibility and effectiveness. Existing infrastructures did not or could not anticipate the specific need for integrating new energy technologies.
- Existing infrastructures of industrial, densely populated areas are likely to have non-adaptive transportation systems, traffic control systems, building designs, processes and industrial areas. This inhibits introduction of new alternative energy resource applications.
- Demonstration of alternative energy resource applications requires new infrastructures found in the regional network concept. Successful implementation may then indicate retrofit potential for existing industrial, densely populated areas and eliminate the chance of premature rejection of new concepts.

Fossil Energy Resources Status *
(25,000 Quads are the estimated proven reserves)**

Kind	Uses	Comments
Coal (Various)	• In combustion; electric power generation, direct heating and metallurgical processes. • As chemical compound; in many products like synthetics, plastics, etc.	Abundant, wide distribution except for large central parts of So. America and Africa and southern Asia.; 67% in U.S.and in former U.S.S.R. Good for about 200-400 years.
Oil (Petroleum	• In combustion; electric power generation, direct heating and transportation. • As chemicals for many products.	Abundant only in small areas of each continent; 67% reserves in Mid-East. Good for about 30-60 years.
Gas (Natural)	• In combustion; electric power generation, direct heating, as methanol for transportation fuel. • As chemical for many products	Abundant distribution except in large parts of Asia, So. America & Africa, U.S.S.R., has 38% of world reserves. Good for 40 years.
Shale Oil	• As fuel in transportation.	Abundant in accessible amounts but in small areas, undeveloped, mostly U.S.
Tar Sands	• In combustion; minor usage.	Exists in limited amounts in special areas.
Peat	• Indirect heating; minor usage.	Exists in limited amounts in special areas.
Uranium *** (Non-fossil)	• In producing electrical power through nuclear fission.	Moderate amounts, not widely distributed.

* "A Survey of United States and Total World Production, Proved Reserves, and Remaining Recoverable Resources of Fossil Fuels & Uranium", J.D.Parent, Institute of Gas Technology, Chicago, Ill., 1978
** A Quad = One Quadrillion Btu
*** Included with current dependencies

    Economic effects of fossil fuel energy resource depletion will be felt acutely in industrial areas within one generation, given continued excessive reliance on these resources as fuels and the absence of serious conservation and alternative measures. Diminished accessibility of these resources will increase their costs and inflate costs of living.

    Any countries with industrial and economic infrastructures that remain highly dependent on fossil resources for fuels are vulnerable. Eventually, most fossil energy resources will not be used for burning but for use in the manufacture of many derivative products that can be recycled. Future generations must also have these valuable resources available to them.

Figure IV-4-A

CHAPTER 4 - ENERGY RESOURCES

Neos begins the discussion. "We have been reviewing quite a bit of information on energy resources and their availability and utilization for specific purposes. Many efforts have been made to introduce new alternative energy systems, but more are needed, especially for regionalization."

Pragma pursues this. "Perhaps more scientists, engineers and managers are realizing that renewable resources and alternative energy systems have less adverse side effects than fossil fuels. They have been concerned with the increasing costs of operations, power generation and industrial processing using fossil fuels. But acceptance of alternative energy resources and their extensive utilization has still not happened worldwide."

Veritor adds, "We ought to briefly review fossil energy resources and their current use. When we think of oil, gas, and coal, we tend to regard them as fuels for combustion. However, there are thousands of products like plastics made from fossil resources which are not used for combustion. Isn't it remarkable that uniquely combined elements were naturally produced many millions of years ago? They were conveniently made for human consumption."

Neos picks up the conversation here and says, "Coal is found on many continents. There seems to be plenty for a while. Oil and gas deposits are abundant but are found only in a limited number of places. There are extensive oil shale deposits in a limited number of countries, but their oil is presently difficult and costly to extract."

Pragma notes, "I think it will be very difficult for most industrial countries to conserve such resources because they desperately need them to trade or to burn. Some of these countries are keenly aware that fossil fuel supplies are finite and deposits are becoming progressively more costly to process and access. How long will nations continue their over-consumption of these valuable resources?"

Veritor reflects and responds, "Most power plants and smelters have been built to burn fossil energy. Many millions of people are dependent on fossil fuels for heating their homes and to perform work. Hundreds of millions of vehicles are dependent on them. Obviously, for the present and near future, many countries are locked into investments that are fossil fuel-dependent."

Neos acknowledges this. "Yes, it will take a long time to wean so many people and industries from such dependency. Scarcity, however, will cause changes in habits and attitudes. I think that alternative energy resources and their systems will gradually gain acceptance, especially in new regions."

Pragma adds, "Fossil resources usually require many expensive processes to make them useful. It becomes even more so when provisions must be made to sharply reduce or eliminate air and water pollution. People have been putting up with these conditions because regulations and acceptable fuel alternatives have not been universally implemented."

Veritor notes, "Many countries do not even have fossil fuel resources. In some impoverished lands, people depend on very cheap kerosene, brush wood and dung for cooking. Oil prices reached levels where they could no longer afford kerosene. One can also go to big cities in northern climates and find similar privation."

Neos insists, "Correcting this situation will take major changes in government policies and greater receptivity to alternative kinds of transportation which require little or no fossil fuels for propulsion. Heavily populated cities relying on outmoded transportation systems will find them increasingly costly, restrictive, fatiguing, dangerous and time-consuming."

Pragma frowns and shifts the subject. "So what are these alternative energy resources? Aren't they being actively pursued by many entrepreneurs, governments and energy companies? People have been burning peat and wood for heating, cooking and the working of metals since there were trees and the discovery of metals. Hydropower, windmills and even some types of solar heating have been in existence for thousands of years. In recent times there have been newer, more efficient concepts of these alternative approaches. Nuclear energy plants have now been built by the hundreds."

Neos answers, "Those are good questions, but they can't all be addressed together. There has been an historical progression in the use of energy. During the industrial revolution, railroad networks, large ocean vessels and modern technology evolved. Then came automobiles, airline networks and large concentrations of populations demanding fuels for combustion, propulsion and the generation of electrical power in convenient, concentrated and deliverable forms. Cities grew where neither fuels nor alternative energy resources were readily available, and they had to be imported. Initial dependency was on coal and natural gas. Wood burning was still used in places where it was abundant. Power was obtained from human effort, animals, mechanical aids and wind and water. I would like to show you a chart I made that briefly describes the evolution of different kinds of energy use through the ages. It also shows possible future trends."

CHAPTER 4 - ENERGY DEPENDENCIES & ALTERNATIVES

Energy Through the Ages

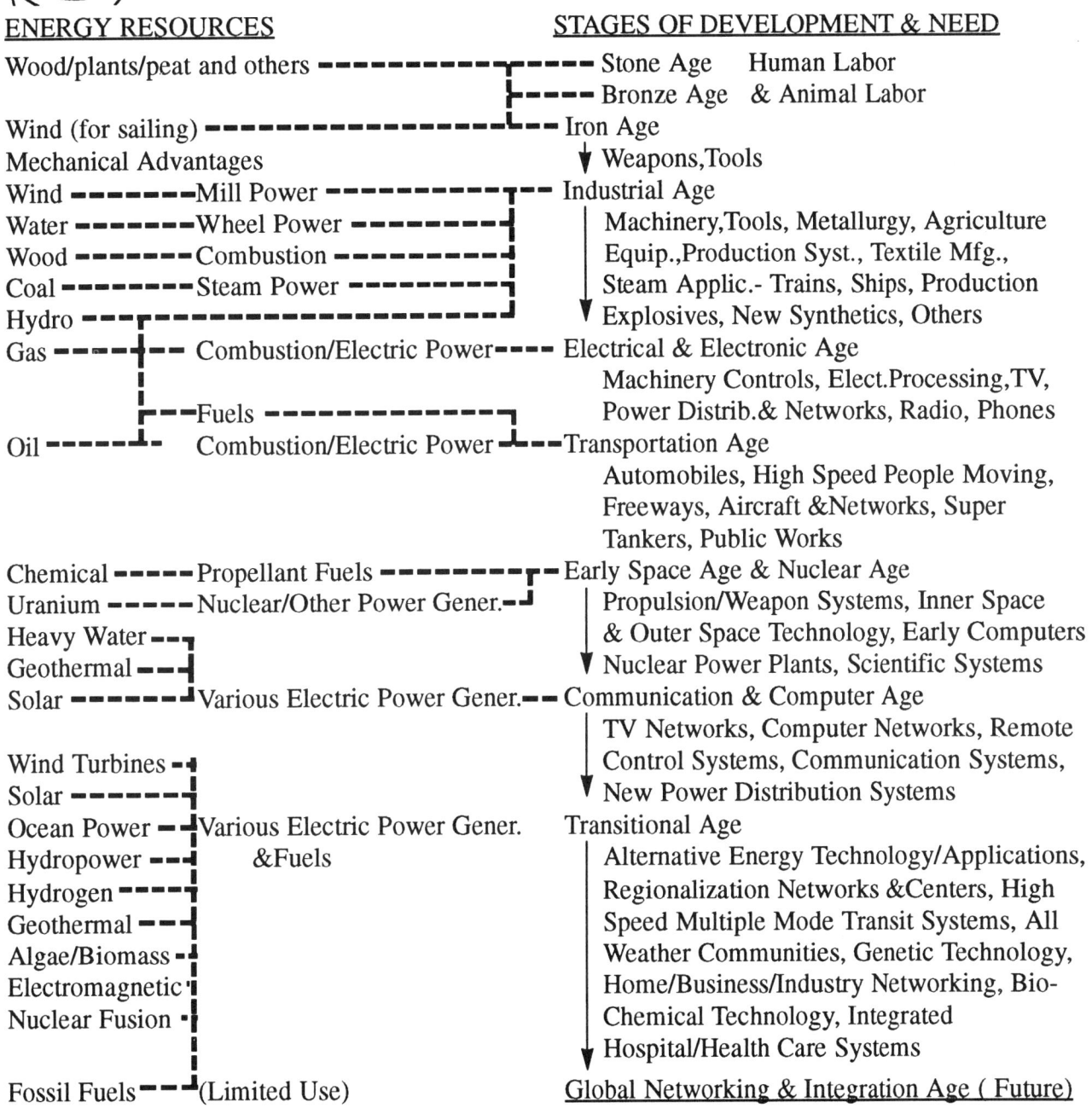

ENERGY RESOURCES	STAGES OF DEVELOPMENT & NEED
Wood/plants/peat and others ------------	Stone Age — Human Labor
	Bronze Age — & Animal Labor
Wind (for sailing) ----------------------	Iron Age
Mechanical Advantages	↓ Weapons, Tools
Wind --------- Mill Power --------------	Industrial Age
Water -------- Wheel Power -------------	Machinery, Tools, Metallurgy, Agriculture
Wood --------- Combustion --------------	Equip., Production Syst., Textile Mfg.,
Coal --------- Steam Power -------------	Steam Applic.- Trains, Ships, Production
Hydro ---------------------------------	↓ Explosives, New Synthetics, Others
Gas ------- Combustion/Electric Power ---	Electrical & Electronic Age
	Machinery Controls, Elect. Processing, TV,
------- Fuels --------------------------	Power Distrib. & Networks, Radio, Phones
Oil -------- Combustion/Electric Power --	Transportation Age
	Automobiles, High Speed People Moving,
	Freeways, Aircraft & Networks, Super
	Tankers, Public Works
Chemical ----- Propellant Fuels ---------	Early Space Age & Nuclear Age
Uranium ------ Nuclear/Other Power Gener.	Propulsion/Weapon Systems, Inner Space
Heavy Water ---	& Outer Space Technology, Early Computers
Geothermal ---	↓ Nuclear Power Plants, Scientific Systems
Solar -------- Various Electric Power Gener. ---	Communication & Computer Age
	TV Networks, Computer Networks, Remote
Wind Turbines --	Control Systems, Communication Systems,
Solar --------	↓ New Power Distribution Systems
Ocean Power -- Various Electric Power Gener.	Transitional Age
Hydropower --- & Fuels	Alternative Energy Technology/Applications,
Hydrogen -----	Regionalization Networks & Centers, High
Geothermal ---	Speed Multiple Mode Transit Systems, All
Algae/Biomass -	Weather Communities, Genetic Technology,
Electromagnetic	Home/Business/Industry Networking, Bio-
Nuclear Fusion	Chemical Technology, Integrated
	↓ Hospital/Health Care Systems
Fossil Fuels --- (Limited Use)	Global Networking & Integration Age (Future)

Figure IV-4-B

"The invention of the automobile, its widespread use and demand for fuel, encouraged the exploration and production for oil and gas wells. Oil and its products became abundantly available and found increasing use in industry and in electric power generation. Also, the invention of the airplane and its popular acceptance as a means of travel greatly increased oil consumption.

"In the meantime, there was a trend towards increasing the size of power generating plants to supply electricity to distant burgeoning cities. Huge dams were built both to store water in large amounts and to generate, through hydropower, large amounts of electrical energy. Considering the demands of distant users, greater efficiency was thought to result from building large power plants, grid networks and transmission of high voltage electricity.

"Then came nuclear power plants, a promising, economical method of producing cheap electrical energy. These plants have been built for large capacity. New starts in the construction of such power plants have since declined. But the surge towards bigness was in response to increasing sizes of cities, industry and transportation.

"If big has been better, it has also brought more vulnerability to catastrophic events. These events, like nuclear plant mishaps, shut-downs and unscheduled downtime affect the load on other networked power plants, and if switch-over cannot be made, there can be major consequences for many users. Consider what happens in a modern city in an industrialized country when electrical power is suddenly curtailed for an extended period of time. Pandemonium! Power producers have since recognized and partly corrected this vulnerability by building networks or grids that can be switched to obtain temporary supplies from other sources. However, these networks must be extended to incorporate switching control at the lowest levels of diverse use. Not so coincidently, the use of networking is one of the things we advocate in regionalization. Networking must accommodate alternate local independent or integrated energy resources and systems as well."

Pragma and Veritor are spellbound by this dissertation and reflect on its ramifications. Veritor asserts,"It's not difficult to see where this is leading us. We definitely need many more smaller alternative energy installations so as to add significantly to the total energy picture. This is not only to reduce vulnerability but to conserve fossil energy resources for subsequent generations to use. As we have already discussed, fossil resources must be conserved as chemicals and for products that can be recycled, when feasible, in the present and the future."

Neos notes. "Certainly, the under-developed countries of the world cannot afford giant facilities. They must borrow only as much capital as they are able to pay back without mortgaging the birth rights of their children. Most poor countries should be able to benefit from the use of smaller alternative energy resources and systems. These would be more manageable and conveniently located."

CHAPTER 4 - ENERGY DEPENDENCIES & ALTERNATIVES

Veritor adds,"There are many competitive alternative energy options emerging these days. A brief look at such choices is encouraging, but it is obvious that infrastructures have to be developed to accommodate and integrate them. One can't just build energy systems anywhere and then ask how they are supposed to serve. The best way is to incorporate them early in the system design and implement them to match anticipated consumer demands."

"Alternative energy systems can be made not only small and decentralized, but mobile as well. Many systems can be applied more directly, requiring fewer subsystems for energy conversion and boosting. This greatly increases the net efficiency to the end user and avoids large transmission losses. Hybrid systems and combined systems, using different kinds of energy resources, are also feasible, and these, too, would produce efficiently."

Pragma observes,"Many alternative energy resources and systems are benign; they do not disturb, destroy or radically change the environment. For regions, these could be installed outside of densely populated areas, resulting in greater public and private acceptance and advocacy."

Veritor responds,"I think we will find many kinds of modular alternative energy systems that can be incorporated into neighborhoods and buildings, vehicular designs and even roadways during initial development. There are whole new ways of utilizing energy. Regional infrastructures could be designed to allow system retrofits after regions and their communities have become operational."

Neos adds,"Special provisions have to be made to utilize solar energy systems. Solar energy is mostly effective where there is little cloud cover for much of the day and when there is sufficient diurnal exposure during the year. Natural obstructions have to be avoided. Man-made structures have to be designed and placed so that they do not cast shadows on neighboring solar collectors."

Pragma answers,"Well, this represents a major problem for many densely populated areas with high rise buildings. Think of the many thousands of buildings that would have to be adapted to install and utilize solar equipment. However, the presence of skyscrapers would continue to obstruct and impose yet another burden on surrounding areas and interests."

Alternative Energy Resources

Solar Energy

Solar Concentrators	• Electrical power generation.
Solar Panels	• Electrical power generation (photo-voltaic) for lighting and small equipment operation; space/water heating/cooling.
Solar Ponds	• Electrical power generation.
Solar Storage	• Heat contribution; electrical recharging of batteries.
Biomass Cultivation (Wood/Corn/Sugar Cane)	• Conversion to alcohol (methanol & ethanol) fuels for transportation and operation of equipment; heating fuel
Biomass Waste (Rice Husks, Dung, and Residues)	• Conversion to alcohol and methane for fuels.
Algae Culture (Saline Tolerant)	• Oil bearing fuel for propulsion and combustion.
Wind Turbines (Various Types)	• Electric power generation.

Ocean Energy

Ocean Current & Tidal Systems	• Electric power generation.
Ocean Thermoclines (Similar to Solar Pond)	• Electric power generation.
Ocean Wave Systems (Vertical or Horizontal)	• Electric power generation.

Hydropower

River Flow & Falls	• Electric power generation.

Hydrogen

Production/Storage	• Fuel for propulsion; electric power generation.

Geothermal

Wet or Dry Systems	• Electric power generation.

Uranium/Plutonium

Nuclear Fusion	• Electric power generation.
Electro-Chemical; Fuel Cells	• Fuel for propulsion; electric power generation.

Figure IV-4-C

CHAPTER 4 - ENERGY DEPENDENCIES & ALTERNATIVES

Neos notes with some excitement, "We've already discussed the use of different forms of energy. We've mentioned uses for solar energy. Now it's time to be more specific. Let's look at solar ponds. They can be installed in special areas of the community or neighborhood where there is enough exposure to sunshine. As passive systems they can be used for producing electricity or for growing algae for fuel. They do not dominate or interfere with the activities of neighborhoods. The solar pond with its high concentration of salinity is best located where there is salt water available. Solar ponds are already operational in the Negev desert of Israel and the southwestern United States."

Pragma asks, "Aren't there thousands of other solar applications to discuss? Even a simple light source is enough to operate instruments and controls, and they are reliable and long-lasting."

Veritor responds, "Yes there are many. However, guidelines, operational limits and legal preparations are needed to instill confidence in companies to invest in the manufacture, installation and maintenance of these solar systems. The regional concept provides an effective approach for establishing criteria, organizing and implementing many different kinds of solar systems."

Neos continues, "New solar energy applications are emerging which are very encouraging because the energy source is free. Besides solar ponds, there are solar stills for chemical processes, using the sun's free energy.

"Like the solar still, there is the solar gas generator which is very appropriate for farming areas throughout the world, especially in the Third World countries. The process uses animal and human waste to produce both methane for fuel and solids for fertilizer. Handling of organic wastes in this manner has greatly increased even in industrial countries.

"Of course, the sun's energy provides for the growth of oil-yielding plants. Oil or fuel is obtainable from the jojoba plant grown in a desert environment. Other plants, as products of solar energy, can also be used for fuel."

"Solar space heating for hot water and room heating has become very prevalent in some industrial and Third World countries. The systems are usually straight forward and simple to maintain. Of course, people have been using the sun for this purpose throughout history. So it is an established candidate for use at the neighborhood level."

"Solar energy conversion to electrical energy is being accomplished by photovoltaic collectors and by solar concentrators of different types and variations. Locally produced electrical energy augments and backs up main energy supplies from interregional grids. Having a back-up is very important to meet peak demands for energy and to minimize vulnerability to catastrophic events."

Pragma interrupts for a moment to ask, "Aren't there other solar energy alternatives like wind turbines? Certainly wind mills have been in use for many years. In windy areas whole forests of different kinds of wind turbines have been installed, and each turbine, when operating, contributes to a local electrical grid system. Turbines have become increasingly competitive cost-wise in producing electricity. Further technological development would greatly improve wind turbine effectiveness and usefulness."

Veritor adds. "I think that any new versions of wind turbine systems should have structures that can be used to provide more than one mode of producing electricity."

Neos responds with enthusiasm, "Of course. Different kinds of systems could be incorporated into a common structure to save on labor and capital. Savings would become very apparent when thousands of them are arrayed across wind-swept plains or passes in many countries. What if a structure were designed with a curved reflecting surface that concentrates the sun's energy to a heat collector for electrical generation? The underside of the curved surface would form a venturi-like deflector to redirect sustained winds to horizontal wind turbines to also generate electricity. The structures would be spaced end-to-end across the land with periodic openings. This would be an example of multiple use of a common structure."

Pragma joins in, "I notice that wind power for commercial ships has also been recently considered again to save fuel. Of course, they do not look like the old sailing ships, but they do use wind turbines. Aircraft and automobiles also use turbines to increase power, efficiency and economy."

CHAPTER 4 - ENERGY RESOURCES

Proposed Concept - Combined Systems for Energy

This concept proposes combined systems of moderate, manageable size that involve more than one function. Many other structures like buildings with flat roofs could support multiple functions. In this concept a curved reflector with extensions and mounting are provided. The curved surface serves as a solar concentrator when facing the sun for the production of electricity. The underside suggests a funnel or venturi that channels higher velocity air into horizontal wind turbines. Air velocities are normally higher further from the ground. The concentrated air flow inpulses the horizontal turbine blades which rotate to generate electricity. When the wind loses velocity, airborne top soil is dropped to create a soil bank for farming.

Solar Input

Wind Turbine/Solar Concentrator System

Horizontally Oriented

Prevailing Winds

Incoming Air

Collector/Conductor Focus

Wind Turbine

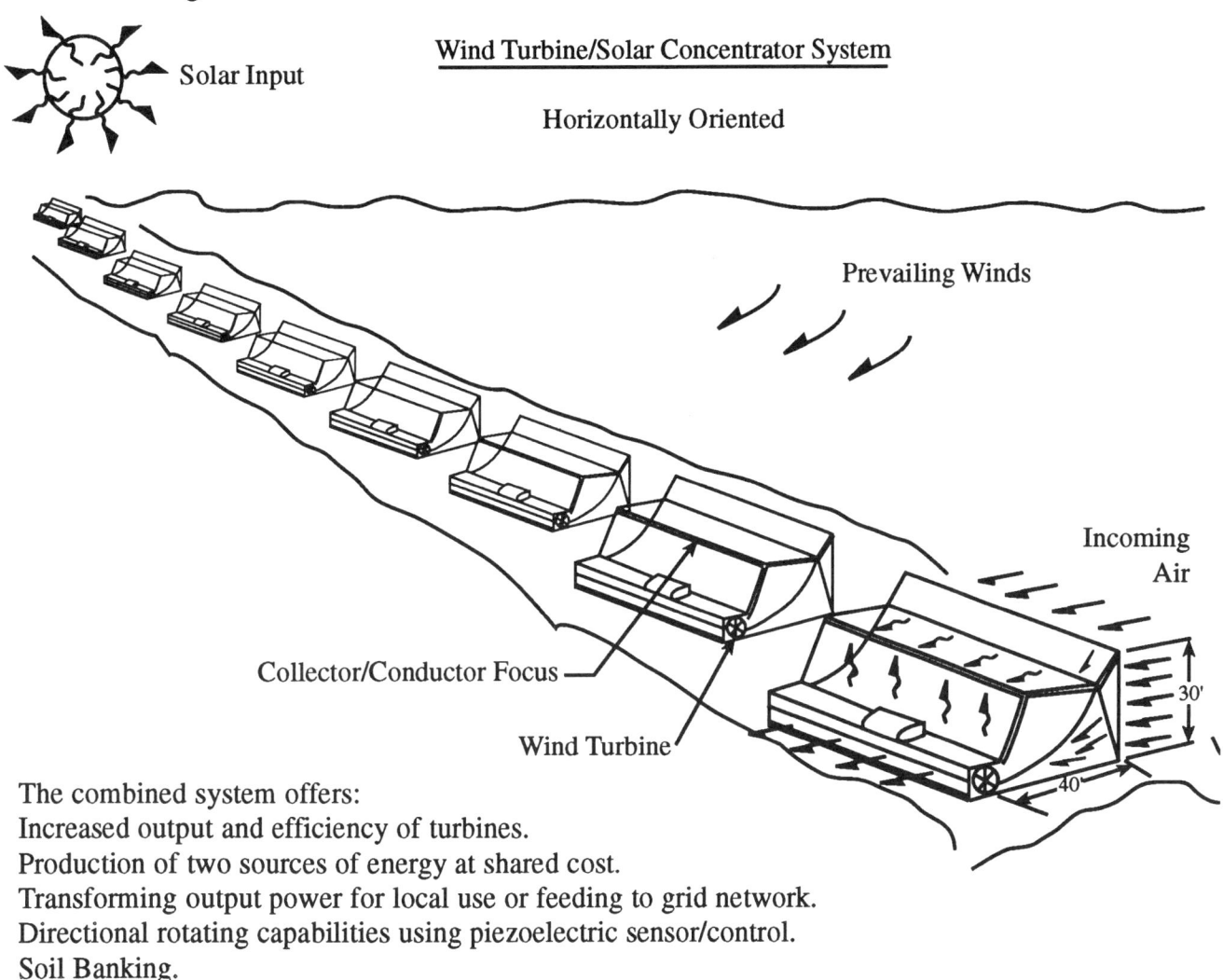

30'

40'

The combined system offers:
Increased output and efficiency of turbines.
Production of two sources of energy at shared cost.
Transforming output power for local use or feeding to grid network.
Directional rotating capabilities using piezoelectric sensor/control.
Soil Banking.

Figure IV-4-D

Neos continues to describe other innovations for regional enhancement. "There are many ways to obtain electrical energy that we have not discussed. But we ought not to dwell on the details of all of them. For instance, nuclear fission reactors have been introduced in industrial countries everywhere. A major obstacle to their use has been fear of accidental radiation exposure and the safe disposal of radioactive wastes that remain hazardous for thousands of years. If such waste could be consolidated and still considered as a viable source of energy, then perhaps it would not have to be shipped elsewhere for disposal. However, nuclear energy plants have been built on a scale that is incompatible with environmental acceptability. Size is important. There are naval ships and submarines that use mini-reactors that have operated for years. Perhaps, for regions, standardized reactors that are smaller, safer and more dependable than those on-line now and the secondary use of safely stored waste may make nuclear power more acceptable."

Veritor responds, "As I see it, there is a finite amount of uranium ore available, and even with breeder reactors, such nuclear plants are questionable as a long term energy solution. We have to worry lest they become a long term threat."

Pragma asks, "How about geothermal energy? Isn't this a promising resource? There are wet geothermal power-generating systems already in operation in the United States. A subterranean inferno exists everywhere under the earth's crust."

Neos reacts positively to this statement. "Yes, favorable conditions for dry rock geothermal energy systems exist in many places worldwide. Surely, we should be starting projects to drill and fracture granite and other rock which is continuously heated by magma or by the presence of radio-active heating in the granite itself."

Pragma answers, "Unfortunately, there are still technological problems in drilling hard rock to depths appropriate for yielding useful heat. The costs and risks of past development have often been prohibitive. However, this resource is widespread and very long-lasting. More creativity is necessary to tap these valuable energy resources. The introduction of regionalization would encourage the pooling of ideas, capital, planning and coordination to develop dry rock geothermal energy systems. Underwriting the cost would be within the scope of the private investors and regional capacity."

Veritor answers, "Such an effort, of course, must still depend on whether specific, hot granitic rock formations exist in the region."

CHAPTER 4 - ENERGY DEPENDENCIES & ALTERNATIVES

Geothermal Tapping of Earth's Furnace *

Mapping of the earth's geological structure has revealed the presence of thousands of hot spots caused by radio-active decay of rocks. Roughly for every kilometer (3,280 ft.) in depth an average of 30 degrees C increase in temperature occurs. This indefinitely large, longtime resource extends down to 10 kilometers (32,280 ft.). Wet geothermal involving hot water and steam resources have been tapped to provide steam for turbine generation of electricity. Dry geothermal implies that the holes and fractures are dry and that water or other heat exchange medium needs to be injected for circulation and use in turbine generation. Such systems are mostly closed loops.

Different Sources:

1. Water percolates down to porous rock heated by underlying magma below. Steam escapes naturally or is tapped for turbine generator use. The product is superheated steam. Potential temperature is as high as 1200 degrees C.
2. Drilling goes down to rock strata containing water trapped under non-permeable layers of rock to produce superheated steam. Potential temperature is 320 degrees C.
3. Drilling goes down to trapped water and methane in porous rock between shale in geothermal pressure zones. Gas, steam and hot water are produced. Potential temperature is 320 degrees C.
4. Drilling is into hot rock that is fractured by explosives or thermal shock. Water is injected for steam production at 320 degrees C.
5. Drilling is into hot radio-active granite intrusions; the rock is then fractured in situ, and a heat transfer medium is injected to obtain a high temperature gaseous product. Potential of 90 degrees C is reached. **

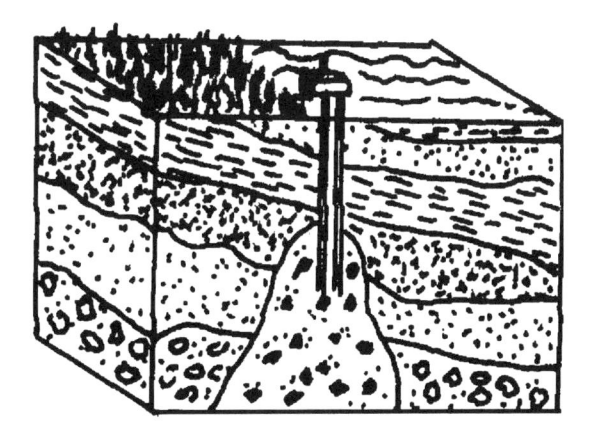

* "Energy, National Geographic Special Report", National Geographic Society, Feb. 1981
** "Hydrojet Drilling Means", U. S. Patent # 4,458,766, G.Siegel, 1984

Figure IV-4-E

Neos ventures along another path. "The dynamics of the sea also offer alternative sources of energy. The tides, ocean waves and thermoclines all provide an inexhaustible supply of energy. Differences in movement for waves and tides or water temperature provide vast amounts of energy. There are many concepts for using these sources. Turbines are already in operation that make use of tidal bores; other mechanisms use wave action to produce electricity. Innovations in alternative energy systems should be diligently studied for coastline regions and other populations."

Pragma answers, "Yes, these alternatives have been neglected, particularly along potentially favorable coastlines. However, the regional concept would be necessary to properly initiate and support such systems. In other words, such systems must be designed as part of a larger picture."

Neos proposes energy innovations in the area of transportation. "Let's concentrate on energy utilization for people-moving. Today's vehicles are totally dependent on fossil fuels which will eventually become scarce. Over-reliance on imported energy resources makes for acute vulnerability and chaos. What must eventually partially replace present dependency on fossil fuels? This is an urgent challenge for today's industrial societies. Unfortunately, the topsy turvey mix and scatter of activities and places where people live, work, shop and do most things in big cities requires a continued reliance on personal vehicles and a limited use of public transportation. The functional design orientation of regional infrastructures would correct this dependency.

"Alternate energy vehicles and supporting systems are urgently needed now. The hybrid vehicle, one that uses electricity and other means of propulsion, has been in the development phase for some time. Some designs use rechargeable batteries for electricity, but where must the electricity to re-charge come from and at what increased demand and cost to existing power plants, resources and means of distribution? What is the net efficiency by the time electricity is used in the vehicle?"

Pragma asks, "What kinds of hybrid systems do you have in mind? It seems to me anything new will also require other related enterprises and tremendous investments."

Veritor responds, "That is true, but there would be differences. The new enterprises and investments would be based on reducing dependency on distant sources of energy supply, and they would be able to be economically competitive and contribute to the restoration of a healthier environment and way of life. What are the alternatives if nothing is done to adapt now?"

Neos proposes an innovation. "We are talking about a gradual and incremental transition to different kinds of hybrid vehicles. They are likely to use combinations of electrical, chemical, and mechanical power. If solar energy is used, the outside construction of the vehicle would have panels or other means for receiving and converting solar energy to charge standby batteries. At least two liquid or solid batter-

CHAPTER 4 - ENERGY DEPENDENCIES & ALTERNATIVES

ies or other means of storing energy would be employed with provisions for switching. Battery recharging, replacement or substitution of cells or liquids would be done at residences, neighborhood terminals or in-transit stations. While the vehicle is driven, mechanical means for regeneration would also provide battery recharging similar to the alternators used in present day vehicles."

Pragma adds, "If the regional network, special centers, communities and neighborhoods are locally producing some of their own energy, re-charging should become much more convenient, economical and less dependent on major electrical power plant generation."

Veritor faces Neos and says, "I think you may have left out another way of battery recharging. A moving vehicle is constantly facing a flow of air that could be scooped to operate a turbine-generator. Such air scoops could be part of the vehicle body design and relatively simple to incorporate. This would convert and save part of the 50% of energy wasted due to vehicle air resistance while moving."

Neos responds, "You are headed in the right direction. The kind of innovation you propose should be aggressively explored. More innovation means more enterprise and progress."

Pragma reflects for a moment and notes, "It is apparent that initial design and development of some alternative energy systems would have to start in industrial, high technology countries. Of course, such development would be driven by the profit motive. The regional infrastructure design would lend support in establishing power regeneration systems."

Propelling Vehicles for a Compelling Future

- Both passenger-carrying and commercial vehicles should greatly benefit from innovations that are predicated on improved safety, reliability, performance, convenience and economy. Basically, innovation must also contribute to a safe environment and not deplete non-renewable resources. We need to re-think our dependence on fossil fuels in transportation. We currently rely on these non-renewable resources because they are expedient, cheap and efficient in a profit-conscious industrial and commercial world. We need to ask other questions. Does fossil fuel dependency lead to an improved collective quality of life or does it detract? What other alternatives are there? What is preventing their introduction?
- Increased innovation and research must be stimulated to devise new hybrid vehicles for carrying people and goods. Technology needs to change direction and discontinue reliance on energy depleting and environmentally damaging means of transportation. Technology must be directed towards creating vehicles utilizing various combinations of energy.
- The future of our changing world is highly dependent on transportation of all kinds. What should new hybrid vehicles be like? Who will accept the entrepreneurial challenges? Conversions toward combinations of electrical/chemical/propulsion, electrical/mechanical/combustion and other combinations of energy must be explored. Hybrid vehicles employing these conversions are likely to require two types of fuel systems. Battery stored electrical energy would be used for normal driving while some higher performance energy would be used for peak demands.
- Batteries may be recharged while traveling or during non-use. Pre-generated power to charge the batteries would be available in homes, centers and places of work.
- A hybrid configuration is suggested as follows:

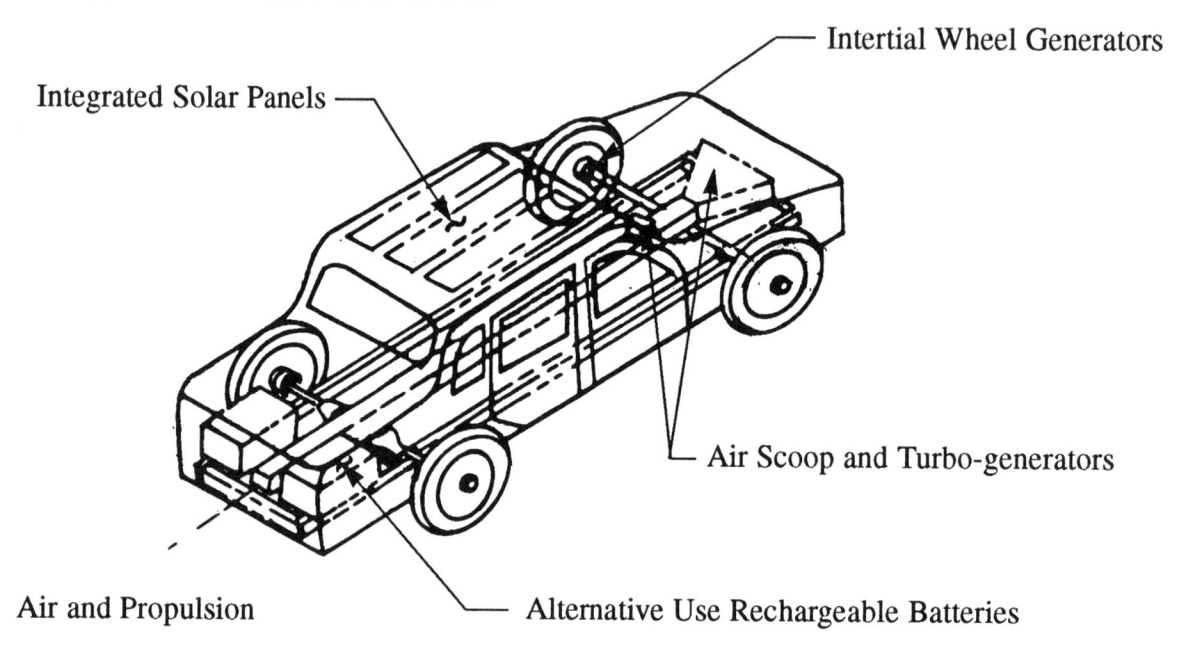

Figure IV-4-F

Part I - Urgent Times & Crowded Places

CHAPTER 5 - TREES AND RESTORATION

The trialogue turns to the subject of forests and cultivated trees and plants. Many kinds of trees and other plant life are diminishing in quantity and variety worldwide. Their depletion affects the quality of the air we breathe, the climate we live in and the products they provide us. We become more aware of the intrinsic value of trees and plant life after they are lost. Casual or indifferent attitudes about their disappearance denigrates their significance. There are some 350,000 species of plants worldwide! They provide wonderlands of beauty and a cornucopia of benefits for mankind.

The aggregate impact that trees and other plants have on people becomes even more significant as populations increase and over-concentrate. The restoration of trees must be first addressed for continents and then for regional sites. Regional designs depend on research findings to intelligently and carefully develop new areas with trees. But this must be a two way street. Research can help regionalization, and regionalization can help research. In regional design and development there would be an unusual chance to experiment with new varieties of plants that could benefit humanity and the specific populations of the region. Diversity of species, their ecology and genetic potential would also be addressed.

Neos, Pragma and Veritor are very aware of the regional implications. Imagine what 5,000 regions that stress resource and environmental issues could do to enhance nature and improve quality of living for millions of humans and other forms of life. Environments differ greatly from continent to continent with considerable variations in terrain, soil, climate and growing conditions. These differences favor the growth of certain species of trees and plants some of which may be indigenous to special areas. Such areas could gradually accommodate adaptive species as well. Regional design and development must encourage and sustain natural bio-diversity, promote the careful introduction of specific flora and fauna and help establish new bio-spheres over time.

Forests, groves and other plants vary on each continent, but the areas have some things in common: depletion of forests and woodlands and the gradual diminishment of arable land. This correlates with population increases and the demand for more cleared lands for agriculture. A brief, general status of forests, groves and other plants suggests an urgent need for system management and restoration efforts.

Neos opens a new part of the discussion. "I think it is extremely important to summarize not only what trees and shrubs presently exist but to project what could exist in the various environments of each continent. Surely, development of regional sites must respect existing local forms of life. Everything that lives today has undergone evolutionary experiments. Humans have to use ingenuity, caution and consideration prior to and during the preparation and development of sites as they share use of the land."

Pragma responds,"This is going to be difficult with fast growing populations and their demands for resources at the expense of rare, valuable or unusual forms of life. Trees and shrubs fall into this category, and people ought to consider replanting them not only for their intrinsic value, but for applications that benefit other life forms as well."

Neos and Veritor readily accept this approach. Veritor notes,"I think it would be extremely wise to consider secondary and tertiary potential benefits during initial development. But there are very different geographical locations and conditions that determine this, and they need to be addressed at the appropriate time."

Neos adds,"Let's consider the global and regional implications of planting of special trees and shrubs on the slopes of mountains and hills."

Pragma thinks about this a moment and answers, "In order to do a comprehensive job, we must also consider projects involving dams, reservoirs, catchment areas and ponds, special access roads, soil stabilization structures, firebreaks and other development projects."

Veritor notes,"I can see a systems approach becomes even more necessary during regional planning and development. As we have mentioned before, justification for a systems approach is obvious. It promotes integration, cost-sharing and greater effectiveness. This approach must be applied to a number of special environments such as plains and farmland, former rain forests, marsh lands and mangroves, and arid barren areas."

CHAPTER 5 - TREES & RESTORATION

Reforestation & Replanting
Global and Regional Renewal Implications

Reforestation and restoration of lands with the planting of shrubs and trees has related implications. It is not a matter of visualizing forests, orchards, shrubs and grasses as just fixed objects, but as life-forms that offer much with the changing seasons. The land must never be made barren and lifeless. That would be a desecration. Trees and shrubs offer homes to multitudes of nature's creatures. They provide functional ecospheres with many processes and inter-relationships.

Reforestation and Planting of Special Shrubs
On the Slopes of Mountains and Hills.

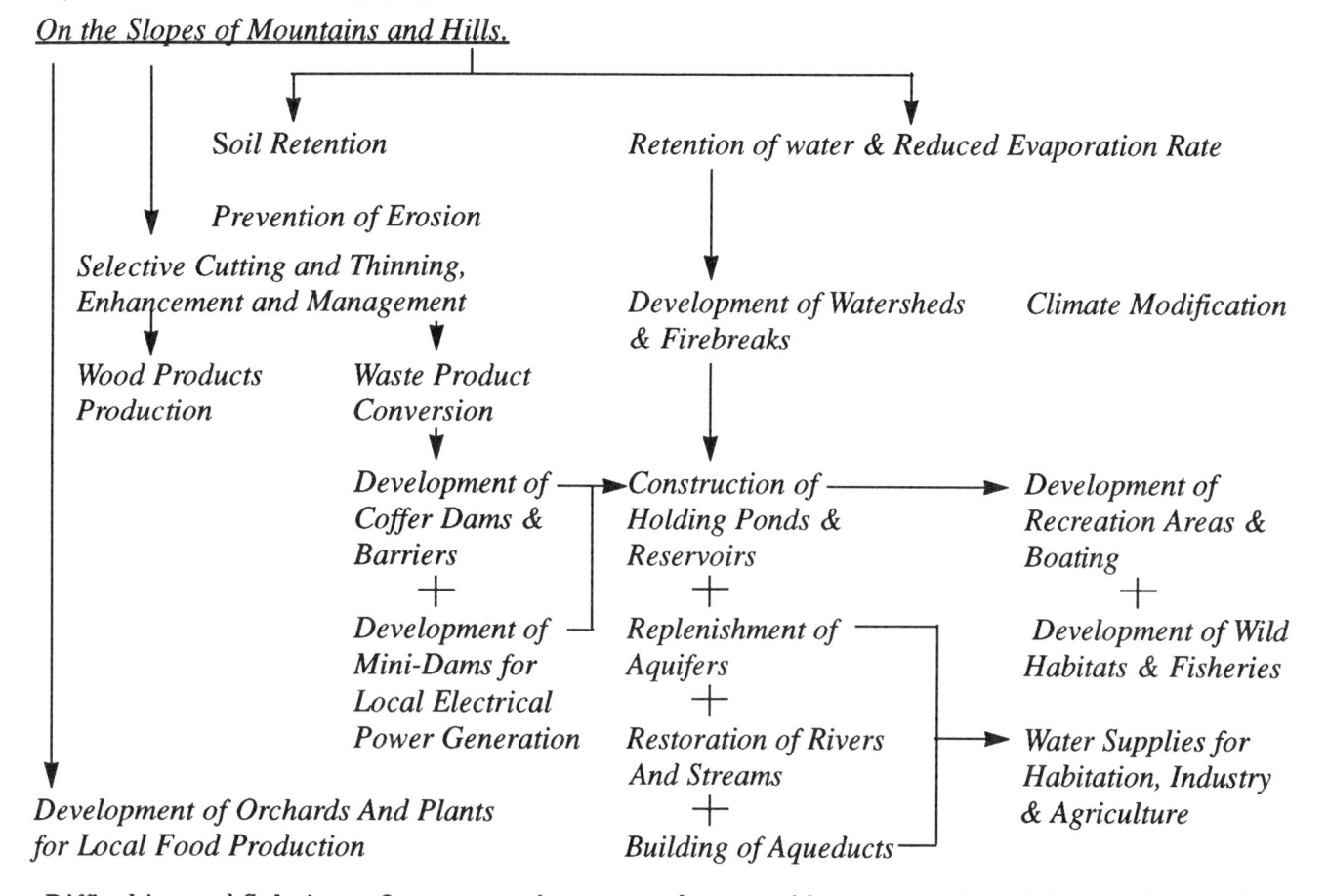

```
                    ┌─────────────────┬──────────────────────┐
                    ▼                 ▼                      
              Soil Retention    Retention of water & Reduced Evaporation Rate
                    │                 │
              Prevention of Erosion   │
                    ▼                 ▼
    Selective Cutting and Thinning,   Development of Watersheds    Climate Modification
    Enhancement and Management         & Firebreaks
         │           │                 │
         ▼           ▼                 │
    Wood Products   Waste Product     │
    Production      Conversion        │
                        │             │
                        ▼             ▼
                  Development of → Construction of ─────→ Development of
                  Coffer Dams &   Holding Ponds &         Recreation Areas &
                  Barriers        Reservoirs              Boating
                        +              +                      +
                  Development of ─ Replenishment of ──── Development of Wild
                  Mini-Dams for    Aquifers              Habitats & Fisheries
                  Local Electrical     +
                  Power Generation  Restoration of Rivers ─→ Water Supplies for
                                    And Streams              Habitation, Industry
                                        +                    & Agriculture
    Development of Orchards And Plants  Building of Aqueducts
    for Local Food Production
```

<u>Difficulties and Solutions:</u> *Over-exposed areas can be caused by clear-cutting of forests, degraded top soil, poor water retention and excessive accumulation of brush susceptible to fires.*
Hardy trees, beginning with hardwoods and then evergreens are required for replenishing. At times, special imported top soil, ground cover and protected seedlings would be needed.

Figure IV-5-A

Reforestation & Replanting (Continued)
Global & Regional Renewal Implications

Reforestation and the planting of shrubs on plains and farm land help retain top soil and prevent erosion. Ground cover and crop rotation, windbreaks, water sharing and cooperative efforts form a part of a regional strategy.

Reforestation, Planting of Groves and Shrubs, Seeding of Ground Cover for Plains and Farm Land

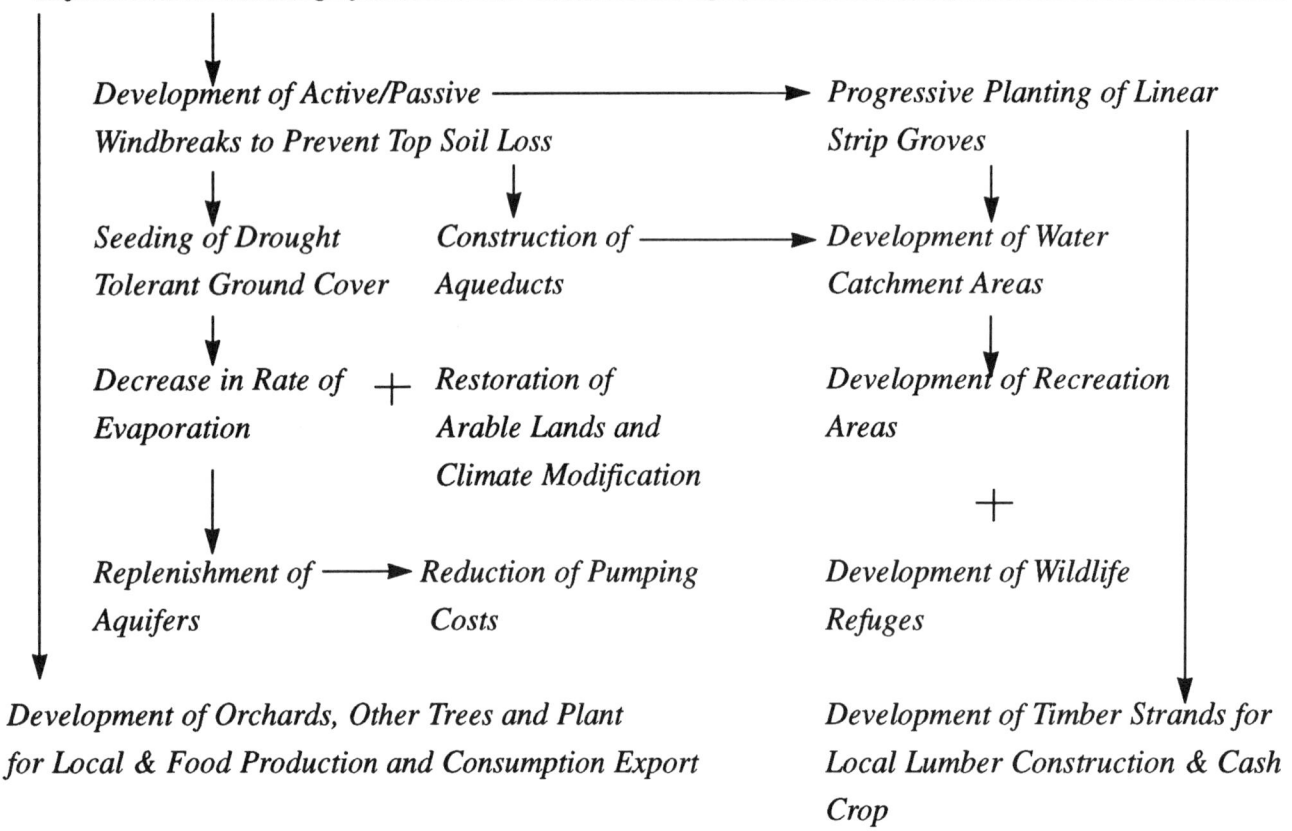

Development of Active/Passive ⟶ *Progressive Planting of Linear*
Windbreaks to Prevent Top Soil Loss   *Strip Groves*

Seeding of Drought   *Construction of* ⟶ *Development of Water*
Tolerant Ground Cover   *Aqueducts*   *Catchment Areas*

Decrease in Rate of + *Restoration of*   *Development of Recreation*
Evaporation   *Arable Lands and*   *Areas*
     Climate Modification
                                         +

Replenishment of ⟶ *Reduction of Pumping*   *Development of Wildlife*
Aquifers   *Costs*   *Refuges*

Development of Orchards, Other Trees and Plant   *Development of Timber Strands for*
for Local & Food Production and Consumption Export   *Local Lumber Construction & Cash Crop*

Difficulties and Solutions:

Drought conditions and sustained high winds make for wind-blown loss of top soil. Extreme seasonal temperatures often exact a large toll on arable land and livestock, wildlife and agricultural production because of water loss making the soil very dry. Replenishing lost top soil is a long, costly process. Soil banking and redistribution, mulching and soil importation may be necessary in increments concurrent with the planting of hardy trees and other plants and the construction of wind barriers. Gradual introduction of non-native species of plant life for commercial crops could lead to necessary restorations. Crop rotation can maintain or replace nitrogen in the soil.

Figure IV-5-B

CHAPTER 5 - TREES & RESTORATION

Reforestation & Replanting (Continued)
(Global & Regional Renewal Implications)

Reforestation and the planting of crops in cleared land requires the restoration of soil nutrients to improve soil quality and to foster productivity in what were once rain forests, mangroves and marshes. Attempts to convert stripped rainforests for crop land and grazing lands has only short-term benefits as the land's fertility plays out in two to three years.

<u>Reforestation, Soil Restoration and the Application of Modern Agricultural Methods for Former Rain Forests, Marsh Land and Mangroves</u>

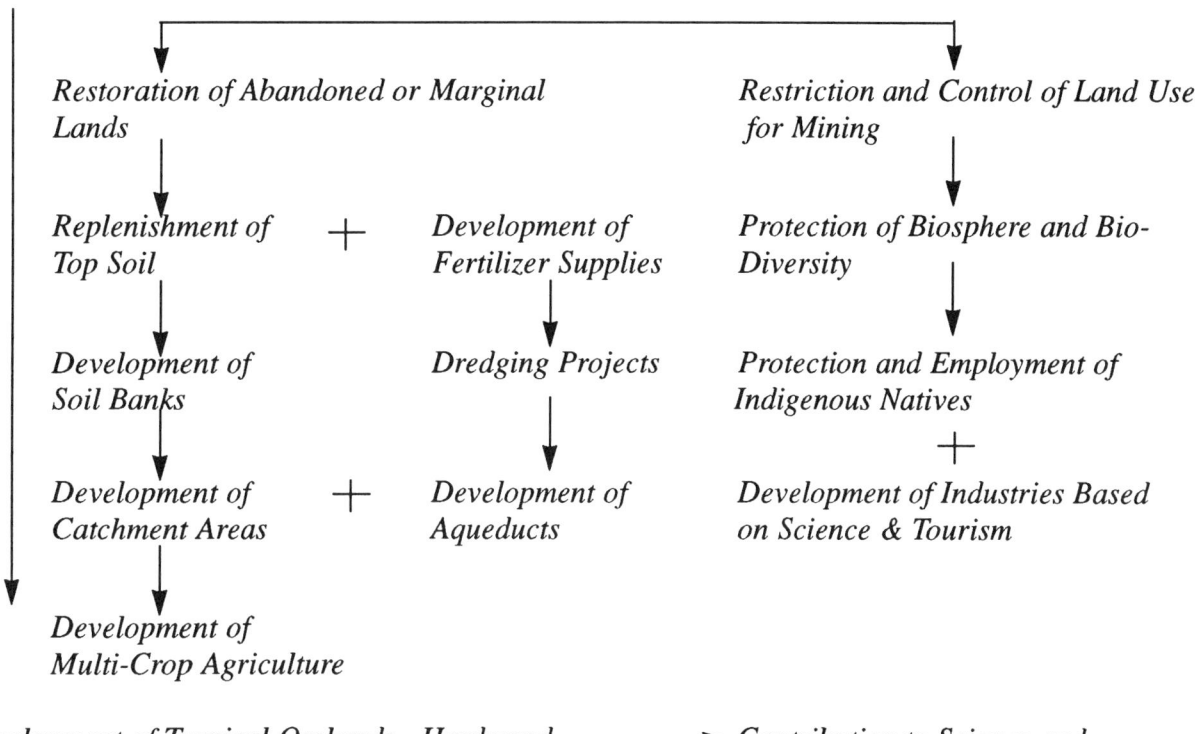

Restoration of Abandoned or Marginal Lands → *Replenishment of Top Soil* + *Development of Fertilizer Supplies* → *Development of Soil Banks* → *Dredging Projects* → *Development of Catchment Areas* + *Development of Aqueducts* → *Development of Multi-Crop Agriculture*

Restriction and Control of Land Use for Mining → *Protection of Biosphere and Bio-Diversity* → *Protection and Employment of Indigenous Natives* + *Development of Industries Based on Science & Tourism*

Development of Tropical Orchards, Hardwood Strands & Plant Conserves and Agriculture for Local and Export Consumption → *Contribution to Science and Climate Control*

<u>Difficulties and Solutions:</u>

Population pressures and greed lead to short-term solutions. Loss of biospheres exposes fragile land to erosion. A changed appreciation of the intrinsic value of the rainforest and marshland must lead to long-term protection and careful utilization. Restoration of abandoned and marginal lands is important, requiring regional emphasis and global support.

Figure IV-5-C

Reforestation & Replanting (Continued)
(Global & Regional Renewal Implications)

Some regions of the world are barren and, for the most part, not suitable for forestation and the planting of shrubs. Where there is ground water, particularly along the fringes of such areas, there may be oases which could support fruit trees and hardy shrubs that require little water and make limited human habitation possible.

<u>Selective Replanting of Certain Fruit Trees and Shrubs for Arid, Barren Areas</u>

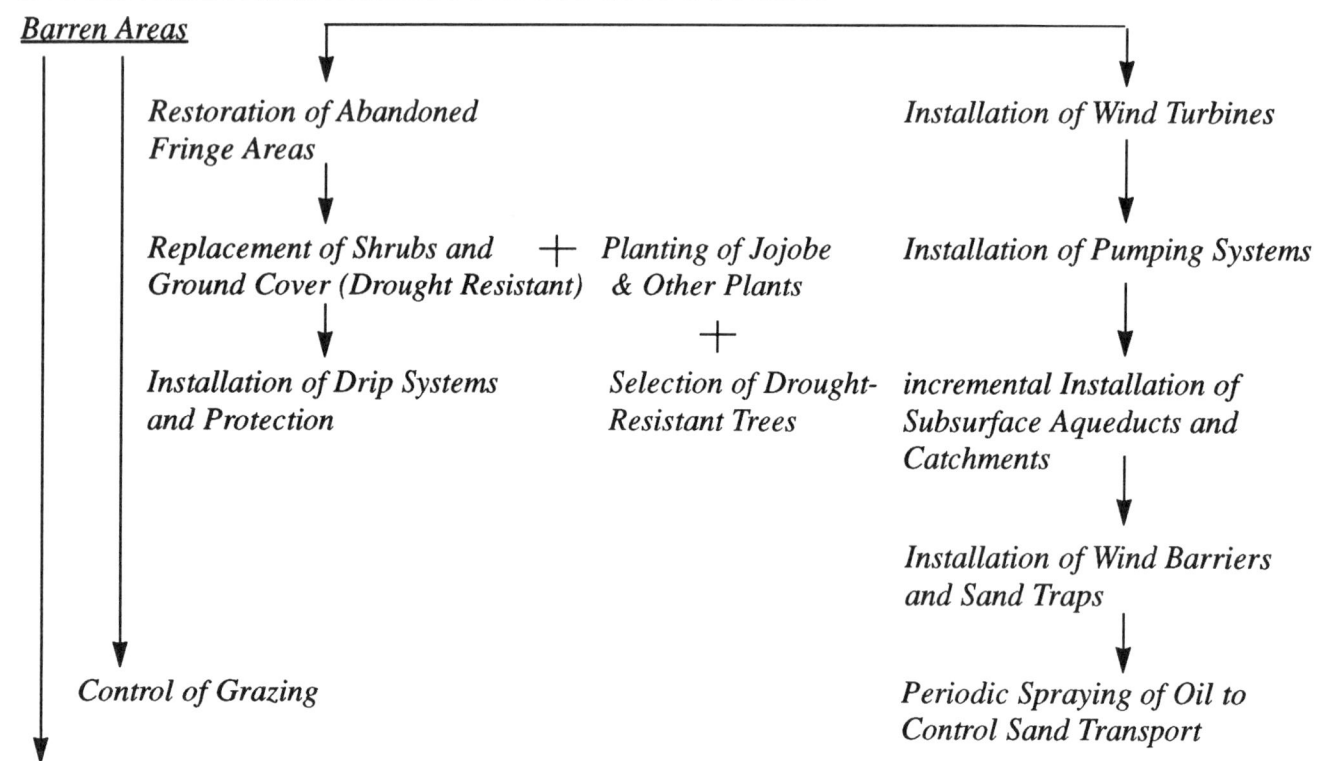

- Restoration of Abandoned Fringe Areas
  - Replacement of Shrubs and Ground Cover (Drought Resistant) + Planting of Jojobe & Other Plants + Selection of Drought-Resistant Trees
  - Installation of Drip Systems and Protection
- Installation of Wind Turbines
  - Installation of Pumping Systems
  - incremental Installation of Subsurface Aqueducts and Catchments
  - Installation of Wind Barriers and Sand Traps
  - Periodic Spraying of Oil to Control Sand Transport
- Control of Grazing

Development of Protected Orchards and Aquaculture

<u>Difficulties and Solutions:</u>

Fierce winds and driven sand encroach on settled areas. These intrusions eventually cover and destroy existing plants. Underground water may exist, but become inaccessible. Over-grazing and the burning of all existing shrubbery for fuel depletes plants and trees. Counter efforts are needed to gradually stem encroachment and to reclaim land with desert-type plants and ground cover. Available oil and gravel would be helpful in stabilizing surrounding surface areas and contain encroachment. Underground channeling or piping of imported water may again be feasible as in the past. Solar energy resources may eliminate dependency on imported fuel.

Figure IV-5-D

CHAPTER 5 - TREES & RESTORATION

Pragma asks "What about cities and other heavily inhabited areas? Don't people in the cities need green spaces? In many places more than 40% of habital land is paved over. This means little in terms of the total area, but it is significant when applied to large, heavily populated areas."

Veritor adds,"You have made a good point. Can over-populated areas be converted from the coldness of concrete, glass, steel and macadam to park-like surroundings? The tide of 'progress' has led to the chopping down of trees to make way for construction and roads in the city. But is this a balanced approach in the long run?"

Neos notes,"Not much positive can be said about the bleakness of such surroundings. Apparently, people become accustomed to buildings and acres of pavement without greenery. Yet, parks are appreciated by so many as a respite from the cold and humdrum realities of their lives and the pressures of technology and commerce. Curiously, plant life is important even to many confirmed apartment dwellers. Witness the line up of plants and flowers in boxes on window sills, landings and porches or the miniature gardens planted in special places. Even well-placed strands of trees and decorative shrubs are attractive. It is an attempt to compensate for the cold, stark look of the surrounding buildings."

Pragma comments,"During periods of population expansion and development, plant life is often largely ignored. Modern concepts of community planning require that high rise buildings be set back. Trees and shrubs are added for landscaping. As people move to the suburbs, they often feel a yearning for foliage and color. These are an important and integral part of creating a home-like atmosphere in the immediate environment."

Veritor sums up the topic of trees and plants."It will be part of any regional scenario to provide large areas without tall buildings and without traffic congestion. This is necessary for both the outlying portions of a region as well as the inner network of communities. Green spaces improve quality of life. They remind people that mankind is also a part of nature. The renewal and preservation of trees and vegetation on a global scale would imply a commitment by mankind to pass on a gift, as well as a challenge, to coming generations. On the regional level, abundant foliage should be included in the grand scheme of things. There is room for nature's unmatchable designs. Regions, with their networks of communities, must have the necessary scope and perspective to express this on a significant level five thousand times worldwide."

The Gift of Trees

- *A world without trees is contrary to nature and, by extension, alien to mankind.*
- *Trees, in a natural and renewable way, fill a multitude of functions and provide thousands of products.*
- *Trees contribute to making life more liveable.*
- *Innovative ways of providing, placing and utilizing trees are part of regional enhancement.*

Provision

- *Grow a variety of saplings in agricultural centers to supply regional centers, communities and neighborhoods.*
- *Grow a variety of saplings for reforestation of the region.*
- *Develop trees that are pest and disease-resistant, using genetic research.*
- *Develop new ways to accelerate growth (genetically or by using intermittent lighting involving photochromes).*

Placement

- *Provide planting information and guidance to home owners, industry and developers for the strategic location of trees in centers and neighborhoods.*
- *Plant and protect forests and provide firebreaks and access to maintain them.*
- *Designate areas for the protection of trees.*
- *Encourage voluntary participation in tree planting.*

Utilization

- *Use trees and shrubs for soil conservation and stabilization.*
- *Use trees for shade or wind barriers to conserve energy.*
- *Use trees for climate modification.*
- *Use trees for absorbing carbon dioxide.*
- *Convert waste wood to methane or alcohol.*
- *Convert wood to wood pulp and fiber products.*
- *Use cultured forests for wood products, structures and surfaces.*
- *Use forests as watersheds.*
- *Use trees as habitats for wildlife.*

CHAPTER 5 - TREES & RESTORATION

Regionalization must be thought of on a level that encourages humans to profoundly respect and enhance nature's creations. The regional concept offers a different vision of the future, one that has many trees and greenery in open spaces everywhere with the designs and works of mankind built in harmony with nature. This is worth striving for. One example is Irvine, California, where the land is respected."

Neos begins again, "Reforestation for watersheds, windbreaks and land preservation has already been proposed. But there is also a need for selected species of trees to be placed throughout communities and centers of the region. Some would shade and cool buildings and others screen large heat absorbing surfaces. Their placement would be carefully made to avoid obstructing solar devices. Trees can reduce the need for energy, and they absorb carbon dioxide and give off oxygen. So there are pragmatic as well as esthetic reasons for having them."

Pragma counters, "How many trees do you think should be planted for each regional community? Wouldn't it be prohibitive in cost? "

Veritor answers, "It is estimated that each regional community in an industrialized society would need about 100,000 three year old saplings.The cost would probably be about $500,000, maybe less with volunteers doing most of the planting and initial nurturing."

Neos notes,"Trees with scientifically accelerated growth patterns would be developed both in nurseries under contract and at the regional farms. These trees would gradually be made available regionally. New techniques could be explored for growing many different kinds of trees as well as other plants. One approach is to use artificial light intermittently at night to keep plants from becoming dormant and allowing them to grow quicker and hardier before transplanting. Temperature, moisture and light control are important factors in this approach."

Part IV - Preparation For Tomorrow

CHAPTER 6 - FIBER: DEPENDENCIES & VARIATIONS

Neos, Pragma and Veritor continue their survey of renewable resources. They are trying to put world resources into a different perspective. They now focus on the availability and value of fibers, another renewable resource. Fibers are derived from natural materials and man-made synthetics. These may consist of organic or inorganic materials and sometimes combinations of both, either in filament form or woven.

Neos begins with an observation. "We have not talked about the resources that give us fibers. Perhaps we can isolate some things that show how prevalent and important fibers are in the lives of human beings. However, we can only introduce the subject to serve the purposes of this discussion. A full presentation of fibers, their composition and their applications would cause us to digress."

"It is easy to digress; so many subjects suggest others," Veritor agrees," because we are discussing resources at this point, some basic resource materials should be identified."

Pragma adds, "Fibers have been in extensive use since the dawn of history. Of course, we can make much greater use of them in modern technology. Some parts of trees, according to species, offer wood for a myriad number of fiber products: furniture, flooring, beams, trusses, framing, sheathing, siding, roofing, built-ins and the like for houses and other buildings. The pulp from trees and other plants furnish material for making paper products and even plastics. Everywhere we look, there seem to be products derived from trees."

Neos continues in this vein of thought. "There are a number of other plants that provide valuable fibers such as cotton, hemp, flax, ramie and jute. Even silk worms depend on a plant. We depended on fibers for woven cloth and rope products. Given the rate of population growth, there would have to be a commensurate increase in cultivating fiber plants were it not for the introduction of man-made synthetic fibers and semi-synthetic fibers."

Veritor agrees with this. "Man-made fibers like Rayon, Nylon, Dynel, Orlon, Teflon have made their appearance just in time. It takes a lot of land, fertilizer and water to increase production of cotton as well as even more fertile land and water for grazing animals that produce wools, furs, skins and sinews."

CHAPTER 6 - FIBER: DEPENDENCIES & VARIATIONS

Fiber Resources

A host of everyday products comes to mind when the word "fiber" is mentioned. Indeed, this mental image is with us when we think of the various functions of the human body and the human diet. We are also aware of an immense array of fibrous products made of organic, inorganic and synthetic materials. Clothing, carpeting, paper, structures, moving parts, cables and filiments are just a small part of those in use today. .

In every day life we come across such expressions as linkage, communication ties, transmission lines, moral fiber, cut from the same cloth, tying the matrimonial knot, pulling strings, tying things down, networking and pulling the wool over someone's eyes, etc. Such figures of speech suggest that fiber and its various forms have left a strong mental imprint on mankind. Fibers are derived from many resources and processes. What are they?

organic	cotton flax hemp jute plant cellulose	wool mohair camel & other hair fur silk	and others.
inorganic	steel molybdenum tungsten lead copper silver gold platinum	silicon carbon asbestos wool rock wool slag wool	and others.
synthetic or semi-synthetic	*Rayon Nylon Orlon Vinyon acrylics Teflon*	and very many more now & in the future.	

Figure IV-6-A

Neos is intrigued by the subject of fibers and the role they have played throughout history. But present and future kinds and uses of fiber resources are the subject of this discussion.

Neos begins,"Today, when we think about selecting a type of fiber for a specific use, we may have a number of options. When we start with a selected fiber of specific composition, we may be curious and ask what can be made from such a substance. It becomes even more intriguing when we start with a given application, so that there are choices of different combinations of fibers to select from."

Pragma laughs,"I can see that making such choices could be puzzling and confusing, but many people may be interested in how well they work and how long they will last. In the world of fiber technologies the selection and production of fibrous materials is serious business."

Neos nods and says,"I'm sure in the coming years there will be a proliferation of new synthetic fibers introduced to replace or be combined with some of the natural ones. The implication is that fewer acres of land may be planted for cotton or left for grazing. Other crops that provide food could be grown on such land. So there will be many changes in the future in the use of agricultural land."

Veritor notes,"We have not talked about inorganic fibers. These are particularly essential, having great use in the modern industrial state. There are many composites with fibers blended with plastics, ceramics and other materials."

"But what of innovations and the invention of new fibers that we discussed earlier?" asks Neos."In our technological age, there are not only woven synthetics but optical fibers and electrical wire conductors, with superconductors a very promising prospect. Great changes in the industrial society are likely to occur because of the emergence of new fibers used in communication and transportation."

Neos, Pragma and Veritor have been centering their interest on both innovations and well known concepts and practices needed for regional enhancement. They are well aware that what they have suggested is merely introductory, serving only as stimuli for further investigation.

Part IV - Urgent Times & Crowded Places

CHAPTER 7 - THE MANAGEMENT OF NON-RENEWABLES

Up to now, Neos, Pragma and Veritor have been dwelling on the subject of renewable resources. They are renewable to the extent that nature or mankind can reproduce or recycle them. The continued supply of many non-renewable resources for present and future generations is in jeopardy. Fortunately, depletion of resources by mankind is gradual and allows human adaptations and adjustments, if recognized in time.

The attrition or unavailability of non-renewable resources is crucial to human existence. It is likely to happen first to those who consume them most and to those who do not have the financial means of obtaining them. The prevailing habit of conspicuous consumption and waste by industrial and heavily populated countries is exacerbated by high concentrations of demand. Countries with supercities are likely to feel the full brunt of scarcity. Experience tells us that rioting, hoarding, thievery and black markets increase. The haves are pitted against the have nots and chaos reigns. This scenario is not hard to visualize. It is unfolding today.

Fortunately, other scenarios exist. Many people recognize the moral and ethical aspects of stability and an acceptable standard of living for those who are in desperate need. Over-consumption and waste are anathema to a healthy and humane society. Many people, worldwide, are becoming more aware of this and are campaigning for recycling and conservation.

Neos, Pragma and Veritor are also advocates of recycling and conservation. They are very concerned about the issue of rapid, continual obsolescence and the scrapping of what is still useful with insufficient attempts to salvage that which could be recycled. Will the next generations have to go to dumps to reclaim non-renewable materials to maintain some semblance of quality in their lives? Neos, Pragma and Veritor see rapid obsolescence as pernicious. Much of what is produced has too short a useful life span and is subject to frequent maintenance and parts replacement. This promotes extra services but does not ensure conservation, since many people prefer to throw away an item rather than repair it.

Neos is ready to pursue this."I think that there is an unhealthy level of the rationalization that prosperity is built on consumption. Increased demand without actual need is promoted as being the 'good life'. Buy now, pay later! There must always be something new to buy and then discard. I see major problems growing from such consumption on a worldwide scale. Increasing population and improved standards of living for more of the world's inhabitants can only mean greater demand for critical non-renewable resources."

Global Resources (Mostly Non-Renewables)*

	Recycling Potential			Future Availability			
	Yes	At Source	By Consumer	Wide Distrib.	Limit. Distr.	Location	Abundance

(Index of Frequency - Number of Locations)

	Yes	At Source	By Consumer	Wide Distrib.	Limit. Distr.	Location	Abundance
Major Metals							
Chromium	x	x	x		21	N.Am.	Africa
Iron	x	x	x	82			Limited
Manganese	x	x	x		29		
Nickel	x	x	x		23	S.Am.	Limited
Minor Metals							
Cobalt		x	x		14	S.Am.	Limited
Molybdenum		x	x		21	Eur, Afr	Limited
Tungsten		x	x		24		Limited
Vanadium		x	x		6	Eur, Afr	Limited
Non-Ferrous							
Copper	x	x	x	72			Moderate
Lead	x	x	x	45			Moderate
Tin	x	x	x	37			Limited
Zinc	x	x	x	57			Moderate
Light Metals							
Aluminum	x	x	x				Ample
Magnesium	x	x	x		17	Afr, Aus.	Limited
Titanium	x				19	Afr, Aus.	Limited
Lithium	x	x			7	Asia, Afr	Limited
Precious Metals						Australia	
Gold	x	x	x	71		Europe	
Limited Silver	x	x	x		30		Limited
Platinum	x	x	x		12		Limited
Diamonds (Metaloid)					20	N.Am	Limited
Uranium							Limited
Mineral Fertilizers							
Nitrates	x	x			24	Afr, Aus	Moderate
Phosphates	x	x			30	Australia	Limited
Potash	x	x			14	Australia	Limited
Sulphur	x	x			19	Afr, Aus.	Limited

* Source: Derived from National Geographic 1990 World Atlas

Table IV-7-A

CHAPTER 7 - THE MANAGEMENT OF NON-RENEWABLES

Pragma responds,"Well, isn't this what free enterprise is all about? Isn't this progress? Isn't it necessary to have greater production of everything to bring prosperity to as many as possible? So what if non-renewable resources are consumed? If they can be reclaimed or recycled, other things can be manufactured from them, and many new services can be created based on waste handling, reprocessing and re-utilization. When new things are produced, people who can afford them and even those who envy them, must feel that this is what it's all about."

Veritor looks up in amazement."You sound as if the possession of material things in life is the purpose of life. It's a way to look at life, but it only emphasizes one dimension of thinking. Supposing one were to be immersed in abundance, but had no friends or family? Suppose one became bored? Suppose suddenly all material abundance disappeared?"

Following this brief philosophical exchange, Neos resumes the discussion of non-renewable resources. "Some of the resources we are referring to are metals and others are minerals for fertilizers. It is quite evident from data that there is considerable uncertainty about their future availability. Recycling and reclamation are mandatory, not optional. We can see from resource maps of the continents that the distribution of metal and mineral resources is neither uniform nor equal. For instance, South America has no significant sulphur deposits. There is no great abundance of non-renewable resources."

Pragma continues,"Probably more sources for both metals and minerals exist, but they are yet to be discovered or made accessible. I am talking about more than physical accessibility. Resources have been becoming extremely difficult to extract and process and still protect the environment without greatly increasing costs. This situation is of growing concern."

Veritor frowns and says with a somber voice,"Because these resources are finite, they must be acquired and processed with skill and not by brute force. To find rich deposits is fortunate. It makes it possible to commercially exploit quickly on a large scale. But as these deposits become depleted, it will obviously be more difficult to depend on them. What can substitute for them? People will surely have to pay premium prices for products made from them. The citizens of most nations will bear the consequences."

Neos adds, "I wonder if mankind will eventually declare these concentrated resources to be world treasures and ration them? Countries that possess them may hoard and control them. Storms of controversy and even wars may erupt if a definitive world policy of conservation, utilization and distribution is not formulated."

Part IV - Preparation For Tomorrow

CHAPTER 8 - SUMMARY OF CONTINENTAL RESOURCES

A continent has been defined as a large extensive land mass established by convention. There are seven continents. But explain the arbitrary separation of Europe from Asia. Certainly, tectonic plates do not define them. The acceptance of the definition of a continent is one of convenience, not significance. It has been a case of mankind exploring the world and attempting to map it as dominant countries lay territorial claims to lands in anticipation of abundant resources. As we know now, such claims have been quickly contested by others. As we have discussed earlier in Part II, Chapters 4 & 5, attempts to create borders and exert territorial control exist to this day.

Agreed upon national boundaries are often distinguished by natural geographical features and environmental characteristics. However, these natural boundaries continue to undergo change. Furthermore, prevailing weather conditions, subterranean geological activities, geographic features and natural resources and deposits do not conform to national boundaries. Such boundaries are, therefore, not a matter of convention but the result of arbitrary territorial imperatives, concessions to power and the control of resources. When we think of national boundaries on an historical basis, we must conclude that all political boundaries are temporary. How many of today's boundaries existed 6000 years ago, and how many will exist 6000 years from now?

All of this must be kept in mind when we approach the concept of regionalization in the context of national boundaries as they presently exist. Nations control specific resources which may span both internal and external boundaries. Oil reserves, mineral deposits, coal seams and forest preserves are but some examples.

. . .

Regional site selection and the subsequent development of infrastructures will take place in naturally defined spaces that may not be solely within a national boundary. If within a national jurisdiction, the region may occupy space in more than one sub-jurisdiction. In this sense, it is analogous to the economic and industrial zones being formed by many nations today in which joint enterprises are carried out to the mutual benefit of all parties. Through many exchanges, there is a sharing of both human and natural resources eventually eliminating, for most part, need for formal borders.

CHAPTER 8 - SUMMARY OF CONTINENTAL RESOURCES

Borderless Regions

The future location of regions is not intended to be limited by man-made borders which historically have offered no prospect of peaceful and economic co-existence. The full breadth of history confirms this.

Regional location must be based on natural, enduring interactions that are in the general best interests of the participating inhabitants within healthy environments. Regional design and networking offer promise of achieving this.

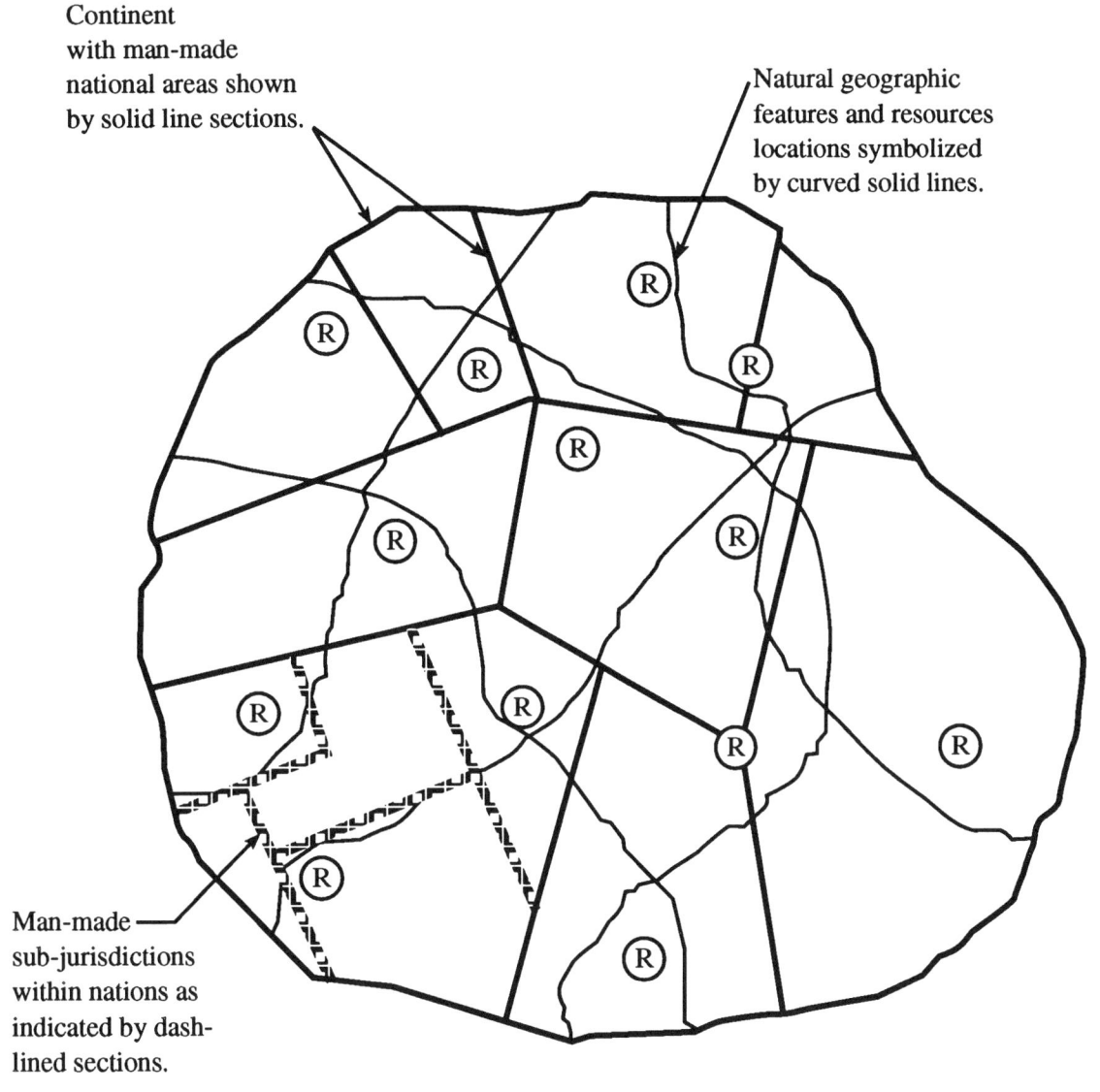

Continent with man-made national areas shown by solid line sections.

Natural geographic features and resources locations symbolized by curved solid lines.

Man-made sub-jurisdictions within nations as indicated by dash-lined sections.

Indicated regional networks R connect to each other, to their nations and sub-jurisdictions of those nations.

Figure IV-8-A

Regions would be designed to interface with other regions and jurisdictions, thereby serving as a means for cooperation and joint ventures. By substituting networking for barriers, the regional concept would become a major promoter of peace and prosperity.

However, those in political power may initially have negative perceptions of regions. Their distortions of the regional intent may mislead the public with fears of temporary losses when actually it would have everything to gain in the long run. If all is in chaos to begin with, protection of the status quo would hardly be worth saving. Neos, Veritor and Pragma are aware of this, but they see how the European Common Market has been evolving as a positive example.

Proper utilization of natural and human resources calls for better management and cooperation. Networking regional implementation would provide orderly, rational and natural transitions and a chance to help society grow. Changes would be made with minimum disruption and waste.

Regional networking would be constructive, not destructive. In short, the regional concept would be open to cooperation, contribution, participation, modification and expansion and dedicated to meeting continuing, long term human needs. Enhancement of continental resources and environments and the preparation of sites for regions are the next phases in our progression. These are fundamental and urgent.

Neos, Pragma and Veritor have been deeply immersed in the examination of phasing programs and their projects requiring joint enterprises. Neos notes,"We have discussed some of the resources and environmental issues, and now it is time to express more specifically what needs to be implemented. Surely there are leaders in the world who are capable of managing essential programs and projects that resolve the problems of food, water, energy, minerals, forestation, fibers and human resources."

Pragma responds,"Those who hold power in the world today have such great opportunities to improve the lives of their people. Progressive programs and projects would make life more bearable and hopeful for all. Why aren't more agencies or people ready to introduce and enact changes? Is it because many leaders do not know how to proceed in the midst of complexity or are fearful of risks and consequences? Is there a lack of comprehensive planning and a larger vision of what development must mean?"

Veritor continues, "Many of the development programs we propose are applicable to all continents. But these programs are only the beginning. Additional ideas, innovations and approaches in a multitude of fields must be brought forth, particularly when the infrastructures of regionalization begin to exist."

Pragma notes,"Enhancement of resources will require considerable funding and great deal of effort. Investments must be made only for well-specified results, not

CHAPTER 8 - SUMMARY OF CONTINENTAL RESOURCES

block allocations of funds for ill-defined or undefined objectives. How can funds and contributions be effectively utilized without objectives that are results-oriented? Without a well-defined direction, haphazard, arbitrary approaches are likely to result in uncontrolled costs, waste and corruption. Investments must focus on the intrinsic value of skills, knowledge and team work in carrying out projects of worth. This is in contrast to 'manufactured' work intended to just keep people busy, diverted and pacified with projects of dubious value. Certainly, there are enough valid things to do to improve human lives and society. The purpose of programs and their projects must be to add value to whatever is produced in order to increase the health and wealth of a nation. It's a matter of acknowledging needs and problems, developing solutions and then implementing them to the extent possible in a timely manner. Of course, resources will need to be diverted from efforts of marginal importance and other wasteful endeavors. I would like to present a summary of different kinds of programs that should be of concern to the countries of each continent."

General Resource Development Appraisal
For Continents of the World

A cursory inspection of renewable and non-renewable resources reveals certain glaring needs for their development and utilization. Selection of regional candidate areas depends on timely innovations in the process of resource enhancement.

Programs Involving Food Resources:

Increased and improved utilization of arable land is necessary. Deserts like the Sahara and Gobi are not the only unproductive areas. Large marginal grazing lands are prone to rapid desertification. Of all the continents, Africa is the only one that does not raise enough food to feed itself. Only 50,000 square kilometers of 23 million square kilometers of land are irrigated in sub-Saharan Africa. Parts of Africa and South America are similar in that severe climate, large population increases, limited capital and weak governmental infrastructures are a deterrent to rapid improvements in food production.

Preliminary Summary of Things to Do:

1. Reclaim desert fringes by planting appropriate ground cover, erect wind deflectors and barriers, spreading oil and gravel over infringing areas. (A, As)
2. Reduce dependency on grazing animals and increase fowl/fish farming. (A, SA, As, Au)
3. Plant wind barriers and erect protective structures for fruit orchards. (A, SA, NA, E, As, Au)
4. Improve irrigation and water management to prevent salinization of soil. (A, As, NA)
5. Introduce alternative foods and growing techniques and induce acceptance. (A, SA, As)
6. Develop experimental plots to introduce new, alternative crops. (A, SA, As)
7. Introduce labor-saving techniques compatible with learning potential. (A, SA, As)
8. Extend research for pest and disease resistant plants. (A, SA, NA, E, As, Au)
9. Introduce effective nitrogen-fixing fertilizer alternatives. (A, SA, NA, E, As, Au)
10. Develop means of storage, preservation & transportation to minimize food losses. (A, SA, As)
11. Import top soil from abundant locations and teach soil conservation. (A, SA, As)
12. Utilize solar energy for food processing and cooking techniques. (A, SA, NA, As, Au)
13. Improve fishing conservation and methods. (A, SA, NA, E, As, Au)
14. Develop businesses to preserve plant varieties and mutants. (A, SA, NA, E, As, Au)
15. Introduce marketing methods and planting strategies. (A, SA, As)
16. Introduce tree farming as an alternative crop. (A, SA, NA, E, As)
17. Develop crops that are tolerant to brackish water. (A, NA, As)
18. Introduce essential nutritional additives to foods to reduce infant mortality. (A, SA, As)
19. Others

A(Africa), SA(So. America), NA(No. America), E(Europe), As(Asia), Au(Australia)

CHAPTER 8 - SUMMARY OF CONTINENTAL RESOURCES

General Resource Development Appraisal For Continents of the World

Programs Involving Water Resources:

Many people in the world are faced with a slow retreat from advancing desertification to areas where there is comparatively more food and especially water. Borders mean nothing to people In desperate straights, fleeing from that which can no longer be endured. Usually, conditions are beyond their control. Witness Mauratania, a country that is literally being blown into the sea. Its lands are barren now with drifting sands from the Sahara that is slowly inundating its cities. Where are the man-made borders now? Are they being redefined in the ocean depths?

The world's rivers and lakes are increasingly polluted. Watersheds are disappearing from lack of trees and ground cover. An increase in water supplies and other key resources requires many small projects tailored and timed to rehabilitate depleted and troubled areas.

Preliminary Summary of Things That can Be Done:

1. Drain and reclaim specific wetlands, without threatening any existing ecopheres, and create ponds and reservoirs. (A, SA)
*2. Build small dams and holding ponds. (A, SA, NA, E, As, Au)
3. Install simple water purification systems. (A, SA, NA, E, As, Au)
4. Provide hydrological studies. (A, SA, NA, E, As, Au)
5. Install pumps and pipelines for water distribution. (A, SA)
6. Install off-shore and shoreline desalinization plants. (A, SA, NA, E, As, Au)
7. Develop catchment areas for rainy season run-off. (A, SA, NA, E, As, Au)
8. Develop and install evaporation and condensation desalting systems. (A, SA, NA, As, Au)
**9. Develop canals and aqueducts. (A, SA, NA, E, As, Au)
10. Provide water injection systems for groundwater replenishment. (A, SA, NA, E, As, Au)
11. Install wells in strategic locations. (A, SA, As)
12. Install water recycling plants and ponds for nearby agricultural run-off and industrial effluent. (A, SA, NA, E, As)
13. Drill holes and pump water from fracture zones. (A, NA, As)
14. Develop in-home water recycling processes. (A, SA, NA, E, As, Au)
15. Provide studies in hydrology for problem areas. (A, SA, NA, E, As, Au)
16. Others

* Also serves as fish pond or solar pond.
** Also serves as access for water or other transportation.

General Resource Development Appraisal For Continents of the World

Programs Involving Energy Resources:

Natural energy resources are not uniformly distributed as deposits nor are most of them likely to be plentiful worldwide. Oil and gas deposits are found heavily concentrated in special areas, and uranium deposits are located mostly in a few remote areas. Curiously, coal deposits exist principally in North America and Asia. The present abundance of these resources permit their export for cash, except when they are already heavily utilized by industry, smelting and power plants. Utilization is obviously limited in underdeveloped countries. Without industry, modern transportation, road systems and energy consuming devices, demand for energy is low. Understandably, some cultures and life styles just don't require much energy. Nevertheless, specific forms of energy are still their life lines. Basic development of resources will depend on forward-looking leaders who are dedicated to serving their own people.

Preliminary Summary of Things That can Be Done:

1. Provide access to undeveloped, remotely located energy resources. (A, SA, NA, As, Au)
***2. Develop & install non-silting small dams for hydro-electric power. (A, SA, As, Au)
**3. Plant oil-bearing shrubs and trees for future fuels. (A, SA, NA, E, As, Au)
4. Develop community power-generating systems using local waste.(A, SA, NA, E, As)
*5. Develop and install community solar ponds. (A, SA, NA, E, As, Au)
*6. Develop and install wind power generators. (A, SA, NA, E, As, Au)
7. Develop and install solar stills for bio-mass conversion for fuels. (A, SA, NA, As, Au)
*8. Provide solar ponds for growing algae-type fuels for cooking. (A, SA, NA, As, Au)
9. Convert human &animal waste to methane fuel for generators. (A, SA, NA, As)
10. Develop & install safe mini-nuclear power plants, but include acceptable way to utilize or dispose of waste. (A, SA, NA, E, As, Au)
11. Develop and install wet & dry geo-thermal systems/power plants. (A, SA, NA, E, As, Au)
12. Convert accessible steam from tectonic plate fracture zones. (A, SA, NA, E, As)
13. Develop new propulsion fuels for transportation. (NA, E, As)
14. Develop new solar/hybrid vehicles and power plants. (NA, E, As, Au)
15. Develop superconductor lines for transmitting electrical power. (NA, E, As, Au)
16. Other

   * *Could be multi-objective project.*
  ** *Could be for more than one purpose.*
 *** *Would be in conjunction with water management projects.*

CHAPTER 8 - SUMMARY OF CONTINENTAL RESOURCES

General Resource Development Appraisal For Continents of the World

<u>*Programs Involving Trees, Shrubs and Other Resources:*</u>

The subject of trees and shrubs would not ordinarily be re-emphasized except for the fact that so much land needs restoration. Unfortunately, much of the desert is not readily restorable by mankind. It would take a major climate change to accomplish this. The best that people can do is reclaim whatever they can and prevent further desertification. The planting and protection of trees and shrubs selected for such purposes requires special strategies. Infrastructures help define and integrate such projects into large scale networks of activities which provide support and markets. But it is not a matter of taming nature; it is a matter of living with it. Many environments require diligent, continuous reforestation along with water management in order to help preserve them. These efforts offer natural buffers and, if protected, could deter mankind's tendency to abuse such environments. It means that trees and shrubs with their many purposes must be planted to provide fuel, shelter, food and fodder as well.

<u>*Preliminary Summary of Things That Can Be Done:*</u>

1. *Create strategies and implement experiments to reduce desert encroachment. (A, SA, NA, As)*
2. *Develop and incorporate wind diverters/barriers to protect plantlife.(A, SA, NA, E, As)*
3. *Progressively plant shrubs and trees tolerant to desert conditions. (A, SA, NA, As)*
*4. Install wind turbine systems to concentrate and collect wind-blown top soil as a by-product. (A, SA, NA, E, As, Au)
5. *Design and build special structures for growing trees and plants to grow food using hydroponic techniques. (A, SA, NA, E, As, Au)*
6. *Develop and protect bio-spheres involving trees and other plant life. (A, SA, NA, E, As, Au)*
7. *Reduce air-borne material by treating dust-spawning areas.(A, As)*
8. *Erect physical barriers to reduce wind velocity of dust storms. (A, As)*
9. *Reduce logging of rain forests to selective cutting. (A, SA, As)*
10. *Establish agricultural experiments introducing new tree and plant varieties that have economic value.(A, SA, NA, E, As, Au)*
11. *Preserve large areas of rain forests for tourism and enhance biospheres.(A, SA, As)*
12. *Plant orchards as an economic alternative to grazing animals. (A. SA, NA, E, As, Au)*
13. *Reforest with both new & indigenous tree varieties.(A, SA,NA, E, As, Au)*
14. *Increase plantlife in urban areas.(SA, NA, E)*
15. *Others*

* Would also be used for power generation.

General Resource Development Appraisal For Continents of the World

<u>*Programs Involving Fiber Resources:*</u>

The technological development of fibers has become a significant man-made accomplishment, encompassing a wide range of applications and sophistication. All fields show promise. Fiber composites and characteristics contribute to versatility and adaptability of design. Yet, fiber technologies are still in their infancy. Great advances in technological development will come when systems, structures and products encourage their further use. Initiation of most system applications are likely to occur within industrial nations first. When regionalization comes about, use of advanced fiber-oriented products and systems will spread to all countries.

<u>*Preliminary Summary of Things That Can Be Done:*</u>

1. *Develop and integrate communication systems and controls using fiber optics. (NA, E, As)*
2. *Develop structural composites made of organic and inorganic fiber materials . (A, SA, NA, E, As, Au)*
3. *Develop functional products that use plant fibers in conjunction with plastics and inorganic materials. (A, SA, As)*
4. *Develop laminar fiber composites for furniture and coverings. (A, SA, NA, E, As, Au)*
5. *Develop walls and roofs from organic and inorganic fiber composites. (A, SA, NA, E, As, Au)*
6. *Develop & incorporate fiber optics into walls and ceilings as a means of light defusion for illumination. (A, SA, NA, E, As, Au)*
7. *Develop fiber matting for protection and stabilization of soil for slopes, agriculture and landing strips. (A, SA, NA, As)*
8. *Develop fine filament insulation composites for outside walls and roofs. (NA, E, As)*
9. *Develop superconductor wire for power transmission lines. (NA, E, As)*
10. *Develop new textile fibers and fabrics. (A, SA, NA, E, As, Au)*
11. *Increase human consumption of high fiber foods. (A, SA, NA, E, As, Au)*
12. *Develop piezoelectric wire fabric network. (SA, NA, E, As)*
13. *Others*

CHAPTER 8 - SUMMARY OF CONTINENTAL RESOURCES

General Resource Development Appraisal For Continents of the World

Programs Involving Non-Renewable Resources:

More people throughout the world are seeking to buy products that use non-renewable materials. Consequently, there is rivalry for resources that cannot be easily replaced, only recycled. The big picture reveals that there is an acceleration of depletion of these critical resources. What will be the eventual cost to all nations when supply begins to curtail consumption, but not demand? How will governments cope without cooperation and the restructuring of their societies so as to become efficient users and savers?

There is no question that conspicuous consumption by the "have" nations is looked upon with awe by many "have not" countries. Given the chance, the latter would shed all restraint and emulate with ardor the practices and life styles of the affluent nations. When people live in quiet desperation, the vision of material abundance, freedom from responsibility, sensuous pleasures and physical conveniences become "heaven" itself. Consumption of non-renewable resources quickens at a rate that ensures that none will be available for necessities in future generations.

There are different directions to go in. For now, these represent a shift rather than a reversal, so that through gradualism, adjustments can be less painfully and more gainfully provided.

Preliminary Summary of Things That Can Be Done:

1. Develop international programs for managing long term usage and recycling of non-renewable resources.
2. Develop alternatives for non-renewable resources, such as material composites, etc.
3. Develop different socio-economic systems, like regionalization, to more effectively use non-renewable resources.
4. Upgrade all kinds of networks (including transportation) to reduce fuel consumption.
5. Reduce military hardware and recover obsolete military equipment for salvage.
6. Develop regional entities that are designed to conserve and recycle non-renewable resources.
7. Develop manufactured goods and equipment, homes and facilities that are designed to minimize dependency on non-renewable resources.
8. Promote (through advertising media) purchase of consumer goods on the basis of improving quality of life rather than in over-indulgence, dissolution and superficiality.
9. Others

Part IV - Preparation For Tomorrow

CHAPTER 9 - HUMAN RESOURCES & HUMAN POTENTIAL

"Responsible world leaders must encourage the enhancement of human potential, " states Pragma. "This is a major, continuing challenge for any nation no matter what its political system may be. The many roads to self-realization for millions of people everywhere are either complex or unknown. Most people are caught up with short term gain. They compare their achievements and living conditions with those in their immediate environment. Many of these man-made environments are detrimental to human growth. Objectivity in developing human potential is largely missing because a larger picture of a healthy and productive society is lacking."

Neos responds, "Very interesting observations, Pragma. They merit a lot of thought. It's important that political and other leaders demonstrate this objectivity and farsightedness by advocating and promoting human development for the long term benefit of all."

Veritor continues, "Emphasis on education and training can improve competency, skills and participation. Help and guidance must be given to millions of people so they can make a living and be able to adapt in this ever-changing world. The public must to be more fully and clearly informed about the deeper issues and prevailing conditions in their society. How else can they become responsible participants and knowledgeable citizens?"

Pragma notes, "Problems occur when people are duped. They become brainwashed and manipulated with slogans and false hopes. They find themselves embroiled in wars, the causes of which may be falsely represented. Cynical and sinister interests may be behind such manipulation in the guise of patriotism. Once duped and frustrated, the public feels betrayed. Tragically, they lose their trust in themselves, in their leaders and in their socio-economic systems."

Neos adds, "We need to emphasize human potential as a resource. The regional concept is meant to provide a fertile environment for the development of this all important resource."

CHAPTER 9 - HUMAN RESOURCES & HUMAN POTENTIAL

Promotion of Human Potential As a Resource

Realization of human potential must not be largely through happenstance. When others dictate circumstances and events, self-realization and opportunity for all may be difficult to obtain.

It is presumptuous and unacceptable that some who have privilege and the chance to grow should deny others this chance. Superior thoughts and deeds are not inherited genetically, but are the gift of prior experience, insight and an environment that favors them.

What is this environment? For one thing, it favors continuity and reverence for life. The environment may be natural, as created, or include mankind's input. Mankind has the sacred opportunity and responsibility to help promote the human potential to achieve an optimum measure of joy, harmony and creativity.

This is what regionalization is mostly about. It offers a general formula with almost limitless possibilities for those who see its merit and who participate in its multiple experiments in order to make this a better world.

Regionalization experiments are directed toward providing infrastructures that organize and integrate human endeavor. These infrastructures are intended to create environments that encourage healthy human growth. In doing this, they help people to focus, to behave responsibly and to participate in what they themselves must consider to be in their best long term interests.

The experiments bring together people and entities with highly varied interests in areas of commonality and emphasis to do what is positive and constructive. By reducing antagonism and conflict, human resource potentiality is conserved and promoted rather than dissipated.

The experiments of regionalization also provide the means for mobilizing a wide range of skills and knowledge in meeting common adversity and in coping with mutual catastrophic events.

Neos, Pragma and Veritor are very interested in human development and progress, but they are not certain whether such development results from the environment, is self-induced or both. Genetic differences and interaction with environmental conditions favor some people over others in the evolutionary processes. However, they can only speculate on 'preferential' genes and where evolutionary processes will lead. They wonder if it is to extinction or to the eventual emergence of a new kind of homo sapiens that is capable of living with and enhancing nature's work, including the correction or modification of genetic defects.

So what have homo sapiens been accomplishing? Has it been a case of mankind going through many experiments in learning and development? Is there some innate sense of direction, and an image of what the world could or should be like? Are individuals aware of how they fit into the scheme of things? For what purpose? Perhaps future generations will know.

Veritor exclaims, "There is a mystery about what life and existence mean. We can only capture a piece of it. How and why do people transcend the conditions in which they find themselves to seek some better life? What assertions and metaphysical conjectures can be made about this? There has been a wide range of dogma, myths and codes of behavior to motivate people to live exemplary lives. Is this meant only for the survival of the species? Has human trial and error been involved? I think so."

Pragma responds,"I have not been too impressed with mankind's individual and collective behavior. Humans seems to repeat in a monotonous cycle preparations for waging war, knowing full well that there can only be wanton destruction and enormous waste. How transient the spoils of war have always been. People become obsessed by hate, fear, greed or power as being some kind of 'normal' way of life. I can see this pattern of behavior as a negative potential for mankind, possibly leading to its extinction."

Veritor nods in agreement,"The irony of all this is that individuals collaborate in the dominance and submission of others. In other words, people get locked into unhealthy behavior patterns without reasoning and without realizing that they are being manipulated. They rationalize. Consequently, they give up integrity, spirit, and their individual rights to self-determination and action."

Neos picks up on this last thought."I think you have expressed an important insight. We must make a distinction between participation and servitude. Both appear in human behavior. The thing is, how much of each is voluntary. Voluntary means free will and freedom."

Pragma poses a question. "Do all individuals know what is in their own best self-interest? Do they have a sense of direction and a heightened self-awareness? It takes maturation, a sense of responsibility and a willingness to learn in order to be able to grow and understand."

CHAPTER 9 - HUMAN RESOURCES & HUMAN POTENTIAL

Veritor is intrigued with this. "It is difficult to account for why some people reject learning and personal growth. Is it some kind of perversity, a rejection of responsibility, poor habits, a general lack of interest, a lack of concentration or a lack of direction? Maybe it is some kind of mind set, a rebellion toward a society they cannot feel a part of. Does it originate in the family setting with a mother's milk or with a parent-child or sibling relationship? There are so many variables."

Neos adds, "All of these observations are relevant to the goal of instilling, revitalizing and developing human resources. But is this goal shared by all people? Wouldn't there be different expectation for people from various backgrounds and environments? Humans start life with genetic potential and then become involved in a learning process with gradual acceptance or rejection of new concepts. As individuals grow, they are stimulated by their environment. Their religious beliefs, social customs, economic statuses and personal sensitivities to new things may encourage, inhibit or prohibit specific activities or exposure to new information."

Pragma also notes, "People are faced with vast differences in environment and in available resources. Humans may have limited choices and control of both man-made and natural circumstances. They may improvise and make the best of things according to their awareness and physical well-being, but they can do no more. When food, water and other necessities are gone, they may try to escape, but to where? Can millions of people in such circumstances be helped?"

Veritor sums up this part of the discussion. "Helping the impoverished and the downtrodden is a major, long-term endeavor. In the meantime, most people will not be able to better themselves, and millions may perish. Nevertheless, there must be persistent, major efforts to alleviate suffering and rebuild society. Progress is likely to be painfully slow, but early and continuous restructuring of the most congested areas is essential. The tide can be turned if there is open-mindedness and cooperation in the implementation of regionalization and the will to develop human potential worldwide."

Enhancing the Potential of Humans on a Community Level

The design of regionalization experiments incorporate networks that are dedicated to enhance human resource potential in the community and neighborhood.

<u>***Projects That Build Human Resource Potential:***</u>

- ***Upgrade Public Health by Improving:***
  Sanitation/waste management, water quality, inoculations/treatment of contagious diseases, vector control and disease prevention programs.

- ***Provide Community Services and Centers for:***
  Infant/pre-school care, elderly care, mentally handicapped care, physically handicapped care, teenage at risk supervision.

- ***Provide Family Planning and Counseling for:***
  Family cohesion assistance, pre-natal care/assistance, birth control and child placement/supervision.

- ***Provide Pre-school Preparation for****:*
  Learning habit stimuli, positive social interaction, early detection of problems, supplemental nutrition.

- ***Provide Teen/Pre-teen Guidance for:***
  Learning habits training, community project participation, exercise/sports/games supervision, basic skills training, multi-cultural and geographic awareness, value awareness, personal hygiene & sexuality, arts/music/crafts awareness, nature awareness, science awareness.

- ***Introduce Community Services such as:***
  Public works assignments, introduction to planning/organizing/managing, voluntary teaching (literacy, etc.), care of disabled, care of young and elderly, emergency assistance, ecological preservation/restoration.

- ***Introduce Apprenticeships for:***
  New technologies, special skills/use of resources, planning /leadership, public/private occupations, group dynamics, home-making, work/learning experiences.

- ***Provide Broad, Balanced Educational Opportunities such as****:*
  Preparation for responsible citizenship, special occupational training, preparation for higher education, exposure to new cultural experiences, physical/psychological health efforts, social skills development.

Part IV - Preparation For Tomorrow

CHAPTER 10 - WELCOME TO INNOVATION

This is but the beginning. The unfolding of ideas which foster improved living conditions and quality of life are but a prelude to countless other benefits. Fertile minds abound, needing only favorable environments, encouragement and direction. Why let the potential of many remain forever dormant? Why let progress flounder? There are many inhibiting factors to the acceptance of improvements; new ideas and ventures tend to disrupt the status quo.

Most people's idea of an acceptable way of life results from generations of accumulated habits and day to day expediency. Despite defects and deficiencies, life is tolerated and even anticipated. Why change, they think? Life's events change this, however. New adaptations become necessary, the old must be modified and the vitality of the new and promising must emerge. New, more effective concepts and methods must be introduced to meet technological and socio-economic changes.

Innovations may be derived from various vantage points which provide visibility, association and applicability. New insights and possibilities relate to what functions are supposed to be performed. Global, national, regional, networked infrastructure, system, special center, community, and its parts all have unique functions and prospects. Lower vantage points provide more detailed and precise innovations. We dare not ignore any vantage point. All are importantly linked and require our understanding and respect.

A wide range of innovation is possible from any vantage point. This must be encouraged for growth. However, innovation serves best when it is meant to elevate humanity and enhance the human condition. Why waste minds and the gift of life? But what makes for significant and enduring innovation?

Neos proposes, "Let's briefly review some aspects involved in growth and innovation."

Innovating For Growth

Enhancement of Natural Resources
Enhancement of Human Resources
— *Innovation & Concept Development* —
New Ways to Organize, Integrate & Communicate
New Ways to Grow and Develop
New Ways to Enrichen Life
New Ways to Prosper, be Healthy and be Productive
New Ways to Simplify

Innovation stimulates other innovation.
Innovation opens the door to the future.
Innovation stimulates enterprise.
Innovation brings about changes to meet change.
Innovation offers possibilities for a better life.
Innovation for peaceful pursuits is in consonance with and enhances regionalization.

<u>Areas of Innovation to be Provided:</u>

Global, National and Inter-regional
- *Health, safety, security*
- *Financial and resource applications*
- *Cooperation, exchange and mutual support*

Regional
- *Conservation and enhancement of resources*
- *Optimization of benefits and integration of networks*
- *Establishment of infrastructures*

Networked Infrastructures
- *Inter-actions of basic functions*
- *Assurance of safety, compatibility, efficiency and effectiveness*

Systems
- *Time-phased flow and interaction of human and machine input / output*
- *Control of rates, quantity, quality and cost*

Sub-system Processes
- *Performance and sequential / parallel control and improvements*
- *Conversion, extraction, separation, fabrication and assembly*

Elemental
- *Enhancement of characteristics such as durability, quality, safety, economy*
- *Utilization of capacity and effectiveness*

CHAPTER 10 - WELCOME TO INNOVATION

Innovational Dependencies

Occasionally, new ideas are born which seem to have no reference or point of origin. They appear mysteriously and spontaneously, seemingly without any apparent imitation of nature or other prompting. They arrive on the scene with some new form, movement, sound or smell as if from outer space. Oftentimes, it is a matter of discovery, and there is amazement as to how something so obvious could have remained unknown for so long. Unfortunately, a concept may be so novel that even its value or direct application may not convince most. Once successfully applied over an extended period of time, the new is finally accepted.

Ideas and concepts, "old" and acceptable through long usage, often become building blocks for further concepts that are now seen in a different light. Anticipated conditions and situations may also give rise to invention and a vision of potential use. It is extremely difficult for pragmatic thinkers to accept what has not yet happened or has not been recognized and proven beneficial. Yet anticipation of projected need requires conceptual thinking in order to meet rapidly changing conditions in a timely matter.

Great ideas motivate and stimulate extensive insights and possibilities. They impact humanity. Improperly interpreted and utilized, they can be destructive; but when properly understood and acted upon, they add to civilization and to the progress of mankind.

This progress is conditional and cannot happen in a vacuum.

Dependency Examples in Technology:

Origin

Discoveries in Physics, Electrical Transmission, Electro-Magnetic & Other Radiation, Microwaves, Etc.

Preparation

Planning & Development of Energy Systems, Applications, Grids, Signal Transmission Theory, Mathematics

Innovation

Inventions-Illumination, Power Generation, Energy Transformation, Micro- Miniaturization, Energy Storage, Phones, Radio, Cable, Television, Etc.

Affect

General Increase in Time for Work, Study, Leisure. Residual Inventions in Products, Machinery & Machine Tools, Instruments, Controls, Computer Systems, etc. Increases in Enterprises and Jobs. Changes in Lifestyles & Information Dissemination

It is at this point Neos, Pragma and Veritor recognize some inherent relationships created by the introduction of the new. New concepts can best modify the old when proposed changes are rational, not too radically different or introduced too fast.

Neos speaks to this issue. "One of the most important factors to consider is the phasing-in of new concepts so that both people and institutions have a chance to absorb them. Direction, understanding, firm commitments and re-associations are necessary to enact the new. Otherwise, there may be subtle or open resistance and sabotaging of well-intended and worthwhile venture or innovation."

Pragma counters,"But how can there be justification for waiting or delaying when conditions become too intolerable and detrimental? Why continue the outmoded and obsolete when they are destructive? Some situations obviously demand urgent change. What must be done then?"

Veritor adds, "I think rapid change will require even greater efforts in communication, coordination and implementation. This should reduce the trauma involved. Also, early efforts and assistance are needed to retrain, relocate, reinvest and reduce present commitments. This must be done with a sense of responsibility and respect for others."

Pragma reflects and notes, "Wars and revolution bring about rapid changes; peaceful changes are inherently slow. Obviously, it's easy enough to destroy, but difficult to build. Results are quicker in war, but are flawed and simplistic. No doubt patriotic or religious fervor and motivation by fear and threats create unambiguous messages.

"However, in times of peace, there are many insidious conditions that should motivate, but people frequently fail to heed warnings which are casually received, quickly dismissed or refuted."

Veritor responds, "I am not sure problems are always ignored. I think it's a matter of people not knowing what to do about complex situations even when they are fully presented. The subject may be too technical or specialized. Rarely are issues carefully analyzed or synthesized and clearly stated. Often, solutions to problems are simplistic, fragmentary or unrelated to the actual issues. Innovative, comprehensive and coordinated solutions require more preparation and a step-by-step presentation."

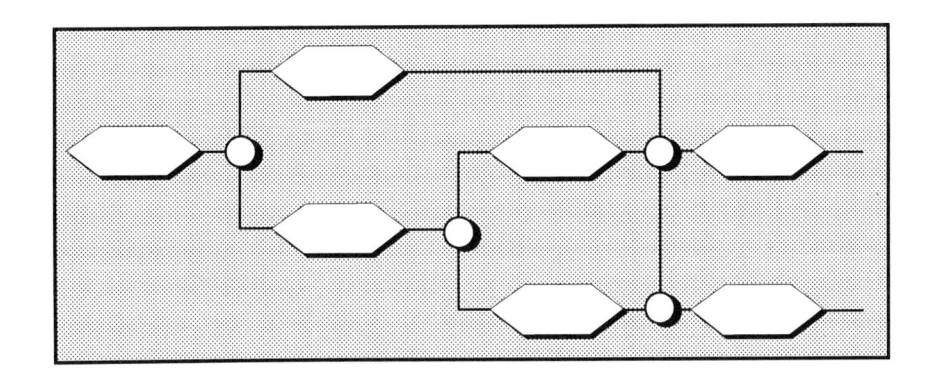

PART V
THE CHALLENGE OF IMPLEMENTATION

Part V - The Challenge of Implementation

CHAPTER 1 - STRATEGY

Worldwide implementation of the regional concept implies comprehensiveness on a grand scale. It has required much planning and experimenting by enterprising people in previous generations to create what we have today. We are only able to appreciate through hindsight how successful yesterday's approaches have been and only through vision can we project what the promise of the future may be. Over the years, management and technological methods have been gradually improving, and increased awareness and knowledge have sharpened the design and analytical tools now available to cope with severe emerging and reocuring socio-economic problems.

Implementation of the regional concept must obviously rely on such experience, insight and skills. The urgent problems confronting the world today are unparalleled in scope and magnitude. Implementing the regional concept demands open-minded, far-reaching and sophisticated strategies. Fortunately, some precedents, using systems management approaches, exist today.

Programs of major proportion and complexity have been developed in the past. Netherlands, for instance, using systems management and engineering along with other disciplines, has developed major public works to stay the onslaught of the sea and to capture and safeguard new lands for habitation. It has been a case of applying major technological advancements to improve the collective quality of life of people. In 1936 the Tennessee Valley Authority came into being in the United States. Power plants and vast public works were developed for a new multi-regional area. Water and power projects, agriculture, industry, recreation and living space were enhanced. This mammoth effort was attempted during a time of economic depression and contributed to the recovery from it. The U.S. Columbia River Authority and the Panama Canal program are but a few more examples. In these and many other major works worldwide, the application of systems engineering management methods has continued to improve the world that we live in.

The strategy for regional implementation begins on a global and continental scale. As previously discussed, efforts to protect and enhance the environment and conserve resources must be greatly increased in scope. By beginning at the global level, countries everywhere will be encouraged to cooperate and become more involved in common causes. The implementation of new regions is one of these common causes.

The strategy proceeds from global preparation to regional site selection, enhancement and development. The regional concept is far more extensive than anything that has preceded it. The strategy involves the implementation of the functionally cohesive infrastructures previously described. We also have indicated that

CHAPTER 1 - STRATEGY

these infrastructures must be networked in order to ensure full regional system integration. This would be made possible by carefully focusing on each phase of their implementation, by anticipating interfaces and by recognizing and resolving problems as they arise.

Pragma, Veritor and Neos have reached the moment when vision and imagination must be transformed into actuality. Pragma begins, "A logical progression of steps called phases must be employed during implementation, especially for large programs."

Veritor interrupts, "We also need to stress the importance of concept networking before any discussion of phases begins. The regional concept has to be widely circulated so that people from diverse disciplines can evaluate, modify and gradually identify with its content and intent."

Pragma continues, "As general awareness grows, people must become motivated to participate in the implementation process. Mobilization would then proceed by first establishing goals and objectives and defining the corresponding functions and tasks needed to attain them."

Veritor notes, "It seems to me that it is also necessary to identify all kinds of resources, elements, limits and constraints that are inherently involved in major programs of regional scope and complexity."

Neos adds, "Logically, I think the next step should be to select and establish the first regional sites on a worldwide basis."

Pragma responds, "Of course. Site selection includes all programs necessary to enhance the specific environments for each potential region and, as we have discussed earlier, it also includes special development of key resources to ensure regional effectiveness."

Neos suggests, "It seems to me once these phases have been progressively completed, the acquisition, planning and design, funding and development phases would then be vigorously implemented in order for the region to become operational. Pragma, would you like to present how these phases must take place?"

Regional Implementation From Concept To Prototype

There is an extreme urgency to bring the first regional concepts to fruition. The world is waiting. What happens to hundreds of millions of human beings if delays occur? Will they or we survive without early implementation of regional prototypes so that expeditious implementation of many more regions can then take place?

The following simple schedule reflects this urgency. Frenetic as it may be, it is realistic in terms of need. Human efforts and resources must become highly focused to accomplish these large efforts.

Phases to be accomplished:

Concept Networking
'94 Initial   '96   Continues for Expansion

Mobilization
'95   Initial   '98   Continues

Initiation
'96   Initial   '99 Continues

Acquisition
'95   '97 Initial   '00Cont

Planning, Design, Development & Funding
95   '96   Prototype Implementation   '00Cont

Figure V-1-A

Part V - The Challenge of Implementation

CHAPTER 2 - CONCEPT NETWORKING

What are the important issues of our day? They are rarely separate and distinct; they are usually related to each other. Issues are conditional and dependent. It is essential that when issues are brought into focus, that system interfaces and other relationships are identified and analyzed before dispositions are made. Likewise, the regional concept must be evaluated within a local and global context.

The regional concept not only offers a philosophical basis for discussion, but a stimulus for innovation. New relationships are combined. The concept also provides a comprehensive model for further understanding major world issues.

A realistic approach to concept networking involves the multi-disciplines of the academic world, the public with its diverse interests and the technological, commercial and industrial worlds. Businesses and corporations of all kinds, governmental agencies with their specializations, and international bodies with their mandates to make this a better world must all be involved. These entities may have different perspectives of reality. Therefore, what more effective approach could there be than to evaluate the regional concept by utilizing all such perspectives? Points of view must be propounded with openness by all who wish to contribute and share. It is also a reality that the regional concept cannot be considered a panacea for correcting all of the world's problems. The concept merely offers an experiment for correcting fundamental ones.

Pragma, Veritor and Neos are very concerned about reaching out to people everywhere. They realize that the regional concept, submitted to millions of people for close inspection and deep discussion, would evoke a wide range of emotions and opinions. In order to gain acceptance by the public and private sectors, especially by those who must lead, the concept must go through critiques and correction. All major efforts and experiments having universal impact require this.

Pragma begins, "The first thing that comes to mind is that although the regional concept should be carefully presented, it is not intended to be placed in a glass case. It is neither a specimen nor a relic. We need to circulate the concept so that it can be acted upon."

Veritor notes, "Won't it be difficult to reach those who are set in their ways, are indifferent or have opposing ideas? Also hundreds of millions of people are likely to have no interest in any concept, who would not understand the regional one in any case or who would only consider the latter in fragmentary fashion."

Neos responds vigorously, "The regional concept is not a threat to the public, just the opposite. Unfortunately, it may be portrayed otherwise by special interests. I think we must gain the early participation of progressive leaders everywhere to counter this."

Pragma asks, "I wonder how many academic disciplines would be interested in the different aspects of the regional concept? Many of these disciplines would gain by expanding, evaluating, modifying and applying the concept. I would like to present diagrams showing academic involvement."

Veritor thinks for a moment and responds, "Faculty and students could further develop parts of the regional concept if assigned or if there is a natural curiosity. Furthermore, I think that many aspects of the region's design and implementation may qualify for research grants from government agencies or private foundations."

Neos is excited by the last prospect and adds, "Regionalization could have a significant impact not only on curriculum development at the college level but at the lower levels of education as well. Regionalization infrastuctures could suggest occupational direction for students, especially for those who are uncertain about what their vocational or professional choices could be and what education and training must be acquired."

Pragma quickly concurs, "Young people with spirit also seek causes and involvement. Regionalization would be a cause supreme. The subsequent implementations of regions would focus on myriad opportunities."

Veritor notes, "Certainly, a chance to help build a better society would have to be considered an immensely worthwhile and satisfying endeavor for present and future generations."

CHAPTER 2 - CONCEPT NETWORKING

The Regional Concept and the Academic World

- *The regional concept may serve as a study model in several academic disciplines. It provides a general background for the study of environmental issues and natural and human resources. The concept is distinctly inter-disciplinary and may help provide a system framework for more extensive expansion, evaluation, modification and application of the concept's premises.*
- *Regional infrastructure groupings and their networks are of particular value because they emphasize key functions in society. These functions and their interfaces must be addressed by the academic community in an objective way. This leads to the study of organizations and their systems. The philosophical basis for regions in different societies must also be thoroughly examined.*
- *Some academic disciplines are tentatively grouped as follows for integrated study programs:*

<u>*Regional Planning and*</u>

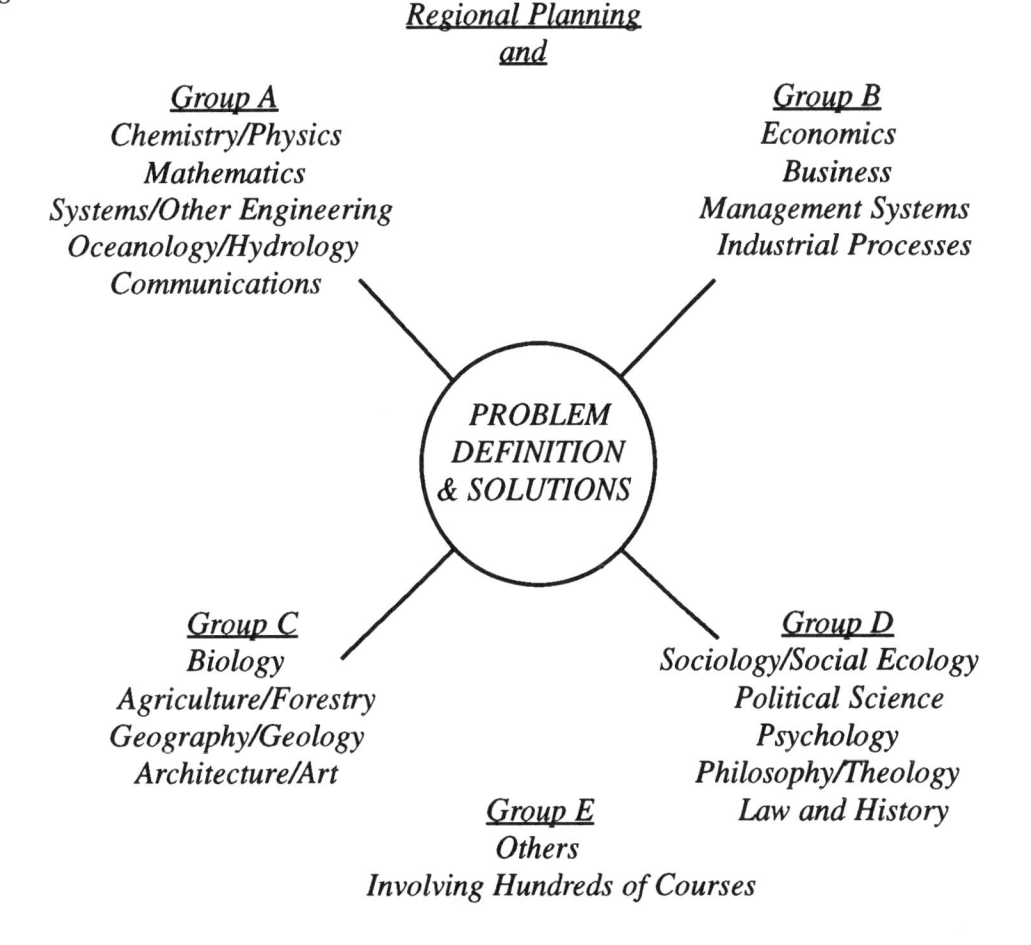

<u>*Group A*</u>
Chemistry/Physics
Mathematics
Systems/Other Engineering
Oceanology/Hydrology
Communications

<u>*Group B*</u>
Economics
Business
Management Systems
Industrial Processes

PROBLEM DEFINITION & SOLUTIONS

<u>*Group C*</u>
Biology
Agriculture/Forestry
Geography/Geology
Architecture/Art

<u>*Group D*</u>
Sociology/Social Ecology
Political Science
Psychology
Philosophy/Theology
Law and History

<u>*Group E*</u>
Others
Involving Hundreds of Courses

Figure V-2-A

Direct Academic Involvement

- *The effectiveness of the regional concept can be observed during mobilization, initiation, acquisition, planning and design, and development. The concept is a dynamic model that, through experimentation, undergoes changes and adaptations to meet long-term human needs.*
- *The part that academia plays is vital for objective and constructive input.*
- *Workshops and study groups focus on the whole picture as well as in areas of specialization. These workshops are part of larger efforts that concentrate on selection, preparation, design, analysis and evaluation required for regional implementation at different sites.*
- *Involvement during implementation with non-academic efforts leads to exchanges in information and feed-back results for curriculum development.*
- *Involvement with regional implementation increases prospects for special study grant awards.*
- *All of the above efforts are involved with regional implementation as follows:*

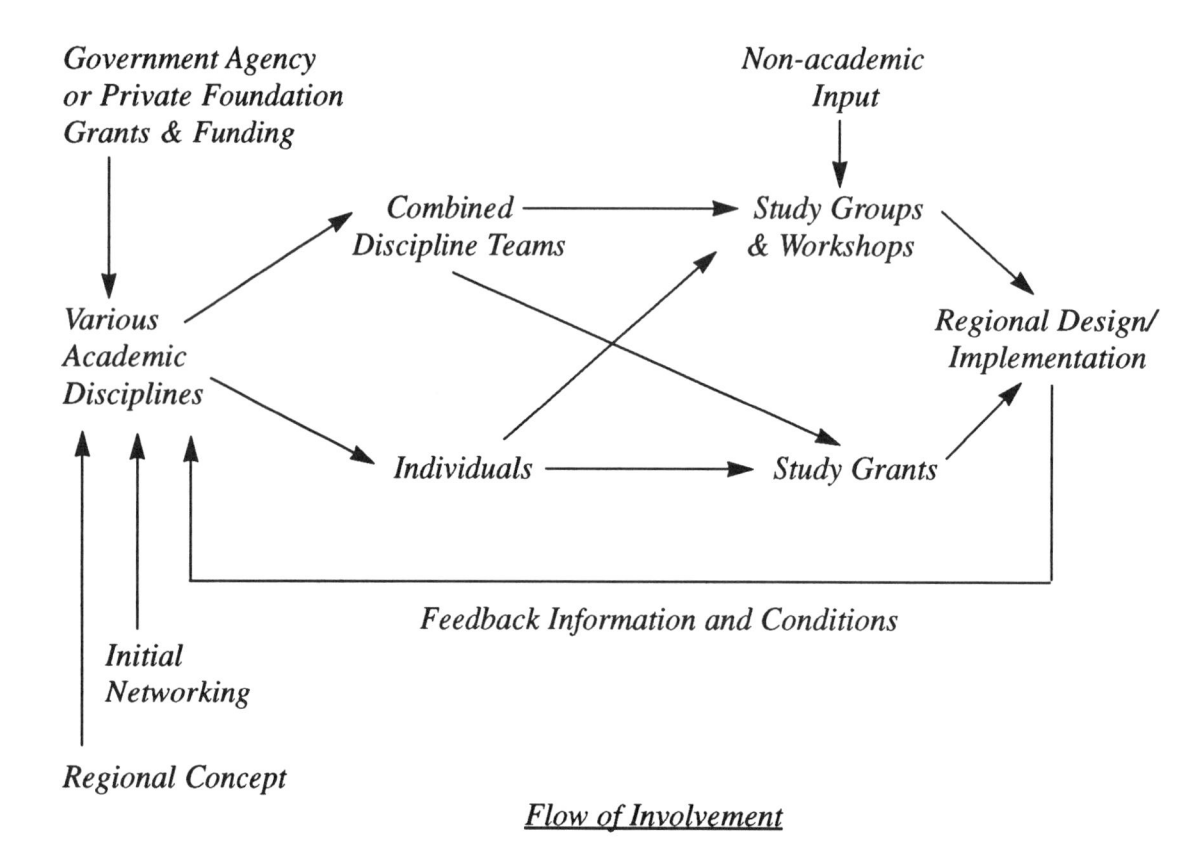

Flow of Involvement

Figure V-2-B

CHAPTER 2 - CONCEPT NETWORKING

Pragma turns to another area that requires concept networking. "Government agencies are vested with the power and the responsibility to enact programs of consequence that will benefit society. Regional implementation would definitely have to be within a governmental range of responsibility."

Veritor notes, "We have already discussed networking in conjunction with regional infrastructures. So the role of government agencies in regionalization must be to mobilize and initiate implementation as early as possible. Transitions will be made as new regions emerge. As regional sites are being developed, other areas like the cities would be able to observe and adopt new concepts as they evolve and become operational. Appointed task forces would be formed to continuously evaluate regional implementation effects on existing socio-economic conditions and the natural environment. These task forces would make recommendations for enabling legislature and initial funding."

Pragma continues, "It will be necessary to obtain different political viewpoints. I feel certain that when people contribute toward problem definition and are open to finding long-lasting solutions, many political differences would diminish and fewer people will be likely to impede progress. We can see this happen when people of different political persuasions come together for the common good during war time."

Veritor returns to the subject, "Program integration is an essential government function. As mobilization proceeds, I can see that government agencies and task forces would have considerable say in establishing goals, recommending organizational structures, suggesting funding sources and defining constraints and limits."

Neos agrees, "We need to realize that government involvement is likely to vary considerably in different countries. The process of networking in democracies, especially for regions, is more complex than in countries with totalitarian governments. But once mobilization begins in democratic countries, I think, the results would be far more impressive and reflect the imaginative thinking and participation of many individuals. In totalitarian governments, the whole process of mobilization would be hierarchal, more direct and quicker but with far narrower results. In any case, the idea is to mobilize quickly so as to gain momentum and to sustain such momentum throughout implementation. This depends on effective government leadership and public responsiveness."

Direct Government Involvement

- *The regional concept provides a ready prototype for governments to develop new, more effective operating procedures. Operations, such as in a giant city, may be in urgent need of change. It is often too risky and costly to experiment on a large scale in long-established or out-moded government operations.*
- *Government agencies, however, must become involved in new regions because they have a leadership responsibility to bring about necessary changes. These agencies would be able to contribute to regional infrastructures and try out ideas that they could not immediately introduce into their own government infrastructure designs. These ideas must have a high probability of being effective.*
- *Regional implementation benefits from the integrated efforts of appointed task forces.*
- *Legislative action for the region requires input information from agency officials who specialize in different fields.*
- *Legislative cooperation with other jurisdictions would be necessary to establish inter-regional and inter-agency networking.*
- *The above interactions are needed to implement regions and are diagrammed as follows:*

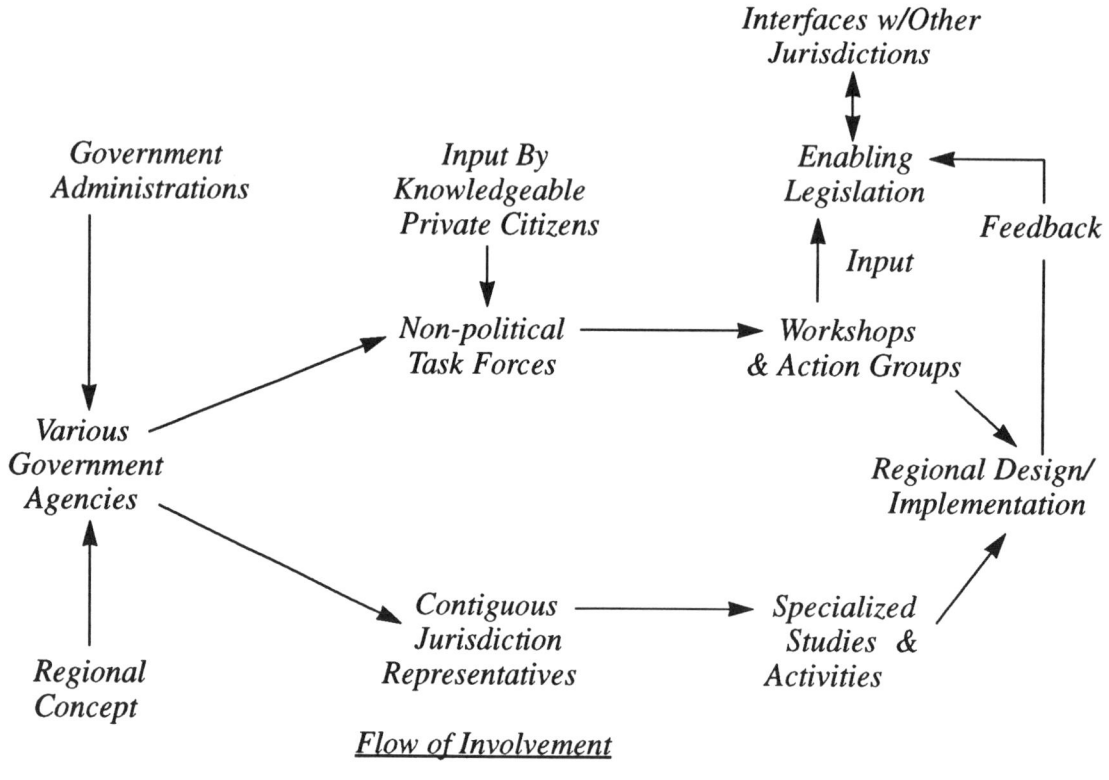

Flow of Involvement

Figure V-2-C

CHAPTER 2 - CONCEPT NETWORKING

Pragma responds, "What you say is true. Sustained momentum is essential. Many people lose interest or become disgruntled when programs drift. But now we come to further participation crucial to the success of any new region, the critical roles of business and industry in the networking processes. They are prime players and significant beneficiaries of a well-planned region and must be involved early in regional implementation. The benefits of being in 'on the ground floor' of promising enterprises are tremendous.

"It would benefit businesses and industrial firms to become very familiar with the regional concept, the planned locations of centers and other information pertinent to their enterprises. They need to learn about proposed zoning laws and other restraints and limits. They have to know what services will exist and what improvements will be already installed such as utilities, transportation and communication. The projected tax structure and the availability of natural and human resources must also be known."

Veritor adds, "This is not a one way street. Prospective businesses and industries should also provide some indication of their interest and intent. However, some companies may be hesitant to divulge certain private information in a highly competitive world. But size of intended operation, potential employment and skill requirements, anticipated civic contributions and investments to be made in the region, anticipated traffic and utility needs all must be provided to the regional designers and planners without fear of espionage."

Pragma continues, "It is very important that business and industry become concerned with environmental constraints and resource conservation prior to and during implementation of the region. Industry must carefully plan, design and locate their facilities so they are in harmony with the regional philosophy. They must also comply with regional guidelines during their planning efforts."

Veritor notes, "I am sure the business and commercial sectors would be amenable to participation in forums and workshops where common concerns and contributions would be discussed. This could lead to the selection of representatives to participate in government task forces. Many highly talented people could then contribute their expertise to ensure regional implementation success."

Direct Business and Industry Involvement

- *The creation of viable regions is closely linked with the early and continued participation of businesses and industries that provide for enterprise and the livelihoods of the regional inhabitants.*
- *Both business and industry require government initiatives in providing guidelines and in defining limits. Not doing so early during regional implementation could lead to subsequent over-restriction, misunderstandings and litigation, particularly in highly industrialized countries.*
- *Participation by various industries and businesses, individually and collectively, must be encouraged. This can best be done when they become familiar with the regional concept and understand and appreciate its comprehensive approach. The concept creates a climate for legitimate and healthy enterprise.*
- *Involvement by business and industry task forces in forums and workshops can generate recommendations for innovative approaches during regional implementation.*
- *Individual businesses and industries must make known their requirements so that planning on a regional scale will help them to operate successfully. In exchange, they must be prepared to assume community responsibilities.*
- *A presentation of the above is expressed as follows:*

Business/Industry Involvement

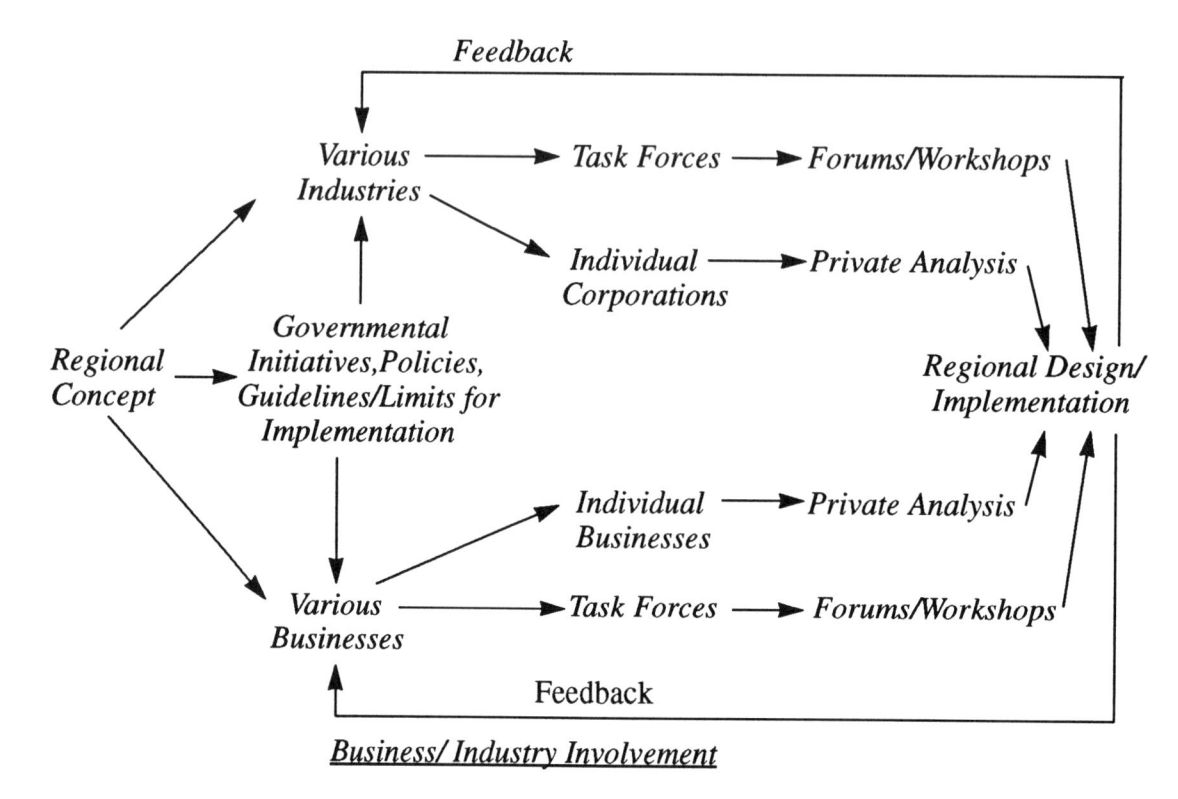

Figure V-2-D

CHAPTER 2 - CONCEPT NETWORKING

Neos adds, "The private sector is not limited to business and industry. The general public is also a part. Concept networking must be established through information dissemination and public forums. The question arises as to how well the salient points of the regional concept will be interpreted and presented locally and to hundreds of millions of people worldwide. An open society will be new for many people in various countries, and it will require many adjustments in thinking."

Pragma responds, "Multi-media presentations of the concept are a serious responsibility. The concept is vulnerable to distortions, speculations and exaggerations. This may be unavoidable, but its fundamental integrity must be sustained. The media's job is to give a clear overall picture of what is being proposed, to encourage participation and to report progress. Initially, public forums must take place outside of the region. People who are gradually inhabiting the region would also begin to initiate forums to discuss local events and problems. I see the forum debates as being a conditioning process that encourages people to think independently and to exchange ideas and opinions."

Veritor adds, "You're right. Public forum summaries and community surveys are needed to sustain the people's interest and participation and to increase regional management awareness. Information derived from such activities are invaluable in a representative government."

Neos suggests, "Perhaps, when helped by a free and responsible news media, civic groups and individual businesses and industries could begin the process of motivating legislators and heads of governments to accelerate regionalization. I suspect that the communication process will be slow and random at first and then begin to accelerate and expand."

Pragma notes, "I think that the eventual success of regions will induce greater motivation. Success speaks volumes. People and their leaders have to go through a process of confidence building to fully accept regionalization. I wonder at times, is it necessary for a society to completely break down before full support and willing participation occurs?"

Veritor concludes this aspect of the discussion by answering. "It seems to me, as problems multiply in both heavily populated areas and under-developed areas, people will either become very protective of whatever remains or reach out for new ideas like the regional concept."

Public Networking for the Regional Concept

- *It is extremely important to introduce the general public to what the regional concept is and what it offers. Simple, straight forward information can stimulate thinking and arouse curiosity.*
- *One of the responsibilities of communication media is to inform the public about the regional concept as an important subject for discussion and action.*
- *Multi-media communications also benefit by becoming a part of an effective regional communication infrastructure.*
- *The furtherance of the regional concept towards implementation relies on timely presentations and exchanges of information.*
- *All regional infrastructures will eventually interact through the communication infrastructure.*
- *The general public must become increasingly involved in forums, presentations and workshops. Leaders will emerge from such participation.*
- *A media-phase relationship is described as follows:*

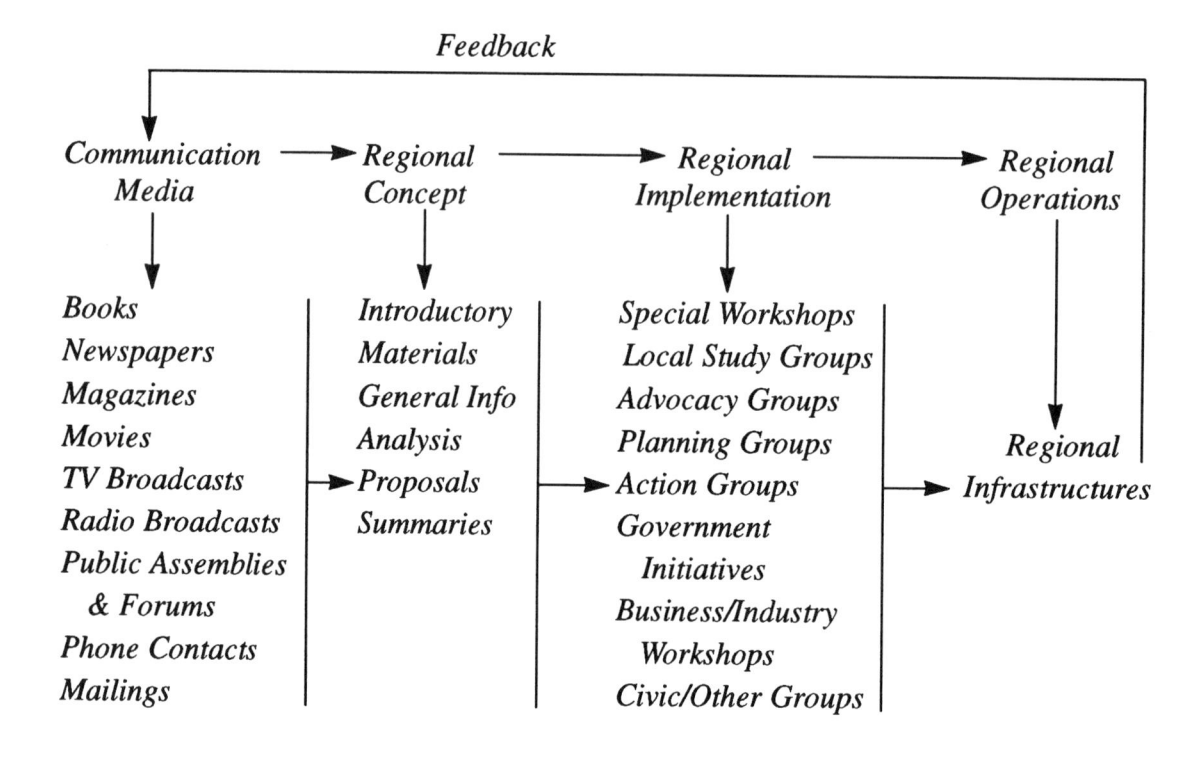

```
                               Feedback
         ┌─────────────────────────────────────────────────────────┐
         ▼                                                         │
Communication ──▶ Regional ──────▶ Regional ─────────▶ Regional    │
   Media          Concept          Implementation      Operations  │
     │              │                  │                  │        │
     ▼              ▼                  ▼                  ▼        │
  Books         Introductory     Special Workshops                 │
  Newspapers    Materials        Local Study Groups     Regional ──┘
  Magazines     General Info     Advocacy Groups        Infrastructures
  Movies        Analysis         Planning Groups
  TV Broadcasts ▶Proposals      ▶Action Groups       ▶
  Radio Broadcasts Summaries     Government
  Public Assemblies               Initiatives
    & Forums                     Business/Industry
  Phone Contacts                  Workshops
  Mailings                       Civic/Other Groups
```

Figure V-2-E

CHAPTER 2 - CONCEPT NETWORKING

Neos has been thinking about regional concept networking on the international level."We have not addressed global networking implications yet. Countries have different legal codes, communication media, socio-economic conditions and experience in public participation."

Veritor answers, "That is true. Also, most people in the world are not concerned with communicating with anyone outside of their own personal spheres of interest. Their future is left in the hands of individuals who may mix personal gain with public trust. With increased media coverage of the regional concept and local meetings, people will begin to see what is going on, how their lives can be improved and how important it is to get involved."

Pragma notes, "Concept networking should also occur in the United Nations when government representatives discover common causes and solutions rather than just differences. Communication within international forums is an important way to introduce the regional concept and demonstrate its importance. The regional concept and its innovations must be presented so that it will become acceptable to different societies. I think many Third World countries would be highly responsive to the implemention of regions, especially those with missing or weak infrastructures."

"The regional approach would also enhance development of international law and attract economic assistance from member nations. The United Nations has many agencies already operational that could immediately participate in regional implementation. Their involvement would also improve their own operational effectiveness by using the regional concept to help integrate and focus related activities. I can also see operational cost reductions through cost-sharing, especially for financially strapped agencies as they become involved in the coordination of regionalization."

"I think that publication and circulation of the regional concept on the international level should arouse interest. Surely, there are enough countries in turmoil trying to find some way to reorganize, attract financial assistance and become operationally effective. These nations will also see new roles for themselves in the planning, implementation and operation of regions. I would think that any promising comprehensive approach that can alleviate world sufferings and prevent major problems should be at the top of the agenda of the United Nations and its member countries."

Development of International Networking

- *The onset of networking of the regional concept must be very deliberate so that its salient points can be absorbed and considered. When the concept's merits and prospects are recognized, the networking process must accelerate and expand.*
- *In order for the regional concept to become a reality, early parallel networking efforts are required to meet projected need for regions in the coming years. The magnitude of this need requires substantial growth and expansion fto provide 5,000 regions by the year 2020 in order to accommodate 7.7 billion people who will inhabit the earth.*
- *On a world scale, dedicated special efforts to meet the goals of regionalization must be adopted by the United Nation's many agencies, international banking, law-making institutions and major international cartels and corporations. These world wide entities and individual nations then become the initiators of the networking process on a global basis in support of universal regionalization.*
- *The following diagram shows this relationship and progression:*

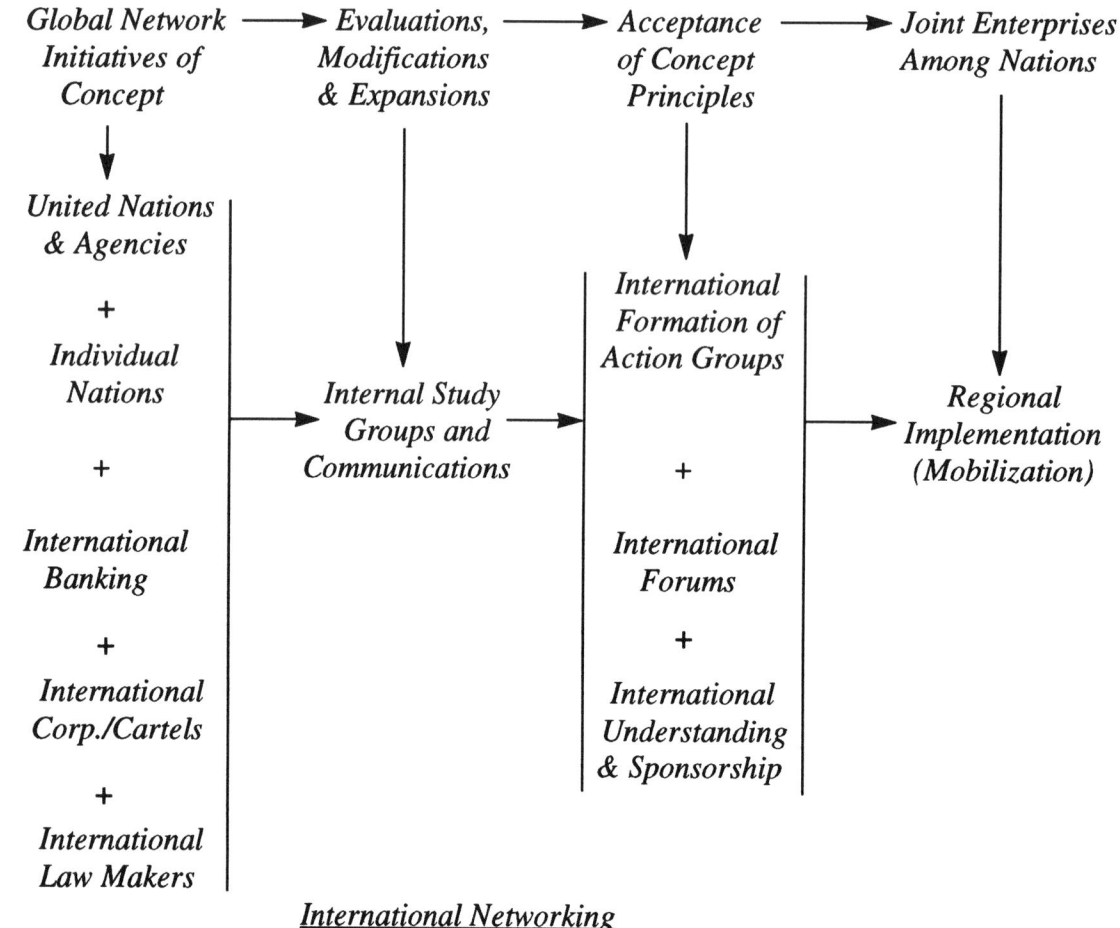

```
Global Network  ──▶ Evaluations,   ──▶ Acceptance   ──▶ Joint Enterprises
Initiatives of      Modifications      of Concept       Among Nations
Concept             & Expansions       Principles
    │                   │                  │                │
    ▼                   │                  ▼                │
United Nations          │          International            │
& Agencies              │          Formation of             │
    +                   │          Action Groups            │
Individual              ▼                                   ▼
Nations           Internal Study    ──▶      +        ──▶ Regional
    +             Groups and                                Implementation
International     Communications         International     (Mobilization)
Banking                                  Forums
    +                                       +
International                         International
Corp./Cartels                         Understanding
    +                                 & Sponsorship
International
Law Makers
```

<u>International Networking</u>

Figure V-2-F

CHAPTER 2 - CONCEPT NETWORKING

Veritor shifts the subject."Science and technology are essential in the development of regional implementation strategies. Their influence must be exerted as the regional concept is being evaluated, modified and applied. Theoretical and applied researchers should concentrate on critical areas of both human need and nature. Applied research, in particular, would be needed for regional development. Some of these improvements have already been discussed, but much more depends on the further efforts of scientists, engineers and other researchers."

Neos quickly concurs, "Research and development efforts must be made in order to better utilize human and natural resources. New approaches and methods will have a profound effect on the societies of the future. It will particularly affect industry and business by greatly expanding their economic opportunities. It seems to me that researchers who are already using scientific networking would be highly receptive to regional networking efforts."

Pragma asserts, "The regional concept must be proven just as any other scientific hypothesis. The same thought processes, zeal and persistence should be employed in all aspects of the regional concept development as well. We have already explored the necessity for introducing regionalization as a series of experiments from which a progression of knowledge will be derived for upgrading quality of life. Surely, science and technology must be major participants in these experiments."

Neos adds, "Regional concept networking will greatly reduce duplication and unproductive efforts. Networking applies to all phases of regional implementation. As we begin to discuss regional motivation and mobilization, we will borrow from general system management experiences and historical accomplishments in order to organize and face what clearly appears to be the greatest impending crisis in human history: population growth and density."

Networking with Regionalization
The Emergence of Research & Development and Enterprise

- *When theoretical and applied research contribute to regionalization, they help create infrastructures which in turn offer stimulating environments. These man-made environments offer new opportunities and direction.*
- *The things that make for a better quality of life suggest a shift away from materialism. In its place must come things that are of more lasting value to humanity. Greed and over-consumption would become alien in a new society with its higher values.*
- *Development of enterprise and other activities also creates a favorable climate for innovation, invention and designs of all kinds, including better living.*
- *Networking is essential in research and development and enterprise. It provides background information and current events on a timely basis.*
- *The following diagram describes these relationships:*

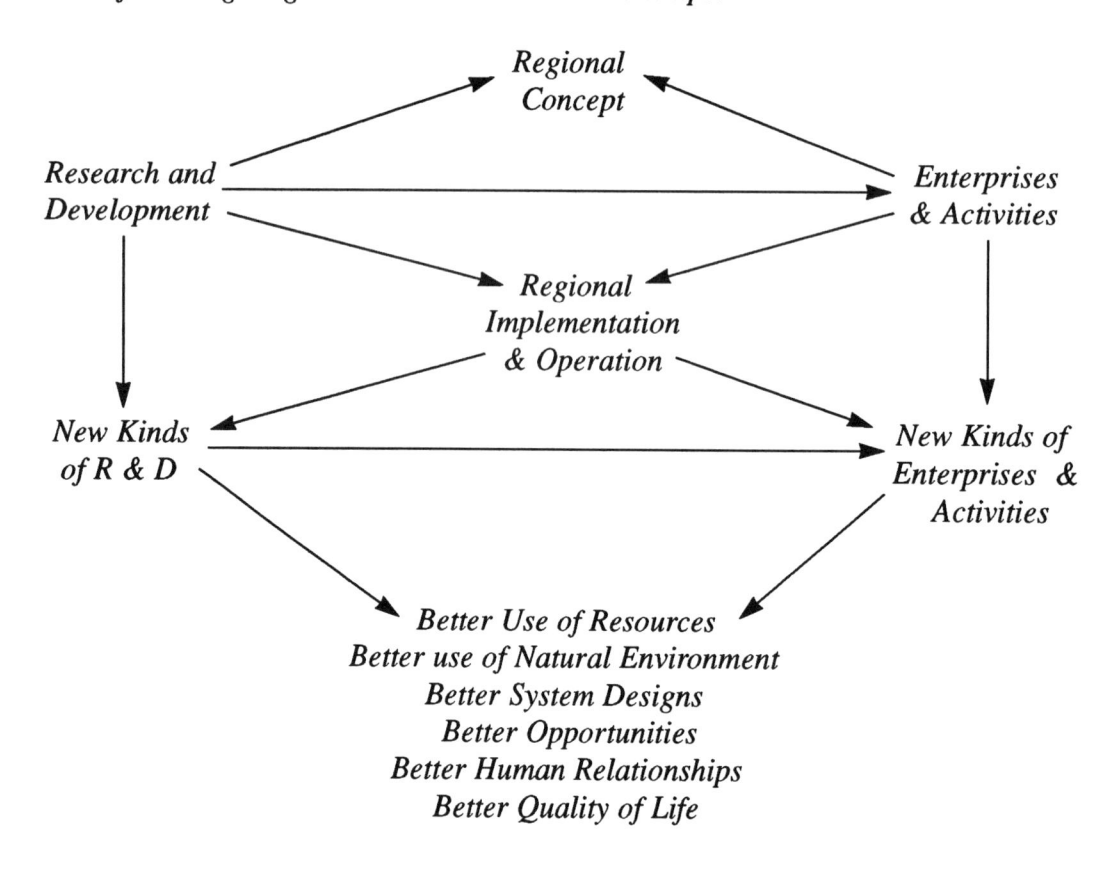

```
                        Regional
                        Concept
                       ↗        ↖
Research and ─────────────────────→ Enterprises
Development    ↘                ↗    & Activities
                 Regional
                 Implementation
                 & Operation
               ↙              ↘
New Kinds ────────────────────→ New Kinds of
of R & D                         Enterprises &
         ↘                  ↙    Activities
          Better Use of Resources
          Better use of Natural Environment
          Better System Designs
          Better Opportunities
          Better Human Relationships
          Better Quality of Life
```

Figure V-2-G

Part V - The Challenge of Implementation

CHAPTER 3 - MOTIVATION

What sort of need fires the desire to bring about monumental changes? If the need is visceral or emotional, we humans almost always spring into action; if the need is reasoned, we sometimes do. In order to influence people of varying cultures to undertake an extensive reorganization of their lives such as implementing regionalization, all three of these motivating factors must be brought into play.

Rational thinking and a sense of direction, careful design and planning, computations and statistics, no matter how clearly, rigorously and comprehensively they may be presented, may not prove sufficient to overcome lethargy and inertia. If they are to be used for regional implementation, it will also take sustained emotional persuasion, prompting and perseverance.

Pragma, Neos and Veritor wish that the concept alone were stimulus enough, but they realize that people are often immersed in their own lives and micro-environments. Only strong stimuli, specifically related to vital needs and vulnerabilities will arouse the public and its leaders to pursue the regional concept.

As the three explorers approach the subject of the mobilization and development phases, they realize up to now they have mostly expressed what regionalization is and why it must be implemented. They have partially presented how regionalization is to take place and have yet to deal with when and where. Motivation must be applied to all these aspects. They know it will take action, direction and implementation to create a better world.

The regional concept calls for extensive exposure and expansion. People must be encouraged to think in terms of regionalization during all its program phases, exchanging ideas and opinions. Networking processes must be intensified so that more people will become involved.

What Will Motivate?

Motivating people to mobilize their resources for regionalization takes various forms. Motivation depends on who is receptive to change and who listens and perceives. Individuals must assume responsibility for motivating and leading. New methods must be employed to excite interest and participation.

When people in all walks of life rise up to be counted,

Will it be through fear of:
- *hunger, thirst and disease?*
- *oppression and tyranny?*
- *loss of means for making a living?*

Will it be repugnance for and repudiation of:
- *decaying societies and alien values?*
- *corruption and greed?*
- *congestion and sub-human living conditions?*

Will it be awareness of:
- *opportunities for personal growth?*
- *chances to try new enterprises and occupations?*
- *opportunities to participate in meaningful and satisfying activities?*

Will it be a yearning for:
- *a better quality of life?*
- *greater spiritual belonging?*
- *social justice and loving relationships?*

Will the regional concept excite and stimulate, attract the attention, resolution and inspiration of enough people to make a difference?

CHAPTER 3 - MOTIVATION

Pragma proposes, "I think the feeling of vulnerability is a very strong motivator, but people have to see enough graphic evidence to appreciate that danger or extreme hardship is imminent. Then we might see action. Until a crisis happens, most people will not respond."

Neos notes, "It seems to me that we have only considered the concept's rational appeal. A way to increase its emotional appeal would be to dramatize what could happen if nothing is done to meet changing world conditions."

Veritor responds, "I think for the present, educators must be encouraged to evaluate the relevance of the regional concept in terms of what is being taught or studied. Because the concept is so comprehensive, it could become a larger scope of reference for many areas of learning. As we have noted, students should then be able to orient their studies and direct their personal aims in life in a meaningful way. Most of all, the concept's implementation would allow them to become involved in a cause as big as life itself. The academic world is one of the areas that holds promise. We have already described other areas where leadership at all levels must be addressed. I think a similar pattern of inducement must be applied to academic leaders as well."

Pragma answers, "You are right. The regional concept should be proposed as a viable solution for urgent problems that mankind is now facing. The validity of problems is more easily defined than their solutions, it seems. Long term problems do not yet sufficiently motivate most people, but short term ones, already impacting their lives, do. People need to wake up to what future consequences might be."

Neos says, "I am most concerned with the people involved in communications. This area is extremely important in presenting the various aspects of regionalization. Of course, there can be negative aspects to this when the public is hyped up with sensationalism, distortions, fragments and false promises. This may be difficult to avoid at times. But as we mentioned before, communication media have a collective responsibility to effectively and completely inform themselves and the public."

Part V - The Challenge of Implementation

CHAPTER 4 - MOBILIZATION

Regional mobilization is faced with prevailing political, social and economic entrenchments. People band together hoping to identify with others, to face uncertainty and to cope with chaos. Will their bonds be loosened enough to allow regrouping? Will they accommodate necessary adjustments in their lives to meet the adverse conditions about them? Will people relinquish dependence on decaying relationships and seek new ones that can benefit all? How well will the challenge of regionalization be embraced?

Regional mobilization involves more than the establishment of transient, random relationships. The bonds that are formed through the development of regional networking are apt to be meaningful, substantial and mutually beneficial to all who will live in and near the new emerging societies. The societies that are to be created will have purpose and direction while maintaining a high level of livability and security for their members. Such purpose involves recognition of the crises of our times.

Can mobilization come about despite recalcitrant human nature? If mankind can mobilize for war and display great efficiency, cohesion and resolve, it can mobilize for peaceful pursuits and exhibit the same characteristics for opposite purposes. The key to successful mobilization is to have common goals and the intelligence to strive for them.

But effective as the mobilization schemes for regions may be in solving major problems, people must still cope with their day to day difficulties. So we cannot realistically expect total involvement in regional mobilization by a great number of people. Involvement is likely to grow in momentum when more people can directly earn their living from the region as it comes into being. Nevertheless, a majority of the population must concur that mobilization is necessary. Mobilization is on a human scale. It requires only what people are able to contribute. It does not ask for people to sacrifice their lives even though the threat of worldwide problems may adversely affect their lives. It calls for people to devote their lives to things that will make life better and safer for themselves and their posterity. It is not too much to ask. It is long overdue.

The process of mobilization involves diverse, dedicated leaders and groups at all levels and areas of competency to effectively carry out necessary functions. Such functions must be related to the program goals established for regionalization in each host nation.

CHAPTER 4 - MOBILIZATION

Basic System Relationships For Regional Mobilization And Beyond

- *Mobilizing for regionalization must begin by bringing together people who are competent at different levels of a system in their own areas of proficiency.*
- *There are direct vertical interactions within general elements and within specific elements of a system.*
- *There is a direct corresponding relationships between general and specific elements of a system.*
- *The general elements are qualitative; the specific elements are quantitative.*
- *Limiting parameters exist for all elements.*
- *Normal progression is from the general to the specific and from a prevailing status to a future status.*
- *The following diagram depicts required system element relationships that must be considered as mobilization begins:*

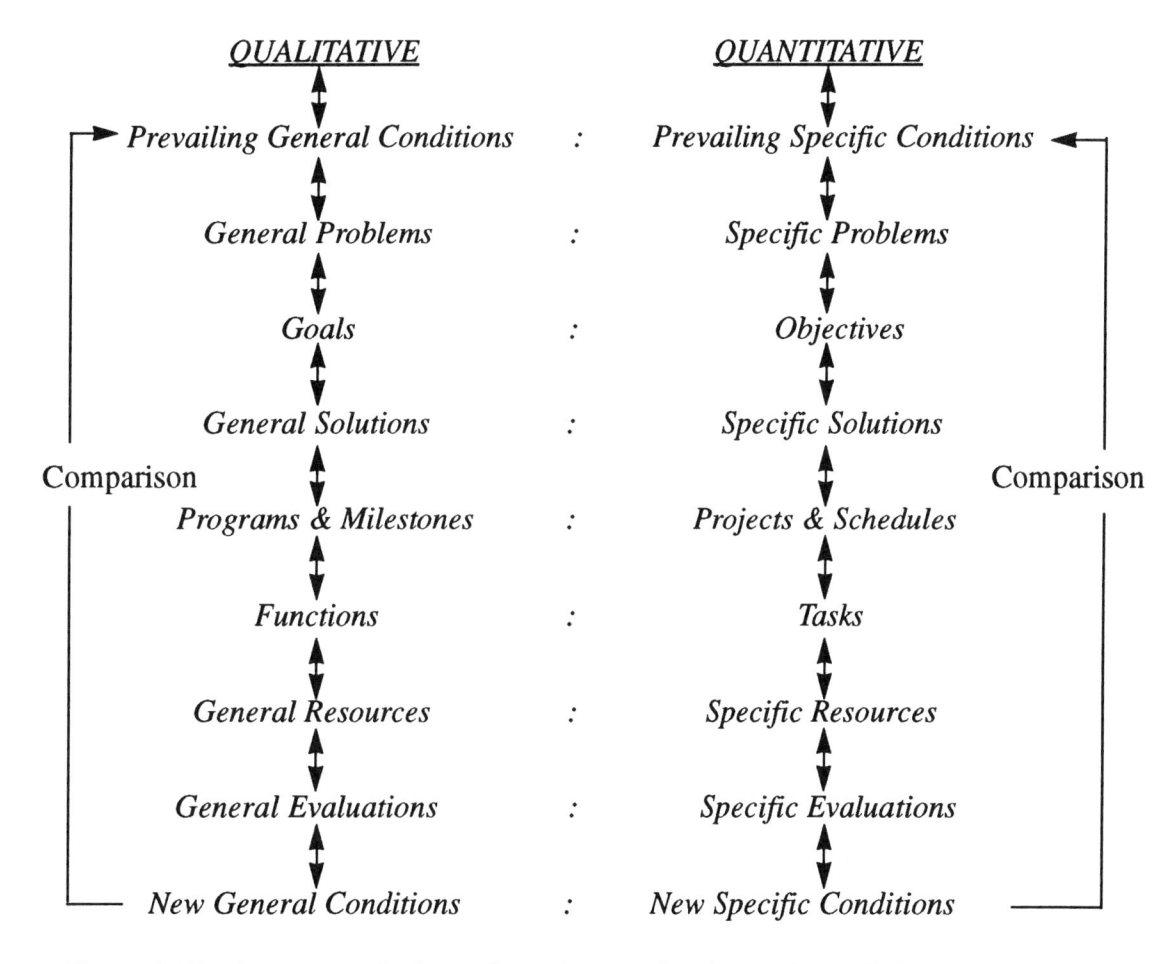

<u>*QUALITATIVE*</u>   <u>*QUANTITATIVE*</u>

Qualitative		Quantitative
Prevailing General Conditions	:	*Prevailing Specific Conditions*
General Problems	:	*Specific Problems*
Goals	:	*Objectives*
General Solutions	:	*Specific Solutions*
Programs & Milestones	:	*Projects & Schedules*
Functions	:	*Tasks*
General Resources	:	*Specific Resources*
General Evaluations	:	*Specific Evaluations*
New General Conditions	:	*New Specific Conditions*

Comparison (left and right brackets connecting Prevailing Conditions to New Conditions)

- *The mobilization proceeds through a mixture of series and parallel events.*

Figure V-4-A

Goals must be established for the implementation of each regional program plan. Milestone dates representing key review points should be indicated on plan schedules. Functional analysis defines types of work to be done for each program. General limits and constraints must also be established.

Specific quantifiable objectives are required for the implementation of projects that make up each program. Task analysis is performed and specific limits and constraints defined for each project. Schedules and manpower assignments follow. The selection of participants and the acquisition of facilities and utilities required to carry out program functions and project tasks continue this progression.

Systems analysis and management approaches and their utilization have been known and increasingly applied in many fields for years. The system methodologies that utilize them will be indispensable throughout regional implementation.

Pragma, Veritor and Neos are well aware that it will take great emotional stimuli, extensive mental and physical exertions and collective perseverance to implement the regions, especially the initial ones, in a relatively short period of time.

Pragma begins,"We have already described general adverse conditions in many environments as well as the status of resources. Some specific examples have also been presented. Much more needs to be done, of course, to define specific environmental conditions and available resources for specific sites in each country on each continent. We have also attempted to define many major problems in both general and specific ways. These must be addressed on a continuing basis. However, many new problems are likely to arise as conditions worsen throughout the world. Let's talk about regionalization goals in several areas that, when combined, represent a new world order. We can see that a goal may be defined as the striving for achievement or state of being within a range of personal or collective acceptance."

Veritor and Neos reflect on Pragma's explanation. Veritor notes,"What you describe appears to be part of a modern management approach. How far should mobilization go? It seems to me that we should explore what organizational structures will be necessary. We ought to identify and define their main functions and interfaces. I'd also like to know how programs will be phased in and activated."

CHAPTER 4 - MOBILIZATION

Organizing for Regionalization

Mobilization and all that follows can be expressed in terms of functions to be performed. By carefully grouping such functions according to their relatedness, organizational names can be assigned to them. This approach avoids the long drawn out struggles for power that often happen when organizations are arbitrarily formed first and political assignments follow. Unfortunately, when this happens, many functions, related or not, are lumped together indiscriminately to form ineffective bureaucracies.

In order for organizations to effectively mobilize to meet program goals and project objectives, adherence to functional orientations is mandatory.

In the following diagram some such functions are briefly expressed. They flow or interact by logical progression:

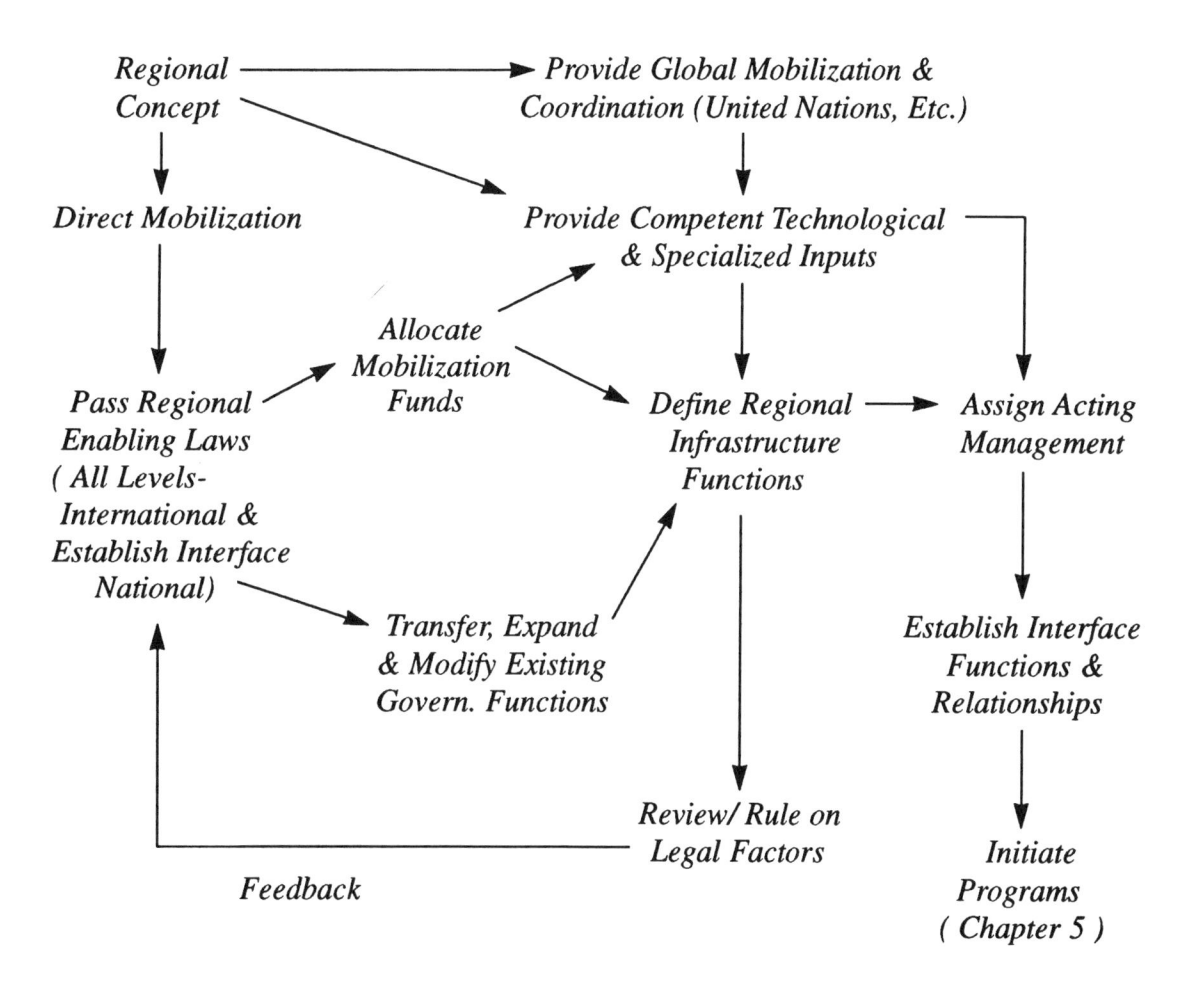

Figure V-4-B

Veritor notes, "It is also necessary for new organizations to interface with existing appropriate governmental agencies. Dependency on many existing agencies will still be necessary, at least until functional transitions can be made and regional operations begin."

Pragma continues to expand on mobilization. "The most critical aspect is that of program resources. For one thing, as the mobilization, initiation, acquisition and development phases evolve, each requires unique combinations of resources. These resource combinations are apt to vary according to level or scope."

Veritor responds to this. "This seems to be a natural way to assign both human, material and monetary resources. These resources not only have to be obtained and allocated, they also must be managed in an open and honest way. Managers at all levels should be given program and fiscal responsibility for functions they are directly and intimately involved in. Then visibility and control become more meaningful."

Neos adds, "Aren't oversight functions also necessary? A separate, independent group of people has to be able to correct, shift or curtail functional activities when unforeseen or varying situations like natural or man-made disasters dictate. The oversight managers can then use contingency or borrowed resources and apply them in a timely manner."

Pragma nods in agreement, "This makes for dynamic and flexible program management. Lower level managers, whose functions may become severely overstressed, could then afford to be open without fear of abusive pressure from those who are not directly carrying out the program. They could request emergency resources and support. This is the way to build a cohesive management team at all levels. The stakes are too great for trivial game-playing and ego enhancement."

Veritor suggests, "I think that when we eventually discuss funding acquisitions, we should review the different kinds and combinations of resources that will be needed for different parts of the world. They may very well determine the rate of completion of regions in such areas."

Pragma and Neos reflect on this and concur. Neos notes, "I think that we will rediscover human ingenuity and enterprise. With proper management and planning, enough incentive and a sense of accomplishment, many things can be done that even money cannot buy. It has to do with behaving in a humane and cooperative manner among fellow humans and achieving something of worth together."

CHAPTER 4 - MOBILIZATION

Regional Resource Application For Multi-Levels & Multi-Phases

Mobilization to carry out the regional concept with its networking avoids pyramid type organizational structures. Because of the number of initial and subsequent regions to be developed, a functional structure with multi-level and parallel relationships would be employed. This approach is more dynamic, allowing portions of programs to be phased in smoothly, encouraging the sharing of resources and permitting mobilization to become more effective.

Special organizational interrelationships need to exist so that regional implementation does not overtax the environment or inadvertently deplete resources. A functional organizational network avoids wasteful duplication of efforts and is less likely to omit key efforts or be untimely.

Four broad functional areas of emphasis are provided for each level during regional implementation. They are depicted as follows:

                                                                Elapsed Time
                            Oversight

<u>Level 1</u>
<u>International</u>

                Phase 1   *Phase 2*   *Phase 3*   *Phase 4*   *Phase n*
    Management Functions
    Main Effort Functions
    Prep./Support Functions

<u>Level 2</u>   Similar To Above With Differences In Magnitude Of Effort & Phase Shift
<u>National</u>

<u>Level 3</u>   *Ditto*
<u>Sub-National/</u>
<u>Inter-Regional</u>

<u>Level 4</u>   *Ditto*
<u>Local/Regional</u>

                                    Figure V-4-C

Pragma continues, "We need to consider preliminary funding and contributions by government agencies, businesses, foundations and individuals throughout the world. It is necessary to attract initial support from many sources. Such resources must be accumulated and utilized according to phase requirements."

Veritor responds, "Of course, the basis of such support is likely to be pragmatic. But those who do contribute must understand that the full impact of regionalization goes far beyond immediate local gain. Neighboring areas and countries are affected, and these in turn will benefit sooner or later. Regionalization calls for a larger awareness and degree of understanding."

Neos adds, "It is apparent that agencies on the international and national levels are primarily involved during initial mobilization, and their organizations must contribute personnel."

Veritor notes, "As you have mentioned, initial support for mobilization doesn't have to occur all at one time, that would be awkward and inefficient. But pledges of support and monetary commitments need to be made by international and national governments and private interests who want to become involved. The rate of mobilization will obviously be influenced by such commitments."

Neos answers, "Also, as mobilization efforts proceed, other activities must start because they, too, need lead time to determine which early preparations to make. Mobilization must always have a sense of direction and focus. Good systems management requires this."

Pragma agrees, "It obviously would be unreasonable to expect initial contributions from different sources without giving such potential donors some idea of where and how such contributions are to be utilized. We should make it clear that these preliminary contributions do not provide for the major acquisition and development phases. The design and planning phases must come first.

Fortunately, extensive international experience has been gained in the mobilization of massive relief efforts. United Nations agencies, many religious organizations and others have a lot of valuable experience in trying to remedy acute socio-economic dysfunctions."

CHAPTER 4 - MOBILIZATION

Initial Contributions For Organizing Mobilization

Different kinds of contributions are required for regional mobilization. They are expected to come from multiple sources. The first initiative may come from one or more large nations and then acted upon by the United Nations. It may be attempted on each continent by either individual countries or groups of them, particularly when they share common economic interests. Wherever regionalization begins, it will then quickly spread from country to country.

<u>Types of Contributions at the International Level</u>

* In Kind Donations And Loans — • For land, buildings, facilities, equipment, furniture.

* Grants And Contributions — • For operational and overhead costs (utilities, supplies, travel, communications, insurance, etc.).

* Gifts, Loans, Volunteers — • For personnel (permanent staffs, temporary and special consultants).

<u>Applied to:</u>

Oversight Functions + Management, Planning Coordinating Functions + Main Technological & Special Functions + Preparation & Support Functions

<u>Provided By:</u>

United Nations Related Budgets And Shared Efforts.
All Nations, Proportionate To Economic Capacity.
International Cartels (Legitimate).
Large Private Foundations.
International Banks
Large Corporations
Religious Foundations
Universities

Figure V-4-D

Initial Contributions (Continued)
For Organizing Mobilization

Types of Contributions at the National Level

Legislative Acts	• For Land Preserves (Potential Future Regional Sites)
** *Budgeted Allocations & In Kind Loans*	• For Centers (Land, Buildings, Facilities, Furniture, Equipment, Etc. at One or More Sites)
** *Government Agency Grants*	• For Operational & Overhead Costs (Utilities, Supplies, Travel, Communications, Etc.)
** *Volunteers, Loans Contributions*	• For Personnel (Permanent, Temporary, Special Consultant)

Applied to:

Oversight + Management, Planning + Main Technological + Preparation &
Functions   Coordinating Functions   & Special Functions   Special Functions

** *Provided By:*

National Budgets
Relevant National Agencies (Shared Efforts)
Major Corporations
International Cartels (Legitimate)
Universities
Large Private Foundations

Figure V-4-D(cont.)

CHAPTER 4 - MOBILIZATION

Pragma becomes more thoughtful as the discussion proceeds. "Of course, as we have already discussed, we can expect opposition from the very beginning of the implementation of regions. However, the greatest resistance is most likely to come during the first phases and for the initial regions rather than subsequent ones. We must face reality and deal with the positive and negative aspects of human nature."

Veritor answers, "Yet, we must also accept the fact that many major worldwide changes have been taking place and require urgent attention. Nothing in history has demanded the magnitude and speed of change that regionalization does. It seems to me that although we have to recognize limiting parameters and acknowledge that there will be opposition, we must move ahead for all aspects of regionalization and exert even greater efforts to help countries having the greatest problems."

Neos adds, "Not only must we identify all kinds of limitations, but we must also have some insight into the residual problems they may create. It seems to me that persuasion, imagination, understanding and perseverance will have to be employed."

Pragma responds to this, "There are some inherent limitations that have to do with nature, such as failure of crops on infertile land, scarcity of water, severity of weather, extensive and debilitating hunger, poverty and high incidence of disease. It is also necessary to respect natural and human productive limitations. We must also recognize that many people may have other plans or special hidden agendas that conflict with regionalization. As we have already noted, other people may just be suspicious or fearful of any change."

Neos and Veritor nod in agreement, and Veritor says, "There are many other reasons why many people may not willingly participate. Regionalization proponents can only hope to eventually gain popular support. As implementation takes place, perhaps, there will be greater acceptance and participation. However, active obstruction to regionalization may take place at any time and even turn violent through provocation. We must acknowledge what these are likely to be."

Dealing With the Realities of Regionalization

- *Some natural conditions cannot be changed by humans. These prohibit or constrain regional design in specific locations for the present and perhaps the future.*
- *Some natural and man-made conditions can be modified to compensate or accommodate regionalization. Such efforts would expand the limits of regionalization.*
- *Still other conditions in supercities appear to be fixed in character but are actually undergoing change. These can be influenced or encouraged to be more in accord- with the goals of regionalization.*
- *Some antagonists to regionalization may be countered by confrontation while others may be diverted or converted.*
- *Some socio-economic conditions represent frivolous, self-indulgent and squandering ways of life occuring in an unstable environment. The more gratifying alternatives offered by regionalization would need to be demonstrated.*
- *Some man-made activities represent hidden agendas that appear to be harmful to our environment. These must be detected, exposed and legally opposed by communities and neighborhoods.*
- *Other human activities are aggressively anti-social. These must be opposed or diverted by legal and psychological means.*

Some Conditions to Consider

Depleted Natural Resources
Hostile Weather & Climate Conditions
Extreme Geographical Conditions
Limited Human Resource Skills
Contrary Cultural & Religious Dogma
Rigid Political Systems
Inadequate Economic Systems
Aggressive, Expansionist Goals
Prevailing Chaos & Capital Dissipation
Unusual Legal Prohibitions
Existing Hidden Agendas
Detracting Extra-Legal Activities

POTENTIALLY LIMITING PARAMETERS

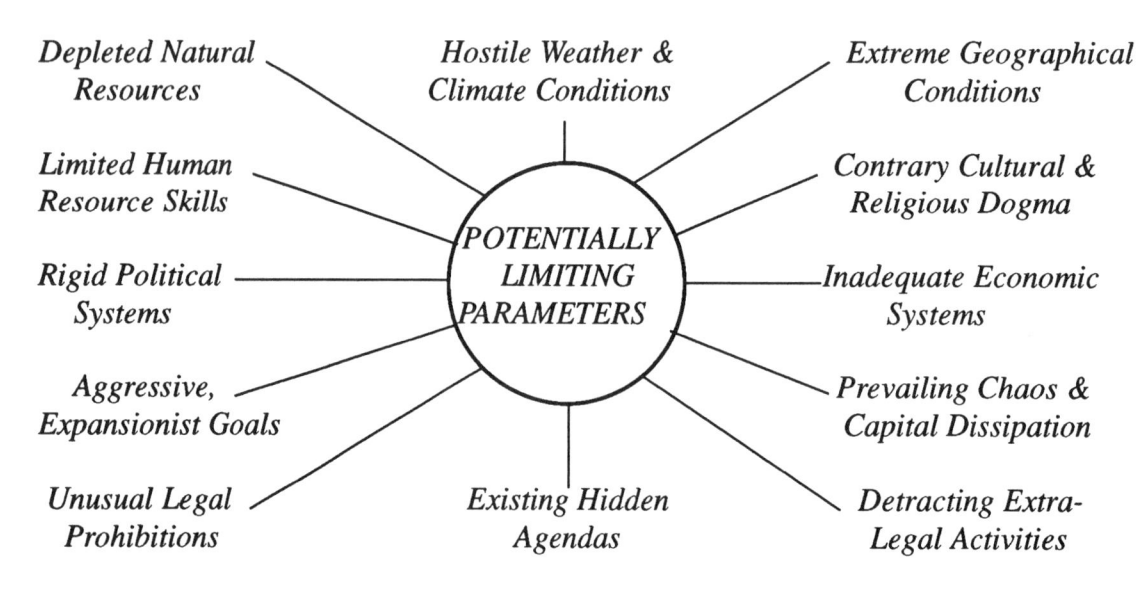

Figure V-4-E

CHAPTER 4 - MOBILIZATION

Pragma notes, "We can hope that leaders everywhere will behave responsibly in coping with major serious problems and not narrowly define them. Perhaps, they may try to be too cautious and end up being indecisive, unrealistic, stagnant and ineffective."

Veritor adds, "I am also concerned. I think that most leaders attempt to identify the symptoms of urgent problems and try to solve them without addressing the causal factors. However, procrastination, the failure to invest resources or the application of only token measures to identify adverse conditions represent irresponsible behavior."

Pragma agrees, "Perhaps the greatest stumbling block and limiting factor will be funding. Certainly it has been in the past. A lack of timely investments in regionalization and its infrastructures would result in reduced cost effectiveness. If this happens, the beneficial impact of regionalization on society might be substantially diminished."

Veritor and Neos both acknowledge funding as being a significantly limiting factor. Neos adds, "This makes it even more important that incremental investments be made in sufficient amounts to match the needs of program implementation. Incremental successes, as we have mentioned earlier, would build confidence for investors as well as the general public."

Pragma notes, "During our previous discussions on concept networking and motivational strategies we emphasized the importance of close working relationships. During mobilization, communication procedures, oversight, support and protocol functions, and regular working or coordination meetings and other special multinational forums would be started. We are talking about program and system management and integration on a grand scale. I think that a special United Nations entity should be formed to arrange and initiate regionalization for countries receptive to the concept. Perhaps even if the regional concept is not initially accepted, the U.N. and its members could adopt some of its premises. This might then lead to the full acceptance of the concept."

Neos answers indignantly, "I cannot see a 'watered down' version as being of great benefit. Is this the time for political compromise that can only produce non-cohesive, ineffectual results?

Pragma nods, "You are right. Sometimes when 'compromise' is thought of as being a convenient or arbitrary political arrangement, it leads to less than acceptable results."

Mobilization Arrangements

An orderly, well-conceived progression of events must occur in order to mobilize the functions of international governments involved in regionalization. Although something of this magnitude and complexity has not been done before, implementation of regionalization is achievable and manageable. It would not do to create societies that cannot be managed. Yet, this is what mankind has often created so far.

There have been significant advances made by creating a United Nations and by groups of nations coming together for common markets, etc. Regionalization is meant to continue this progression.

Mobilization for regional initiation may be described as follows:

Describe Regional Concept → *Involve U. N. Agencies In Regional Development*

- *Define Purpose & Directions*
- *Define Organizational Functions*
- *Identify & Obtain Participants*
- *Define Acquisition Of Operational Resources*
- *Identify Limiting Parameters/Problems*

→ *Establish Worldwide Program Centers* →

- *Establish Communication Functions and Procedures*
- *Establish Protocol Functions*
- *Establish Regular Working, Coord. & Formal Meetings*
- *Provide Support Functions*
- *Establish Oversight Functions*

↓

Develop Individual Program Management Capabilities

→ *Initiate Worldwide Regional Programs*

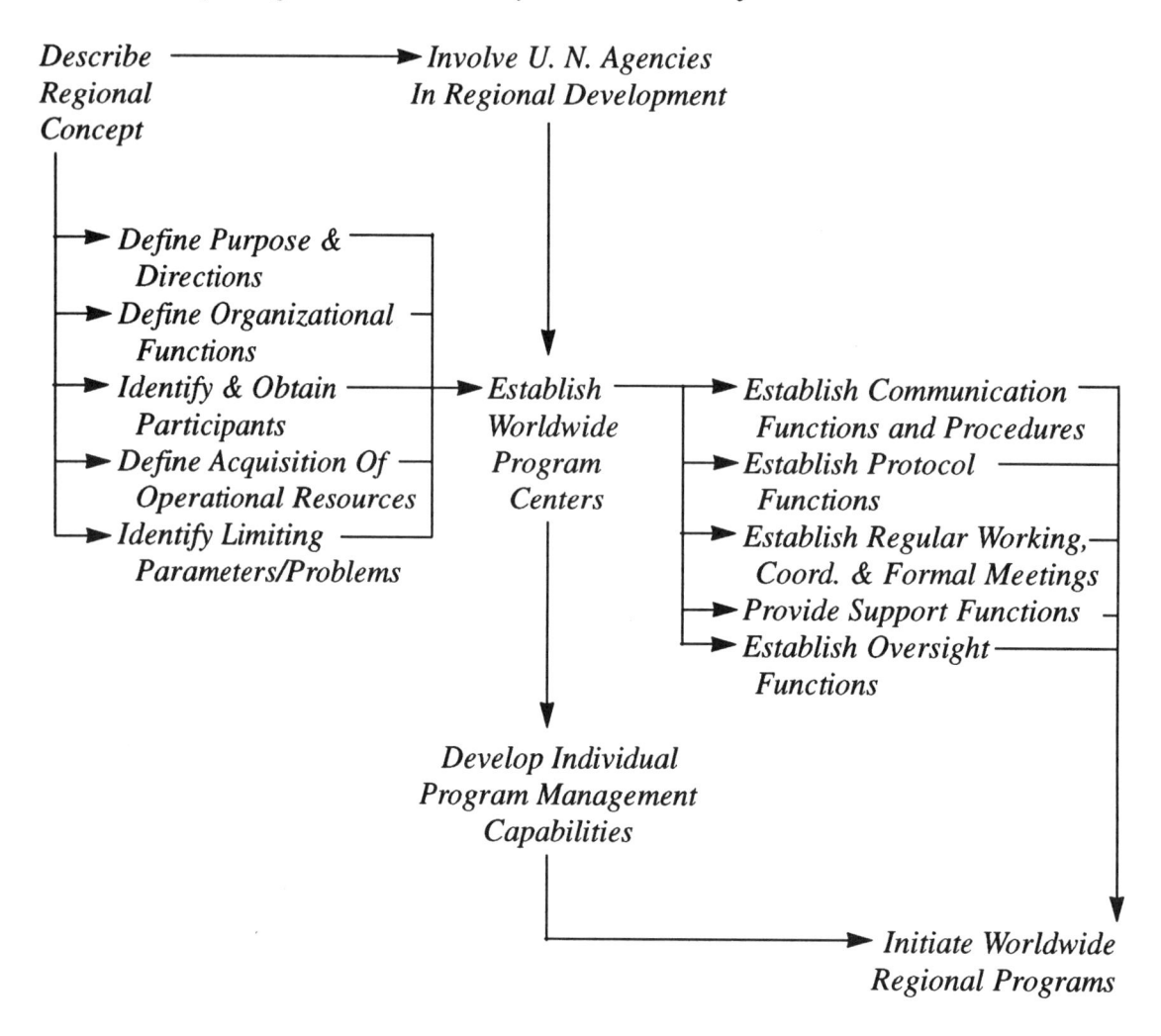

Figure V-4-F

Part V - The Challenge of Implementation

CHAPTER 5 - INITIATION OF PROGRAMS

The initiation of regional implementation involves different kinds of programs. Some of these have been described in Part IV, Preparation for Tomorrow, and relate to the general and specific restoration and enhancement of global and regional environments and the enhancement and conservation of resources. The overall global efforts are intended to be successive, dedicated programs of long duration which may require periodic re-initiation. The shorter term regional programs focus on continental sites that are appropriate for development.

There are many legal and economic global ramifications. They require special programs to codify and clarify international laws such as laws of the sea, air traffic control regulations, rules of commerce, and resource exploitation as they affect the implementation and operation of new regions. New regions depend on these efforts and in turn provide unique opportunities to orient and focus such laws. They also help in structuring both legal and economic relationships.

Initiation of the programs associated with regional site selection, enhancement, preparation and development require individual nations or groups of nations. The transition of responsibilities from the U.N. to individual countries or groups of countries offers the potential for new, healthy relationships that involve trust, cooperation and support.

As the regional programs are initiated, many lower levels of government, businesses and society in general gradually become involved. It should become very apparent to host countries that regionalization unifies, stimulates and permits societies to organize in unique ways.

Pragma, Veritor and Neos now shift their attention to the global efforts of initiating resource programs. There are different kinds of resources to consider. They are faced with how to begin such changes. These require definitive programs that carefully utilize both natural and human resources.

Pragma speaks first, "A variety of both long and short term strategies must be considered in order to avoid depletion of non-renewable natural resources. However, it takes a world body of all nations to challenge excessive use by one or more countries. If such resources are, in the short term, the life blood of such countries, use is not likely to stop unless alternatives are available to them. Economic help to make changes and reduce dependencies must be forthcoming from all the affluent nations. However, the continued attrition of natural, non-renewable resources by those who control them should be discouraged. Eventually, such exploitation can only cause abject misery for millions of dependent and susceptible fellow human beings. I propose that existing world organizations expand their scope by creating a world resource conservation organization."

Veritor adds, "I think this organization should initiate programs such as recycling, substitution of resources for various applications, prohibition of wanton destruction and waste, modification of situations that lead to excesses and coordination with other agencies and governments to help enforce these efforts."

Neos nods, "Such an organization would start out as a nucleus, and as it grew, would progressively network with countries and their emerging regions."

Pragma continues, "This world program management organization would focus on both non-renewable and renewable energy. It would initiate action projects to investigate and resolve regional and non-regional problem areas. Special sub-groups would be involved in resource analysis and related research to advocate or substantiate positions taken. Regional design and planning offer ways to conserve resources without causing undue hardships. Certainly, new alternative approaches to conservation are necessary."

CHAPTER 5 - INITIATION OF PROGRAMS

Program Initiation of Regional Natural Resources

A worldwide program center under the auspices of the United Nations and other world organizations provides services to both regional and non-regional entities through specific programs for renewable and non-renewable resources and energy and water as special emphasis.

Before this can happen, the nucleus of a program organization must be formed so that more efficient and effective decision-making and coordination can be made.

Description of the interrelationship of such an organization is shown as follows:

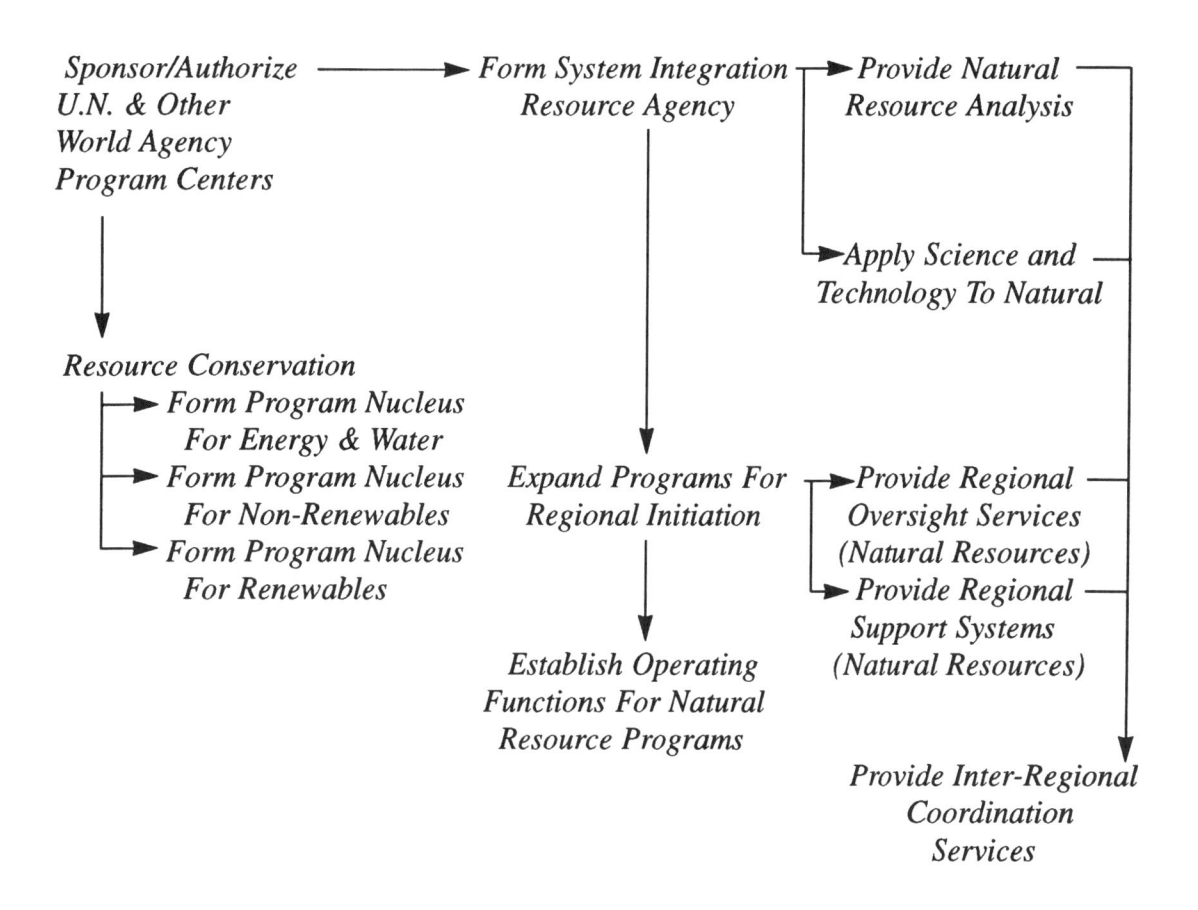

```
Sponsor/Authorize ──────▶ Form System Integration ──▶ Provide Natural
U.N. & Other              Resource Agency              Resource Analysis
World Agency
Program Centers
                                                    ▶ Apply Science and
      │                                               Technology To Natural
      ▼
Resource Conservation
   ├─▶ Form Program Nucleus
   │   For Energy & Water
   ├─▶ Form Program Nucleus      Expand Programs For ──▶ Provide Regional
   │   For Non-Renewables        Regional Initiation     Oversight Services
   └─▶ Form Program Nucleus                              (Natural Resources)
       For Renewables                                 ▶ Provide Regional
                                                       Support Systems
                                  ▼                    (Natural Resources)
                             Establish Operating
                             Functions For Natural
                             Resource Programs        Provide Inter-Regional
                                                      Coordination
                                                      Services
```

Figure V-5-A

Veritor addresses human resources. "We have already discussed the enhancement of human potential and its application throughout the world and specifically for regions. Much has been done in this area by the U.N. and other world agencies. Regionalization would provide a new stimulus for human productivity and growth. How can the initiation of regionally-oriented efforts in this area begin?"

Pragma says, "It seems to me that such efforts must be initiated at the national and regional levels with exchanges of knowledge and skills."

Neos agrees, "That is sensible, Pragma. Many highly specialized skills, of course, take more than short term training, particularly those necessary for managing the complex regional programs throughout the world. It takes years of both formal education and experience to master such skills."

Pragma answers, "How about people who are educated, but lack experience because there are few opportunities available? Regionalization would offer many programs requiring their skills, knowledge and participation. In Third World countries, especially, many qualified people work at jobs that are much below the training and education they have received. This is a tragic loss. We would expect the United Nations and other world agencies to provide technical as well as management assistance during regional implementation to help employ and guide such people."

Veritor notes, "But it is at the national and regional levels that the highly educated with vision and scope are likely to have a better chance to develop their skills and produce what they are capable of."

Neos remarks, "As we have already mentioned, it would be self-defeating to only import the highly skilled and experienced and not help qualified indigenous people build self-reliance. Even manual labor must be upgraded by introducing use of new tools and methods. Regional development offers an excellent opportunity to help people grow by introducing a number of challenging projects. I believe that what they accomplish will be phenomenal and fulfilling."

CHAPTER 5 - INITIATION OF PROGRAMS

Initiation of Human Resource Development Programs

- *Initiation of human resource development programs requires the forming of a management nucleus to direct efforts for primary training and teaching. The major emphasis would be to provide apprenticeship programs for different kinds of skill requirements. Such management groups have to be formed under the United Nations or other world organizations and include national and regional sponsorship as well during regionalization.*
- *Formation of the human resource management program functions is as follows:*

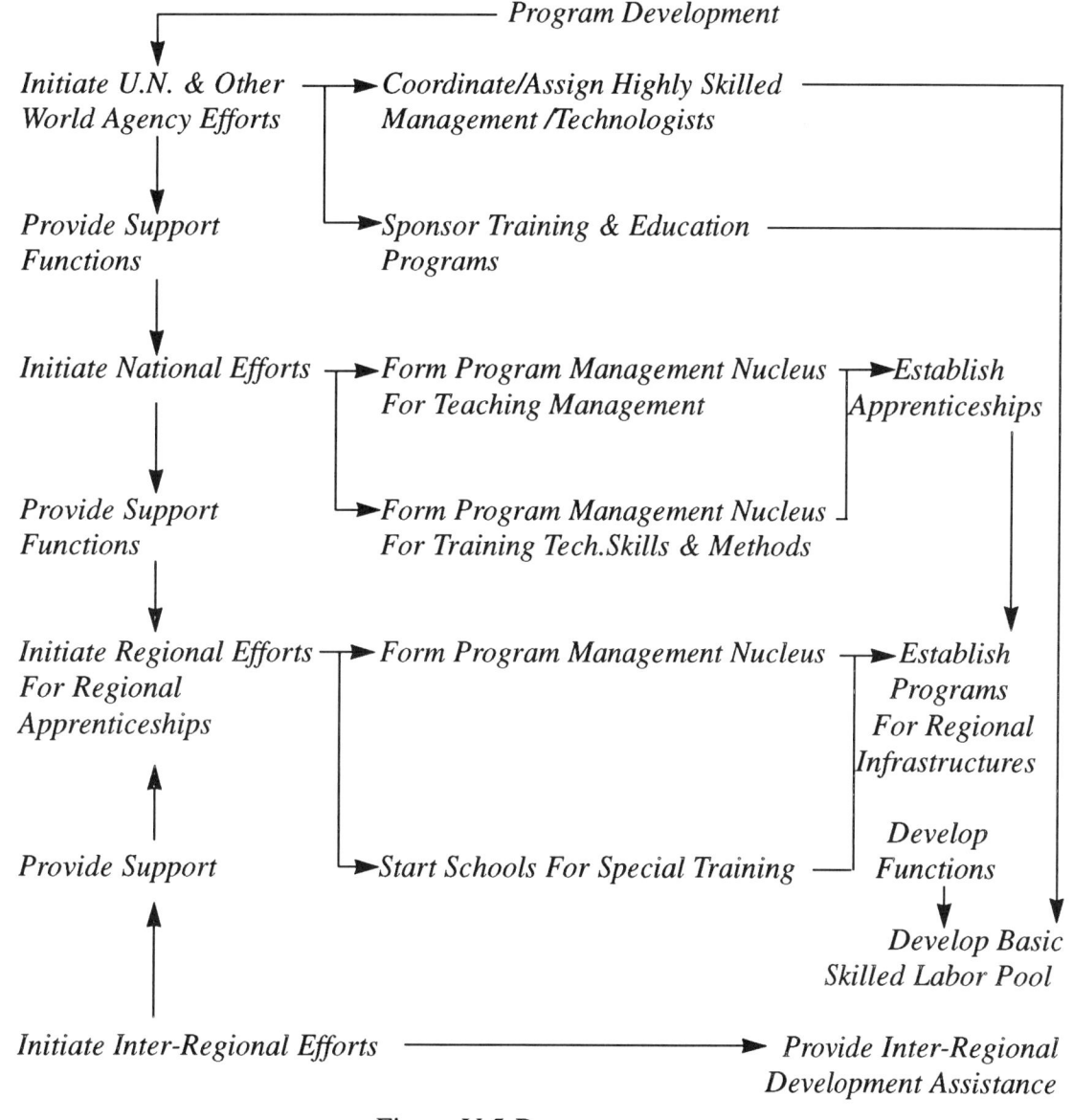

Program Development

Initiate U.N. & Other World Agency Efforts → *Coordinate/Assign Highly Skilled Management /Technologists*

Provide Support Functions → *Sponsor Training & Education Programs*

Initiate National Efforts → *Form Program Management Nucleus For Teaching Management* → *Establish Apprenticeships*

Provide Support Functions → *Form Program Management Nucleus For Training Tech.Skills & Methods*

Initiate Regional Efforts For Regional Apprenticeships → *Form Program Management Nucleus* → *Establish Programs For Regional Infrastructures*

Provide Support → *Start Schools For Special Training* — *Develop Functions*

Develop Basic Skilled Labor Pool

Initiate Inter-Regional Efforts → *Provide Inter-Regional Development Assistance*

Figure V-5-B

The U. N. and other world agencies have been initiating programs that produce, store and distribute food to areas of need. These persistent needs represent both short and long-term problems for many countries, especially in the Third World. The regional concept includes an infrastructure for providing food resources. Therefore, it closely conforms with the intent and purposes of world organizations. The initiation of regionalization is actually an extension and augmentation that will benefit their work.

The initiation phase for developing food resources is a multi-level effort that includes world organizations as well as individual or groups of nations and regions. Many nearby non-regional areas may also receive assistance. Therefore, oversight functions of the U.N. become even more essential in providing aid. Groups of countries gain economically from their combined initiation of programs for developing agriculture and in their implementation of regions. As regions are initiated in each country, cooperation can take the form of special equipment loans, advice and new techniques. This kind of inter-regional exchange and cooperation forms a common shield against outside economic exploitation and usurpation.

Pragma begins the discussion, "I can see that regionalization would also encourage the establishment of agricultural research stations. These stations would be started by private firms as well as government entities, often as joint enterprises. The private sector has many food companies and pharmaceutical corporations that could become involved. Regions would provide the organizational means for initiating cooperation and accelerating efforts. As mentioned earlier, new kinds of plants would also be introduced experimentally and then developed commercially under appropriate management."

Veritor answers, "Research in food processing, storage and distribution are likely to be greatly accelerated in a regional setting. Again, sponsorships and residual benefits would be shared."

Neos adds, "I think that it is important to initiate special water conservation programs in close conjunction with research and farming. We also have to consider limitations that exist in many Third World countries where water may be very scarce."

Pragma responds, "You have brought up an important point that we have already touched on when mobilization was being discussed. Of course, there are implied limits for everything that may be initiated, and certainly availability of water is one of them."

CHAPTER 5 - INITIATION OF PROGRAMS

Initiation Of Food Resource Development From Global To Regional

- *The regional concept can greatly enhance world efforts to save humans from starvation and malnutrition. Many private and government channels have established networks that attempt to reach such people under hazardous and desperate conditions. The programs have been designed primarily to relieve the suffering of millions of innocent people.*
- *The regional concept offers a definitive correction or reduction of many of the underlying conditions associated with food resource scarcity. Each region represents the means for creating new environments and new potential. Therefore, each region acts as an integrator, combining activities that would ordinarily have been accomplished in part or not at all.*
- *The initiation process is described as follows:*

Initiation Process

Provide U.N. Oversight and Coordination → *Establish World Food Bank* → *Establish Distribution Systems* → *Distribute Food*

→ *Establish World Food Research* → *Disseminate Findings*

→ *Support Regional & Non-Regional Devel.*

Initiate National And Inter-National Agric. Research Programs → *Establish Agricultural Research Network* → *Form National Agricultural Management Nucleus*

↳ *Initiate Private Sector Support*

Provide Support

Initiate Regional Agric. Programs → *Form Management Nucleus* → *Integrate Research & Applications*

→ *Integrate Concepts (Growing, Process., Storage, Distrib.)*

→ *Establish Experimental Farms*

Disseminate Findings

Initiate Inter-Regional Exchange/Support

Disseminate Findings

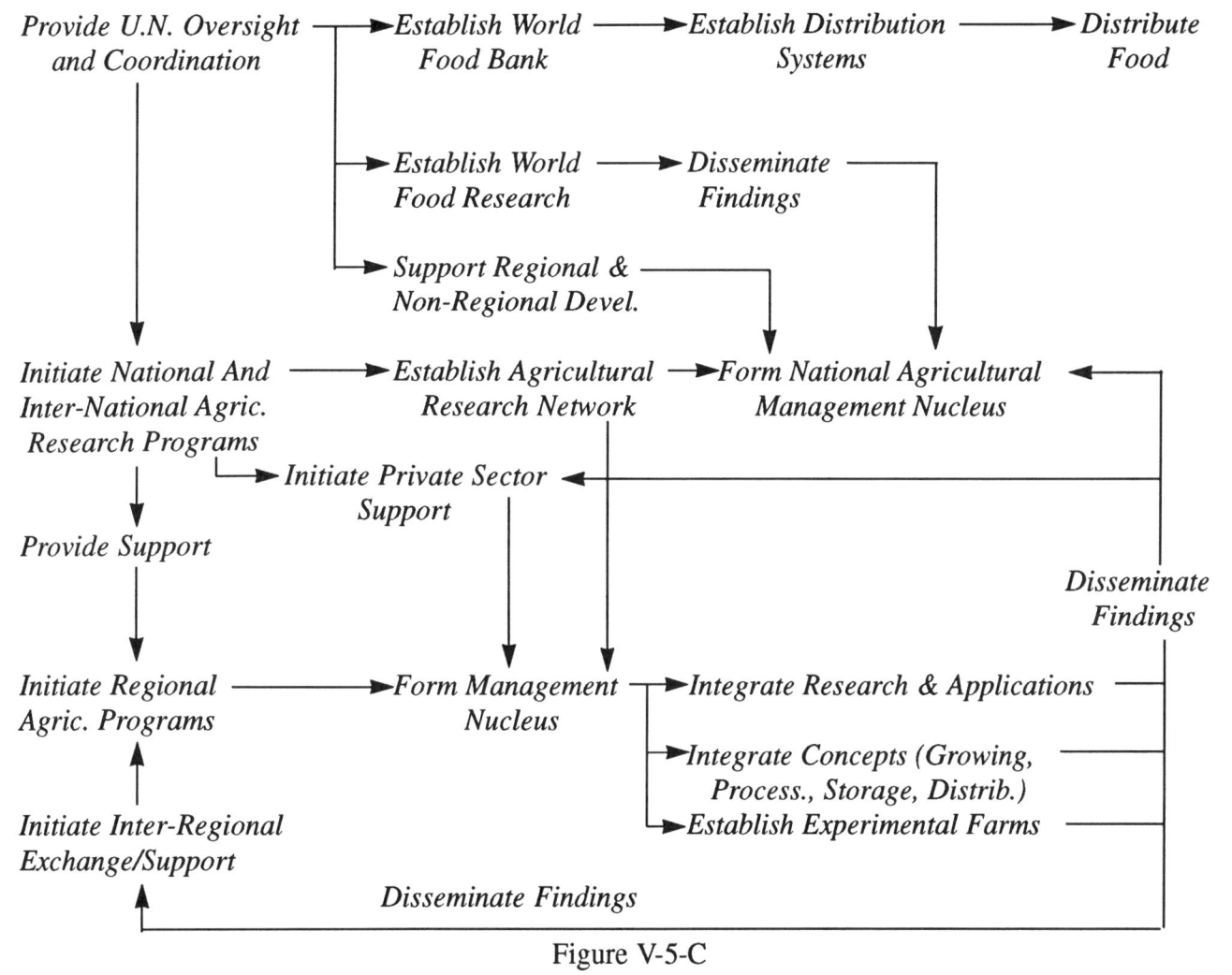

Figure V-5-C

Veritor says, "When we talk about limits, we have to include the introduction and up-grading of laws at the international and national levels in anticipation of regional need. These would provide the uniformity and common agreements that guide international behavior and relationships. Without such accord there would be total reliance on opportunistic behavior and values of convenience. Rules based on the convenience of the moment often produce short term advantages but long term inequities and friction. This latter approach is contrary to the regional concept."

Neos adds, "The development of legal codes doesn't necessarily mean that they are meant to only prevent or control dishonesty, curb aggression or avoid disagreements. The laws are also meant to encourage equity and reasonableness and to increase participation of all countries that are interested in promoting good will, peace and harmony."

Pragma continues the discussion, "National and international forums should address significant issues and their legal relationships. Issues must be faced in a comprehensive way before legal analysis and lawmaking is attempted. Also, laws that are too limited in scope or too biased are often superceded by higher laws that are more inclusive and sound. So there have to be legislative forums at different levels based on larger principles and impact. Certainly, many existing laws will have to be modified or expanded to accommodate regionalization."

Veritor asks, "Don't we need to discuss different areas of law that affect various kinds and levels of activity? The world is fortunate in that all nations have become involved in U.N. forums, councils and assemblies where international law is fostered."

Neos answers, "It seems to me that all of the nations will have to address the problems of global law and continental deterioration of the environment. Many environmental conditions extend far beyond the borders of nations. They will also have to concern themselves with the global management of natural and human resources. Attrition and misuse of resources seriously impact all nations. However difficult it may be to formulate laws on the basis of technological predictions and environmental expectations, it must be done. Such laws may give the world a chance to 'look before it leaps'."

Pragma notes, "The application of and compliance with laws must begin with managers at every level. These laws guide, direct and determine limits for further acquisitions, design, planning, implementation and operations. From the international level of law we can approach the national and regional levels. From such levels we must then formulate laws governing the functions of different infrastructures. This continues down to the neighborhood level with the laws provides for legal continuity for corresponding levels of functions."

CHAPTER 5 - INITIATION OF PROGRAMS

Initiation of Lawmaking from Global to Regional

Regional infrastructures form the focus for much of regional lawmaking. Although global laws may not be able to address regional infrastructure design and development directly, they may influence and elevate the scope of lawmakers. Initiating new laws at the regional level must take into account the body of laws that prevail locally and in contiguous areas or regions. Existing laws are utilized until newer regionally oriented ones displace them. Infrastructures for water and power networks, transportation networks, communication networks and some of the others cannot begin in isolation, despite the capacity of the region to be operationally semi-autonomous.

The overview of regional infrastructure groups is a convenient reference. Management of these infrastructures is guided and directed by laws formulated at all levels as follows:

<u>International Lawmaking Level I</u>	<u>Infrastructure Groupings</u>	<u>National Lawmaking Level II</u>
	L - Court Management	
	A - Government Admin./ Plan. & Management	
	M - Health Services Mgt.	
	S - Social Services Mgt.	
	D - Law Enf./ Emergency Services Management	
	H - Recreation, Culture/ Spiritual Devel.Mgt.	
	E - Educational System Mgt.	
	T - Transportation Systems Mgt.	
	P - Water /Pwr / Waste Mgt.	
	F - Food Resource Mgt.	
<u>Inter-Regional Lawmaking Level III</u>	C - Communication Syst.Mgt.	<u>Regional Lawmaking Level IV</u>
	N - Environment/Res. Mgt.	
	B - Business, Mfg., Sales Mgt.	

<u>Community Lawmaking Level V</u>

Figure V-5-D

becoming more definitive as they descend from level to level. In a systems sense, this Veritor nods approvingly and comments, "That is a very interesting observation. There is considerable continuity among the many functions within each infrastructure group and at different levels. Laws, rules, regulations, guidelines and other codes governing such functions can then be grouped and related."

Neos adds, "I think that many legal codes are fragmentary or have missing or contradictory logic. We discover these omissions and conflicts when attempts are made to apply them under real life conditions and in the courts. Anticipated operational functions and conditions must help in defining constraints, restrictions, prohibitions, limits, precautions and performance criteria. We will then have meaningful functional laws."

Pragma agrees, "Such relationships suggest a better approach in the formulation of laws in all fields. We can see that this is true because natural laws are predicated on natural functions. If man-made laws are to be relevant and meaningful, they must also be based on one or more man-made functions. So further functional definition is needed if we want to have better laws."

Veritor responds, "It seems to me that lawmaking and functional definition must also be used to fully describe programs for the various phases of regionalization long before such phases are implemented. This also applies to codes and functional definitions that are needed at the various program levels before they are attempted. Early preparation will help control the implementation of all activities in a timely manner."

Neos adds, "Less program friction should occur, and when conflicts do arise, they could be resolved more rapidly. If laws, codes or guidelines have not been provided in time, then those of a higher functional level must be utilized."

Pragma answers, "There are many ramifications to what we have discussed. I believe these are novel ideas that will open new perspectives. This contrasts with laws written only on the basis of precedent or in response to past crises. Such laws may no longer be needed because of changing societies and new functions."

Veritor notes, "The selection of regional sites will require prior lawmaking and reliance on precedent. The lawmaking function must be a part of the investigation of potential regional sites. This is because existing conditions are likely to reveal legal obstacles and other problems that would hinder enhancement, restoration and comprehensive regional planning. Also, private interests and people who may be occupying potential sites would deserve compensation if they have to move because of eminent domain seizures."

Neos responds, "What you say has merit. It permits the initiation of other regionalization processes. But the investigation of potential sites must be broad and

CHAPTER 5 - INITIATION OF PROGRAMS

more general at first to avoid triggering speculation and deliberate obstruction. There is a significantly greater imperative involved than quick profit-making."

Pragma concurs, "There must be a strategy to screen areas that are in need of enhancement of resources and environment before selection. This screening must include analysis to determine whether prevailing conditions will be suitable for regionalization."

Veritor considers this carefully and says, "There should also be progress reports that indicate degrees of readiness for potential sites as they are being enhanced. Regionalization should not come as a great shock to the existing populations, government entities and economic interests. The enhancement and preparations must be expeditious, yet gradual enough not to overwhelm them. All parties must have a chance to adjust and participate."

Neos adds, "Even if an enhanced area does not become a selected regional site, everyone would still benefit. It is in the best interest of local inhabitants to improve areas that have been previously neglected or allowed to deteriorate."

Pragma responds, "There is still another benefit. Regional site selection and eventual development will not ignore people in contiguous areas. They, too, will become involved through employment opportunities and services. Surrounding areas will require some enhancement because of the proximity of regional development. In a way it is similar to Olympic Game site selection. Countries and cities compete for the opportunity to host the games and improve certain sites just to do so. However, the regional concept is far more than a game, and there will ultimately be thousands of selected sites. In the case of new regions, however, site selections must not be made in areas that are contiguous to supercities to merely become their extensions. Restoration and restructuring of supercities would require special emphasis and attention if they are to be converted to regions and maintain their unique identities."

Investigation & General Enhancement of Potential Regional Sites-(Investigation)

- *Investigation and general enhancement of potential sites is ordinarily a long process encompassing many years. But long before completion of such efforts there must be some indication from management, analysis and field research teams that specific sites have reached a state of readiness for early selection and subsequent implementation. This will allow management functions to aggressively pursue acquisitions.*
- *United Nation agencies initiate and direct site investigations and enhancement and form management, field and analysis teams with their members drawn from all member countries who are able to participate. These teams must be autonomous and objective, however, and must not represent any one country.*
- *The initial site investigations are general. They are independent surveys to determine the viability of areas that, with enhancement, would qualify them as potential sites. These efforts would significantly address complex issues and would be of great value to potential host countries.*
- *The investigatory phase is as follows:*

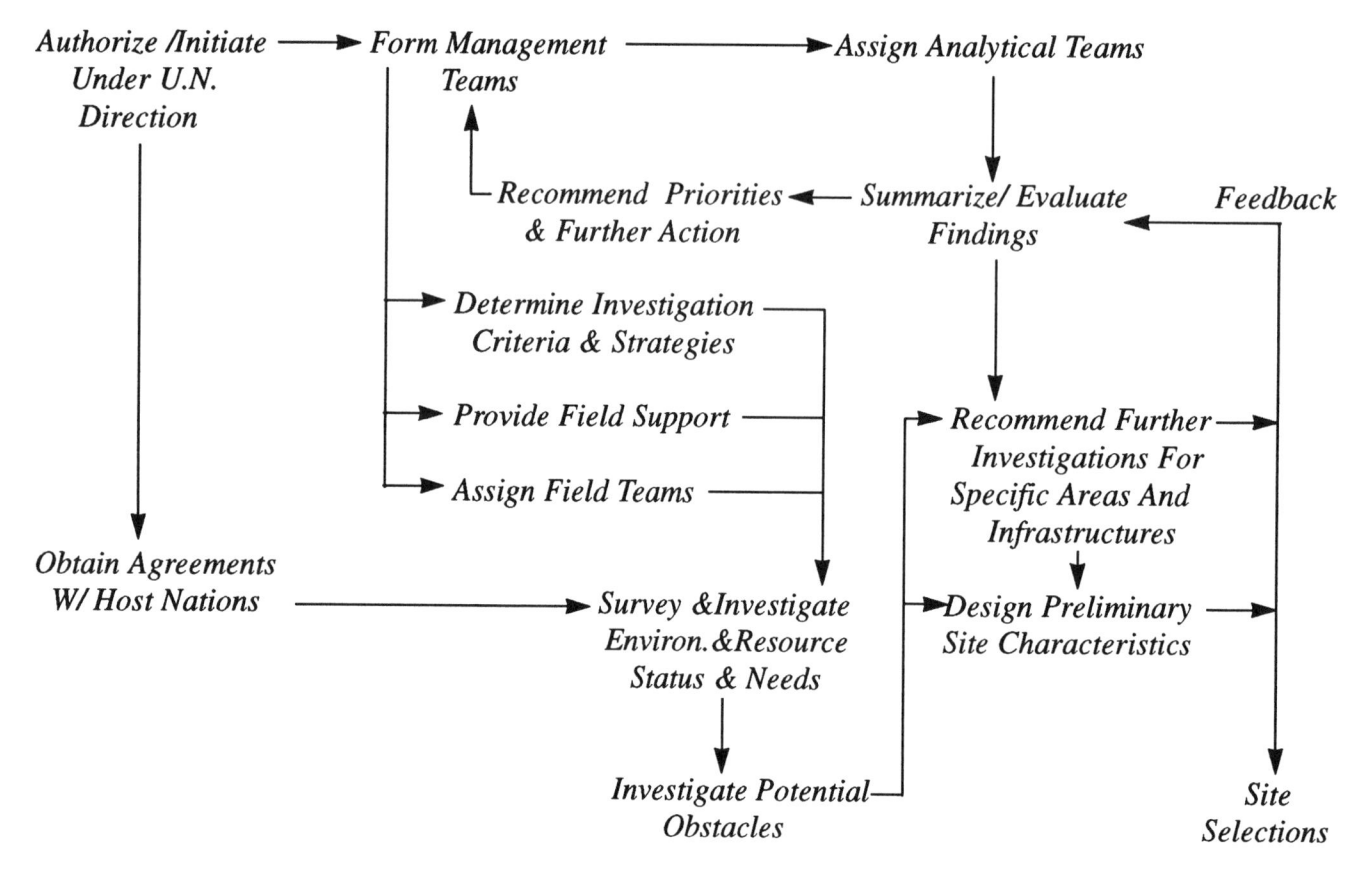

Figure V-5-E

CHAPTER 5 - INITIATION OF PROGRAMS

Investigation & General Enhancement of Potential Regional Sites (Enhancement)

- *The enhancement phase leads either to direct regional site selection with specific enhancement or to continued general enhancement within the limits of host country response and support.*
- *Progress reports for enhancement projects are provided to the management teams, the United Nations representative and the heads of host nations.*
- *The enhancement phase is shown as follows:*

Authorize & Initiate U.N. Direction → *Form Management Teams*

Provide International, National & Inter-Reg. Support

Determine Enhancement Needs & Strategies

Obtain Enhancement Resources

Form Enhancement Team

Coordinate W/Host Nations

Form Project Teams

Initiate General Enhancement Projects

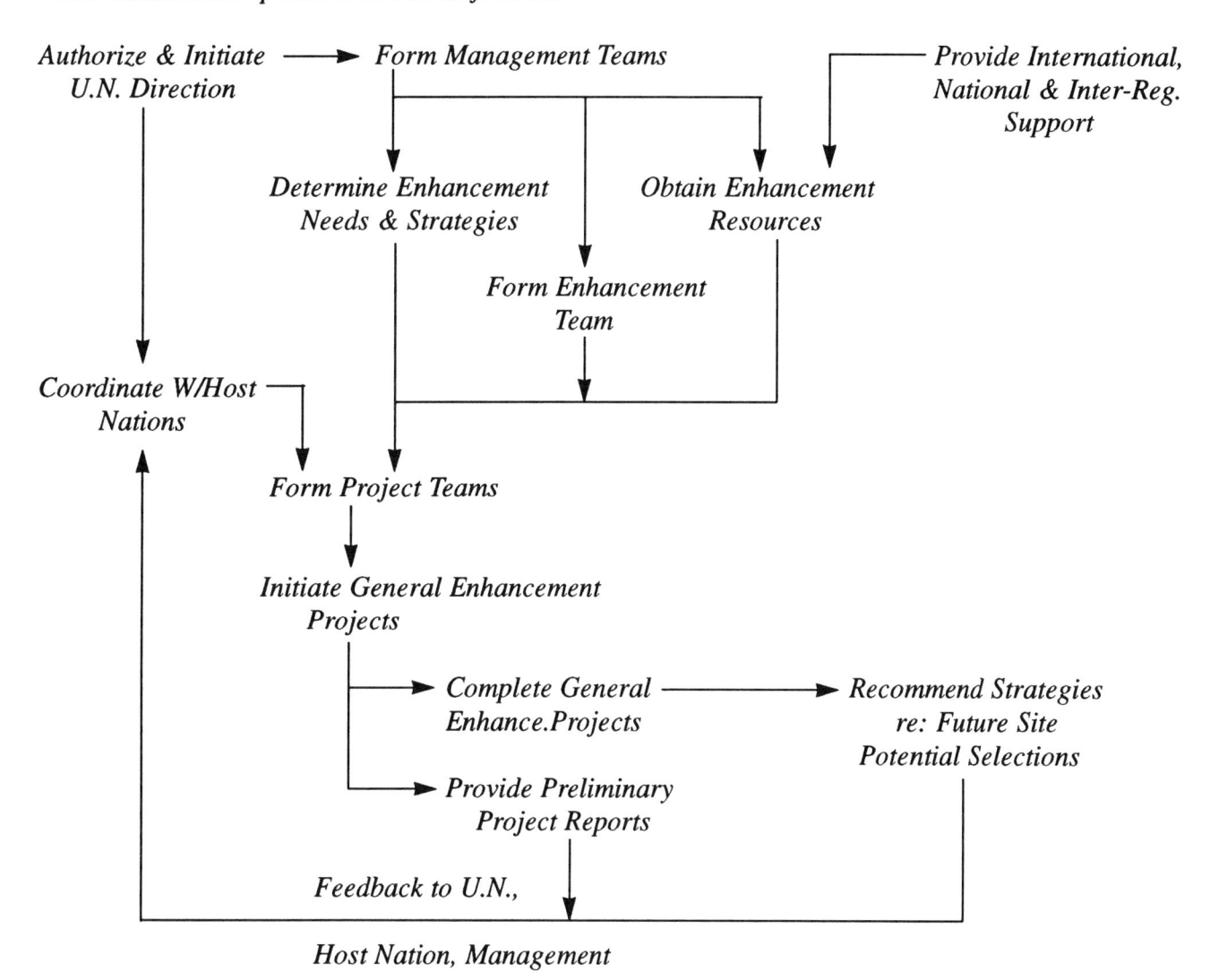

Complete General Enhance.Projects → *Recommend Strategies re: Future Site Potential Selections*

Provide Preliminary Project Reports

Feedback to U.N., Host Nation, Management

Figure V-5-F

Veritor notes, "We have reached the time for site selection. Both gradual and rapid transitions must now take place. Selections need to be made by a special, technically-oriented team, probably under United Nations auspices. The team would work very closely with potential host nations. The team would also establish criteria for scheduling development of selected sites occurring over many years."

Neos says, "There must be full cooperation from the host countries. Their most urgent needs would have to be considered. All countries would eventually become beneficiaries, but I can see that some crisis-ridden Third World countries would require accelerated efforts and considerable help."

Pragma begins to discuss site selection requirements. "Once the selection team determines the order in which regional sites are to be implemented, the negotiation procedures and activation guidelines must then be formulated. Negotiations and indications of need would proceed and continue progressively as the host nations begin to respond and marshal their resources."

Veritor notes, "Host countries give to the regionalization process as well as benefit from it. It would be wrong if the host countries became completely and perpetually dependent on outside help. Once a host nation becomes self-sufficient, it would help others in turn."

Neos adds, "You're right. The host nations definitely have to be closely involved in developing site plans. Actually, they should gradually take the lead as regionalization progresses so that when the regions become operational, there will be sufficient managerial and technological personnel with experience. Host nations must first thoroughly understand and adopt the underlying philosophy of the regional concept so that it is not distorted. In other words, if power groups cynically use regionalization as a means for increasing power over the public, it would seriously erode the intent of the concept."

Pragma responds, "Indicators of misuse are likely to be the diversion of resources for personal use, over concentration of resources for implementation of but a few infrastructures, and the exclusion of competent people from direct participation. Obviously, independent oversight of all activities would be necessary."

CHAPTER 5 - INITIATION OF PROGRAMS

Criteria for Regional Site Selection

- *What makes an area suitable for regional site selection? We know it must have the prospect of eventually sustaining at least one and one-half million people. This means key resources must be available or made so by gradual enhancement. It means that the environment must be restorable in order to be inhabitable. Obviously, some areas are initially more appropriate than others. Selections would be made using a detailed set of criteria concerning when and where regions are to be implemented. Priority of site selection must be given for relief of supercities, to under-developed countries undergoing critical deterioration and to demonstration regions that can be expeditiously implemented.*
- *There are other factors, however. For instance, the positive response and cooperation of potential host governments. Their task is to implement and operate effective regions as well as help other nations in such a quest.*
- *Selection of sites leading to successful regionalization is dependent on:*

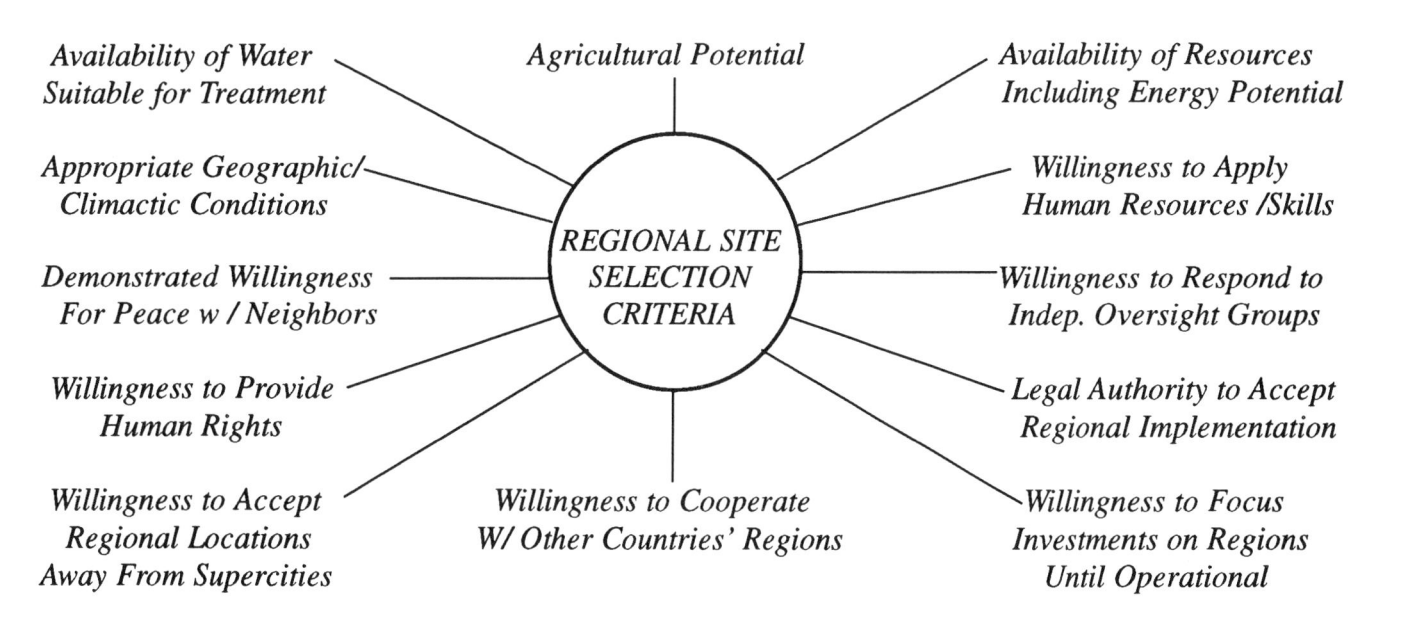

REGIONAL SITE SELECTION CRITERIA

- Availability of Water Suitable for Treatment
- Agricultural Potential
- Availability of Resources Including Energy Potential
- Appropriate Geographic/Climactic Conditions
- Willingness to Apply Human Resources /Skills
- Demonstrated Willingness For Peace w/ Neighbors
- Willingness to Respond to Indep. Oversight Groups
- Willingness to Provide Human Rights
- Legal Authority to Accept Regional Implementation
- Willingness to Accept Regional Locations Away From Supercities
- Willingness to Cooperate W/ Other Countries' Regions
- Willingness to Focus Investments on Regions Until Operational

Figure V-5-F

Neos concurs, "Yes, this is true, especially for unstable governments. Realistically, they may only be able to respond in a tentative manner. Cooperative agreements have to be made, however, despite uncertainties."

Pragma adds, "In order to secure firm agreements, a sufficient amount of the host country's existing infrastructures and diverse interests must become involved. Their participation and involvement must be encouraged through forums, workshops and other close working relationships."

Veritor observes, "By having these multiple interests involved there is a much greater likelihood that changes in power will not disrupt the regional site selection process and subsequent regional implementation and operation."

Neos comments, "The presence of all interests in workshops, especially during the planning phase, would no doubt benefit all participants. Everyone would be exposed to cross stimulation and become aware of limitations and possibilities. Domination by one narrow interest could be countered, and distortion of the regional concept could be prevented."

Pragma answers, "It seems to me a variety of people with different interests would have to become involved in studies as well. They would have to determine how quickly and extensively the regional approach should be integrated in their countries. Most of all, they would become involved in the creative process."

Veritor suggests, "For one thing, those who represent host nations would have a chance to express preferences that reflect the economic and political structure and the cultural, religious and social make-up of their respective countries."

Pragma states, "Everything that we have discussed up to now has been preliminary to the main effort of regional development. It has been necessary to present such a general approach for the initiation phase which is actually a continuation of the mobilization phase and its processes. I think we should now discuss policy making, because it is essential for implementation."

Veritor agrees, "I am greatly encouraged by the future prospect of having so many talented people involved in regional implementation policy making. It would mean participation on the basis of reasoning and competence rather than on political power."

CHAPTER 5 - INITIATION OF PROGRAMS

Initial Participation
Policy Making for Regions

- *Policy making during the initial planning stage is best made by people of varied backgrounds who are able to make valuable contributions. In order to be effective, policy making must have this kind of representation. Many perspectives are necessary. Where will they come from?*
- *Viewpoints and information can come from both the inside and outside of the region that is to be implemented. This increases the objectivity necessary for complete policy making. It also allows outside experience to be utilized for policy making decisions that will ultimately affect people on the inside. Some of the outside advice would be specialized, while other advice would be associated with economic and legal matters and, therefore, provide constraining factors.*
- *The inside regional policy makers must have combinations of skills and specialized knowledge. This suggests that policy making teams would need to exist with one member acting as chairperson for each.*
- *There would be different levels of policy making within the region. These are noted as follows:*

At the Inter-regional Level	• *Contributions would come from representatives of contiguous regions and other neighboring jurisdictions.*
At the Regional Level	• *Contributions would come from representatives of each regional infrastructure and special center complex.*
At the Community Level	• *Contributions would come from representatives of neighborhoods and neighborhood centers.*

Regular meetings as well as periodic meetings must take place to elect representatives to new policy making teams. Policy making representatives would be appointed or be on loan from outside of the region on an interim basis until the operational phase begins.

Policy Making As a Function of Regional Program Phases

- *Policy making must not only exist at various levels but for different phases of regional implementation. Each phase requires a separate set of decisions to be made that are derived from such policy making.*
- *Policies provide the basis for rules and regulations that are intended to be consistent and reasonable. Deviations from such fixed policies, of course, are sometimes necessary to accommodate unusual and unforeseen conditions. But any deviations would still have to be in consonance with the philosophies and intent of the regional concept. Directors, managers and others with leadership responsibilities for program implementation would provide regional goals that comply with established policies.*
- *Specific policies must exist for each of the phases as they are implemented. They are concerned with the following:*

<u>Conceptual -</u>
Why concept is used; who organizes / directs total effort; what are responsibilities; when are activities to start; where; how are preliminary funds obtained?

<u>Definition -</u>
What are possible concept variations; who defines regional application; when and where should they take place; what countries are initially involved; what are their needs and problems?

<u>Mobilization & Initiation -</u> Who defines regional programs; what is the protocol and / or communication approach; how are meetings to be arranged; when is technological support needed?

<u>Design -</u>
What is the planning and design approach; who is to carry it out; who is to do analysis; when, where and ; how is reporting to be done; who is to review and respond; what are the total resource needs?

<u>Acquisition & Funding -</u>
Where do regions go; how is land to be acquired; what are program needs for each phase; who is committing funding and other resources; how are they to be obtained and managed?

<u>Development -</u>
Who has responsibilities; how must the programs unfold; what oversight methods must be used; what are the project objectives and schedules?

<u>Operations -</u>
When do the programs become operational; who will operate and maintain on-going programs; how will transfer of responsibilities occur; where will operating funding and support come from?

CHAPTER 5 - INITIATION OF PROGRAMS

Neos asks, "But who will shape policy? Will it be the U.N. and other world agencies or will it be individual host countries? It seems to me both must be involved. There would have to be a gradual shift of responsibility for policy making as implementation takes place."

Pragma answers, "It's apparent that the regional concept has to be presented to the U.N. and its member nations for debate. World leaders must become aware of the regional concept's enormous potential and decide if and when commitments will be made to explore it."

Veritor says, "Once commitments are made, some method of selecting policy makers must be developed. Representative policy makers should be selected in working committees all over the world."

Neos notes, "If all these activities are done in a sequential manner, the whole process of commitment and selection would take forever. Whenever possible, activities should be done concurrently to save time. Selection committees would simultaneously be appointed in the U.N. and member nations. Some of the national members may already be serving in the U.N. and can perform this extra function. Perhaps this would be a good indication of how extensive world interest in regionalization has become."

Pragma asserts, "The process of selecting policy makers brings up the matter of when they should serve. The criteria for their selection must consider changes in background requirements for each phase of implementation. Different combinations of skills and background are required for each. For example, people selected for the development phase may not be appropriate for the operational phase."

Veritor adds, "It seems to me that policy making is a function for boards of directors. Continuity is necessary from phase to phase. Some board members and policy makers should serve for longer periods of time and, therefore, have wider experience. The shorter term policy makers would most likely have high specializations in some technology, law, economics or banking, compatible with specific phases. All members must have proven records of integrity."

Neos agrees, "This sounds like a very plausible approach. It's particularly important to attract and select highly competent individuals who are also high-minded, innovative and practical. I am confident that there will be many and that they will provide important points of view."

Veritor brings up another program phase. "What I have in mind has to do with the design of regional infrastructures. We have discussed this topic at length earlier, but now we must be concerned with the preliminary design functions for these infrastructures. The region is born when its infrastructures are fully designed and implemented."

Neos adds, "The preliminary designs and planning are highly creative. Because of new functional groupings and networking possibilities, fresh ways to resolve problems and establish working relationships would be applied for each infrastructure."

Pragma states, "It seems to me significant opportunities for freedom of expression will arise as each infrastructure design evolves. We must remember that innovative designs and methods offer a chance to cut eventual implementation and operational costs, greatly improving infrastructure effectiveness. Preliminary designs would offer the first opportunity to compute preliminary costs. These estimates are essential for attracting funds and other resources and for allowing development strategies to be formulated."

Veritor adds, "Preliminary designing and planning requires surveying, mapping, analysis and, of course, studies in climatology, hydrology and seismology. There will have to be close inspections of natural resources and environmental conditions and constraints. There may also be existing activities going on that have to be accommodated or changed."

Neos answers, "This would require three dimensional mapping to account for air, ground and underground characteristics. Terrain, geographical locations of mountains, rivers and other natural features must be considered. Layouts would have to be made to identify all such features so that options for placing basic infrastructures, centers and communties can be evaluated in depth. Consideration must be given to flooding, extreme weather exposure, known earthquake faults, soil quality, natural hazards, archeological sites and special ecosystems with their unique flora and fauna. In short, a macro-systems approach would be necessary."

Pragma considers this for a moment and notes, "I can see that this is a key effort because it is critical to all that follows. Certainly, there would have to be considerable use of computers and graphics to present all this information to many different kinds of disciplines."

CHAPTER 5 - INITIATION OF PROGRAMS

Preliminary Design Sequences For Subsequent Regional Development

- *Preliminary designs are critical for the eventual effective operation of the region and its infrastructures. Costs of operation directly affect taxation. Preliminary design involves trade-offs and analytical processes that are more rational than adversarial in combining ideas for design and planning optimization and decision making.*
- *Following site selection, various overall schemes are proposed by special planning and design teams. Background materials, layouts and graphic representations are provided to support a series of design and planning functions. Specialists ensure concept reasonableness, legality and practicality.*
- *Preliminary design teams are formed and perform as follows:*

Prepare Background Material and Layouts
↓
Obtain Information on Existing Activities
↓

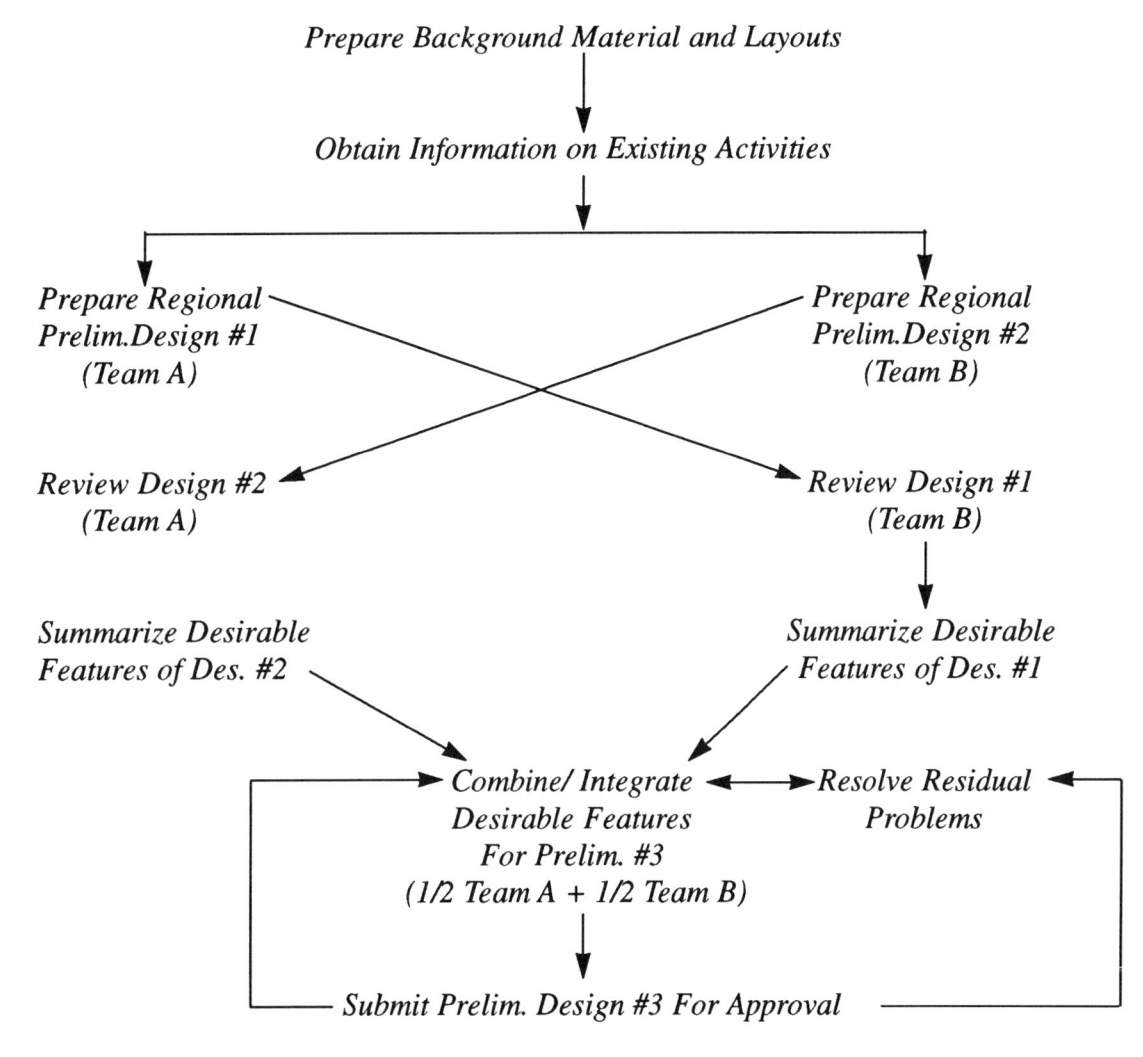

Prepare Regional Prelim. Design #1 (Team A)   *Prepare Regional Prelim. Design #2 (Team B)*

Review Design #2 (Team A)   *Review Design #1 (Team B)*

Summarize Desirable Features of Des. #2   *Summarize Desirable Features of Des. #1*

→ *Combine/Integrate Desirable Features For Prelim. #3 (1/2 Team A + 1/2 Team B)* ↔ *Resolve Residual Problems*
↓
Submit Prelim. Design #3 For Approval

Figure V-5-H

Preliminary Design Sequences (Cont.) For Subsequent Regional Development

- *Infrastructure preliminary designs are dependent on external overall regional designs and conditions. This is true for most infrastructures because they are more dependent on limits, direction and external support and communication.*
- *It is folly to attempt to develop infrastructures as though they were completely autonomous because absolute independence and isolation are incompatible with regional networking. In the region al setting, the special functional groupings of the infrastructures are more likely to provide greater options and support when they are semi-autonomous yet freed of interference in performing their normal functions.*
- *Preliminary design of infrastructures reflects such sequences as:*

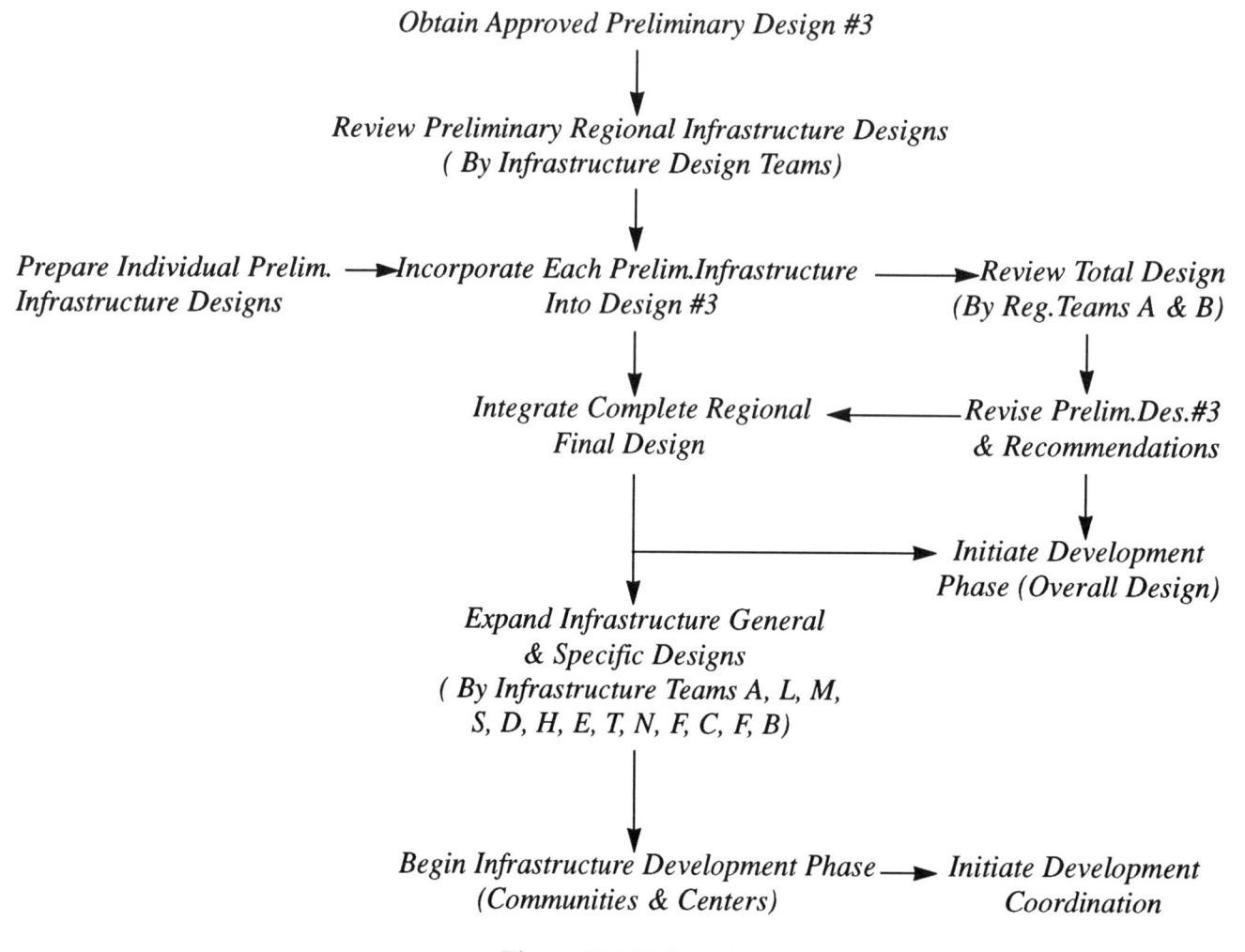

Obtain Approved Preliminary Design #3
↓
Review Preliminary Regional Infrastructure Designs (By Infrastructure Design Teams)
↓
Prepare Individual Prelim. Infrastructure Designs → *Incorporate Each Prelim. Infrastructure Into Design #3* → *Review Total Design (By Reg. Teams A & B)*
↓ ↓
Integrate Complete Regional Final Design ← *Revise Prelim.Des.#3 & Recommendations*
↓ ↓
→ *Initiate Development Phase (Overall Design)*
↓
Expand Infrastructure General & Specific Designs (By Infrastructure Teams A, L, M, S, D, H, E, T, N, F, C, F, B)
↓
Begin Infrastructure Development Phase (Communities & Centers) → *Initiate Development Coordination*

Figure V-5-H (cont.)

CHAPTER 5 - INITIATION OF PROGRAMS

Veritor answers, "There is also the need for extensive system integration to put all of this information into useful context for analysis. This would permit further detailed design and planning to proceed."

Neos adds, "The systems integration of the total region and its infrastructures represents a very complex design and analysis effort. There has to be a definite strategy employed to ensure the effectiveness and compatibility of each infrastructure with the total region."

Pragma answers, "Fortunately, there has been considerable experience gained in the design and development of other complex systems at the infrastructure level and to some extent at the regional level. Computerized systems and special systems management programs have been especially effective in the design and control of such efforts."

Veritor proposes, "Multiple network designs incorporating all infrastructures indicate that some must be initiated earlier than others. Critical design benchmarks would need to be established as references. Timelines are important."

Neos adds, "It is apparent that the infrastructures must be progressively designed and developed as interfaces are defined and resolved. The public works, transportation and communication infrastructure designs would support the development of all the others."

Veritor comments,"This would be the appropriate time for both public and private developers to become involved and to integrate their unique design requirements. Many of the conflicts and discrepancies that usually arise could be resolved. They would have to know where to put things, what they have to work with and what they have to provide. Obviously, much duplication and waste can be avoided by using a systems integration approach."

Part V- The Challenge of Implimintation

CHAPTER 6 - DEVELOPMENT OF THE REGION

The development phase of regional implementation is a dramatic period of time. Tangible evidence of progress begins to make the skeptical observer less so. Participants realize something of significance is taking place. All who have been involved in the emergence of the region will now be able to look forward to new opportunities.

The rate of development for the region is incrementally controlled. The region's size and tentative population limit allow definitive planning. Progressive installation of major public works can more precisely match the future needs of the inhabitants and centers. As infrastructures materialize and centers appear throughout the region, communities begin to evolve. Developers progressively plan and build as people begin to move into neighborhoods. Infrastructures continue to expand services and create new jobs. Prospective inhabitants can now make their choice of neighborhoods and homes. Developers would compete to give value and provide healthy environments, conducive to quality of life. Good workmanship, safe conditions and good business practices would be enforced.

Until the population of a region has grown sufficiently to elect representatives to the regional and community governments, an interim trust and caretaker group must assume responsibilities. Special management and technological development teams are established. Their members would be experts in relevant fields, representing a mix of both public and private interests. Public appointees must be chosen by a higher level of government. Private appointees would be selected for their unique qualifications by university senates and from various professional fields, willing to work in the development of specific infrastructures. These development teams would be responsible to the national government and other supporting agencies until the operational phase is about to begin and elections have taken place. The development teams must also be responsible for carrying out program goals and project objectives based on guidance derived from established policies.

Variations in the above approach are likely. However, the essential ingredients for all approaches must be that the people who participate be competent, have integrity and demonstrate "working wisdom".

Pragma, Veritor and Neos have been discussing various approaches to the development phase. They recognize that what has been expressed must be enlarged upon many times and in great detail in order to establish working models and procedures for effective development.

Pragma notes, "It does not serve our purposes to over-expand and become too detailed. Neither is it beneficial to explore different development approaches and philosophies. However, we should explain some relationships and sequences that are

CHAPTER 6 - DEVELOPMENT OF THE REGION

involved during the development phase."

Veritor agrees, "Yes, specifications and diagrammed analysis, normally employed in a detailed design and development of something as complex as a region, would be very confrontational and confusing. It would take many flow diagrams and networks to fully describe regional systems for even those capable of systems analysis."

Pragma continues, "As we have noted, it should be apparent that none of the infrastructures can be completely developed until all of them have gone through extensive design and planning or are at least partially built. All infrastructures are interdependent and should be phased in. I have briefly expressed this requirement earlier."

The Development Phase

- *Development of a region is a gradual, controlled process. Some infrastructures precede others of equal importance, and some can be completed more quickly than others and become operational sooner. However, a sufficient number of people must reside and participate in the region before infrastructures are fully operational and viable.*
- *The development of a region is accomplished by completing a number of programs and projects based on goals and objectives, respectively. All program activities must be networked so that their projects are not completed at the wrong time and, therefore, be out of phase. If so, they may have to be totally or partially redone. Other projects that are late would delay their becoming operational.*
- *Except for temporary habitation and conveniences for on-site workers, community development is started when enough of the infrastructures are ready to become operational. This allows the communities to be developed more quickly and fully and become integrated with the rest of the region.*
- *Development of the infrastructures begins in approximately the following order:*

Acquire, prepare, protect land and and obtain land use rights. - Infrastructure N
  Establish courts, interim legislation, program management. - Infrastructure L
  Establish interim administration, coordination and planning centers. - Infrastructure A
    Prepare interim communication systems. - Infrastructure C
    Prepare basic and interim transportation systems. - Infrastructure T
    Prepare and build public works and utilities and habitation sites. - Infrastructure P
      Begin business, commercial and manufacturing centers. - Infrastructure B
      Begin agricultural system and centers. - Infrastructure F
        Begin medical systems and centers. - Infrastructure M
        Begin emergency and law enforcement systems. - Infrastructure D
        Begin educational systems and centers. - Infrastructure E
          Begin social service systems and community development. - Infrastructure S
          Begin spiritual, cultural and recreational centers. - Infrastructure H
            Begin special research and development centers and infrastructure.

CHAPTER 6 - DEVELOPMENT OF THE REGION

Neos notes, "When lands are set aside for regional site development, privately owned parcels may also be acquired because they fall within the selected regional site location. The concept of public and private lands varies considerably in certain countries. If private land are to be acquired, some owners, especially those who are well established, may object strongly to being displaced. The right of eminent domain may have to be exercised in some countries. There is no problem when the land has not yet passed into private hands."

Pragma states, "Acquiring and designating land use is a very important step in development. Some land must be prserveded as open land and preserved, particularly when certain ecosystems need protection. Land for forests to provide water sheds and recreation must also be set aside. Various plans must be provided for waterways, farm lands and access. Special centers and general patterns of habitation must be defined and zoned accordingly."

Veritor answers, "Zoning is an important consideration for regional development because it is essential for quality of life. The development teams who recommend zoning, as well as the legislators who pass zoning laws, must respect the underlying requirements for quality of life. Otherwise, they would be incompetent to carry out their functions in meeting the goals of regionalization. The framework for a healthy region lies in the effective organization and placement of its infrastructures, centers, communities and neighborhoods."

Neos comments, "We've only briefly mentioned zoning for the optimum placement of communities and centers. There are other kinds of zoning that are concerned with traffic control for air, land and water and for zoning within the communities themselves."

Prgama states, "If a zoning philosophy is strongly adhered to, it will help prevent over-concentrations of population in the future. It will also diminish the number of special laws and rules which are necessary when space is overused along with their attendant conflicts."

Veritor responds, "This brings up the need for developing regional Infrastructure N which includes functions that oversee and ensure zoning and proper use of air, land and water. This infrastructure development would be in a unique position for defining environmental protection codes and enforcing them throughout the region. Industry, farming, mining and other activities of the region would be developed according to firm, clearly defined laws and guidelines. Private planning and development, therefore, would automatically be in greater compliance."

Development of Regional Infrastructure N

- *Regional Infrastructure N begins with the site development and evolves into two functional branches. One is concerned with protection and conservation. The other involves the enhancement and development of land, water and other resources.*

- *Background from surveys and existing maps and other data are made available. Development can now proceed.*

- *The parallel paths of functional flow are as follows:*

Initiate Infrastructure Development

Establish, Identify Protected Zones & → *Prepare Installation Sites Development Installations*

Define Environmental Protection Requirements → *Develop Forest Preserves*

Obtain Protection Laws (From Legislation) → *Develop Water Resources*

Enforce Environmental Protection Laws → *Develop Land/ Air/ Water Protection Projects*

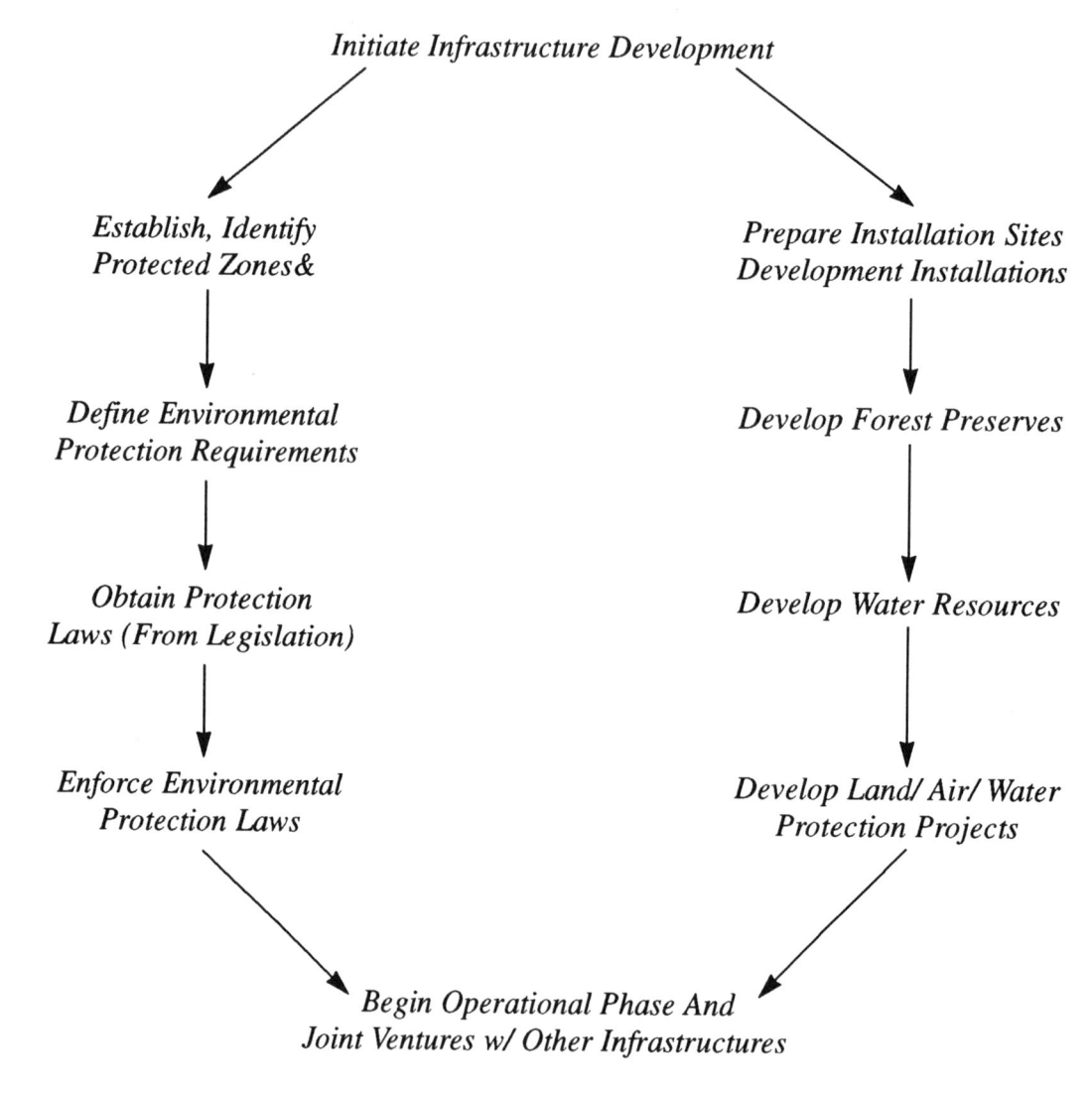

Begin Operational Phase And Joint Ventures w/ Other Infrastructures

Figure V-6-A

CHAPTER 6 - DEVELOPMENT OF THE REGION

Pragma continues, "Legal challenges are apt to arise during Infrastructure N development. Infrastructure L and its legislative bodies will need to pass laws in anticipation of legal conflicts. Therefore, early legislative research and legislature must completed to meet a regional requirement for swift adjudication and conflict resolution so the development of all infrastructures will not be blocked."

Veritor reflects, "Of course, as the region's growing population becomes more politically involved, legislators and judges would be locally elected. Carefully selected competent appointees without conflicts of interest would serve in the interim."

Neos contributes, "The range of legislation during the region's formative stages is likely to involve land use, access, jurisdictions, environmental concerns and key resource utilization. However, many projects have complex technology and phase relationships during development. These projects could benefit more from optimization analysis, trade-offs and established policies rather than by political debate. When the region becomes operational, elected formal legislative bodies could perform their duties without becoming involved in development problems."

Pragma and Veritor both agree with this appraisal. Pragma adds, "Certainly, program managers must have the freedom to carry out programs without undue distractions. But they must adhere to existing laws and be guided by policies from higher levels of government. Legislative bodies at higher levels should provide enabling legislation and address how to overcome major legal obstacles."

Veritor notes, "Closely allied to Infrastructure L would be the administrative and managerial functions of Infrastructure A. There are budget allocations to be made and management controls, including auditing, to be applied during infrastructure development."

Neos responds, "Regional coordination is very essential during the development of the infrastructures. So administrative functional groups must be involved with both intra and inter-regional matters. This is where regional system integration is especially important in the development of all program interfaces."

Veritor pauses and answers, "That is true, but integration would definitely require at least the initial development of the Communication Network Infrastructure C to handle program coordination."

Neos notes, "For one thing, a computerized information exchange system must be developed to meet the expanding needs of each infrastructure. Both working and formal meetings would utilize many new techniques to speed up integration."

Pragma responds, "Of course, we cannot ignore both the conventional postal service and newer types of mail delivery. The development of this communication function is the responsibility of the host government, however."

Veritor adds, "It's apparent to me that a communication complex and sub-centers should be developed as the other infrastructures begin to grow. In addition to special, dedicated computer systems for each infrastructure, there also must be a regional level integrated computer system to link them. Independent, mobile auxiliary power sources would back up all communication systems in case of power failure."

Neos continues, "A phone system network has to be installed early in the development phase. The final design and development of a telephone system must allow for such innovations as light and micro-wave transmissions. This expandable system will be adapted to new community and center operational needs."

Veritor responds, "Of course, there would be a big difference in technological development in regions throughout the world. Some would be able to accommodate and utilize costly, advanced systems; others wouldn't. Some regions may never need such sophistication."

CHAPTER 6 - DEVELOPMENT OF THE REGION

Regional Communication Development

- *A distinction must be made between the communication required during development of the region's various infrastructures and during the operational phase.*
- *During development, prior to their operational phases, different communication media would provide impetus and improve coordination.*
- *During the operational phase communication systems would evolve to handle the changing needs of each infrastructure as well as the common need for networking. Media for general information to the public via radio, television, newspapers, books and magazines come next.*
- *As the region grows and its communities and centers develop, expansion of communication systems will continue.*
- *Communication system development is likewise essential within each community and center.*
- *Communication system development is as follows:*

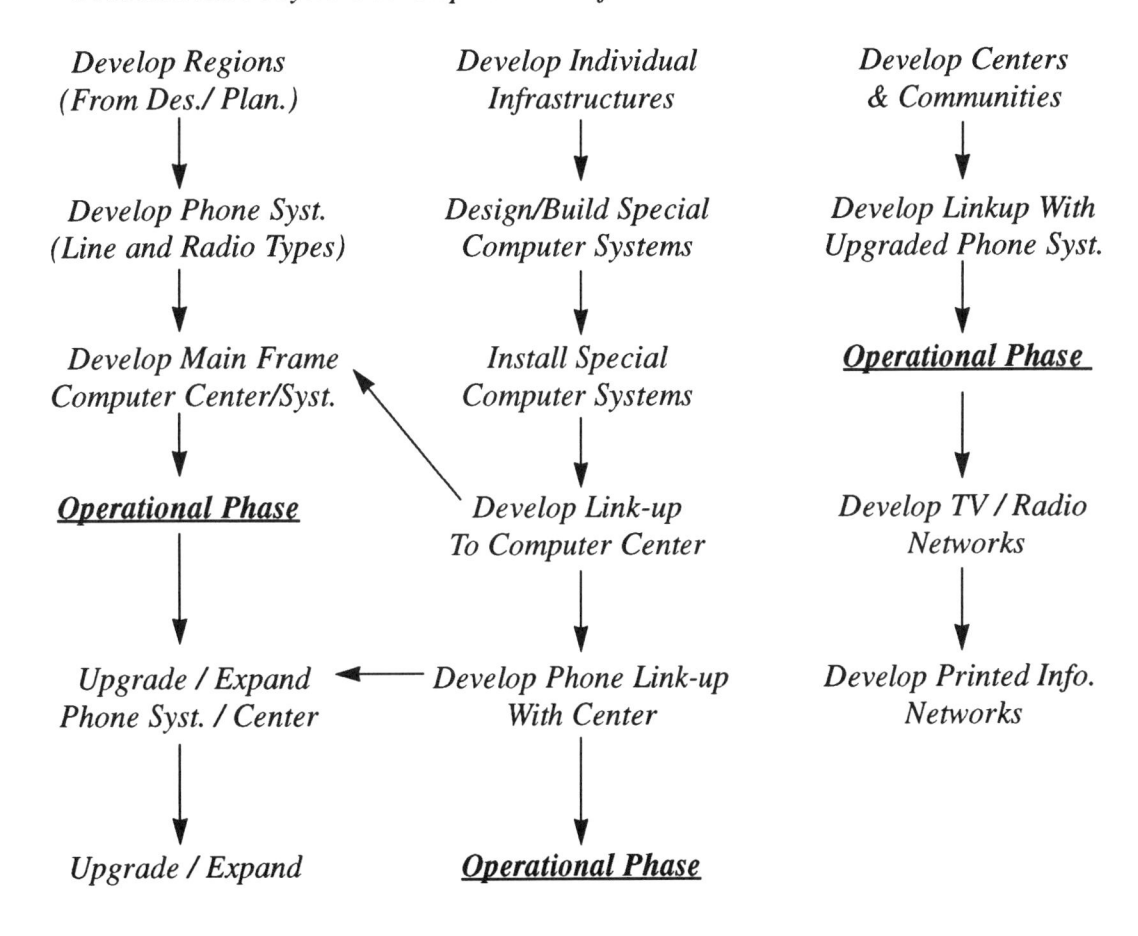

Develop Regions
(From Des./ Plan.)
↓
Develop Phone Syst.
(Line and Radio Types)
↓
Develop Main Frame
Computer Center/Syst.
↓
Operational Phase
↓
Upgrade / Expand
Phone Syst. / Center
↓
Upgrade / Expand

Develop Individual
Infrastructures
↓
Design/Build Special
Computer Systems
↓
Install Special
Computer Systems
↓
Develop Link-up
To Computer Center
↓
Develop Phone Link-up
With Center
↓
Operational Phase

Develop Centers
& Communities
↓
Develop Linkup With
Upgraded Phone Syst.
↓
Operational Phase
↓
Develop TV / Radio
Networks
↓
Develop Printed Info.
Networks

Figure V-6-B

Veritor continues the survey of infrastructure development, "Transportation Infrastructure T also evolves in stages, but there is a distinct pattern to its development. There will be a number of transportation modes with special kinds of transportation vehicles to consider."

Neos answers, "It seems to me that during initial regional development new special access roads would be built to traverse and penetrate the site area. These roads would be primarily for delivering and moving materials and equipment to the many installations under construction. Later, some of the roads would be upgraded for heavy duty, all weather purposes."

Pragma states, "The land must be surveyed for these main roadway networks meant for heavy trucks and trains. Branch spurs will be built for farming, industry, mining and processing centers. This approach has been in use for many years, but in the case of regionalization, it must now comply with a larger master plan that has more than exploitation in mind."

"The construction of dedicated high speed highways, tunnels, elevated structures, bridges and underpasses will quickly follow as the pattern of communities and various centers begins to evolve. Canals and waterways would be built to add another mode of transportation as well as provide water to farming areas. Most construction development would be used for multiple purposes.

"An air terminal and other transportation terminals and substations will be built and, if the region is near a coastline, jetties and harbors also developed. There would certainly be a beehive of activity."

Veritor counters, "It seems to me that environmental protection is to be included in the building of roadways. When ecosystems are involved, development must cause minimum intrusion even if at higher immediate cost. It is not a matter of how fast or how cheaply roadways are built, but how well. This means that there must be concern for future overall costs and for quality of life over many generations."

Neos and Pragma agree. Neos adds, "For instance, this may call for elevated or submerged sections of road with tunnels and overpasses to eliminate intersections and, therefore, future accidents."

CHAPTER 6 - DEVELOPMENT OF THE REGION

Regional Transportation Development

- *Like the communication infrastructure development, the transportation Infrastructure T is progressive. Development of roadways, bridges, tunnels and canals would be in parallel with the installation of centers, depots and terminals and the multi-mode transportation systems. Community and neighborhood access follows a third development path in which local roadways are designed and built according to a strategy that minimizes collisions and obstructions.*
- *Gradually, a large pattern of multi-mode transportation evolves. Main arteries, including rapid transit systems begin to develop and expand to complete the regional network.*
- *Public departments develop road systems at the community level and private developers build the road systems for neighborhoods. All construction must be in accordance with the regional concept.*
- *Transportation system development is briefly described as follows:*

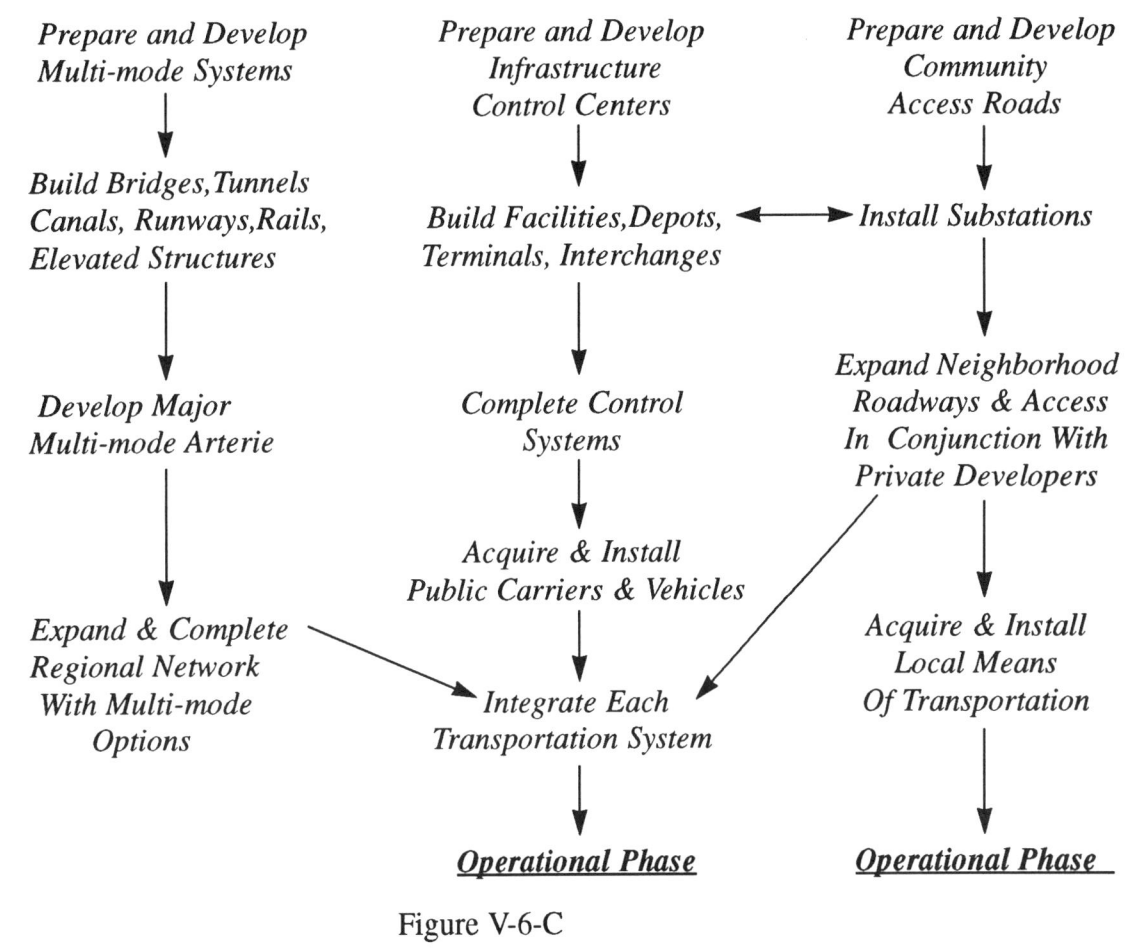

Prepare and Develop Multi-mode Systems	*Prepare and Develop Infrastructure Control Centers*	*Prepare and Develop Community Access Roads*
↓	↓	↓
Build Bridges, Tunnels Canals, Runways, Rails, Elevated Structures	*Build Facilities, Depots, Terminals, Interchanges* ↔ *Install Substations*	
↓	↓	↓
Develop Major Multi-mode Arterie	*Complete Control Systems*	*Expand Neighborhood Roadways & Access In Conjunction With Private Developers*
↓	↓	↓
Expand & Complete Regional Network With Multi-mode Options	*Acquire & Install Public Carriers & Vehicles*	*Acquire & Install Local Means Of Transportation*
→	*Integrate Each Transportation System* ←	↓
	↓	
	Operational Phase	***Operational Phase***

Figure V-6-C

"It seems to me that private builders of communities and neighborhoods have an excellent opportunity to develop housing and centers that minimize travel for most of the neighborhoods and centers," Pragma notes. "In line with this, developers would provide special types of low speed transportation and access for the neighborhoods."

Veritor shifts the topic, "The development of transportation must coincide with the development of Infrastructure P which has to do with public works and power generation and transmission. As we have noted, laying out and installing public works is a tremendous job. Public works are required early in regional development because of complexity, accessibility and maintainability difficulties during installation. Litigations and other complications would be much more prevalent if public works are installed after the fact."

Neos answers, "Of course, pre-design of the region allows such early development. Predictions of future power loads and water demand must avoid unnecessary over-design or out-sizing of machinery, equipment and facilities. Fortunately, the regional concept specifies a finite population and pre-determination of locations, densities of population and special centers. Public works development can, therefore, be more accurately estimated and result in less cost and risk."

Pragma adds, "This becomes more apparent when the numerous regional public works projects are considered. Many of these projects must start years in advance so as to be completed in time for other regional infrastructures and their centers and communities."

Neos answers, "I think we can describe in general, the parallel paths of development for major functions. For instance, the first series of functions has to do with developing the land for many different purposes, including habitation. Electric power generation and distribution must be developed in conjunction with the building of dams and waterworks as well. Functions pertaining to waste conversion, recycling and disposal along with sewage processing must also be initiated. The integration of all functions must be controlled on a regional level."

"Most of the functional areas don't have to be completed during the development phase," Pragma notes. "Basic systems, however, must be well established and, when fully operational, must be expandable to meet planned infrastructure and population growth."

Veritor responds, "I think it is essential that functional areas employ up-to-date technologies and system management methods during the design and development phases of Infrastructure P so that lower operating costs will result."

CHAPTER 6 - DEVELOPMENT OF THE REGION

Public Works Development

- *The importance of timely development for Infrastructure P is apparent from the dependence other infrastructures have on it for their own development and operations. The coordination of separate development paths is presented generally as follows:*

Develop/ Enhance Environmental Conditions
→ *Develop Agricultural Areas*
→ *Develop Watersheds & Soil Erosion Protection*
→ *Develop Land Areas For Special Centers*
→ *Develop Land Areas For Habitation*
→ **_Operational Phase_**
→ *Develop Land Improvements*

Install Electrical Power Plants &
→ *Install Power Grids, Towers, Cable, Etc.*
→ *Develop/ Integrate Alternative Energy Syst.*
→ *Develop Regional Substations*
→ *Integrate Projects W/ Private Developers*
→ **_Operational Phase_**
→ *Expand Syst. Distribution*

Install Dams/ Reservoirs/ Pumping Stations
→ *Install Water Treatment Plants*
→ *Install Water Reclamation Plants*
→ *Install Canals/ Pipelines*
→ *Develop Local Water Conversion Measures*
→ *Integrate Efforts W/ Private Devel.*
→ **_Operational Phase_** *& Expand Distrib.*

Install Main Waste Conversion Facil.
→ *Develop Waste Collection System*
→ *Develop Waste Disposal & Recycling System*
→ **_Operational Phase_**
→ *Expand System Collection*

Install Sewage Treatment Facil.
→ *Develop Sewage Collection Syst.*
→ *Develop Sewage Solid Treat. Disposal*

Develop Special Waste Disp.Syst. ← *Develop Sewage Solid Treat. Disposal*

Figure V-6-D

Neos begins, "It is time to discuss the development of the other essential infrastructures. It seems to me that the sooner development starts, the sooner employment opportunities will materialize. Infrastructures F and B are concerned with agriculture and business, commerce and manufacturing and would be developed starting at the regional level."

Pragma responds, "Of course, such infrastructures depend on both local and external demand for services and products. Population influx must be sufficient to utilize them. Various infrastructure centers would become operational as soon as possible to provide stability and to satisfy growing needs. Entrepreneurs interested in establishing businesses to engage in commerce or manufacturing would also need preparation time."

"Is it prudent to develop all of the communities simultaneously?" asks Veritor. "I think it is better to incrementally expand in order to maintain a more stable work force. This means that all levels of agriculture, business, commerce and manufacturing have to be carefully phased in. Development program managers need to project when new enterprises should be started."

Neos notes, "The phasing in problem is somewhat less critical for agriculture and industries that are not located near populated areas, especially when they are not too labor intensive. Probably, they should be developed early and utilize outside workers."

Pragma agrees, "That's true. However, enterprises located close by or integrated into the community or special centers are likely to be directly dependent on a local work force. Therefore, private builders, community planners and special business efforts must synchronize development. This approach would result in better community design and cohesion."

Veritor adds, "Community development planning, preparation and support measures should be worked out long in advance so that an optimum number of the community inhabitants benefit from the emerging infrastructures."

Neos continues, "I think it is important to note here that fully functional agricultural centers would be developed early on so that crops could be harvested in time to help feed a growing population."

Pragma answers, "Yes, crops have to be cultivated, orchards have to be planted and animals raised in increasing amounts as the population grows. We must remember that the region is intended to be largely independent agriculturally. Farmers need markets that are likely to provide price stability. People in the region would provide this."

CHAPTER 6 - DEVELOPMENT OF THE REGION

Business, Commerce, Industrial and Agricultural Development

- *The rate of initial development for agriculture and businesses, commerce and industries depends on how quickly their centers can be integrated with community design and development.*
- *Centers, although independent in development, must be considered as early as possible so they can be more closely integrated with land preparations and transportation, communication and public works development. The new centers would then be in a better position to network with emerging communities and draw much of their management and labor force from the growing number of inhabitants.*
- *Many of the businesses and commercial developments would operate in special centers located within the communities, convenient to neighborhoods. Private developers would integrate their designs and development with these centers as follows:*

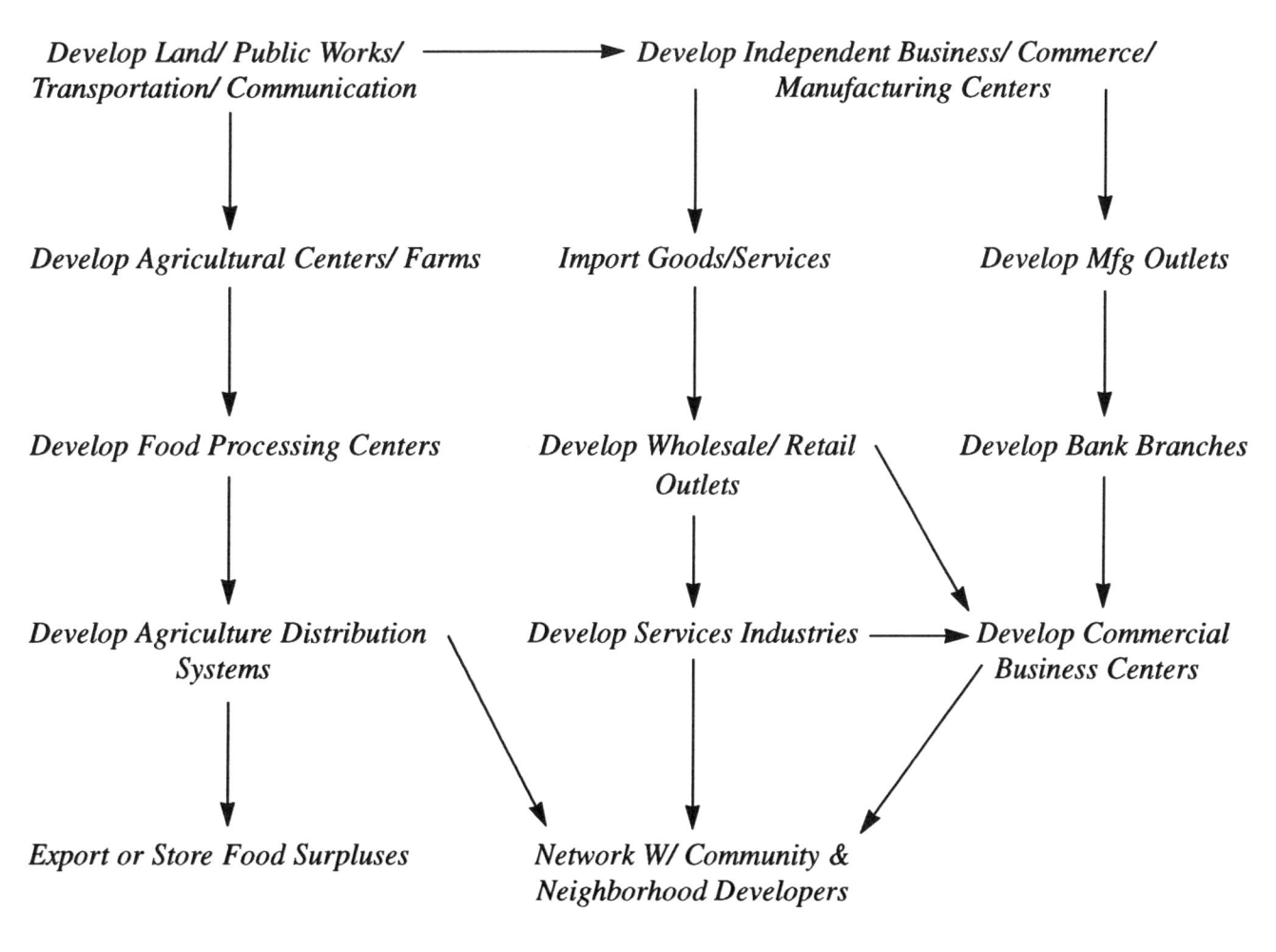

```
Develop Land/ Public Works/      ───►  Develop Independent Business/ Commerce/
Transportation/ Communication            Manufacturing Centers
         │                                      │                         │
         ▼                                      ▼                         ▼
Develop Agricultural Centers/ Farms     Import Goods/Services     Develop Mfg Outlets
         │                                      │                         │
         ▼                                      ▼                         ▼
Develop Food Processing Centers         Develop Wholesale/ Retail   Develop Bank Branches
         │                                   Outlets
         ▼                                      │                         │
Develop Agriculture Distribution        Develop Services Industries ─► Develop Commercial
         Systems                                                          Business Centers
         │                                      │
         ▼                                      ▼
Export or Store Food Surpluses          Network W/ Community &
                                        Neighborhood Developers
```

Figure V-6-E

327

Veritor agrees, "Although developing agricultural independence in the region is essential, this may not always be possible because of prevailing climate and extremes in weather conditions. In this case, farming schemes must be designed to protect crops as we mentioned earlier. Why plant crops that cannot be harvested? Also, those who live in the region should benefit from locally grown food that is as good as that exported. Quite frequently countries will ship their best produce in order to obtain higher prices, leaving less desirable food for local consumption. This is not the way to achieve quality of life."

Neos notes, "Development of food processing adds value, and development of food storage allows better market timing. Both can be cost effective and worthwhile investments. These developments provide employment, and their profits and wages would add to the regional economy."

Pragma continues, "We now come to three infrastructures that have similarities in their incremental development. They directly impact quality of life in the region. Infrastructure M for medical systems and centers, Infrastructure D for emergency and law enforcement systems and centers, and Infrastructure E for educational systems and centers all require early development and expansion as the population grows."

"There would be a need for interim medical clinics, fire-stations, security forces and mobile educational facilities from the very beginning of development," Veritor adds. "We can expect many families to quickly locate in or near the region, some escaping socio-economic or political pressures elsewhere. Some people may already be living in the regional area when regional development starts."

Pragma notes, "At the community level of the educational infrastructure, colleges must be planned and developed as each community becomes operational. Regional universities would be planned and built when at least three communities have become operational. Attention must be given to both a growing tax base and increasing educational needs."

Neos states, "As the operational functions of the centers and communities begin to materialize, private developers and public agencies would begin to develop new kinds of neighborhoods. These neighborhoods must provide a balance between the need for individual privacy and the opportunity for the inhabitants to participate together in local affairs."

CHAPTER 6 - DEVELOPMENT OF THE REGION

Infrastructures M, D and E Development
Medical, Safety / Security and Education

• *Early regional development cannot be without at least some essential medical care, security, protection, and educational opportunities.*
• *During this initial period, full, comprehensive planning and progressive development of the infrastructures will be accomplished. Subsequent development must be on a region-wide basis to meet the growing needs of the communities and centers. Each of these infrastructures would be developed in parallel; yet they must be integrated with each other.*
• *The infrastructures are to be developed at all levels of the region as described:*

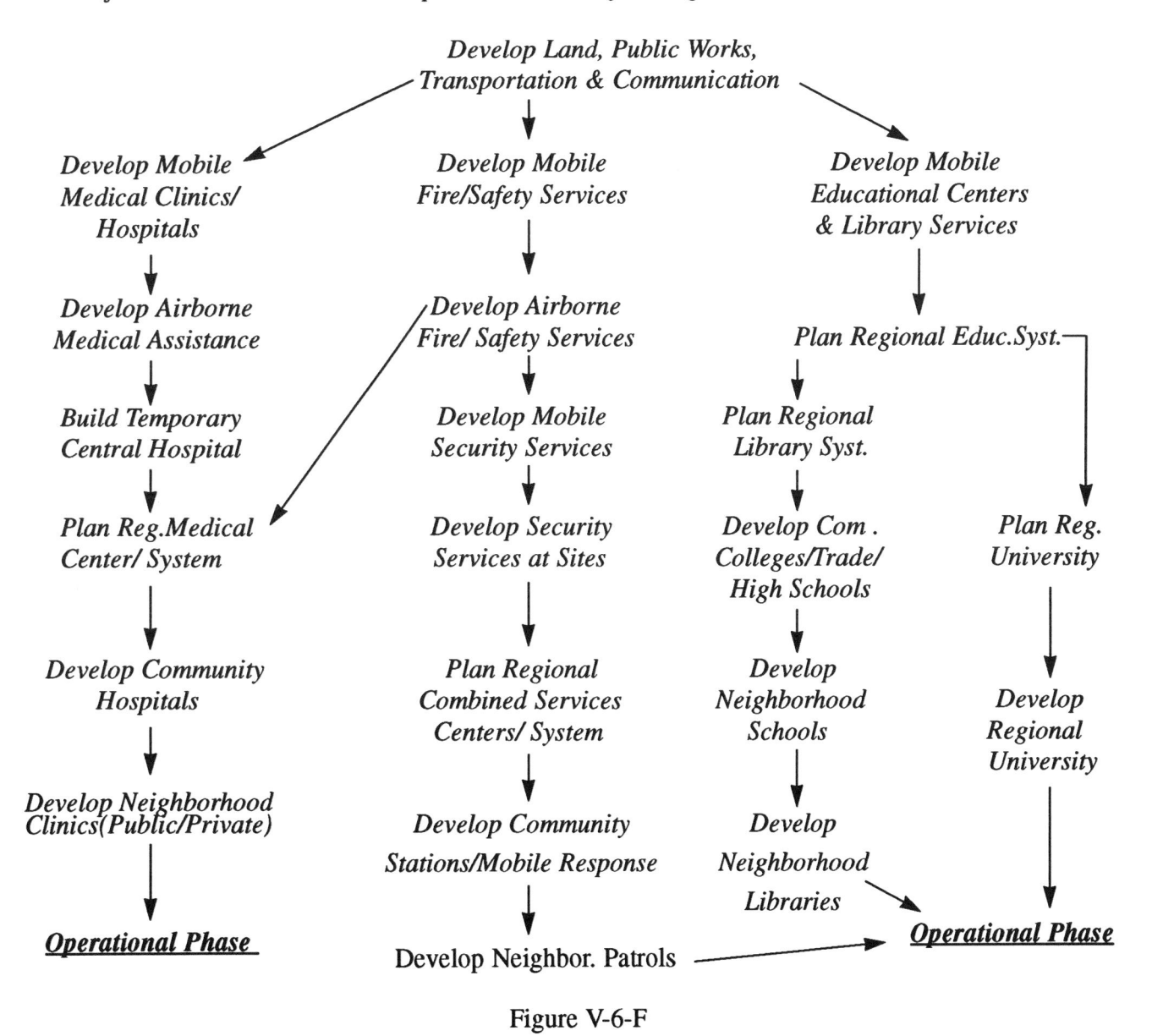

Develop Land, Public Works, Transportation & Communication

↓

Develop Mobile Medical Clinics/ Hospitals	*Develop Mobile Fire/Safety Services*	*Develop Mobile Educational Centers & Library Services*
↓	↓	↓
Develop Airborne Medical Assistance	*Develop Airborne Fire/ Safety Services*	*Plan Regional Educ.Syst.*
↓	↓	↓
Build Temporary Central Hospital	*Develop Mobile Security Services*	*Plan Regional Library Syst.*
↓	↓	↓
Plan Reg.Medical Center/ System	*Develop Security Services at Sites*	*Develop Com. Colleges/Trade/ High Schools* — *Plan Reg. University*
↓	↓	↓
Develop Community Hospitals	*Plan Regional Combined Services Centers/ System*	*Develop Neighborhood Schools* — *Develop Regional University*
↓	↓	↓
Develop Neighborhood Clinics(Public/Private)	*Develop Community Stations/Mobile Response*	*Develop Neighborhood Libraries*
↓	↓	
Operational Phase	*Develop Neighbor. Patrols* →	***Operational Phase***

Figure V-6-F

Pragma notes, "It's essential that each neighborhood enhances family safety and stability and provides everyone with a local network of support. Communities and their neighborhoods would be physically and functionally designed with this in mind. Developers would build more than housing. Public facilities in the neighborhood must also become operational to serve effectively. As private developers compete with each other in planning and development, they must provide the kinds of construction that further quality of life."

Veritor heartily agrees, "This makes a lot of sense. If the developer builds what is needed, it is worth added costs. Also, the developer would probably receive more cooperation from government agencies and a positive marketing response from the public because everyone would be gaining. Creating good will is clearly better than creating antagonisms."

Pragma reacts to this. "Private developers can only provide so much and still make a profit. Most of them try to anticipate public preferences in the communities and neighborhoods, and some furnish a variety of activities and facilities as well as housing."

Neos changes the subject, "No community or neighborhood can ever be complete without the development of Infrastructures S and H. Infrastructure H pertains to spiritual and cultural activities, recreation and sports, theater, art and music and health development programs. Infrastructure S provides facilities and basic services to assist individuals and families who are in need of help. Both are major factors in attaining individual and collective quality of life."

Pragma concurs, "The placement of these activities is very important. Places of worship, cultural centers, schools, recreation, shopping and local services, as well as social services, should be convenient for each neighborhood, although some major activities and events may require large facilities to be developed on a community or regional level."

Veritor begins a new topic. "We have been talking about public and private development, but it seems to me that we have to be more definitive in describing who does what in the development of various infrastructures. Who should carry out various programs and projects? Should they be public or private developers? Who oversees the developments?"

CHAPTER 6 - DEVELOPMENT OF THE REGION

Developing Regions, Communities, Neighborhoods & Centers
(For Social Systems and Social/Spiritual & Recreational Purposes)

• *Two Infrastructures, S and H, are involved. Infrastructure S with its emphasis on social systems must be developed regionwide. Although special regional centers would be established, the main part of the infrastructure is at the community and neighborhood levels where specific assistance can be directly provided to families, children, the elderly and the disabled. Facilities built in select locations would do this.*
• *Infrastructure H would be developed concurrently. Some of this development such as large parks, sports centers, theaters, concert halls, museums and halls would be at the regional level. Other Infrastructure H developments pertain to local activities such as theater, art, music, physical fitness facilities and particularly spiritual/cultural centers for each community and its neighborhoods. Infrastructure H would bring the communities and neighborhoods together.*
• *The following is a three pronged development effort:*

Develop Regional Centers

- *Develop Social Service Centers/System*
  - *Develop Local Family Assistance Centers*
  - *Develop Local Child Assistance Centers*
  - *Develop Local Elderly Assistance Centers*
  - *Develop Local Disability Assistance Centers*

- *Develop Community Civic Centers*
  - *Develop Neighborhood Residential Areas*

- *Develop Large Scale Presentation Stadiums, Parks, Theaters, Halls, Etc.*
  - *Develop Community Recreation, Theater, Art, Music Centers*
  - *Develop Neighborhood Spiritual/ Cultural/Sports/ Physical Fitness Centers*

→ ***Operational Phase*** ←

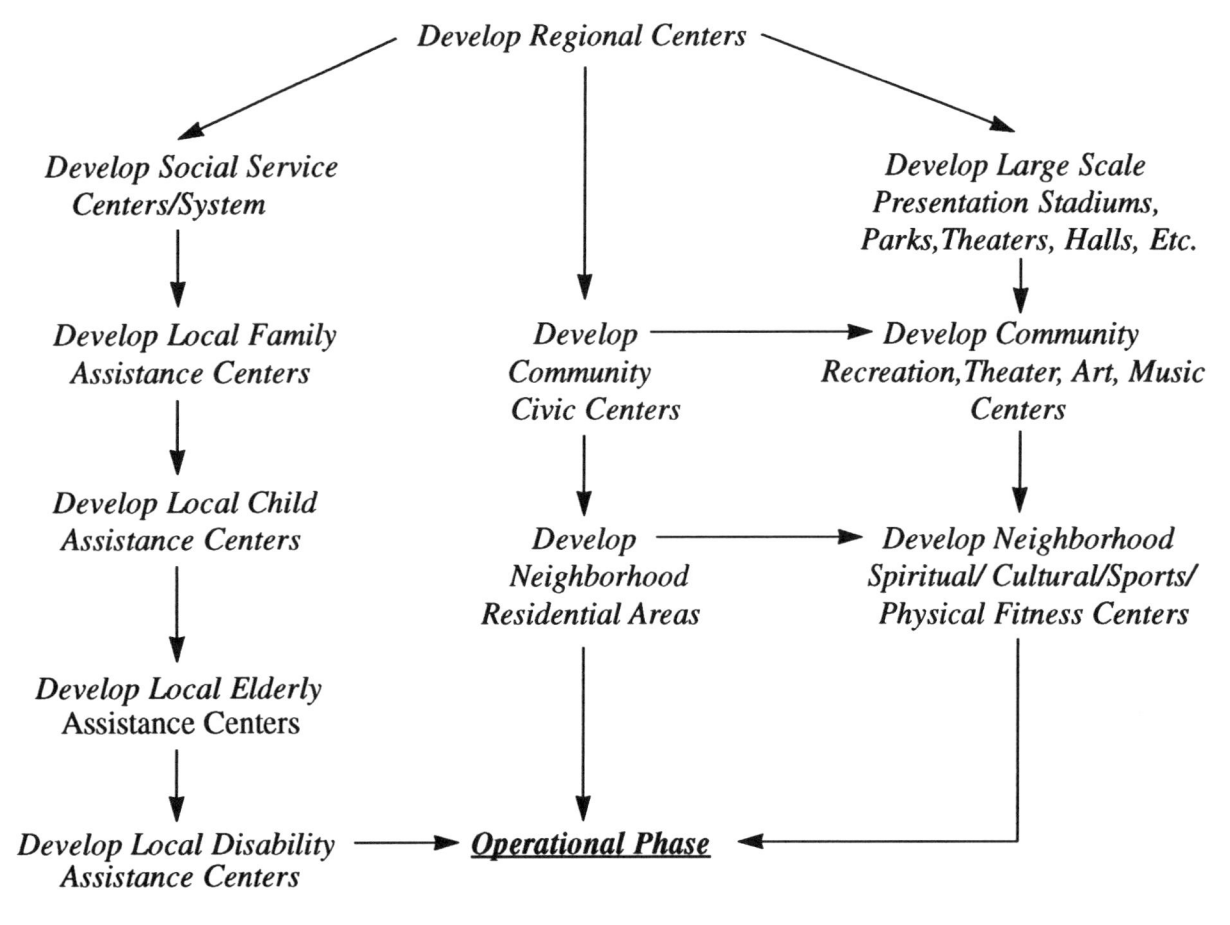

Figure V-6-G

Neos notes, "Some developments seem to be more appropriate for public developers, some for private developers and some for a combination of both. Of course, on a regional level, public agencies assume the responsibility and may contract with private firms to carry out development. In some public works, certain government departments, military entities or other personnel may carry out the development. Buildings and installations are usually built under contract by private architectural and engineering companies."

Pragma adds, "Development of electric power, gas production and other energy provisions could be done by either public or private means. In either case, it is for public use. Telephone and other communication systems are often provided by private developers who have personnel knowledgeable in special fields. I think there are certain basic principles involved when determining whether public or private developers are more appropriate to carry out major projects."

Veritor responds, "I think that one such principle has to do with investment. If development of public works and installations are not funded or initiated by the government, then private developers and operators usually assume responsibility. With private operations, profit-making is necessary, and individuals in the general public and private companies must pay according to prevailing rates. If the public decides to pay for a development through taxation, then long term bonds would be sold to private investors for immediate funding. Financing the bonds would be spread over one or more generations, which is appropriate, if they would also be beneficiaries. Oftentimes, financing requires trade-off analysis to determine which is a better and more economical way to serve the public. However, for regions, much development precedes the population influx, and, therefore, the internal tax base would not yet have been established."

Pragma asks, "Isn't this where higher government entities and larger, existing tax bases would be needed? Wouldn't other regions also have to help with loans and in-kind services? More rapid and effective development of the region's programs must provide part of the answer because shorter term loans could then be borrowed at lower rates, and this would result in less taxes levied on incoming populations. We have to remember that much of the infrastructure development must come from private and corporate investments. This brings us to another important subject: funding and resource utilization."

CHAPTER 6 - DEVELOPMENT OF THE REGION

Developing What Is Public And What Is Private

- *There are many kinds of developers and developments. Development may be accomplished by public or private means or a combination of both.*
- *In the regional concept, public works activities would generally begin before private developments. This allows for basic infrastructures to be planned, initiated and completed in time for the development of communities and special centers.*
- *As public infrastructures are being completed, increasing information on sizing, style, limit, access and availability of utililities would become accessible for private planning and development. Guidelines and codes contribute to a reduction of risk and cost. Much "red tape" would be eliminated. Participating private developers could make their needs and plans known during the development of public works and utilities. This information is of considerable benefit in estimating.*
- *Combinations of public or private development are:*

General Order of Development

Devel.Water/Elect.Pwr Syst.
Devel.Transport.Facil./Syst.
Devel.Sewage/ Waste Syst.
Devel. Parks/Recreation
Devel. Land Reserves
Devel.Courts/ L.E./Fire Syst.
Plus Others

Access to Land Resources
Access to Housing
Access to Special Centers
Devel. Scientific Research
Plus Others

1. Develop What is Public for Public Use
2. Develop What is Public for Private Use
3. Develop What is Private for Public Use
4. Develop What is Private for Private Use

Devel. Business/Commerce
Devel. Recreation Centers
Devel. Shopping Centers
Devel. Manufacturing Centers
Devel. Communication Centers
Devel.Elect.Pwr Facil.(Alt.to 1)
Plus Others

Building of Homes
Building of Apartments
Building of Soc./Rel.Centers
Devel. of Local Utilities
Devel. of Personal Farms
Plus Others

Figure V-6-H

Part V - The Challenge of Implementation

CHAPTER 7 - INVESTING IN LIFE AND LIVING

The regional concept offers a means to focus investment in a way that could better the lives of people everywhere. The definition of regionalization and how to achieve it offers a strong sense of direction and magnitude of effort. It has given us a glimpse of what the future could be. This picture will be enlarged and re-described many times. Descriptions must be penetrating and forward-looking when exploring what is possible and realistic.

The investments are for experiments. Mankind has been involved in experiments in living since the very beginning. As in all experiments, there can be no guaranteed results, only exploration and discovery. Mankind has continued to invest, gaining knowledge and growing in the process.

The regional concept is meant to produce experiments designed for the real world. A succession of regional experiments are, therefore, purposeful and necessary. Each will most likely meet many obstacles that must be overcome. The investing public must assume that there will likely be setbacks and difficulties in the attainment of individual and collective quality of life. By implementing regional experiments, the world can be made safer, wiser, more compassionate, more creative and a happier place to live in.

There is more than enough peril, insecurity and vulnerability in the real world. These hazards often become dominant features of everyday life. They become increasingly so when no deep thought is given, no comprehensive plans are utilized and no dedicated efforts are expended to create a better tomorrow. Investments must be made in life and living. Without doing so, can there be any satisfactory returns?

Lack of investment in quality living is a precursor to the more costly and less effective lifestyles that we commonly see today. Because this omission has been repeated so many times, we must come to the conclusion that insufficient investments or misdirected spending will yield attrition, deterioration and extinction of human hope for a better world.

Investments in regional experiments cannot be trivial or timid. In order to be cost and performance- effective, they must be persistently and sufficiently applied according to well-defined goals and objectives. We have to know what must be achieved and then do it. The future of humans everywhere awaits our collective will and decision.

Pragma, Veritor and Neos are well aware that the extent of regional implementation is totally dependent on willingness to invest. They have been exploring this subject thoughtfully. Pragma notes,"There will be considerable differences in the investments required for each of the regional experiments. Some of these differences relate to the specific designs selected for the regional infrastructures. Some will be

CHAPTER 7 - INVESTING IN LIFE AND LIVING

primarily agrarian, others industrial. Investment differences can also relate to environmental conditions, social structures, cultural affinities and available local human and natural resources. We have discussed these before, but repetition is warranted because they significantly affect investment characteristics and strategies."

Veritor joins in, "The kinds and amounts of investments needed will also vary because the costs of simpler or less developed infrastructures will be much lower."

Neos asks, "So how do these different regional developments obtain investment experience? How can the investment experiences of regional development in an industrial country, for instance, be of help to those in the Third World which are not industrialized? What common approaches can be made?"

Pragma responds, "It will be necessary in any case to utilize modern management approaches in making estimates. Prevailing market costs, as well as inflation, have to be considered for purchased materials and equipment. In order to compute estimates of total labor costs, it is necessary to determine programmatically what kinds of work or functions need to be done during infrastructure development. Specific task definition is derived from this data and provides the basis for estimating labor, material and energy costs. The national labor rates of specific areas would be relevant. In this way, considerable investment experience can be gained and extrapolations made for common functions of most regional developments."

Veritor adds, "Although there are many variables, abundant experience and standards exist in the development of public works, buildings and other construction for most countries. Of course, styles, materials, complexity and methods will vary, and there will always be special cases."

Neos comments, "I think that it's impossible to respond to the question of how much regional development will cost until preliminary designs and planning have been completed and major problems disclosed and analyzed. Basing estimates on things built at another time and place is always risky. Prematurely setting aside blocks of funds for undefined efforts is also risky. Wage standards vary considerably in the performance of common functions. Even purchasing power varies widely from country to country."

Pragma poses a question, "How can an undeveloped country afford investments in regionalization when everything that needs to be done is at an unreachable funding level? How can Third World countries hope to participate?"

Veritor responds, "A common practice has been for economically undeveloped countries to borrow money in desperation from world banks and more affluent countries. Unfortunately, these undeveloped countries have been considered to be 'poor risks', and money lent to them has been at exorbitant interest rates, often requiring natural resources to secure such loans. For agricultural countries the loans may be for growing specific export crops destined for a manipulated market that may produce huge losses to the producing country. Loans for only a minimum amount of infrastructure development are provided to permit delivery. Because this cycle induces attrition and deterioration of resources and even greater indebtedness and neglect of all other infrastructures, it leads to the devastation of countries and world destabilization."

Neos adds, "This is extremely serious because such countries have no chance to address their internal problems. Eventually labor rates are suppressed to a level that leaves much of the population without sufficient means for survival. Relatively few people profit. Eventually, violence and destruction prevail. This is the very opposite of regionalization."

Pragma continues, "It seems to me that other imaginative approaches must be attempted. There must be a worldwide effort, led especially by the affluent nations, to stabilize and revitalize impoverished countries. The number of such countries continues to increase. It is time to reverse the trend with regionalization."

Veritor adds, "Of course, the leaders of host countries must reach accord on the regional concept and be willing to help implement most of the regional infrastructures. This is a far better strategy than isolationism and indifference. World markets can be stabilized by storing surpluses and by establishing interregional price stability for specific critical resources. However, the enhancement of human and natural resources is a better way to achieve stability and viability in an undeveloped country."

Neos notes, "It is apparent that regionalization utilizes various kinds of investment resources, including investments in human and natural resources. In this way, healthy, long term growth can be achieved. Investing in such basic resources is an integral part of all phases and levels of regional implementation and operation."

CHAPTER 7 - INVESTING IN LIFE AND LIVING

Human Resources
Primary Regional Investment

- *Enhanced human resources are primary investments in the implementation of regions. Without such enhancement regionalization or any other concept will fail.*
- *Enhanced human resources are better able to add value to natural or man-made raw materials. This produces new and negotiable wealth. The greater the enhancement, the greater the eventual capacity and wealth. Also, the greater the capacity, the greater the quality of life.*
- *Other means of investment for regional implementation are directly dependent on the existence of such wealth and capacity.*
- *Implementation of regional infrastructures, itself, also provides increased wealth and capacity (and competitive position).*
- *Other regions and host governments through mutual support, receive direct benefit from the region's wealth and capacity.*

Paths of Enhanced Investments

Trained/Skilled Human Resources → *Devel. of Concepts, Mat'ls, Machinery, Services & Organization* → *Increased Capacities, Wealth & Earnings* → *Derived Taxes, Special Assessments* → *Government Investments (Allocations, Grants, Loans, Contracts)*

Natural Resources & Enhanced Environment → *Direct Utilization By Region*

Unskilled Human Resources → *Enhancement of Skills by Training* → *Increased Capacities, Wealth & Earnings* → *Derived Taxes, Special Assessments*

Investment In Bonds, Shares, Capital, Savings

Investment In Bonds, Shares, Capital, Savings

Investments, Loans From Other Regions, Etc.

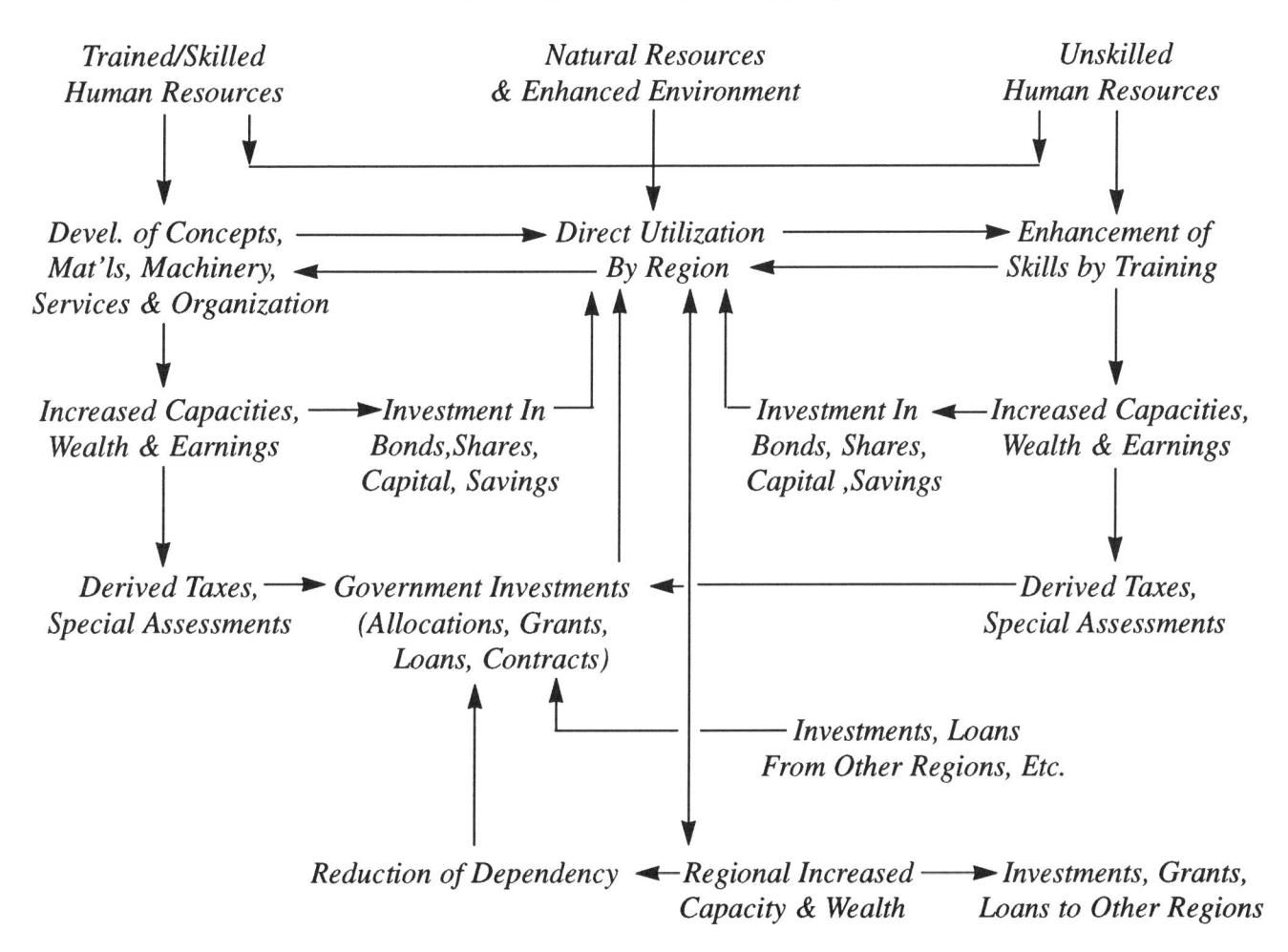

Reduction of Dependency ← *Regional Increased Capacity & Wealth* → *Investments, Grants, Loans to Other Regions*

Figure V-7-A

Pragma continues, "We have been discussing investments that enhance human potential. This potential must now be converted and focused building regions. Human effort must be mobilized, assigned and given direction. Without major, concerted efforts, little of consequence can be accomplished in regionalization."

Veritor responds, "You're right. This has always happened, and we must clearly realize this. I am particularly concerned about the undeveloped countries of the world that have few natural resources but very large numbers of people. Many of these people are untrained or only semi-skilled. These countries must go through the extremely difficult process of trying to utilize their workforce while simultaneously attempting to train and upgrade their capabilities while regionalization is going on. This process is bound to be slow, but it is unavoidable."

Pragma states, "All national accomplishments have been brought about through major human endeavor. It doesn't matter whether a country is rich or poor. This essential ingredient is where achievement has to start. If people don't have money to buy other people's labor, then they have to do it themselves or pool efforts. This brings up an important point. Leaders in both rich and poor countries are likely to claim that there is not enough money for regionalization even though regionalization is essential. Capital reserves may be limited, missing or already committed. Money for investment can be gradually raised by adding intrinsic value or profit to whatever is produced. The increased productivity from improving health and safety, as well as organizing and concentrating effort will result in sustained growth. Improving quality, efficiency and effectiveness increases value still further. Temporary, short term loans at low rates, equipment bought on credit or consignment, and shared equipment all provide alternative assets. But there must be specific, attainable objectives and sustained efforts to achieve results."

Veritor adds, "Regional infrastructures in poor countries may not immediately require as much capital because large infusions of funds at one time are likely to exceed the capacity to utilize them properly. Such capital is very likely to be dissipated before results can be obtained to pay back debt. Fortunately, regionalization develops incrementally, so need for capital is also incremental."

Neos asserts, "The time to borrow capital is when the benefits of doing so can be clearly defined. But it is also essential to anticipate need. This is likely to happen as regional implementation gradually unfolds. Lead time is required to implement programs and projects in a timely manner, and it does take time to acquire necessary capital."

Veritor expands on this. "It's apparent that regions do not have to be fully capitalized and mobilized before they start. Capitalization and the mobilization of human effort must obviously be phased-in in time for the development of various regional programs. This means that when peak demands for capital occur, only short or

CHAPTER 7 - INVESTING IN LIFE AND LIVING

mid-term loans at lower cost are needed. The loans are paid back during the operational phase. As for human effort, careful mobilization and better utilization of people for greater effectiveness is needed."

Pragma responds, "That is a good observation. We need to discuss how investments in human labor and capital are to be utilized during the preparation and subsequent phases of implementation. Certainly, during general preparation, countries everywhere should be applying concerted efforts to enhance their lands in anticipation of new regional site selection. There should be great incentives for them to do so because the implementation of new regions will bring large infusions of all kinds of help and benefits."

Veritor agrees, "This is a particularly important time because human labor and perhaps borrowed equipment, more than capital, are necessary for planting trees, improving watersheds, modifying agricultural practices and so forth. Even aqueducts, small dams and certain other structures can be built by hard labor in many cases. Whatever can be accomplished will ultimately pay off."

Neos notes, "As we have said earlier, this situation is similar to when countries prepare for the Olympics, world fairs and expositions. Such investments are meant to attract capital and improve human and economic climate."

Pragma adds, "This is just the prelude to even greater and more concerted efforts that must be expended when site selections are prioritized. Virtually all countries are candidates for one or more regions. So it is a case of when selections will be made, not if they will be made."

Veritor answers, "This should be an incentive for even the smallest of countries, even those that are smaller than a region. They can still benefit immensely by adopting some of the regional infrastructure concepts, experiences and overall development."

Pragma continues, "Of course, during networking and mobilization, there will be no great need for capitalization. However, there must be organizational efforts and arrangements whereby some of the early funding needs can be identified and commitments obtained. I would like to present a simple graph of how investments for each region would be applied."

Regional Investments According to Phases

- *The amounts and kinds of investments needed for regional implementation vary according to the preparatory and subsequent implementation phases.*
- *Preliminary investments in manpower and capital are required of all countries according to their capacity to participate and their anticipation of benefits. This occurs during global preparation and then increasingly during specific regional site preparation.*
- *Networking and mobilization involve mostly efforts by people. Comparatively little capital is expended.*
- *Investments for specific site preparation involve an infusion and utilization of capital from multiple sources.*
- *Planning and design are mostly labor intensive, requiring some increase in funds.*
- *Investments during initiation and acquisition require a significant increase in the need for both capital and labor. The need for capital, labor and materials accelerates and peaks during the development phase.*
- *Investments for the operational phase are derived from different and more diverse sources as the general population grows. A more uniform level of labor, material and capital expenditure gradually takes place.*
- *These changes are shown graphically as follows:*

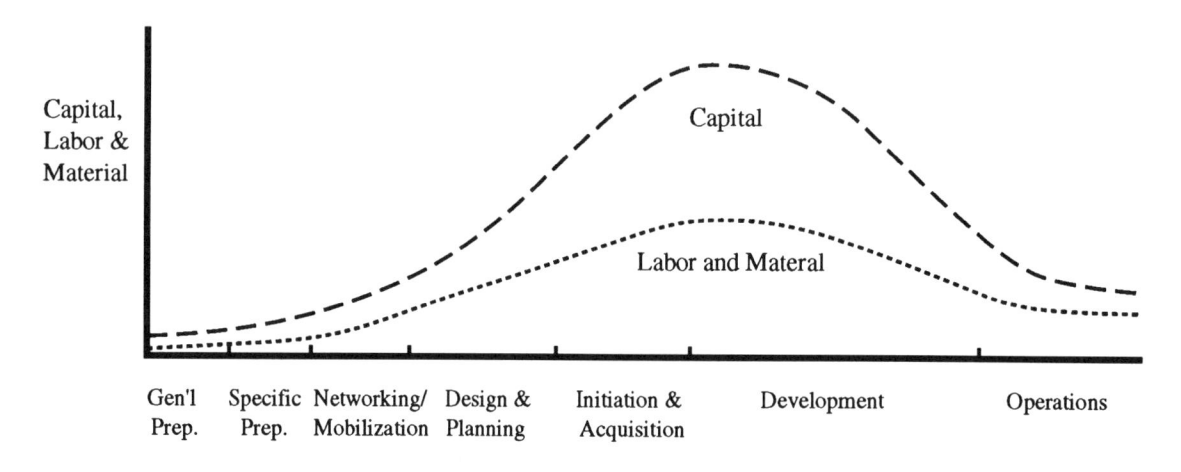

General Investment Curve

Figure V-7-B

CHAPTER 7 - INVESTING IN LIFE AND LIVING

Neos concurs, "Further efforts to obtain investment sources must be exerted as the designing and planning of sites begin to solidify. This is when programs are more fully identified and defined so that specific estimates of expenditures and rates can be determined at the regional level."

Veritor says, "The big expenditures in capital, labor and material take place during the initiation, acquisition and development phases. We are talking about billions of dollars, more so in industrial countries where the economies are much greater. These are likely to be astronomical numbers."

Neos adds, "Eventually, the operational phase is reached. This implies that the regional, community and neighborhood levels and special centers are now functioning with some stability. It also implies that many more kinds of investment sources can be utilized to maintain the infrastructures of the region."

Pragma continues, "Once the basic infrastructures have become operational, there will still be internal development necessary to meet gradual increases in population and commercial and business activities. Private investments would greatly increase."

Veritor adds, "It is a time of great vitality and promise. It is during the operational phase that many new innovations would pique the public's interest for further enterprise. People living in the region would be continuously involved in bettering living conditions and ensuring that successive generations will have opportunity to also contribute and participate."

Neos notes, "I think that greater public service and community and neighborhood participation in the region would inspire a higher sense of individual responsibility."

Pragma adds, "Another significant change we can look forward to is that investments in time and effort would be increasingly thought of in terms of quality of life. It's hard to put a price on voluntary cooperation and a spirit of belonging."

Veritor has been listening carefully and says, "As regions are implemented, there should be great economic shifts in capital for investment. After all, regions mean new growth, stability and opportunity, and this is where capital is likely to go. But, eventually, as we have already noted, the established regions must invest in other regional development as well."

Investing in the Infrastructures

- *Each infrastructure requires a variety of investments according to the functions to be performed. This variety relates to the regional, community and neighborhood levels of each infrastructure.*
- *Investments are first required at the regional level. These investments continue to change according to each phase.*
- *Investments at the community level are furnished by public and private sources and continued throughout the operational phase.*
- *Investments at the neighborhood level are intially made mostly by private funds and are maintained by private funds except for certain infrastructures which are mostly publicly funded.*
- *Investments for special centers for Infrastructures A, L, D, S, P and N are mostly from public sources. Investments for special centers for Infrastructures M, H, E, T and C are from public and private sources. Investments for special centers for Infrastructures F and B are mostly from private sources.*

* Regional Level
   Government borrows directly from investors (bonds and other paper).
   Government raises general tax revenues.
   Government raises special taxes (sales, excise, service,use, etc.).
   Government incurs long term debt and borrows from banks.
   Military & public agencies lend personnel with special skills (in-kind services).
   Private foundations donate funds, give grants and other support.
   Private investors develop certain kinds of public facilities.
   Public resources are traded or sold for public benefit.
   Government raises special tax revenues for education, medical and other infrastructures.

* Community Level
   Government borrows directly from investors (bonds and other paper).
   Government raises local tax revenues.
   Government derives revenue-sharing and pass-through funds.
   Government raises funds from special assessments and improvement bonds.

* Neighborhood Level
   Private investors build properties, lend mortgages and other money.
   Volunteers donate services.
   Funds are donated by private individuals for public benefit.

* Centers
   Public and private entities invest in buildings, facilities, etc.
   Private foundations donate funds, give grants and other support.

CHAPTER 7 - INVESTING IN LIFE AND LIVING

The Search for Human Resources and Funding Alternatives

- *The marshalling of human resources during regional implementation has similarities with mobilization for wars, except that it is for opposite purposes.*
- *A number of prospective funding sources have been noted in "Investing in the Infrastructures", but many others exist or have been suggested. In the State of the World 1991,** one such suggestion proposes "that green taxes be put on products and activities that pollute, deplete or otherwise depend on natural systems to pay for environmental costs".*
- *All kinds of funding and human services will be needed, however, and there are many ways to obtain these. Some are proposed as follows:*

    * *Grants and endowments through estates and foundations.*
    * *Loans of personnel by large corporations.*
    * *Donation of blocks of labor to build housing by prospective tenants.*
    * *Cooperative building and other projects.*
    * *Requirement for universal public service for one year.*
    * *Tax deductions for conservation of fossil fuels and water.*
    * *Voluntary services to help the needy.*
    * *Voluntary or paid child care and teaching services for parents at work.*
    * *Performance of public work at reduced wages in exchange for educational benefits.*
    * *Utilization of prison labor on environmental projects or in conjunction with apprenticeships.*
    * *Fees for heavy use of roadways and increased gasoline taxes.*
    * *Increasing import surtaxes on products of domestic companies produced by foreign labor.*
    * *Increasing taxes on products found to be harmful to human health.*
    * *Military participation in the construction of public buildings, public works, etc.*
    * *Military participation in providing interim transportation for regional site development.*
    * *Others*

- *When the public is encouraged and motivated, new ways and means for accomplishment will materialize from many sources.*

** Brown, L.R., et al, State of the World, A Worldwide Institute Report on Progress Toward a Sustainable Society, W.W. Norton, N.Y. 1989

PART VI
Expansion Of Regionalization & Beyond

Part VI - Expansion of Regionalization and Beyond

CHAPTER 1 - EXPANSION

On each continent where population crises exist, the absence of socio-economic viability beckons regionalization or some other form of infrastructure development. But there remains a dearth of comprehensive concepts that can lead to the alleviation of severe socio-economic problems that plague most countries. Leaders in countries with the most intractable problems should welcome ways to cope with them.

The regional concept however, cannot be simultaneously applied worldwide. Even if early concurrency were possible, it would be unwise. The initial regions and a gradual implementation of subsequent new starts must reflect a controlled, well-managed utilization of human and natural resources. Each region would offer other newly initiated regions the opportunity to gain experience and avoid the repetition of recognized errors.

Countries should anticipate the prospect of regionalization by improving environmental conditions for regional site selection to take place. Socio-economic adjustments and cultural accommodations will have to be made. Blind ideologies will have to be overcome. A common failing throughout history has been to ignore inherently harmful side effects when making large scale changes. History reveals that adherence to rigid social experiments fails to provide necessary, periodic modifications and self-corrections. When the operational phase is reached, the experiment ends, as if frozen in time. Rigid practices leave no room for improvement and growth. People who question specific practices in such experiments are accused and punished or ostracized as trouble makers or deviationists.

Therefore, any regional concept must contain the means for periodic change and renewal even after it has become operational. As the number of regions increase and inter-regional relationships develop, experiences and ideas must be exchanged so that new regions can adopt and apply them.

Pragma, Veritor and Neos have been reviewing their earlier discussions on the need for worldwide regional expansion. Pragma states, "The greatest number of regions to be developed must be in countries like China, India and others where populations have skyrocketed. Even a modified or limited version of regionalization would be of enormous help in these countries."

Neos adds, "Fortunately, the infrastructures of the regional concept have modular characteristics. These modular characteristics may have the best chance of being incrementally adopted and developed. The newness of the regional concept and its networking principles are apt to cause apprehension at first. Ironically, it is the twin extremes of chaos and over-regimentation that people in such countries would be giving up."

CHAPTER 1 - EXPANSION

Pragma continues, "It seems to me that expansion of the regional concept must occur in two basic ways. When it takes place on the international level, development impetus must come from agencies of the United Nations, the host nations and affluent nations. When host countries are able to sustain their own regional expansion, the U. N. must still continue to play a major role in fostering international support, cooperation and peace to safeguard progress."

Veritor answers, "Looking ahead, many new national and international governments are likely to evolve. Unlike the past, they will be compelled by population growth, limited habitable space and diminishing resources to interface and cooperate. If they do not, chaos, war and oppression accompanied by hunger, sickness and death will prevail until either sanity and peace are restored or the extinction of homo sapiens occurs. It should be more than apparent that regional networking would provide one of the more important means of achieving world peace and prosperity."

Neos concurs, "Without doubt, world regionalization would represent an enormous advance in the history of mankind."

Pragma notes, "As we mentioned earlier, during the expansion of regionalization, sites for new regions must not be placed too close to supercities or other densely populated areas. Appropriate site locations that do not impinge on existing population centers are less likely to create major hardships for jurisdictions not directly involved in regionalization."

Veritor adds, "Of course, when proximity is unavoidable, such as in densely populated countries, new regions would have to be carefully developed. An overlay of infrastructure networks would gradually incorporate existing towns and villages. Perhaps, in most cases, people might even remain in their same homes and neighborhoods to minimize disruptions."

Neos summarizes by saying, "Expansion of regionalization may be disrupting to many, but it will be miniscule compared with what is likely to happen if socio-economic deterioration continues as it has been during coming years. All changes bring disruptions; all we can do is minimize hardships."

Part VI - Expansion of Regionalization and Beyond

CHAPTER 2 - POPULATION SHIFTS & REGIONAL INFLUENCES

New regions are meant to divert population away from supercities as well as attract those who are trapped in such environments. As noted in Part II, without reducing population pressures, there can never be optimum solutions to supercity problems. Furthermore, persistent chaos will make supercities increasingly ungovernable. More stringent emergency measures will have to be applied, and more oppressive laws passed in futile attempts to provide "law and order". Quality of life will be elusive.

Therefore, regions must directly influence the supercities by relieving pressure and giving them a chance to recover, reorganize and cope. It is extremely urgent to relieve pressure because the cost of doing so is many times less than resulting socio-economic damage if nothing is done. In other words, we cannot afford not to act. Implementing and operating pressure-reducing regions represents a viable alternative.

The positive influence of regions extends far beyond benefiting supercities. It also affects the well-being of host countries as they redirect resources to accomplish regionalization. Investments revitalize and stimulate the whole economy. As regions are implemented, they profoundly influence the functional interfaces and activities of the government, causing new political alignments, different land usage, new economic patterns and improved social behavior. This is as it is meant to be. It is essential, however, that all transitions and adjustments be made as smoothly as possible with minimum friction, deprivation and inconvenience to the people needing help. The newness of regions is bound to impact the old and established ways of societies. This rejuvenation should dramatically advance quality of life and diminish the negative attributes of overpopulation and societal deterioration.

Pragma, Veritor and Neos have been thinking about the regional influence as this new concept expands worldwide. Pragma notes, "Certainly, the regional concept is not a threat but an opportunity that allows countries and their supercities to survive. Regional experiments are bound to reveal how existing supercity infrastructures must be corrected. Far from being something to fear, regional influence on supercities and other growing cities offers hope and solutions. But I think that we should examine some of the positive changes that may take place as population pressures are reduced and infrastructure developments impact present-day systems. Obviously, supercities will change for the better physically, socio-economically and politically as population density is reduced, communities and neighborhoods are reorganized and reorientations take place."

CHAPTER 2 - POPULATION SHIFTS & REGIONAL INFLUENCES

Conversion of the Supercities

* *There will be many positive changes in the supercities and perhaps other cities as regions are progressively developed and become operational. Once excess population has been redirected and supercity populations are allowed to decline, pressures on all infrastructures will also decline. Loads on many diverse functions of these infrastructures will be reduced, allowing more human and monetary resources to be concentrated on problem solving.*
* *The following possibilities are apparent:*

   * *Infrastructure A - More tax revenues could go for upgrading services and investment.*
   * *Infrastructure L - Court cases could be greatly reduced in number; trial dates could be moved up; legislation could be made more effective .*
   * *Infrastructure M - Trauma cases could be greatly reduced; public health case loads would be reduced; hospitals could become more effective; medical outreach to neighborhoods could be established.*
   * *Infrastructure S - More housing would be made available; neighborhoods could be improved and re-established; social service caseloads would be reduced.*
   * *Infrastructure D - Overcrowding of jails would be eliminated; law enforcement could shift more resources to direct neighborhood services and crime prevention; street safety would be ensured; other safety services would be more effective.*
   * *Infrastructure N - Neighborhood parks could be restored, developed and maintained; local cultures could be revitalized; neighborhood extended families could be fostered; theaters, art and music could flourish; sport activities could redirect youthful energy; cooperative projects could restore the environment.*
   * *Infrastructure E - School class size would be greatly reduced; remedial help for learning and child care would be provided; educational resources could be more effective; teachers would be treated with greater respect and rewarded for dedication.*
   * *Infrastructure T - Traffic congestion could be greatly reduced; old roadways and structures would be repaired and modified to be more effective and safe; new transportation systems would become more feasible to implement.*
   * *Infrastructure P - Less electric power and water would be used; sewage and trash system overload could be reduced and new methods of processing introduced.*
   * *Infrastructure C - Postal delivery would be simpler; public forums could be introduced.*
   * *Infrastructure F - Food distribution could be simplified; local gardens would be encouraged.*
   * *Infrastructure B - Remaining work force would stabilize; less merchandise would be stolen; new enterprises would flourish.*
   * *Infrastructure H - The environment would be less abused; restorations could begin.*

Veritor continues, "The first initiatives for reorganization must be taken by existing government functions. Interestingly, governments must become the instruments of their own change as well as participants in regional implementation. However, as has been discussed earlier, the national government must provide regional coordination and support. The top leaders of host nations must take bold initiatives to ensure regional implementation. Considerable pressure and regional advocacy by other leaders in the host countries may be necessary to sustain momentum. The most difficult adaptation for existing governments would be the designation and sharing of powers and responsibilities with counterparts in regionalization."

Neos nods and says, "Other key adjustments will vary from country to country. This means that as new regions become operational, the transfer of powers to newly created authorities must take place for all emerging infrastructures. Like parents encouraging their grown children to leave the 'nest', the regions must be encouraged to become semi-autonomous and viable."

Pragma adds, "Emerging regional political subdivisions will require new legal jurisdictions which may be included in or separated from those of contiguous areas. I believe regions are large enough to have their own political identity, and functionally they should. New political alignments often establish jurisdictions to tap any existing industrial and commercial tax bases. By contrast, regionalization will develop its own tax base through infrastructure and human and natural resource development.

"We must also anticipate opposition or at least extreme caution. Many people might not be fully convinced that the regional experiment will be good for them. The region may be considered to be competition, something to be feared. I expect that opposition groups will continue to exist both within and outside regions even when they become operational. This could be reasonable and necessary because it might take outside opposition to detect excesses and irregular behavior within the region."

Veritor notes, "New regional areas may occasionally overlap or contain existing jurisdictions. When this happens, there may be conflicts that cannot be immediately resolved. Regional site selection must include negotiation to settle conflicts or site development might have to be deferred until conflicts are resolved. "

CHAPTER 2 - POPULATION SHIFTS & REGIONAL INFLUENCES

Expansion Adjustments

- *There are always difficulties when it is necessary to accommodate the new. The regional concept is no exception. There have to be adjustments and re-arrangements within most countries and with areas contiguous to the new regions.*
- *It is essential that contiguous jurisdictions, as well as host nations participate in the birth of new regions. All will ultimately gain.*
- *Adjustments and re-arrangements are required both during regional implementations and operations. An attempt to briefly summarize these processes is as follows:*

During Regional Implementation

Host Government

Contiguous Jurisdictions	*Select/Define Regional Site* *Prepare Environment* *Provide Management* *Establish Funding/ Resources* *Establish Interfaces* *Obtain Resource Investment* *Establish Infrastructures* *Establish Networking* *Establish Communities &* *Neighborhoods*	*International Government* *&* *Inter-Regional Government*

During Regional Operations

Host Government

Interim Courts & *Appointed Officials*	*Establish Permanent Courts* *Establish Legislature* *Establish Political Divisions* *Elect Officials & Representatives* *Establish Administration* *Establish /Maintain Budgets*	*Regional Public &* *Private Entities*

Part VI - Expansion of Regionalization and Beyond

CHAPTER 3 - REFLECTIONS

Pragma, Veritor and Neos have at last returned to their mountain retreat. It has been a long journey of the mind that has ranged from the philosophical to the conceptual to the practicable. The journey has produced visions of a world made safe and sane, a world made peaceful through good will and creative endeavor. What they have witnessed, however, has been far different. So much needs to be urgently done. How many are aware and are willing to change what needs to be reshaped or to create what needs to be built? They have asked themselves questions; pondered solutions to problems. Now they would like to ask the reader some questions.

"What kind of world do you think we live in? We ask you to think about this very carefully from various perspectives as you frame your answer for yourself. If it isn't what you would like it to be, try to picture what would make it better for yourself and for others. Try to think, feel and sense what fulfillment of this vision might mean for the people who live in your general area, in your country and in your world.

"Have you thought about general and specific changes that would benefit your environment? How would you shape your goals and objectives and what direction would you take in order to produce a better world? What are your criteria for establishing them? Are they based on achieving a better quality of life? For yourself? For others?"

Pragma, Veritor and Neos have been examining these very same questions. They are interested in you and all humanity. They have been seeking knowledge about how future generations might also survive and thrive. In so doing, they have been building the future.

Now they ask your help in seeking and building such a future. They need your thoughts; they need your deeds. Whatever your background, your intellect, your competence, your sensitivity or your occupation, you are the world. You are someone who must become involved. Don't wait for others to perform for you. Be responsible for yourself, so that you will count. Be responsible for others so that they will count. Each day of noble endeavor will bring you the joy of living. Each passing year will bring you fulfillment.

> We are the product of the past.
> We are the process of today.
> We are the promise of the future.
> Let us begin!

APPENDIX - GLOSSARY

bench mark - a surveyor's permanent landmark used as reference giving a known position and altitude.

brackish - salty, briney.

centers - dedicated or special facilities and complexes within the region or communities that focus on special functions of infrastructures at all regional levels. Centers for infrastructures include administration, legal and legislative, public safety, public and commercial utilities, public works, transportation, communication, industry, commerce, finance, agriculture, medical services, public health, scientific research, education, recreation, culture and religion. Centers of different size, scope and complexity serve the region, infrastructures, communities and neighbor hoods.

community - a subdivision of a region that provides for the needs of approximately 150,000 people grouped into networked neighborhoods. Public and private services in dedicated centers provide the civic, economic, educational, health and safety, cultural, recreational functions needed by local residences and enterprises.

desalination - desalting of ocean or brackish water

distillation - the evaporation of a liquid by heating and followed by cooling and condensation of the vapor to produce a more nearly pure substance.

ecosphere - any area in which life can exist; an ecosystem is made up of a community of organisms interacting with their inanimate environment and each other.

electrodialysis - the speedup of the passage of ions through a membrane by applying voltage across it.

electromagnetic levitation - an electrical current passed through a conductor (monorail) creating an magnetic field and causing repulsion (levitation) of the like-charged wheel of a vehicle.

economic imperative - complex human needs involving production, distribution, exchange and consumption that contribute or detract from economic well-being.

environmental imperative - pertains to mankind's need to protect and augment natural surroundings, conserve natural resources and promote optimum living conditions.

evolutional progression - the positive assumption that mankind's development is on the ascendency.

function - the performance of a particular type of activity (both mental and physical for humans).

Gaia hypothesis - conditions necessary for life are created and maintained by life itself in a self-sustaining process of dynamical feedback.

goal - a desired state of being or a particular accomplishment that one strives to attain.

halophytes - salt water tolerant plants

hectare - an area metric measurement equal to 2.471 acres.

hybrid vehicle - a vehicle using more than one means of propulsion (ex. solar battery/combustion engine).

infrastructure - one of a number of functional groups consisting of special systems necessary to develop, operate and maintain the activities of the region. Approximately thirteen infrastructure groups apply their functions through networking.

linkage type network - closely interrelated and combined physical and functional interactions.

milestone - a strategic date or completion date of a program.

megalopolis (supercity) - a complex population center with more than two million people which characteristically expand in random fashion to absorb neighboring cities, towns andvillages.

network - multi-faceted elements of a system that physically and functionally interconnect, integrate, coordinate and support communities, neighborhoods and special or dedicated centers of the infrastructures of a region. Regions are also networked with other regions and governmental entities. Networking involves the communication of information and ideas, the transfer of tangible items, and the physical interaction of people and people and machines.

neighborhood- a subdivision of the community involving a diversity of life styles and social, ethnic, religious and economic groupings. Subdivisions provide for unique combinations of activities such as creative and cooperative efforts for the mutual benefit and support of neighbors. Neighborhoods have close-by schools, medical clinics, recreational facilities and parks, religious and cultural facilities, local entertainment facilities, meeting halls for local events, emergency and safety services, commercial outlets and maintenance and repair services.

objective - an attainable quantifiable accomplishment, reachable through the performance of tasks.

ownership - implies the exclusive right to use land and its resources in any way that does not conflict with the interests of owners of adjoining properties.

phase - one of a logical progression of events such as design, planning, acquisition, development, installation, operation, maintenance and evaluation of a program during its life cycle.

photovoltaic collector - panels with solar photo-cells that collect and convert sunlight to electrical energy.

program - a goal-oriented, planned effort that is divided into a series of phased events.The planned efforts are subdivided into projects with tasks to meet specific objectives.

project - an objective-oriented, planned effort that is subdivided into tasks for assignment.

quality of life (individual) - individual life has optimum quality when it is given meaning and is appreciated, when there is hope for the future and, within limits, the freedom of choice.

APPENDIX - GLOSSARY

quality of life (collective) - in a community, consists of vitality and a spirit of cohesion and participation, accomodation for different lifestyles and beliefs, and respect for the welfare of all inhabitants.

region - a special area providing a unique living environment and key resources that is dedicated to serving the public and private sectors. It consists of a network of infrastructures, communities, centers and support areas. These areas include arable and buildable lands and open spaces for conservation, resources and recreation. The total area of approximately 600 square miles is defined by natural boundaries, to the extent possible, and characterized by close proximity to such features as oceans, rivers, lakes, wetlands, valleys, mountains, hills, desert fringes or plains. The region's area must contain resources sufficient to sustain an optimum population of approximately 1,500,000 people and a maximum of 2,000,000.

reverse osmosis - the separation and exclusion of salt as sea water passes through a semi-permeable membrane under pressure.

solar energy - energy supplied by the sun.

solar concentrators - Curved reflectors used to focus the sun's rays on the concentrator's heat-conducting fluid for the steam turbine generation of electricity.

system - an approach to defining the functional interactions of humans and machines in order to attain goals and objectives throughout all program and project phases.

system integration - the analysis and synthesis of interacting functions and the resolution of compatibility problems, spheres of responsibility, human and machine involvement, performance evaluation and trade-offs in meeting goals and objectives.

task - specific work defined by hours needed for accomplishment over a specified period of time.

thermocline - a permanent or temporary boundary layer formed in oceans and lakes between warm and cold water masses.

tidal bore - a wall of water that travels up some rivers about twi or three times as fast as the incoming tide. It is formed on those rivers where the mass and momentum of the incoming tide are concentrated into a narrow front by the river channel, by the rise of the river bed or both.

timeline - one of a number of methods of scheduling series and parallel events or tasks. Milestones and completion dates are indicated.

territorial imperative - the need to acquire land or a place to settle where there are sufficient resources and a favorable environment for surviving and thriving, enjoying the bounty of the earth.

trialogue - conversation involving three perspectives.

usership - implies the right, along with responsibilities, to use or have access to lands held in common or the legal right to use resources or space above or below ground without dispoiling property.

APPENDIX - SPECIFIC REFERENCES

Introduction
Gleick, James, *Chaos*, Viking Press, 1987

Part I, Chapter 1
Bookchin, M., *The Ecology of Freedom*, The Cheshire Books, 1982

Buber, Martin, *The Knowledge of Man*, Harper & Row, Publishers, Inc., 1965

Goodman, Percival and Paul Goodman, Communitas: Means of Livelihood and Ways of Life, Vintage Books (Random House) and Alfred Knopf, Inc., N.Y., 1947, 1960

Dice, L.R., *Man's Nature and Nature's Man*, Univ. of Michigan Press, Ann Arbor, 1955

Muller, Robert, New Genesis, Shaping a Global Spirituality, Doubleday and World Happiness and Cooperation, 1979

Newman, Joseph (Editor), *1994: The World of Tomorrow*, U.S. News & World Report, Inc., Washington, D.C., 1973

Part I, Chapter 2
Frankl, Viktor, *Man's Search for Meaning*, Washington Square Press, Inc., 1963

Minsky, Marvin, *The Society of Minds*, Simon & Schuster, N.Y., 1985

Part I, Chapter 3
Giedion, S., Space, *Time and Architecture, 4th Edit.*, Harvard University Press, Cambridge, 1962

Rusmeyer, R., *Space Places,* Collins, San Francisco, 1990

Scheflen, A. with N. Asheraft, *Human Territories: How we Behave In Space-Time*, Prentice-Hall, Englewood Cliffs, N.J., 1976

Part I, Chapter 4
Adler, Mortimer, *The Idea of Freedom*, Doubleday & Co., Inc., 1960

Louis Harris & Associates for U.S. Department of Housing & Urban Development, 1978 Survey *Quality of Communal Life*

Rosenthahl, B.G. and J.E. Mayer, *Crowding Behavior and the Future,* Irvington Publishers, N.Y., 1983

Spilker, B., Edit., *Quality of Life Assessments in Clinical Trials,* Raven, N.Y., 1990

Part I, Chapter 5
Aiello, R., A. Baum, Edit., *Residential Crowding and Design,* Plenum Press, N.Y., 1979

Altman, I., L.S. Wrightsman, Edit. Consult.,*The Environment and Social Behavior: Privacy, Personal Space, Territory, Crowding,* Brooks/Cole Publishing Co., Monterey, California, 1975

Baldassare, M., *Residential Crowding in Urban America,* University of California Press, Berkeley, 1979

Baum, A., Y. M. Epstein, Edit., *Human Response to Crowding,* L. Erlbaum Assoc. and Hasted Press, N.Y., 1978

Bookchin, A., *The Limits of the City,* Harpers & Row, N.Y., 1974

Booth, A., *Urban Crowding and Its Consequences,* Praeger Publishers, N.Y., 1976

Dasman, R.F., *The Destruction of California*, MacMillan Co., Ltd, London, 1960

Freedman, J.L., *Crowding and Behavior,* Viking Press, N.Y., 1975

Humphries, D., *Household Crowding, Population Density and Their Relationships to a Number of Pathological Indicators*, California State University, Fullerton, Calif., 1982

Insel, P.M., H.C. Lindgren, *Too Close For Comfort: The Psychology of Crowding,* Prentice Hall, Englewood Cliffs, N.J., 1978

Sax, K., *Standing Room Only: The Challenge of Overpopulation,* Beacon Press, Boston, 1955

Part II, Chapter 1

Barkai, H., *Growth Patterns of the Kibbutz Economy*, North Holland Publishing Co., Amsterdam, 1977

Kelman, H.C., *A Time to Speak: On Human Values and Social Research*, Josey-Bass, San Francisco, 1968

Olswewska, A. L.K.Roberts, *Leisure and Lifestyle: A Comparative Analysis of Free Time*,Sage Publications, London, 1989

Park, R.E., *Human Communities: The City and Human Ecology*, Free Press, Glencoe, Ill., 1952 Service, E.R., *Primative Social Organization,* Univ. of Michigan, Random House, N.Y., 1990

Thomas, W.L., Jr., Edit., *Man's Role in Changing the Face of the Earth,* Wenner-Gren and The National Science Foundation, University of Chicago, 1956

Part II, Chapter 1

Carver, H., *Cities in the Suburbs,* University of Toronto Press, 1962

Chesen,G., et al , *Fodor's Japan,* Fodors Travel Publications, Inc., 1988

Crumpton, M.J., T.M. Dexter, Edit., *Growth Factors in Differentiation and Development*, Royal Society, London, 1990

Dubos, René, *Man Adapting,* The Yale University Press, New Haven & London, 1965

Golledge, R.G., G.Rushton, Edit., *Spatial Choice and Spatial Behavior: Geographic Essays on the Analysis of Preferences and Perceptions,* Ohio State University Press, Columbus, 1976

Gregor, H.F., *Spatial Disharmonies in California Population Growth,* Geographical Review, 1963

Hannerz, V., *Exploring the City: Inquiries Toward an Urban Anthropology,* Columbia University Press, N.Y., 1980

Hicks, U.K., *The Large City: A World Problem,* MacMillan Co., Ltd, London, 1974

APPENDIX - SPECIFIC REFERENCES

Michelsohn, D.R. & Associates Editors, *The Cities in Tommorrow's World: Challenges to Urban Survival,* J. Messner, N.Y., 1973

Mumford, L., *The Culture of Cities,* Harcourt, Brace and Co., N.Y., 1961

Mumford, L., *The City in History,* Harcourt, Brace and World, N.Y., 1991

Searles, H., *The Non-human Environment,* International University Press, N.Y., 1960

Sillo, D.L., Edit., *International Encyclopedia of Social Sciences, Vol.2,* The Macmillan Co., N.Y., 1968

Sukopp, H.S., S. Hejny, I Kowarik, *Urban Ecology,* S.B. Academic, The Hague, 1990

Walton, J., D.E. Carns, *Cities in Change : Studies on the Urban Condition,* Allyn and Bacon, Boston, 1973

Wright, W.D.C., D.H.Stewart, Edit., *The Exploding City,* Edinburgh University Press, 1972

Part II, Chapter 2

Lee, R.H., *The City: Urbanism and Urbanization in Major World Regions,* Lippicott, Philadelphia, 1955

Robson, W.A., *The Great Cities of the World: Their Governments, Politics and Planning,* Allen and Unwin, 1957

Stanley, J., D.Brunn, J.F. Williams et al, Edit., *Cities of the World: World Regional Urban Development,* Harper and Row, N.Y.,1983

Summerfield, J., *Fodor's Republic of China,* Fodor's Travel Publications, Inc., 1988

Thomlinson, R., *Urban Structure: The Social and Spatial Character of Cities,* Random House, N.Y., 1969

Toynbee, A.J., *Cities of Destiny,* McGraw -Hill, N.Y., 1967

Part II, Chapter 4

Angell, R.C., *Free Society and Moral Crisis,* University of Michigan Press, Ann Arbor, 1958

Bromfield, L. et al, Edit. E.T. Peterson, *Cities Are Abnormal,* Greenwood Press, Westport, Conn., 1971

Exline, C.H., G. L. Peters, R.P. Larkin, *The City: Patterns and Processes in the Urban Ecosystem,* Westview Press, Boulder, Colo., 1982

Ghurje, G.S., *Cities and Civilization,* Popular Prakashan, Bombay, 1962

Jones, E., E. Van Zandt, *The City: Yesterday and Tomorrow,* Aldus Books, 1974

Morgan, E., *Falling Apart: The Rise and Fall of Urban Civilization,* Stein & Day, N.Y., 1977

Naesa, A., *Ecology, Community and Lifestyle,* Cambridge University Press, N.Y., 1991

Norbeck, E., *Changing Japan,* Rice University Press, Holt, Rhinehart & Winston, 1967

Rodwin, L., R.M. Hollister, Edit., *Cities of the Mind: Images and Themes of the City in a Social Scenario,* Plenum Press, N.Y., 1984

Rodwin, L., et al, *Cities and City Planning,* Plenum Press, N.Y., 1981
Reisman, D., *The Lonely Crowd,* Yale University Press, New Haven, 1950
Sennett, R., *The Uses of Disorder: Personal Identity and City Life,* Knopf, N.Y., 1970

Part II, Chapter 5

Bird, J., *Centrality and Cities,* Routledge and Kegan Publishers, London, Boston, 1970
Fransman, M., *The Market and Beyond,* Cambridge University Press, N.Y., 1991
Glazer, N., *Social and Cultural Factors in Japanese Economic Growth,* Patrick and Rosovsky Edit., Asia's New Giant, 1976
McGaugh, M. E., *A Geography of Population Settlement,* W.C. Brown Co. Publishers, 1970

Part II, Chapter 6

Berger, J.J., *Environmental Restoration,* Island Press, Washington, D.C., 1990
Kemp, D.D., *Global Environment Issues,* Routledge, N.Y., 1990
Pawley, M., *Building for Tomorrow: Putting Waste to Work,* Sierra Club Books, San Francisco, 1982
Rapaport, A., *History and Precedent in Environmental Design,* Plenum Publishers, N.Y., 1990
Reinfeld, N.V., C.M. Layman et al, *Community Recycling: System Design to Management,* Prentice Hall, Englewood Cliffs, N.Y., 1992
Winton, H.N.M., Compiled and Edited, *Man and the Environment: A Bibliography of the United Nations System, 1946-7,* Unipub, N.Y., 1972
Young, J.E., *Discarding the Throwaway Society,* Worldwatch Institute, Washington, D.C., 1991

Part II, Chapter 7

Blowers, A., C. Hamnett, P.Snare, *The Future of Cities,* Hutchinson Educational Associated with Open University Press., 1974
Carver, H., *Cities in the Suburbs,* University of Toronto Press, 1992
Clarke, J.I., *Geography and Population: Approaches and Applications,* Pergorman Press, N.Y.,1984
Defries, R.S., T.F. Malone, Edit., *Global Change and Our common Future,* National Academy Press, Washington, D.C., 1989
Dickenson, R.E., *City, Region and Regionalism: A Geographical Contribution to Human Ecology,* Routledge and Paul, London, 1947
Dutt, A.K., *Growth, Distribution and Uneven Development,* Cambridge University Press, Cambridge, N.Y., 1990
Hebbs, D.O., *The Organization of Behavior,* John Wiley & Sons, N.Y., 1949
La Patra, J.W., *Applying the Systems Approach to Urban Development,* Dowden, Hutchinson & Ross, Stroudsburg, PA, 1974

APPENDIX - SPECIFIC REFERENCES

Mantell, M.A., S.F. Harper, L. Propet, *Creating Successful Communities,* Island Press, Washington, D.C., 1990

Morgan, A.E., *The Community of the Future and the Future of Community,* Yellow Springs, Ohio Community Service, 1957

Nehru, Jawaharlal, *Glimpses of World History,* The John Day Co., 1939

Nisbet, R. A., *The Quest for Community,* Oxford University Press, 1953

Pool, Ithiel de Sola, E.M. Noam, Edit., *Technologies Without Boundaries,* Harvard University Press, Cambridge, 1990

Vyskosil, P., C. Reigber, P.G. Gross, Edit., *Global and Regional Dynamics,* Springs-Verlag, N.Y., 1980

Part III, Chapter 1

Babcock, R.F., *The Zoning Game,* The University of Wisconsin Press, 1969

Cameron, G.C., L.Wingo, Edit., *Cities , Regions and Public Policy,* University of Glasgow and Oliver-Boyd, Resources for the Future, Washington, D.C., 1973

Condon, P., P.Batey, Edit., *Advances in Regional Demography: Information, Forecasts, Models,* Belhaven Press, London, N.Y., 1989

Friedmann, G., *Industrial Society,* The Free Press, N.Y., 1964

Fry, R., *Vision and Design,* Meridian Books, 1956

Galbraith, J.K., *The New Industrial State,* Houghton Mifflin Co., Boston, 1967

Ghosh, P.K., *Third World Development: A Basic Needs Approach,* Greenwood Press, Wesport, Conn., 1984

Leinwand, G., R.E.Shutz, *The City As a Community,* Washington Square Press, N.Y., 1970

Neutra, R., *Survival Through Design,* Oxford University Press, N.Y., 1954

Miller, M.L., R.P. Gale, P.J. Brown, *Social Science in Natural Resource Management Systems,* Westview Press, Boulder, Colo., 1987

Speas, J., L. Cherryholme, Sr. Edit., C. Cherryholme, G. Manson, *Exploring Communities,* Webster Div., McGraw-Hill, N.Y., 1979

Stewart, F., *Basic Needs In Developing Countries,* John Hopkins University Press, Baltimore, 1985

Sussman, M.B., *Community Structure and Analysis,* Crowell, N.Y., 1959

Part III, Chapter 2

Duffy, J.C., Edit., *Health and Medical Aspects of Disaster Preparedness,* Plenum Pub., N.Y., 1990

Horwitz, A.I., *The Logic of Social Control,* Plenum Publishing, N.Y., 1990

Hoskin, F.P., *The Functions of Cities,* Schenkman Publishing Co., 1973

Humphries, D., *Household Crowding, Population Density and Their Relationships to a Number of Pathological Indicators,* California State University, Fullerton, Ca., 1982

Wolfe, A., *Whose Keeper? Social Science and Moral Obligation,* University of California Press, Berkeley, Ca., 1979

Part IV, Chapter 1

Baade, F., *The Race to the Year 2000, Our Future,* Doubleday, N.Y., 1962

Clarke, J.I., et al, Edit., *Population and Disaster, (on Population Geography),* Basil Blackwell, Cambridge, Mass., 1989

Dregne, H.E., *Desertification of Arid Lands,* Harvard Academic Publishers, N.Y., 1983

Erlich, P.R., A.H., Erlich, *The Population Explosion,* Simon and Schuster, N.Y., 1990

Haragen, D.R., *Human Intervention in the Climatology of Arid Lands,* Symposium, University of New Mexico Press, Albuqeurque, N.M., 1990

Johnson, R.I., P.J. Taylor, Eds., *A World in Crisis,* Basil Blackwell, Cambridge, Mass., 1989

Mexico (page 81) and World Population Explosion (page179), Vol.66, No.2, National Geogrphic Magazine, Washington, D.C., August, 1984

Middleton, N., *Atlas of the World, Facts on File,* N.Y.and Oxford, 1980
Our Magnificent Earth,: A Rand Mcnally Atlas of Earth Resources, Rand McNally, N.Y., 1979

The World Food Problem, Pres. Johnson's Science Advisory Committee, 1967 Report

Revelle, R., *Food and Population,* Scientific American, September, 1974

Ridker, R.G., Edit., *Changing Resource Problems of the Fourth World,* Resources for the Future and John Hopkins University Press, 1976

Rudiger, P., Edit., *Conflicts and Cooperation in Managing Environmental Resources,* Springer-Verlag, Berlin & N.Y., 1992

The 1990 Information Please Almanac, Houghton Mifflin Co.

Santos, M.A., *Managing Planet Earth,* Bergin and Garvey, N.Y., 1990

Trewartha, G.T., *A Geography of Population: World Patterns,* Wiley & Sons, N.Y., 1969

Woods, R., *Population Analysis in Geogrphy,* Longman, N.Y., 1979

Part IV, Chapter 2

Boyko, H., *Salt Water Agriculture,* Scientific America Magazine, March, 1967

Brown, L. et al, *State of the World,* A Worldwatch Institute Report, 1989,1990 & 1991

Campos-Lopez, E, R.J. Anderson, Eds., *Natural Resources and Development in Arid Regions,* Westview Press, Boulder, Colo., 1983

Cowen, R. C., *Frontiers of the Sea,* Doubleday and Co., 1960

Crossum, P.R., K.D. Frederick, *The World Food Situation: Resource & Environmental Issues in the Developing Countries and the United States,* Resources for the Future, Washington, D.C.1977

APPENDIX - SPECIFIC REFERENCES

Goldstein, J., *Demanding Clean Food and Water,* Plenum Publishing, N.Y., 1990

Lal, R., *Soil Erosion in the Tropics,* McGraw-Hill, N.Y., 1990

Major World Crop Areas and Climatic Profiles, Joint Agricultural Weather Facility, U.S. Department of Agriculture, World Agricultural Outlook Board, 1987

National Geographic Atlas of the World, 6th Edition, National Geographic Society, Washington, D.C., 1990

Newman, L.F. et al, Edit., *Hunger in History,* Basil Blackwell, Cambridge, Mass., 1990

Research News, Vol.248, Science Magazine, May 25, 1990

The Desert, Vol.156, No. 5, The National Geographic Magazine, Washington, D.C., 1979

Tompkins, P., C. Bird, *Secrets of the Soil,* Harper & Row, N.Y., 1990

Part IV, Chapter 3

Abelson, P.H., *Desalinization of Brackish Water and Marine Waters,* Science Magazine, Mar.1991

Coombs, H.C., *The Return of Scarcity: Strategies for an Economic Future,* Cambridge UniversitY Press, Cambridge, N.Y., 1990

Maybech, M., D.V. Chapman, R. Helmer, Edit., *Global Fresh Water Quality,* Basi Blackwell, Cambridge, Mass., 1990

Parent, J.D., *A Survey of United States & World Production, Proved Reserves, and RemainingRecoverable Resources of Fossil Fuels & Uranium,* Institute of Gas Technology, Chicago, 1990

Popkin, R., *Desalination: Water for the World's Future,* Frederick A. Praeger, N.Y., 1968

Siegel, G., *Vision and Venture for the Continental Shelf,* West Coast University, 1965

Siegel, G., *Undersea Storage and Distribution,* U.S. Patent No. 3,610,194, 1971

Singh, R.P., J.F. Farr, B.A. Stewart, Eds., *Dry Land Agriculture,* Springer-Verlag, N.Y., 1990

Part IV, Chapter 4

Cullingworth, J.B., Edit., *Energy, Land and Public Policy,* Transaction, New Brunswick, N.J. 1990

Energy, The National Geographic Special Report, National Geographic Soc., Washington, D.C., 1981

Fossil Energy Resources, National Coal Association, Washington, D.C., 1974

Siegel, G., *Hydrojet Drilling Means,* U.S. Patent No. 4,458,766, 1984

Zweibel,K., *Harnessing Solar Power,* Plenum Publishing, N.Y., 1990

Part IV, Chapter 5

Gradwohl, J., R. Grounberg, *Saving the Tropical Forests,* Earthscan Publications, London, 1988

Mathews, J.D., *Sylviculture Systems,* Oxford University Press, Clarendon, N.Y., 1989
Natural Resources of Humid Tropical Asia, UNESCO, Paris, 1974

Postel,S., L.Heise, *Reforesting the Earth,* Worldwatch Institute, Washington, D.C., 1988

Reynolds, E.R.C., F.B. Thompson, *Forests, Climate and Hydrology: Regional Impact,* United Nations University, Tokyo, 1988

Richardson, S.D., *Forests and Foresting China,* Island Press, Washington, D.C., 1990
Technologies to Sustain Tropical Forest Resources, Office of Technological Assessment, U.S. Congress, 1984

Part IV, Chapter 6

Glass, J.E., G.Swift, *Agriculture and Synthetic Polymers,* American Chemical Society Symposium, Washington, D.C., 1990

Galasio, F.S., *Advanced Fibers and Composites,* Gordon and Breach, N.Y., 1989

Part IV, Chapter 7

Anderson, S., W. Ostreng, Eds., *International Resource Management,: The Role of Science and Politics,* Belhaven Press, London, N.Y., 1989

Church, A.m., *Taxation of Non-Renewable Resources,* Lexington Books, Lexington, Mass., 1981

Kharbanda, O.P., E.A. Stallworthy, *Waste Management,* Auburn House, N.Y., 1990

Klee,G.A., *Conservation of Natural Resources,* Prentice-Hall, Englewood Cliffs, N.J., 1991

Page, T., *Conservation and Economic Efficiency: An Approach to Materials Policy,* Resources for the Future by John Hopkins University Press, Baltimore, 1977

Part IV, Chapter 9

Friedman, M.S., *The Confirmation of Otherness in Family, Community and Society,* Pilgrim Press, N.Y., 1983

Schumacher, E.F., *Small Is Beautiful,* Perenial Library, Harper & Row, N.Y., 1973

Part IV, Chapter 10

Englert, R.D., *Winning at Technological Innovation,* McGraw-Hill, N.Y., 1991

Part V, Chapter 1

Anderson, W., *Politics and Environment,* Goodyear Publishing Co., Inc., California, 1970

Garvey, G., *A Framework for Environmental Policy,* W.W. Norton & Co., Inc., N.Y., 1972

Part V, Chapter 6

Baylin, E.N., *Procedural Diagramming for System Development,* Baylin Systems, 1990

APPENDIX - SPECIFIC REFERENCES

Hall, A.D., *A Methodology for Systems Engineering,* D.Van Norstrand Co., Inc., N.Y., 1972

Part V, Chapter 7

Brown, L.R., et al, *State of the World,* A Worldwide Institute Report on Progress Toward a Sustainable Society, W.W. Norton Co., N.Y. 1989

Keynes, J.M., *The General Theory of Employment, Interest and Money,* Harcourt, Brace & Co., 1936

Weitzman, M.L., *The Share Economy-Conquering Stagflation,* Harvard University Press., Cambridge, Mass., 1984

ORDER FORM

Published by: UNIWORLD Publishing
9392 Canterbury Lane
Garden Grove, CA 92641 U.S.A.
(714) 530-7586
FAX (310)427-0440

Your Name: _____

Address: _____

City: _____ State: _____ Zip Code _____ - ____

Telephone: (_____)_____ FAX: (_____)_____

Number of Book(s) @ $24.95: Number ordered _____ $_____

Sales Tax: Please add 7.75% for books shipped to a California address: $_____

Shipping and Handling: Please include $2.50 for the first book, .75 cents $_____
for each additional book. (Normal Shipping may take three to four weeks.)

Air Mail: $3.50 per book $_____

Total Enclosed $_____

Payment: ☐ Check (Do not send cash)
☐ Money Order

* Note: For quantities greater than two, please phone for terms.

Policy: I understand that I may return any book(s) for a refund for any reason, no questions asked. However, all returns must be in resalable condition.